S0-BFI-186

SOUTHWEST HERITAGE

SOUTHWEST HERITAGE

A LITERARY HISTORY WITH BIBLIOGRAPHIES

THIRD EDITION, REVISED AND ENLARGED

BY
MABEL MAJOR
AND
T. M. PEARCE

First Edition (1938) and
Second Edition, Revised and Enlarged (1948)
by Mabel Major, Rebecca W. Smith
and T. M. Pearce

ALBUQUERQUE
UNIVERSITY OF NEW MEXICO PRESS

HOUSTON PUBLIC LIBRARY

73-053173

RO1185 28850

In *BCL*

© 1938, © 1948, and © 1972 by the University of New Mexico Press. Manu-
factured in the United States of America by the University of New Mexico
Printing Plant, Albuquerque. Library of Congress Catalog Card No. 77-175507.
Third Edition—Revised and Enlarged

ACKNOWLEDGMENTS

Rebecca W. Smith, our collaborator, who participated so generously in the research and writing of the first two editions, was unable to join us in preparing the third, but she shared our interest in the project and wishes it every success.

For material used in Chapter VII of Part Three on Southwestern books for children, the authors are indebted to Faye Devine of Tucson, Arizona, and to Siddie Joe Johnson, children's librarian at the Dallas Public Library. Miss Johnson also gave indispensable aid in the preparation of the bibliography of juveniles. Frances Gillmor, author and folklorist at the University of Arizona, contributed helpful suggestions about Arizona writing.

Those who gave active assistance in the Third Edition are: the librarians at the Albuquerque and Fort Worth Main Public Libraries; the Reference Librarians at the University of New Mexico and Texas Christian University, especially Mary Charlotte Faris, Johnween Gill, and Ann Jarvis McDermott; Emma Normand, Huntsville, Texas, and Joyce Roach, Keller, Texas for assistance in research; the late Mody Boatright, for suggestions, especially with regard to "Westerns"; C. L. Sonnichsen, for his helpful booklet, "The Southwest, The Record in Books," and his publications as acknowledged in footnotes to the chapter on fiction.

Frances Gillmor read the chapter on folklore and provided valuable supplementary data. A number of poets and teachers helped to write the chapter on poetry: Richard Shelton and Ethel Sure for Arizona; Arthur M. Sampley and William Bard for Texas; Leslie McRill and Winston Weather for Oklahoma; and Anna Nash Yarbrough, Sue Abbott Boyd, and Ben Kimpel for Arkansas.

The chapter on literature for young readers gained by advice and guidance from Patricia Taft and Edith Beck of the Children's Room and from Katherine McMahon of the Southwest Room, Albuquerque Main Branch Public Library; Evaline E. Schunk, Coordinator of Work with Children, Tucson Public Library; Carolyn Abernathy, Children's Services, Oklahoma

County Libraries, Oklahoma City; and Camilla Campbell, Anne Pence Davis, Loula Grace Erdman, and Siddie Joe Johnson—all Texas authors.

PREFACE TO THIRD EDITION

Thirty-four years ago, SOUTHWEST HERITAGE, A LITERARY HISTORY with Bibliography by Mabel Major, Rebecca W. Smith, and T. M. Pearce was published as a pioneering critical guide to books about the region for students, libraries, and the general reader. In 1948 the authors revised and enlarged the 1938 volume, retaining the central plan of a division of the literature into three parts, determined by chronology. Part Three was originally called Literature of the Contemporary Scene, c.1918-[1948]. By 1970, the cut-off date for the third edition, that shifting word "contemporary" no longer was applicable to the years 1918 to 1948. In the past twenty-two years literary activity in the Southwest has accelerated, with more books in the field published in a year than during decades in earlier times. Population has increased; rural areas have become urbanized; presses, bookstores, libraries, and colleges have multiplied. All of this is reflected in the nature of books written, as well as in the number.

Except for the correction of errors and the combining of indexes, the 1948 version of SOUTHWEST HERITAGE is reprinted virtually unchanged in this third edition as still valid for the perods covered. Part Four, Literature from 1948-1970 —we avoid being trapped again by that word "contemporary" —is added, including Selected Bibliographies. The final chapter is titled Literature for Young Readers, with works for adolescents included as well as those for children.

Published plays that can be considered literature are too few in number, we feel, to warrant a separate chapter; hence we have incorporated them into chapters on folklore, fiction, biography, and poetry as content or form suggested. Had space and our knowledge permitted, a chapter called "Dramatic Activities" might well have been included which would have considered the few published plays for the legitimate stage, but drama has become chiefly movie scripts, television plays, musicals, historical pageants, and traditional religious and entertainment folk-practices. Likewise had space and our expertise permitted, our definition of the Southwest as set forth in the Introduction might well have been expanded to include southern California, which increasingly is thinking of itself not only as the southern part of California but also as the most westward thrust of the Southwest.

MABEL MAJOR, PROFESSOR EMERITUS
Texas Christian University

T. M. PEARCE, PROFESSOR EMERITUS
University of New Mexico

CONTENTS

PART THREE

Literature from c.1918—1948

PART FOUR

Literature from 1948—1970

INTRODUCTION

THE SOUTHWEST as an area of American culture has been variously defined. At the beginning of the nineteenth century the name was given to the lands occupied by the Five Civilized Tribes of Indians east of the Mississippi, the lower Mississippi Valley, and the adjacent Spanish territories to the west of it. Historians now speak of that as the "Old Southwest." Today the term "Southwest" is sometimes used to designate the upper Rio Grande Valley in New Mexico and the arid lands surrounding it. But to most people, not only students but travelers and business men and dwellers in the region, the Southwest includes the region from the Mississippi Valley westward to the valley of the Colorado River, and from the broad watersheds of the Arkansas on the north to the Mexican border on the south. That is to say, approximately the states of Arkansas, Texas, Oklahoma, New Mexico, and Arizona. The "Southwest" is a term more easily felt and understood than defined, like the "Orient" and the "West." It connotes the final thrust of American colonization toward the south and west, the last push of the frontier into new lands. Here the Old South and the West joined to wrest a borderland from the aborigines and the Spanish, and, in turn, to fuse with them in a new pattern of living.

Geographically the Southwest, as we have defined it, is very diverse. To the east it is a wooded country with sufficient rainfall for rich agricultural crops of rice, grain, and, especially, cotton. Then, irregularly, at the timber line or about the ninety-eighth meridian, rise the semi-arid plains naturally adapted to grazing; and farthest west is an arid desert broken by narrow, rich river valleys and high, timbered mountains. The region has hot summers and, on the whole, temperate winters, except in the higher altitudes. Over all, the southern sun shines brilliantly; and the wind blows almost continuously, whether the Gulf breeze, the dry plains wind, or the sudden cold northers. Sun and wind and ever wider horizons greet the traveler who journeys to the Southwest.

Racially and politically, the Southwest has been the home

I

of many peoples: Indians, Spaniards, Mexicans, Anglo-Americans, immigrant Europeans of different nationalities, Negroes. In this respect it is like other American frontiers but with a salient difference, that here each race has stubbornly remained rooted and so has become a part of its modern life. The present culture is therefore cosmopolitan and diverse, the result of the mingling of geographical and racial and economic elements.

Just as the older historians were too long preoccupied with political events, so students of literature have characteristically limited themselves too closely to habitual language and racial patterns. Most Americans, young and old, have read only books made in the traditions of Europe and written in the English language. It would be desirable and profitable to include in this guide to the literature and life of the Southwest all the works, oral and recorded, in Indian, Spanish, English, and other tongues, that have sprung from the section. Some day we shall attain that breadth of vision. This study does undertake to consider much writing besides belles lettres and much that is derived from languages other than English. However, in a limited space we can include only works written in English or those available in translation. Moreover, we shall frankly relate all other cultures in the Southwestern scene to our contemporary American life. There are good reasons besides expediency for our doing this. While civilization here is greatly enriched by contacts with other cultures and languages, today the dominant strain seems clearly to be Anglo-American, with its ever increasing tendency to spread its influence and to absorb its competitors. Inevitably, then, we adopt America in the Southwest as a focal point, and set as our goal an understanding of the region, past and present, a vision of it as it is related to its own contours and resources and to the rest of the world with which it is now so inextricably entangled. To see how the region is unique and, at the same time, how it is like other areas will surely deepen our comprehension of its cultural values.

We have repeatedly used the word culture. What do we mean by culture? Not merely refinement or education or esthetic appreciation, but the "round of life in its entire sweep of individual activities."[1] We mean every way in which a group of homogeneous people continuously adapt themselves to living successfully in a given environment: food, shelter, clothes, warfare, transportation and travel, worship, marriage and rearing children, property rights.

The unifying element in culture is the body of ideas and beliefs a people hold; but the factors that determine such ideas seem to be primarily socio-economic forces. In other words, the culture of the Eskimo centers in his food, clothes, travel, basic ideas. He builds a domelike house of snow, eats blubber, uses dogs for transportation, and chooses his wife according to his own ideas of female desirability. All this springs directly from his Arctic background. The Euro-American, on the other hand, builds a boxlike house of wood, stone, or cement; eats grain and vegetables and fruit as well as meat; travels over land or through water or air propelled by machines; and finds women fair for his own reasons. These two cultures are clearly different. Most groups have complex blends of cultures, the result of historical and geographical contacts with other peoples. For example, the Southwest reveals a confusing complexity in its culture traits whether we study the early peoples who lived here or the present dwellers.

We can show plainly what we mean by culture traits and also illustrate the influence of geographical areas by considering briefly the Indians who were the earliest inhabitants of the Southwest about whom we have any knowledge.[2] The map of the region shows a broad woodland area in the Arkansas and Red River valleys and along the eastern Gulf coast where several tribes of Indians lived, among them the Quapaws, Caddos, Wacos, and Tankawans. These tribes, especially the Quapaws, shared the basic cultural habits of their eastern neighbors across the Mississippi. They were farmers, living in settled houses, eating maize and vegetables and melons; they wore clothes of skin, made good baskets and fair pottery, and held elaborate agricultural rituals. Those tribes to the west, however, such as the Wacos, tended to blend woodland traits with certain plains ways. On the adjacent plains roamed such tribes as the Comanches, Apaches, Kiowas, and Wichitas, who

1. Clark Wissler, *Man and Culture* (1932), p. 2.
2. Clark Wissler, *The American Indian* (1931, second ed.), Ch. XIV.

characteristically hunted and ate the buffalo, wore buffalo skin
clothes, lived in movable skin tipis, rode constantly on their
wiry ponies,[3] made no pottery or baskets but did excellent bead
and leather work, and preserved a warlike sun dance ritual.
They had contact on the west with the sedentary pueblo folk
that lived along the rivers or in protected valleys. Certain
border tribes mingled the plains and pueblo characteristics, as
was the case with the Navajos; but the typical pueblo culture
was distinct. They dwelt, as they still do, in adobe houses or
shelters in the cliffs, farmed intensively to raise grain and
melons, domesticated a few animals and fowls, wove cloth for
their loose garments, made baskets and particularly fine pottery, and cultivated elaborate rituals for social, agricultural,
and religious ends.

How clear a picture we thus have of the influence of
regional differences on the lives of primitive peoples. These
distinctions are still apparent among the Indians. No tourist
should confuse a Taos with a Navajo Indian; certainly no
Oklahoma teacher should fail to consider the temperamental
divergences between a Kiowa and a Cherokee in the classroom.
We have cited these comparisons, however, to suggest that
similar differences between dwellers in the woodland and plains
and arid areas of the Southwest still persist among the modern
inhabitants and may be understood today by any sensitive observer as well as by scholars and artists. A white pillared home
in Little Rock is as fitting among the tall trees there as a ranch
house on the plains of West Texas or an adobe *casa* in Albuquerque. You may properly order ham and hominy in the piney
woods country of East Texas, but take beef on the plains, and
fowl and fruit along the Rio Grande. In the same manner, the
books that emanate from the Southwest reflect these differences
if they are true to the background. More subtly but just as
surely the poems and chronicles are shaped by the land and the
peoples who live there.

Geography is not the sole factor in determining culture.
Races adapt themselves according to their previous history and
the time-spirit. Thus the Indians inhabiting the woodland-

---

3. See Walter P. Webb, *The Great Plains* (1931), Ch. III, for the introduction
of the horse, among the Plains Indians, by the Spaniards in the sixteenth
century.

plains-desert-area of the Southwest from the dawn of historic times until the coming of the European white man conformed to the conditions imposed upon them by sky and land, with no apparent desire to break the regional pattern.

Early in the sixteenth century the *conquistadores* of Spain carried the cross and their gorgeous banners northward along the coasts of the Gulf and the Pacific and over the line of the Rio Grande into the Indians' land. They meant to establish a New Spain for gold and glory and the salvation of heathen souls. In 1528 Cabeza de Vaca, one of a party of explorers, was shipwrecked on Galveston Island and wandered for eight years before he reported his strange adventures to the Spanish officials in Mexico City. In 1541-42 Hernando De Soto led his men up the Mississippi and over much of what is now Arkansas and Oklahoma before he was struck down by disease and buried secretly in the great river. Meanwhile the Spanish leaders in Mexico were still eager to spread their power by sending overland expeditions northward. In 1540 Francisco Vásquez de Coronado set out with a large train, sending ahead the Franciscan, Fray Marcos de Niza, and the Moor, Estevanico, who had been a castaway with De Vaca. Coronado first explored the upper Rio Grande Valley but found no gold, and therefore pushed on across the Llano Estacado and perhaps into what is now Kansas before he turned back, baffled by the sunburnt plains. Not until 1595, when Juan de Oñate was commissioned to colonize New Mexico, did the Spanish get firm hold on the territory that lies above El Paso del Norte. It remained under Spanish rule for two centuries and a quarter; the native Indians were officially converted to Christianity; and a new race of intermingled blood was reared.

To the east the Spanish colonized less diligently. Only in 1684 when the French Chevalier La Salle attempted to claim the wooded region from La Vaca Bay up into the Red River Valley were the Spanish officials aroused to send expeditions of soldiers and priests into what is now southeast Texas to found missions and forts. In the eighteenth-century chess game of war, played in the Old World and the New, Spain won these western borderlands; but Mexico declared its independence in 1821. Then the border country offered irresistible attractions to hardy, land-hungry Americans who wanted new frontiers and trading opportunities.⁴ First they poured into Texas, and within two decades rebelled against Mexico, established the Republic of Texas in 1836, and were annexed as a state in the Union in 1845. The tide of English-speaking immigrants into the rest of the Southwest, despite prohibitions and treaties, could not be stemmed. It was an integral part of the great frontier migration. The Santa Fe Trail lured traders to the upper Rio Grande Valley; the territory allotted to the Indians could not be denied to the competitive Americans. A picture of the progress of American settlement is the succession of new states added to the Union.⁵ The woodland regions were possessed first; the plains and arid sections later.

Besides the Indians, Spanish-speaking peoples, and English-speaking Americans, other peoples came to the Southwest, though less powerful in numbers. The settlers from the Old South brought their Negroes to the farming sections, where they are still a large and economically important part of the population. In the middle of the nineteenth century, French and German immigrants established colonies, the Germans notably near San Antonio. Except for the white man's virtual expulsion of the Indians from Arkansas and Texas, however, these races have tended to settle in communities, neither overwhelming nor exterminating each other.

It is easy to see the differences between the various areas and races that meet in the Southwest. It is more important to look beneath the surface of its life to see the unifying forces, the traits common to the whole. We have already noted the prevalence of sun and wind and wide horizons; the persisting frontier; the tenacity with which the many races remain on the soil perpetuating themselves and accepting each other. Such forces operate all the more freely in a land where there is still room enough to turn round in, a land which is not industrialized or urbanized to any great degree.

It is more difficult to point out specifically the common customs and attitudes of the region, but we may suggest some of

4. See F. L. Paxson, *History of the American Frontier* (1924), Chs. XVI, XXXIV, LVI, LIX.
5. Arkansas (with Missouri) admitted as a territory 1812, as a state 1836; Texas as a state 1845; Oklahoma (with Indian Territory) as a territory 1890, as a state 1907; New Mexico as a territory 1850, as a state 1912; Arizona (with New Mexico) as a territory 1850, as a state 1912.

them. Southwesterners live much out of doors, working and amusing themselves and often eating under the open sky. They travel much and cover long distances for business or pleasure. Where one can see twenty-five miles to the horizon, mileage shrinks. They are inclined to be informal, friendly, unconventional in manner, speech, and dress, except the more prosperous women, who often follow fashion's dictates. They are confident and optimistic, especially in economic enterprises, and inclined to take long chances. Why not, they subconsciously reason, in a land where drouth or flood, oil or gold or sulphur may suddenly dislocate planned and prudent frugality? In a region that seems destined to preserve frontier conditions longer than the rest of America, the inhabitants move about, change their plans, rebuild their dwellings, and cheerfully begin again.

These attitudes are reflected in the changing ways of the older groups, the groups which by Anglo-American standards are regressive and primitive. The Indian is less and less a primitive in his customs every day, what with soil conservation introducing small dams and windmill wells for grazing areas, and list furrows for dry farming. The Indian riding a tractor is no less noble than his forbears, but he has new means to live in harmony with nature. The little Spanish towns will not be long without neon signs and the disturbing world awareness brought by radio. Inevitable is the march of modern scientific living, but the spirit and manner of a people change gradually. There are centuries of a slower tempo, of an easier courtesy, and a less material advance lingering in the Southwest.

(Literature is a mirror in which this unchanging land of the Southwest and its changing panorama of peoples are reflected. At first simple and unselfconscious, it recorded achievement and action.) It was utilitarian and practical. As leisure has increased, belles lettres have flourished; today writers can live and make a living in Dallas and Santa Fe and Oklahoma City. Native critics begin to take stock of cultural resources and to evaluate artistic achievements. This self-consciousness is a sign of approaching artistic maturity.

The most pointed literary criticism the Southwest has produced has centered about the doctrines loosely known as regionalism. This creed, which was formulated and christened in

America shortly after 1918, is at bottom a protest against the mechanization and regimentation of modern life. It seeks its justification in those recent findings of social scientists that relate man to his environment. To create literature, most regionalists will agree, we must root ourselves in an environment, and even then we can produce only such blossoms and fruit as are proper to it; otherwise we are a weedy growth. This generalization is probably as much agreement as could be secured among the regionalists, who apply the central principle in divers directions. Thus the Nashville Agrarians would use literature to restore the intrinsic values of the ante-bellum South; while the Middle Western group have leanings toward social and economic liberalism. In the Southwest the literary movement has concerned itself chiefly with the arts and so has avoided public controversy, perhaps at the cost of vitality.

Regionalism in the Southwest has been variously understood. B. A. Botkin, spokesman of the Oklahoma group during the heyday of the matter, defines it from four angles: *localistic* with roots in one place, *naturistic* with roots in the land and the folk, *traditional* with roots in personal heritage, and *cultural* with roots in inter-regional backgrounds. Such a view is broad enough to challenge a hearing and to inspire creative writers. Indeed, Mr. Botkin's *Folk-Say* (1929-31) and *Space* (1934) did so. The trouble is that so comprehensive a creed permits of different interpretations and heresies not only among the infidels but among the believers. Therefore, as early as 1929, the *Southwest Review,* then edited by John H. McGinnis and Henry Smith, opened its pages to outstanding Southwestern writers for a Symposium on Regionalism. "Do you think the Southwest landscape and common traditions," the editors asked, "can (or should) develop a culture recognizable as unique and as more satisfying and profound than our present imported culture and art?" The responses, as published in the *Review,* sum up the whole problem. Need for contact with the land, the perils of over-standardization, the rich heritage of the past are stressed; but warnings are sounded against provincialism and sentimental romanticism.[6]

---

6. A discussion of regionalism will be found in the following publications: Mary Austin in *English Journal,* XXI (February, 1932), 97-107. Joseph E. Baker

So stands the case for regionalism in the Southwest as a specific literary movement. Undoubtedly it was sometimes too glibly accepted as a final word, and as often it was bally-hooed; but it was and still is an important influence. Out of it continue to come good results.[7] The discussion itself stirred intellectual activity and bred new critics and bold little magazines. It has stimulated creative writing in many fields, fostered regional presses, and encouraged bookshops.[8]

The discussion of regionalism is by no means the only manifestation of the critical spirit in the Southwest. Much good literary appreciation appears in the various periodicals and newspapers. Book pages in the press of the larger cities review current books with considerable attention to writings near home, maintaining, in most cases, a high standard of values. The most consistent of them are, naturally, those which are conducted over a long period by a good editor. *The Southwest Review, The New Mexico Quarterly Review, The Arizona Quarterly, Texas Quarterly*, and other journals contain reviews and critical articles. An even wider reading public is reached by critics whose reviews and articles relating to the Southwest appear frequently in national periodicals.

7. Henry Nash Smith in an essay written in 1942 ("The Southwest: An Intro-duction," *The Saturday Review of Literature*, XXV (May 16, 1942), 5-6) points out that the schools of regional criticism contributed to overthrow the standards of the genteel tradition which so thoroughly permeated American thought in the nineteenth century. The regional critics objected to an "ideal of a cultivation and refinement of the human being without reference to place and social setting" and maintained "the human need for a harmonious adjust-ment to nature—not an abstraction, but a specific, tangible terrain; and to society—not a featureless aggregate, but a concrete group of individual persons engaged in a joint enterprise, governed by shared references to a historical tradition, and bound together by the common conditions of their life."

8. Among the non-commercial presses and publishers of books in the Southwest are the presses of the University of Oklahoma, the University of New Mexico, the University of Texas, Southern Methodist University, and such societies as the Quivira Society and the Book Club of Texas.

and Paul Robert Beath in *Saturday Review of Literature*, XV (November 28, 1936). B. A. Botkin in *Frontier Midland*, XIII (May, 1933), 286-96; *English Journal*, XXV (March, 1936), 181-84. John D. Clark, Kyle Crichton, John Gould Fletcher, Philip Stevenson; Dudley Wynn in *New Mexico Quarterly*, V (February and May, 1935), 7-14, 21-26, 40-47, 71-87. Paul Horgan in *Southwest Review*, XVII (Summer, 1933), 329-59. Carey McWilliams in University of Washington Chapbook Series, No. 46 (1930). T. M. Pearce in *New Mexico Quarterly*, I (August, 1931), 195-209; *New Mexico Historical Review*, VII (July, 1932), 210-32; *Space*, I (September, 1934), 63. Symposium in *Southwest Review*, XIII (Summer, 1929). Lowry Wimberly in *Prairie Schooner*, VI (Spring, 1932), 214-21.

There is now a sufficient body of Southwestern writing and a widespread enough interest to justify a literary history of the subject. The authors of SOUTHWEST HERITAGE will apply three standards of value. First, we recognize the informative records and chronicles and descriptions. Second, we appreciate racy and indigenous revelations of character and custom, however crudely set down. Finally, we seek beautiful expressions of the human spirit, whether in the chant of the Indian, the folktale of the backwoodsman, the limpid style of a modern novel, or the clean-cut prose of a scholar. The quality of Southwestern experience caught in memorable words—that is our quest.

PART ONE

LITERATURE BEFORE THE ANGLO-AMERICAN,
TO 1800

I

POETRY AND PROSE OF THE INDIAN

HE TRADITIONS of the American Indian are more evident in the Southwest than in any other section of America, because many of the Southwestern Indians have continued to live in the same places where their ancestors built permanent homes more than a thousand years ago. Poetry and story telling among them have been intimately associated with localities in which they have lived for centuries, during which they built up myths about the forces in the universe, legends about the heroes and leaders who moved freely between god-world and man-world, and folktales about friends and neighbors, animal as well as human. The mythology of the American Indians is a storehouse of imaginative beauty and spiritual significance. Prometheus, befriender of mankind in Greek myth, giver of fire, is no more splendid than Johona'ai, the Turquoise Man of the Navajos, carrier of the sun. The Roman Jupiter never sent his messengers to mankind with greater dignity than the mysterious Shalakos approach the pueblo of Zuñi in December to bless there the new houses and the indwellers. The Indian is today the greatest practitioner in America of verbal literary arts, both in poetry and prose. Although some books have been prepared by Indians, they have not yet fully learned to practice these arts in English. We must depend upon interpreters who know the Indian, his thinking, and his speech. We are fortunate to have so much of the treasure of Indian imagination, wisdom, and wit made known to us through their efforts.

INDIAN POETRY

All poetry has aboriginal roots. Poetry in English goes back to lines sung to the chords of a harp and later recorded in manuscripts, which show these lines and the rhythmic pauses but leave no marks of the musical tones in which the poet sang. Early poetry in other tongues was also sung. David, the poet of the *Psalms,* sang before Saul, and his words of the wisdom of Jehovah and the beauty of his handiwork were recorded for future generations. Yet the modern reader does not hear the tones of David chanting. We read only his words, rich in thought and imagery, but divorced from the wealth of sound they carried as the poet himself delivered them.

The poetry of the American Indian is nearly all sung poetry, chanted to the tone and rhythm of drum beats, occasionally with flute notes added, and frequently with sounds of gourd or shell rattles. The singers are shamans or Medicine Men, singing for the blessing of hidden powers, the forces in nature which can cure illness, produce an abundant harvest, bring victory in war, bless new homes, guide the individual and the tribe along The Road of Life and Death. Very little modern European or American poetry is written in this primitive mood of thankfulness or awesomeness toward nature. It is necessary then for a modern reader who wants to appreciate the poetry of the Indian first to understand the world of thought and feeling in which it was composed. The Southwestern Indians have a unified view of Nature and Man, expressed with varied symbolism and various rites in a dozen or more tribal nations. Life and death are not separate forms of existence, but one *living* under different circumstances within the same spiritual environment. The world in which the Indian lives this present life is a world alive with forces identical with those in the after-life. The sky, earth, mountains, animals, streams, springs, and rocks have an inner nature as vital as man's, and this inner nature with its supernatural forces may be either malevolent or benign. The Indian tries then, through his poetry (which is one with his religion), to live in harmony with universal forces, for he knows that he is a part of nature, dependent upon nature for his survival and for his peace of mind.

The second fundamental difference between Indian poetry and European and American poetry is that the Indian expression is largely impersonal. Poetry is not often a medium for his personal experience, but is generally expressed in the interests of others and their well-being. Indian poetry is not so introspective and subjective as most modern poetry. Song is not simply self-expression among the Indians, but expression to relate him to the outer powers, to "Those Above," the friends or potential enemies in the world about him. In a sense, Indian poets are always "Poet Laureate," chosen for their fine character as well as for their literary gifts. The songs they sing are considered as gifts from "supernatural powers," as in old English times the poet Caedmon received his gift of song from God. Frank Linderman, in his book *American,* tells how a young Indian boy fasted for days on a lonely mountainside waiting to receive his song; this song was the gift of the gods, naming the lad and defining his character and way of life. He as a person did not create the song. It was directed to him, so that he might serve more worthily as a member of his group.[1] Tribal singers who chant the great Indian ceremonies today believe that poems came in just the same way to earlier singers who afterward handed the poems down from generation to generation by word of mouth.

"It is the peculiarity of American Indian poetry that its full meaning is never expressed in the words it utters," writes Mary Austin, life-long student of Indian song and ceremony. "These are, in fact, only a sort of shorthand note to what the Indians themselves call the 'Inside Song.'"[2] Compression of meaning and clarity of image is the third fundamental of Indian art expression. The earliest imagist poetry in America was composed by Indians, not by twentieth-century Americans. Some lines of Indian poetry are pure images phrased in sequence to suggested relationships of idea or feeling. Take, for illustration, the "Painting Black Song" as it is reproduced by Mary Roberts and Dane Coolidge.

PAINTING BLACK SONG

Black ashes, black ashes, beautiful black ashes.
  Heaven ashes.
  Everlasting.
Black ashes, black ashes, beautiful black ashes.

Black ashes, black ashes, beautiful black ashes.
  Earth ashes.
  Everlasting.
Black ashes, black ashes, beautiful black ashes.[3]

---

1. Frank Linderman, *American* (1930), pp. 34-44.
2. Mary Austin, "Medicine Songs," *Everybody's Magazine,* XXI (1914), 413-15. Mrs. Austin has an excellent essay on Indian poetry in her Introduction to *The Path on the Rainbow* (1918), a collection of Indian poems edited by George W. Cronyn. Ruth M. Underhill, in her book *Singing for Power* (1938), stresses the community significance of Indian song as it calls upon the powers of nature.
3. Dane and Mary Coolidge, *The Navajo Indians* (1930), p. 179; see also, "Red Paint Song," p. 180.

The image stands alone here, repeated, until it suggests not another image, but a religious meaning in the healing ceremony to which the poem belongs. The remedies given to the patient are not enough. There must be curative singing to drive out evil spirits afflicting the body. The blackening with ashes keeps the ghosts from re-entering.

Not all the magic of imagery and sound is directed at ghosts or spirits, but at such natural forces as sun, wind, rain, clouds, and thunder. In what Ruth Underhill calls "Songs to Pull Down the Clouds," a series of Papago poems, every image in the sequence of songs is used to suggest rain, to concentrate the mind, desire, and will of the people upon rain. Imagery here is an "imitation of nature" in perhaps the deepest sense. Aristotle used the phrase in defining poetry. The Indian poet tries to produce a counterpart of nature in the human mind, by the use of words with their imagery, sounds with their onomatopoetic values, and movements of hand and body.

SONGS TO PULL DOWN THE CLOUDS[4]

The little red spiders
And the little gray horned toad
Together they make the rain to fall;
They make the rain to fall.

Upon the Children's Land
The waters run and overflow,
Upon the stream-bed Mountain
The waters run and overflow.

Corn is forming,
Corn is forming.
Beside it, squash is forming.
In the yellow flowers
The flies sing.

At the edge of the world
It is growing light.
The trees stand shining
I like it.
It is growing light.

---

4. Ruth M. Underhill, *Singing for Power* (1938), pp. 26-27. Gladys Reichard in *The Compulsive Word* (1944) and Margot Astrov in *Introduction* to *The*

> At the edge of the world
> It is growing light.
> Up rears the light.
> Just yonder the day dawns
> Spreading over the night.

Imagery and the association of imagery with thoughts and feelings is the pure substance of all good poetry. In the Navajo healing rites, sand paintings are made which reproduce the symbols of gods and natural forces. Then the poetry of prayer for peace and beauty is chanted.

> I have made your sacrifice . . .
> Restore all for me in beauty,
> Make beautiful all that is before me.
> Make beautiful all that is behind me.
> Make beautiful my words.
> It is done in beauty.
> It is done in beauty.
> It is done in beauty.
> It is done in beauty.[5]

Although the great bulk of Indian poetry is ceremonial, there are personal songs dealing with love, with death, with individual exploits. Even here, however, the Indian poems are more reserved and dignified than many modern European and American lyrics. One of the finest personal poems in Indian literature is called "Last Song."

> Let it be beautiful when I sing the last song.
> Let it be day.
> I would stand up on my two feet singing!
> I would look upward with open eyes, singing!
> I would have the wind to envelop my body,
> The whole world would I have to make music with me,
> Let it be beautiful when Thou
> Wouldst slay me, O shining one!
> Let it be day when I sing my last song.[6]

---

5. Washington Matthews, "Mountain Chant," *Bureau of American Ethnology,* V (1883-1884), 456-76. See also "The Mountain Chant of the Navajo," in G. W. Cronyn, *The Path on the Rainbow,* pp. 82-83.
6. Hartley B. Alexander, *God's Drum* (1927), p. 63.

Winged Serpent (1946) stress the Indian faith in reiterated words to produce power. "Whenever the Indian ponders over the mystery of origin, he shows a tendency to ascribe to the word a creative power all its own. The word is conceived of as an independent entity, superior even to the gods." (Astrov.)

As a fourth element, we must understand the structure of Indian poetry. It is a kind of free verse disciplined by the drum beat and certain devices of phrasing and chanting. There is no recognized foot measure, like the English iamb, trochee, anapest, or dactyl. Indian poets recite their verse with a steady *beat, beat, beat, beat, beat, beat, beat,* against which the sung line flows with recognizable pauses, governed by words in breath groups, by thought units, by the Indian language formations called holophrases or long compounds like "hither-whiteness-comes-walking" for "dawn," or "the-two-top-feathers-of-an-eagle's-wings." There are no rhymes in Indian verse. The lines are of different length though they are repeated in parallel form in many passages. The structure of Indian verse resembles that of the Hebrew Psalms with their freely rhythmed cadences, the repetitions of phrase, the loose stanzaic groupings.

Impressive feats of memory are performed by the Indian poets who sing the long ceremonies on festival days. Fine examples of ceremonial song are the "Creation Myth" of Zuñi pueblo[7] or the "Story of the Coming of the Navajo."[8] In them one follows the mind's singing as the Zuñi people of the Middle Place emerge with the shaping of the earth through darkness, water, mud, into a world of wings and breathing—to Awonawilona, the breath of the light of day. Here is the dignity and symbolism of a world pilgrimage. Navajos sing of a great flood at the time they came from the Underworld into the present Earth, where they climbed by means of a hollow reed. There are myths for the creation of light and darkness, of human and animal life, of seeds for earth, of good and evil influences in life and the mixture of the two in the animal Coyote, who is the Loki of the Indian world, a prankster combining fun with wisdom. Songs of the Spider Woman, sky weaver who brought the loom to mankind, of the rainbow trail of the deities, of Fire God who made the stars, Songs of

7. Matilda Coxe Stevenson, "Zuñi Creation Myth," *Bureau of American Ethnology, Twenty-third Annual Report* (1901-02), pp. 73 ff.
8. Dane and Mary Coolidge, *The Navajo Indians* (1930), pp. 121-31; Washington Matthews, "Story of the Emergence," *Navaho Legends* (1897), pp. 63-179; William Whitman, *Navaho Tales* (1925), pp. 3-28; Franciscan Fathers, *An Ethnologic Dictionary of the Navaho Language* (1910), pp. 346-61; Dorothy Hogner, *Navaho Winter Nights* (1935), pp. 3-23; Hasteen Klah and Mary Wheelwright, *Navajo Creation Myth* (1942), pp. 9-125.

Blessing—hundreds of long and short songs make up the
Navajo world of myth and medicine. Superstition and witchery
are the motives for some, but many more are for healing or for
the celebration of household events from the birth of a child
to "lucky songs" for prosperity and well-being.

This brief introduction to Indian poetry may well conclude
with a Tewa song which holds the living reality for Indians of
the god-world. It is a hunting song translated by H. J. Spinden. In it the phrase "Road of Magic" connotes the Road of
Life which runs before birth and beyond death. Along it pass
the souls of the unborn, the ghosts of the dead, and the gods
themselves.

THE ROAD OF MAGIC

Yonder on White Mountain Plain
It was good in the long ago!
San Juan girls and San Juan boys,
Together they used to walk
Where lies the Road of Magic.

Yonder on Cactus Stalk Plain
It was good in the long ago!
Together we used to walk,
San Juan girls and San Juan boys,
Where lies the Road of Magic.

Here on Medicine Hill Plain
Again we talk together!
San Juan girls and San Juan boys,
Again we walk together
Where lies the Road of Magic.[9]

INDIAN PROSE

Indian stories in prose may be classified as myths, legends,
and folktales. The myths recount the deeds of gods and
founders, the divine or semi-divine ancients who founded religion or explained natural phenomena. The legends describe
the exploits of historic or typical individuals who shaped
tribal destiny by notable exploits in contact with either supernatural or natural figures. The folktales treat of the familiar
and humorous everyday world frequently exploiting animal
lore as a satire on wit and cunning wherever they are found.

9. Herbert Joseph Spinden, *Songs of the Tewa* (1933), p. 72.

Many of the figures in ceremonial poetry appear in the prose accounts of myth and legend. Anecdotes remove Old Man Coyote from his role in the Creation Myth to the prankster in folktales. The Isleta Indians tell a story in prose about a man who married the Moon, a Pueblo Endymion, opposed by evil forces whom he at last overcomes with the help of Moonmaiden.[10] The supernatural characters in this story are borrowed from the ceremonial chants, but the transition is easily made from the medium of poetry to that of prose. The circumstances of telling and the tone of the story teller are different.

Indian story telling was a household art, for the Indian family circle boasted no library shelf with the children's set of "Journeys Through Bookland." Pueblo young ones gathered with their elders to hear stories told before the adobe fireplace in the winter months as Navajos gathered around fires in their hogans and Plains Indians in their tipis.[11] Tales were told in the kivas and medicine hogans, and in general they are brief, for frequently there were series of stories told by more than one teller. With smoking, the tales sometimes went the length of rolling, lighting, and finishing a single ceremonial cigarette.[12] Indian folktales have the artistic qualities of concrete phrasing, universal wisdom, and brevity.

Frank Cushing's tale of how the twin gods, Áhaiyúta and Mátsailéma, stole the thunderstone and the lightning shaft of the gods and by the death of their grandmother brought the chili plant to mankind is an example of the myth type of prose narrative.[13] So, too, are the feats of the Slayer, the war-god of the Navajos, chief of which was the destruction of Yeitso, enemy of the Sun and greatest of all evil gods, who loved the Turquoise Goddess, mother of the Slayer. Tales descriptive of the Navajo fourth world, or of the Pueblo world-wombs, are in this oldest group. Frances Gillmor in *Traders to the Navajo* (1934) includes transcriptions of very early legends among the

---

10. Charles F. Lummis has the story of "The Man Who Married the Moon" in his *Pueblo Indian Folk-Stories* (1910), pp. 53-70. This is an excellent collection of folktales.

11. Charles Lummis gives a pleasant picture of Indian story telling in his introduction to *Pueblo Indian Folk-Stories* (1910), pp. 6-11; originally issued as *The Man Who Married the Moon* (1894).

12. See Introduction to Mary Austin's *One-Smoke Stories* (1934), pp. xi-xiv.

13. Frank Cushing, *Zuñi Folk Tales* (1931), pp. 175-84.

Diné, as the Navajos call themselves. Dorothy Hogner's "Tales of Big Long Man" also illustrate the legend form. Big Long Man, or First Man, as he is called elsewhere, fights with giants, but he also has a very human experience with his wife when he neglects his corn patch to go hunting. Anecdotes such as Walter Prescott Webb's "The Singing Snakes of Karankawas" belong in the group of legendary tribal accounts, as does the story of "The Giant Killer Twins" reported by Elizabeth Willis DeHuff in "Pueblo Versions of Old World Tales." This legend is a highly serious version of two Jack the Giant-Killers, who overcome the giant Tsah-ve-yoh living upon the summit of Black Mesa and after they have replaced his witch heart with a good one, bring him back to life and make of him a good giant who visits the pueblos each Christmas rewarding the obedient children and punishing the bad.[14]

The mischief and cleverness of Coyote are the substance of many folktales exemplary of the third type of prose narratives. He is the central figure in a cycle of folktales some of which are humorous and others profoundly wise. Lillian Elizabeth Barclay in "The Coyote: Animal and Folk-Character" has discussed Old Man Coyote in his various roles as pest and benefactor, Great Spirit or World Creator, and just creature of wit and learning. She draws upon folktales about coyote found among the Indians from Canada to Mexico and recorded by such writers as Mary Austin, J. Frank Dobie, Ernest Thompson Seton, Enos Mills, and Charles F. Lummis. "Coyote and the Rock Lizards" in Dorothy Hogner's *Navajo Winter Nights* is typical animal lore.[15] Coyote appears in a number of stories which have parallels in other languages. The story of The Pine Gum Baby found in both Pueblo and Navajo lore is very like the Tar Baby story in Joel Chandler Harris, if we change Coyote for Br'er Rabbit; and the Coyote and the Turtle story found among the Hopis is analogous to the Briar Patch episode in *Uncle Remus,* too. The trick by which Coyote gets Fox to jump into a pool after what appears to

14. For Mr. Webb's tale, see *Southwest Review,* XXII (July, 1937), 325-37; for Mrs. DeHuff's, see "Coyote Wisdom," *Publications* of the Texas Folk-Lore Society, XIV (1938), 104-26; for Mrs. Hogner's, see *Navaho Winter Nights* (1935).
15. Lillian Barclay's article is in "Coyote Wisdom," *Publications* of the Texas Folk-Lore Society, XIV (1938), 36-103; Dorothy Hogner's tales are also available in *New Mexico Quarterly,* IV (1934), 83-86.

be half of a round cheese is not unlike the famous European tale of the Fox and the Wolf, with the variant that it is sheep and other viands that the Wolf has in mind, and buckets in wells were not known to Indians.[16] Among the most interesting parallels found between Indian story lore and European is the Cinderella story told in terms of the little Turkey Girl treated unkindly by her sisters, Yellow Corn and Blue Corn.[17]

The analogy of the Celtic gift to English literature comes to mind when one thinks of American aboriginal tradition. It took six centuries for Arthur and his Celtic world to find their way first into English poetry and then into English prose. We have begun much sooner to realize the glories of our American literary inheritance.[18] Mary Austin in her poem "Western Magic"[19] writes of the Spider Woman mending "with thin-drawn cloud, torn edges of the sky"; of the Hunchback god, the fluteplayer, who plays "in deep rock crevices where springs are found"; of the Rainbow Boy who dances with the "many-footed rains." She concludes:

> There are no fairy-folk in our Southwest,
> But there are hours when prairie dog and snake
> Black beetle and the tecolote owl
> Between two winks their ancient forms will take.
>
> Clad in white skins with shell shield glittering,
> The Sun—their chief—the ancient road will walk,
> And half in her sleep the mothering earth
> Of older things than fairy-folk will talk.

The Indian world is a simpler and, if anything, more profound world than the European. "I always remember what the old men told me: that the world is God," said an old Indian.[20]

---

16. Elizabeth Willis DeHuff, *Taytay's Tales* (1922), "The Coyote and the Turtle," pp. 18-29; "The Coyote and the Fox," pp. 3-7.
17. DeHuff, *op. cit.,* "A Little Cinderella" (Picuris Pueblo), pp. 186-90; and "The Turkey Girl," *Pueblo Versions of Old World Tales, Publications* of the Texas Folk-Lore Society, XIV (1938), 104-26. Frank Hamilton Cushing has the story from Zuñi, with the variant that it is not the sisters who cause the little Cinderella's distress, but her own forgetfulness of the turkeys who have befriended her, *Zuñi Folk Tales* (1931), pp. 54-64.
18. T. M. Pearce, "American Traditions and Our Histories of Literature," *American Literature,* XIV (November, 1942), 277-84.
19. Mary Austin, *The Children Sing in the Far West* (1928), pp. 55-56.
20. Mary Austin, "Non-English Writings, Aboriginal," *Cambridge History of American Literature,* IV (1921, 1923), 614.

When someone criticized the Indians for spending too much of their time in dancing and ceremony, a young Jemez lad answered, "Indian spend as much time in other world as this." The Indian believes in immortality for animal as well as human life. Men are part of the world creation, not the final achievement or lords of it. The world is made up of entities—men, plants, lands, waters, rocks—that have souls which interact upon one another through individual powers. The Indian thought is always to produce harmony among these powers. What higher end can literature work to achieve?

Although Indian poetry and prose represent a world of symbol and experience more elemental than our own, there is universality and beauty in them to nourish and vitalize modern conceptions which have in complex societies grown too far from the roots of peace and understanding.

II

NARRATIVES OF THE SPANISH EXPLORERS
AND COLONIZERS

We turn now from the beginnings of Southwestern literature in the myth world of the Turquoise Man and the folktales of Coyote to a world of literary values which spring from the soul of another race, whose mysticism, courage, and materialism are born of the traditions of Europe and not of America. Where pictographs and the memories of tribal singers had briefed the chronicles of Indian movements, the first Europeans in the Southwest left their *relaciones*[1] on a thin, flat sheet which is white like the Indian wafer bread and as thin, but tougher and quite indigestible. One can read the lines and in between the lines to relive the experiences of Cabeza de Vaca and his companions as they made their way in the years between 1528 and 1536 from the Florida coast to Northern Mexico. These first Europeans to traverse territory now in the United States built boats and launched them in the Gulf, only to be shipwrecked in Galveston Bay and forced back upon an overland route which probably led through southern New Mexico. There were only four of them, Cabeza de Vaca, two other Spaniards—Andrés Dorantes and Alonso del Castillo—and a Negro named Esteban who was a serving man to Captain Dorantes. If the Indians had chosen to destroy these four, reports of the land embellished by fanciful tales of wealth in gold and jewels would never have reached Mexico. On the contrary, the Indians were hospitable to them, offering food, clothing, and shelter and winning a response from Cabeza de Vaca, at least, which was warm and grateful. He recounts how the Christian prayers of Castillo, Dorantes, and himself seemed to perform miracles of healing among the natives. From shared hardships, sickness, and want, the barriers between Indian and European were broken down until on one occasion Cabeza de Vaca remarked to Andrés, "If we reach Spain I shall petition His Majesty to return me to this land,

1. Reports, narratives, memoirs.

with a troop of soldiers. And I shall teach the world how to conquer by gentleness, not by slaughter."

"Why then a troop of soldiers?" asked Dorantes, smiling. "Soldiers look for Indian girls and gold."

"Perhaps I could teach them otherwise," Cabeza de Vaca replied.

"They would kill you, or tie you to a tree and leave you. What a dunce you are, Alvar Nuñez !"[2]

Yet the Spaniards travel on, unfettered and unmolested by their Indian companions until they encounter their Spanish countrymen mounted on horses and in search of Indian slaves. Cabeza de Vaca is astonished to find how different his attitude toward Indians is from the attitude of the Spanish who have never lived among them on equal terms. "Who are the true Christians?" he asked of the King, "Spanish wayfarers living in harmony and helpfulness with the natives of the land, or the *caballeros* in armor and pride, driving herds of men, women, and children before them into slavery?" The *Narrative* of Cabeza de Vaca presents as clear a picture of basic motives in human behavior under primitive conditions as any account in early American history.

Later chronicles deal with larger groups of explorers and colonizers. Don Francisco Vásquez de Coronado led an expedition of three hundred soldiers, a group of friars, and three hundred Mexican Indians into Arizona and New Mexico in 1540, and his forces in whole or in part remained in the region the space of two years, exploring as far west as the Grand Canyon and as far east as western Kansas. The chronicler of this expedition, Pedro de Castañeda, has left a graphic account of the *entrada* into New Mexico, the discovery of the Rio Grande, and the Grand Canyon, the democratic political organization of the many Indian tribes and cities throughout Cíbola (the earliest name for the northern Indian country adjacent to the Rio Grande), the agriculture, social organization, religion, and handicrafts of the peoples. Coronado withdrew when Cíbola did not yield wealth in precious stones and metals, but so impressed was his chronicler Castañeda by the

---

2. Taken from Haniel Long's *Interlinear to Cabeza de Vaca* (1936); the original text in translation may be found in *Spanish Explorers in the South-western United States, 1528-1543. "The Narrative of Alvar Nuñez Cabeza de Vaca"* (1925). Edited by F. W. Hodge and T. H. Lewis.

promise in the land for colonization that he comments: "For although they did not obtain the riches of which they had been told, they found the means to discover them and the beginning of a good land to settle in and from which to proceed onward. . . . I say this because I believe that some of those who came from there would today be glad if they could go back and try to recover what they had lost."[3]

The Spanish *relaciones* or chronicles have nothing of the Indian philosophy of nature with its dancing to the harvest gods or singing to the nature forces of rain and sun. Like other chronicles of the sixteenth century, in English or French, they appraise the land and its peoples and present an inventory of the wealth in minerals, agriculture, and humankind. But there is a lot of firsthand reporting of interesting personal experiences, of heroism, cunning, and deception on the part of both natives and Europeans. Castañeda's account of the Indian called "The Turk" who led Coronado probably three or four hundred miles into the hot, arid plains on a fruitless adventure just to have his revenge upon the Spanish is a classic among early American records.

It is not generally known that the historian of the colonization of New Mexico was a poet, Gaspar Pérez de Villagrá, graduate in letters from the University of Salamanca, Spain, and a true Renaissance gentleman in the combination of arms, courtesy, and letters. Villagrá, like all Renaissance writers, in his *History of New Mexico* (1610)[4] exhibits his knowledge of classic writers by overmuch reference to their works and imitation of their poetic practices, but he does sing of "arms and of the deeds of that heroic son," Don Juan de Oñate, who in 1598, after opposition on the part of the King and viceroy, finally led five hundred men (one hundred and thirty of them with families) from Taxco, Mexico, to San Juan on the Rio Grande some thirty miles north of Santa Fe, the present capital of New Mexico. It was not until twelve years later, in 1610, that the Spanish under Peralta, Oñate's successor, moved to the new location at Santa Fe. Villagrá is a source for information on much that has made the Southwest a distinctive

3. *Narratives of the Coronado Expedition, 1540-1542.* Translated and edited by G. P. Hammond and Agapito Rey (1940), p. 194.
4. Gaspar Pérez de Villagrá, *History of New Mexico* (1610). Translated by Gilberto Espinosa (1933), with Introduction and Notes by F. W. Hodge.

region in the culture of the United States. He tells of the first observance of Holy Week (with the scourging still observed by the Penitente Brotherhood), of the staging of the first dramatic performances in this country, such as the impromptu drama written by Captain Farfán describing the conversion of the Indians[5] or the drama on horseback called "The Moors and The Christians,"[6] of the character and customs of the people ("They are quiet, peaceful people of good appearance and excellent physique, alert and intelligent. They are not known to drink, a good omen, indeed."),[7] of the siege of Acoma, a fortified citadel on a mesa three hundred and fifty feet high, which was taken by less than one hundred soldiers resisted by five or six times that number of defenders. In this assault, Villagrá himself participated, contributing to the success of the attack by a prodigious jump across a chasm to put in place a log which was to serve as a bridge for the other soldiers.[8] Villagrá's poetic chronicle must be accorded place as the first poem about America by anyone who had visited the territory and could give firsthand observation of what he saw.

The missionary zeal of the Franciscan friars found its chroniclers, notably in the book by Alonso de Benavides, called *The Memorial* (1630). Friar Benavides writes of what he hopes for rather than what he sees, but his picture of the Indians at the useful tasks of carpentry, leather-working, music, and letters is the idyllic view of happy people everywhere. Father Benavides hoped for greatly increased financial aid from the Spanish crown in order to expand the mission work in the province of New Spain. When one recalls that his *Memorial* was written more than a century after Thomas More had published his *Utopia* and that only four years earlier Tomaso Campanella, another religious, had written a philosophical work describing an ideal country, *The City of the Sun,* Benavides' view may be pardoned if it occasionally idealized the state of American society at this early date.

It is clear from these chronicles that in the settlement of the Southwest the Conquistadors were not pinched by as much

5. Villagrá, *op. cit.*, p. 129; also p. 149.
6. *Ibid.*, p. 141.
7. *Ibid.*, p. 143.
8. It is not known just where "Villagrá's leap" was made, but the details are clear as to how it was accomplished; *History of New Mexico* (1610), p. 243.

want as the English in the first years at Plymouth; that they found more of civilization at hand on which to build; that life was enlivened by more gaiety than life in the colonial periods of either Virginia or New England. With the help of Indian labor, great mission churches went up in the Indian villages where the friars as architects directed and trained workers who built some of the most impressive monuments on the American continent. There were few if any buildings along the eastern seaboard in the seventeenth century which in size or beauty could equal the great church and monastery at Gran Quivira in New Mexico or the massive structure at Acoma. Centers of culture, the intermingling of Indian and Spanish elements, dotted New Mexico in the seventeenth century. After the Pueblo Rebellion in 1680, Spanish and Indian life never again had the same standing. With the reconquest, priests returned to the Pueblos but the Pueblans remained Indian. Spanish culture drew apart. The two traditions remained separate.

It is important for Americans to know what the colonial way of life was like in the Southwest where the life of the Indian was well integrated and where a culture stemming from ancient Mediterranean traditions was to clash and merge in the nineteenth century with the Anglo-Saxon stream moving from the east and south. The average New Englander, steeped in English traditions, knows little about the colonial period in the Southwest, never dreaming that it parallels his own history with interesting events and characters. The average Southwesterner has a vague idea, hinged to a few isolated dates, that the Southwest was settled a century before any other part of the United States and can rest complacently upon the antiquity of its institutions. A careful study will show that Portuguese John Cabot's voyage, under the patronage of English Henry VII, followed by only five years the voyage of Italian Columbus, under the patronage of Spanish Ferdinand II, and that the English left more permanent settlements in Nova Scotia in 1563 than Coronado established in New Mexico in 1540. The French were in Canada in 1534 and in South Carolina, Georgia, and Florida in the 1560's but not to stay. Raleigh's unsuccessful colonial ventures in Virginia between 1584 and 1589 parallel the efforts of Chamuscado and Espejo in New Mexico during approximately the same period. Oñate's colony at San Juan anticipated John Carver's colony at Plymouth by twenty-two years. So the story goes. Discoveries, explorations, settlement are never more than a few years apart in the Southwest and along the Atlantic seaboard; the Englishman is always on the heels of the Frenchman or the Spaniard. But the Englishman is English and the Spaniard Spanish, and therein lies the interest for the historian of culture. Dates can never reveal how close or how far apart peoples may be who bear the features of two different nations.

In art, in social, educational, and religious attitudes, the colonial traditions with the chronicles that bear witness to them are. exceedingly important for contemporary thought. "This has always been a people of government and a republic," Fray Benavides remarks of the Indian civilization as he observed it in 1625, "the old men coming together with the chief captain to confer and judge the things that were suitable. And when these had been determined, the *capitán mayor* went forth in person proclaiming through the pueblo that which was ordered. And this is, even today, an action of great authority, this proclaiming by the chief captain what has to be done in the pueblo." Spanish authority, however, did not manifest itself through democratic machinery. The governors of the northern province of Mexico maintained such royal splendor at Santa Fe as was possible for a town on the edge of civilization, but the *villa real*, nevertheless, of a kingdom larger than Europe.

The Southwestern colonizers were not so bookish a people as the New Englanders. There was no printing press in New Mexico until the mid-nineteenth century, two hundred years after Stephen Day had set up his establishment for publication in Boston. Doctrinal discourses and manuals of devotion came for the clergy from Spain and Mexico where there were presses. The wills of Spanish colonists are not replete with such bequests of books as the wills of the Massachusetts Bay colonists or the settlers at Plymouth.[9] But books such as the plays of Lope de Vega or the romances of Cervantes were read, by some of the colonists at least.[10] More active was the folk tradition

9. Thomas Goddard Wright, *Literary Culture in Early New England, 1620-1730* (1920).
10. Eleanor B. Adams, "Books in New Mexico, 1598-1680," *New Mexico Historical Review*, XVII (July, 1942), 226-70; also Eleanor B. Adams, "Two Colonial New Mexico Libraries," *New Mexico Historical Review*, XIX (April, 1944), 135-67.

of story telling and ballad singing. The historical *relaciones*, as we have seen, were vivid and rich in both documentary and literary details. It is the chronicles which keep alive the deeds of the two most important groups in the colony, the church and the state.

The Gentleman of Elvas reports a John Smith and Pocahontas episode in the heroic story of De Soto in Spanish America.[11] The secret burial of the Adelantado in the great river he had discovered is among the tragic annals of American history. Don Diego de Peñalosa, Governor of New Mexico (1661-64), incurred the wrath of the Inquisition by permitting the Indians to worship with their pagan ceremonials. His tolerance, however, did not save either priests or laity from the Pueblo Rebellion in 1680, led by Popé.[12] The Pueblo Rebellion is magnificent material for a drama or novel that can realize the clash of powerful pagan forces fighting to reclaim a continent from the will and mastery of an alien culture. Peñalosa, champion of the Indians was later imprisoned in Mexico, deprived of rank and possessions, and so humiliated that upon his return to Europe he volunteered to serve England and France against his native Spain. The Alarcón expedition into Texas, with the romantic figure of the Frenchman St. Denis, captured by love of the Spanish captain's granddaughter, is the human side of history instead of the factual. The chronicles of Arizona yield Padre Kino,[13] among the greatest of the missionary figures, whose adventures for the cross are as hardy as those of any of the crusaders for the sword or money chest.

So for the seeds of drama, of narrative, of history, even of poetry, and of the transitional culture pattern, these old Spanish chronicles are precious.

---

11. *Spanish Explorers in the Southern United States, 1528-1543* (1907), "Narrative of the Expedition of Hernando de Soto," p. 151.
12. See Eugene Manlove Rhodes, *Peñalosa* (1917, 1934).
13. Herbert E. Bolton, *The Rim of Christendom* (1936).

III

SPANISH FOLK DRAMAS, SONGS, AND TALES
FOLK DRAMAS

How we would like to have the comedies of Captain Farfán, mentioned by Villagrá, or a record of all the Moorish and Christian games with which the *caballeros* entertained themselves at San Juan in the season when the fields were springing green with the planting of Indian corn and the drums sounding in the pueblos for the summer rain dances. We do have a very old play called *Los Moros y Los Cristianos* which is largely a matter of action on horseback and of text little more than the speeches addressed by the captains of the opposing sides.[1] Yet who can tell when from these sources a drama will spring like the drama which grew from Shakespeare's Holinshed and the other chroniclers in the time of Queen Elizabeth. The free materials from which theatre grows are everywhere present in the Southwest. The struggle of races and individuals is there. Since a soldier poet and a soldier dramatist were among the

---

1. The cast consists of six main characters with supporting soldiers in armies: there is the Christian general with two captains, Frederic and Eduardo; the powerful Sultan of the Moors with two captains, Moma and Selín. The setting is an open place large enough for movement of the armies, with an altar on one side and the Castle of the pagans on the other (the Sultan is called the Turk in one place, Captain of the Moors in another). After an opening military procession in which the captains place the Cross on the altar, the Turk speaks to his men in the Castle, exhorting them to attack the Christians. Moma, a Moorish captain, offers to get the Christian sentinel drunk and steal the Cross. Eduardo, the Christian captain, falls with his head in the wine-bag, and Moma carries the Cross to the castle. Don Alfonso, leader of the Christians, gathers his men to attack. There are three skirmishes and the Christians fall back. Apparently the action of the play was then carried over until the next day, with players on both sides remaining more or less on the scene of the battle. The next day the Sultan offers to accept a bribe from the Christians but Don Alfonso refuses to recover the Cross in any way but by battle. In three skirmishes this day the Moors are defeated and the Cross recovered. Don Alfonso pardons his enemies and there is music and singing in praise of God. (A manuscript of *Los Moros y Los Cristianos* is to be found in Spanish in the Mary Austin Collection, Laboratory of Anthropology, Santa Fe, and mimeographed in translation by Aurora Lucero White, State Department of Education, Santa Fe, N. M. An interesting pictorial representation was done in 1936 by Dorothy Stewart as a mural for the portal of the Albuquerque Little Theatre. For a copy of text, see "*Los Moros y Los Cristianos*: Early American Play," by T. M. Pearce in the *New Mexico Folklore Record*, Vol. II, University of New Mexico Press, June, 1948.

31

first settlers, we should look for poetry and drama in an ever richer stream as the opportunity for expression grows.

As in the European drama, there is a background in the Southwest of religious plays. Riva Palacio describes the early religious theatre:

Theatrical performances began in Mexico shortly after the arrival of the Conquerors. The subjects represented were usually scriptural, or concerning the wars of the Christians and the Moors, in which explication of Christian doctrine occupied an important place. In all religious and political celebrations care was taken to include some sacred comedy or Corpus Christi Play, which was usually performed in the open air, so that all might attend. In the famous festival of Corpus Christi at Tlaxcala, in 1538, an elaborate *auto* was given, the subject being the sin of Adam and Eve. This *auto* was performed by native converts, for whom it had been translated into their own language.[2]

The *auto* and the *coloquio*, which seem to correspond to the English morality play and interlude, though the terms are not clearly distinguished, were the first sources of dramatic representation among Europeans in the New World. *Auto sacramental*, as it is represented by the *Adán y Eva* in Mexico in 1538[3] or in New Mexico later,[4] is a typical miracle play of the French-English type. *Auto* as it is applied to the *Conversion of the Four Kings of Tlaxcala*, which Dr. Castañeda calls the first American play,[5] fits the more secular type of morality production in England, a development from the miracle cycles. The contest between representatives of good and evil, with attendant abstractions personifying the Deadly Sins and the Angelic Virtues is the stock plot in this type of *auto*, with varying degrees of realism and action in portrayal. *Los Moros y Los Cristianos, Conversion of the Four Kings of Tlaxcala*, the

2. *México á través de los Siglos,* quoted in M. R. Cole, *Pastores, A Mexican Play of the Nativity* (1907), Introduction, xi.

3. See the description from Toribio de Motilinia in C. E. Castañeda's "The First American Play," *The Catholic World,* January, 1932. Reprinted by Texas Catholic Historical Society, Vol. III, No. 1, January, 1926.

4. A. L. Campa, "Religious Spanish Folk Drama in New Mexico," *New Mexico Quarterly,* II (February, 1932), pp. 4-8.

5. Dr. Castañeda objects to Charles P. Daily's statement, in 1886, that the first play in North America occurred in 1718 in Williamsburg, and states that two hundred years beforehand *autos* and *coloquios* were being presented at Tlaxcala and elsewhere in Mexico. The comparison is not quite fair between a belated stage of the religious drama and the presentation of a formal play. One might say that two hundred years before the *autos,* the Shalakos were enacting a drama, in December at Zuñi, of sacred and ceremonial sort in honor of the winter solstice and the coming of the gods to bless the life of the tribe.

New Mexican *Los Comanches* [6] are each of this type of representation.

There are two versions of *Los Comanches* in New Mexico and Colorado. The play in its earliest form commemorated the defeat of Indians in 1774 by the Spanish up in Colorado, north of Taos, and like *The Moors and the Christians* was a mock battle staged between threats and heroic speeches. Later the popular play and dialogue came to be staged at Christmas and was adapted to the theme of Christmas eve. The Comanches attack a village and carry off the Christ Child. The Christians pursue the Indians, offering to trade a blanket for the Child. When the Indians hear the miraculous story of the Holy Child, they agree to return Him and they make offerings of blankets, bows, and arrows. In the neighborhood of Albuquerque, this Christmas *Comanches* is given independently.[7] In more rural localities, it is frequently added to a Christmas dialogue and ceremony called *Las Posadas* (The Inns).

The entire community takes part in the production of *Las Posadas*. In older days, the ceremony was acted on nine nights before Christmas. Each night the people would carry images of St. Joseph and The Virgin to various homes supposed to represent the Inns of Bethlehem. Bonfires or *luminarias* would light the roads and a voice of St. Joseph would ask "Who will give lodging to these pilgrims wearied from travelling the highways?" From within the houses there would come answers on eight nights, "There is no room here." On the eve of Christmas, however, the images are admitted and everyone kneels before a decorated altar where the figures are placed. Later in the evening, the Infant Jesus in his cradle is placed

6. A lengthy Spanish text of *The Moors and the Christians* is recorded by Frances Gillmor in *Spanish Texts of Three Dance Dramas from Mexican Villages,* University of Arizona *Bulletin,* Vol. XIII, No. 4, October 1, 1942. In a later publication, Miss Gillmor discusses dramatic elements in this play and another sword-play related to it: "The Dance Dramas of Mexican Villages," University of Arizona *Bulletin,* Vol. XIV, No. 2, April 1, 1943.

7. An edition of *Los Comanches* was published by Aurelio M. Espinosa in 1907, University of New Mexico *Bulletin,* Language Series, Vol. I, No. 1. A translation of this by Gilbert Espinosa was published in *New Mexico Quarterly,* I (May, 1931), 133-46. The most recent text is that edited by A. L. Campa; see "Los Comanches, A New Mexican Folk Drama," University of New Mexico *Bulletin,* Language Series, Vol. VII, No. 1, April 1, 1942. Honora De Busk Smith describes the two forms of Los Comanches in "Mexican Plazas Along the River of Souls," *Publications* of the Texas Folk-Lore Society, IX (1931), 71-72.

beside his parents on the altar. Today *Las Posadas* is usually celebrated in nine successive visits to houses on Christmas eve.[8] Then a folk play of the type called *Pastorela* will follow, presented in a larger hall at the church, school, or community center.

Of the "miracle play" type of *auto* the *Pastorelas* are representative. "Los Pastores" in various versions is still presented in many Spanish communities in the Southwest, and has even been presented in English as a radio production. In 1893, Captain John G. Bourke induced one of the actors in a miracle play in San Antonio to put the play down on paper. This manuscript, after careful study, was published by M. R. Cole, and a second text from San Rafael, New Mexico, printed in the same book as a comparison.[9] The general plot of these *Pastores* plays tells of shepherds often named Rotín, Tubero, Tubal, and Tetuán who hear the angelic annunciation of the birth of Christ and decide to go to Bethlehem. They are joined by other shepherds, and there are dancing, singing, and exchange of personal remarks. One of the shepherds desires to carry the Christ Child off and play with him. His companion has to suppress him just before Lucifer enters to find out whether the Messiah has really come. Christ is defended by the angel Michael in several contests before Lucifer is overthrown. When the shepherds proceed to Bethlehem, an altar at the front of the hall, they circle the playing place a number of times during which a lazy shepherd named Bartolo has to be continually prodded to keep him from lying down and resting or going to sleep. In one version Bartolo remarks that the only thing he is violent in is eating. In the play the shepherds eat tomatoes and fritters (*buñuelos*). There is a character called the Hermit who aids the shepherds to reach Bethlehem. Whether or not the Hermit and Bartolo in *Los Pastores* draw any inspiration for their roles from the New World in the production of the Nativity play, the costumes, lines, and action reflect native folk elements. The paper flowers, tinsel, and

---

8. No extended discussion reproducing text and music of *Las Posadas* is available. Ruth Laughlin Barker describes the festival in *Caballeros* (1931, 1945), p. 241; Honora De Busk Smith in *Publications* of the Texas Folk-Lore Society, IX (1931), 76-77; Vicente T. Mendoza in a two-volume unpublished manuscript, entitled *The Folk Music of New Mexico*, now in the library of the University of New Mexico, gives both text and music.
9. M. R. Cole, *Los Pastores, A Mexican Play of the Nativity* (1907).

the ribbons in costume and stage decoration come from the local property box.[10] Bartolo is a rival to Mak, the amusing shepherd who steals a sheep in the Towneley "Second Shepherds' Play," and the acting of both Bartolo and of Satan requires genuine talent.

Why did the native tradition fail to develop in the Southwest? It is sometimes said because of the invasion of the eastern Americans who did not appreciate at first the values of folk culture. Though Spanish life did suffer from the first impact of strangers who were on the edge of an industrial society, still there had been ample time for the dramas to flower in the Southwest under the old culture if the encouragement had been there. It was not. Two things which occurred in England did not occur here: first, the drama became entirely divorced from the educational direction of the church and, second, the stage learned about the formal and cultural elements in the drama of antiquity. The English theatre thus came of age. It played to an audience that wanted plays for the sake of entertainment, and it learned how the playwrights of Greece and Rome entertained audiences in their day. In the Southwest, the religious plays remained in a state of arrested development, interesting in their acting and staging conventions but unresourceful in their texts, and still primitive and naïve.

---

10. Printed versions of the folk plays are presented by M. R. Cole, *Los Pastores, Memoirs* of the American Folklore Society, IX (1907); Mary Van Stone, "El Niño Perdido," *Publications* of the Texas Folk-Lore Society, XI (1933), 48-89; A. L. Campa, "Spanish Religious Folk Theatre in the Southwest," University of New Mexico *Bulletin,* Language Series, V (February 15, June 15, 1934). Aurora Lucero White has published a *Pastorela* in mimeograph, *Estrella,* State Department of Education, Santa Fe, N. M. A typed play, *Coloquio de Los Pastores,* copied from the ms. of Prospero S. Baca, Bernalillo, New Mexico, is in the library of the University of New Mexico. A manuscript in the possession of Felipe A. Chavez, of Albuquerque, has been used for a number of performances in the Albuquerque High School since 1929. This text, in both Spanish and English, is available in the unpublished thesis of Fred Meza Brewer, University of New Mexico Library, August, 1948. Critical comment on plays is also found in A. L. Campa, "Religious Spanish Folk-Drama in New Mexico," *New Mexico Quarterly,* II (1932), 3-13; J. E. Engelkirk, "Notes on the Repertoire of the New Mexican Spanish Folktheater," *Southern Folklore Quarterly,* V (1941), 127-31; Sister Joseph Marie, *The Role of the Church and the Folk in the Development of the Early Drama in New Mexico* (Philadelphia, 1948).

Folk Songs

No people in Europe preserve a greater tradition of folk music than the people of Spain. In somewhat the same degree, the Spanish peoples in the Western hemisphere have kept alive the traditional music inherited from Spain and perhaps to a greater degree created a new and lively *cancionero,* "treasury of song," in Mexico, Cuba, Argentina, Brazil, and other Latin American countries. The traditional materials live on in the American Southwest, where in such early cultural centers as the Santa Cruz Valley north of Santa Fe or the old mission quarter of San Antonio, Spanish *romances* and *décimas,* both types of old ballads, live on. Here and elsewhere in Texas, Arizona, and New Mexico, *corridos,* a later narrative form, are being written from week to week as events occur which inspire them.

Many of the *romances* illustrate old courtly themes, like that of *Gerineldo,* which treats of the love of a court attendant for a king's daughter. The father discovers them embraced, and he places a sword between them. Having tested their fidelity, he allows them to wed.[11] Other *romances* are light and joking, such as "The City of Jauja," a ballad about a sixteenth-century dream-world where the hills are of cake, the rocks of candy, and for all the idlers it is quite a place because anyone who wants to work is punished. Among other assets of Jauja is a tortilla tree.[12] A romance very generally known through the Southwest and sung by children is called "The Wedding" or *La Boda.* It tells of the marriage plans of a louse and a nit, and of the help the other animals gave them: the cow offers to give bread, the calf promises money, the spider promises dishes to eat, and the cricket offers wedding bells. Everyone is helpful, even the mouse who agrees to be best man if they will tie up the cats. This marriage is celebrated and the guests are enjoying the wedding banquet when the cats break loose

---

11. See annotations to individual *romances* and bibliography of collections by Menéndez Pelayo, Agustín Durán, Aurelio Espinosa, Menéndez Pidal, Vicente T. Mendoza, and others listed in A. L. Campa, *Spanish Folk Poetry in New Mexico* (1946).
12. This ballad is sung by Prospero S. Baca of Bernalillo, New Mexico. It appears in his manuscript collection, and is reprinted by A. L. Campa, *op. cit.,* p. 50.

and end the ceremony by devouring the best man.[13] Such a ballad as *La Boda* is a parallel to *The Frog's Courtship* as given by Carl Sandburg in his *American Songbag* (1927).

The old ballads or *romances* have been modified in the Southwest. The long sixteen-syllable line has been divided into octosyllables. These are grouped in quatrains for the popular form called *corrido*. In the *décima,* however, they are grouped in four ten-line stanzas, which are preceded by a quatrain giving lines repeated in the stanzas. The *décima* is popular for philosophic, political, or religious subjects. A well known *décima,* sung in Mexico and New Mexico, is called *Rico y Pobre* (The Rich and the Poor). Its content is just what might be surmised:

> El rico en palacio vive
> y el pobre in los campos crece,
> y en medio de los cuidades
> Siempre el pobre desmerece.

> The rich live in palaces
> And the poor grow up in the country,
> And in the heart of the city
> The poor always get a raw deal.

The song goes on to contrast the lot of the poor lad from birth, through school, in courtship, and in business. An original *décima* by Prospero S. Baca of Bernalillo, New Mexico, is addressed to the members of the Republican Party in a neighboring county, urging them to unite to defeat the Democrats who have just won an election.

The *décima* and the *corrido* are a good deal alike in theme, but the *décima,* on the whole, is more serious and formal in its intentions. The *corrido* is the true ballad expression of Spanish-speaking people in the Southwest. *Corridos* treat of accidents, disasters of fire or flood, murders and other crimes which in the currents of community life have resulted in emotional stresses. The Spanish *corridos* rival such American ballads as Missouri's "Jesse James," Texas' "Sam Bass," or New Mexico's "Little Joe the Wrangler." About twenty years ago a young Mexican was sentenced to death at Tombstone,

---

13. *La Boda* appears in A. Espinosa, "Spanish Folklore in New Mexico," *New Mexico Historical Review*, I (1926), 154, and in A. L. Campa, *op. cit.,* p. 83.

Arizona, for a crime he had not committed. The *corrido* of "Guillermo Daniel" tells how the youth confessed to protect a friend, how he escaped shortly before his day of execution, and how he is now at large enjoying his freedom from an unjust sentence. In 1920, there was a New Mexican *corrido* about the San Marcial flood.[14] In 1936, a *corrido* was written and sung about the trial of the Gallup coal miners who, during a strike, had exchanged shots with the sheriff and his men, causing loss of life. When Senator Bronson Cutting was appointed to the United States Senate, one of his humble followers in Albuquerque addressed an imperfect *décima* to him praising Cutting's defense of the soldiers, and of the under-privileged people of the state. Then the folk-poet reminded him that all people have their dignity. "I see that you were born in the largest city in the United States and I in the smallest city which is the Ranchos de Tomé. I see that you are very rich. I very poor. You very smart and I very ignorant. But watch the papers, Senator Cutting; they are dying who have never died before, and so we will go to death, you and I. When they start crying and they put us on a Ford, they will take us to the cemetery, and from there we will come back no more." And the poem closed with:

> Ud. se come sus coles
> Con su pan y mantequilla
> Y yo me como mis frijoles
> Con un pedazo de tortilla.

> You eat your cabbages
> With your bread and butter
> And I eat mine with beans
> And with a bit of tortilla.

A type of song composition practiced by Spanish popular singers and even more spontaneous than the writing of *corridos* is known as *hacer coplas,* "making coplas." These are quatrains improvised at a wedding, a fiesta, at any celebration where there is singing and an occasion to celebrate. *Coplas* in praise of the bride, in honor of the groom, out of respect for the families that are being united, in praise of a visiting guest

---

14. A. L. Campa, "Spanish Folksong in the Southwest," University of New Mexico *Bulletin,* Language Series, Vol. IV, No. 1 (November 15, 1933), p. 10.

—this is the practice of *coplas,* a musical custom still very much alive.[15] The old practice of *los trovos,* a singing contest between rival troubadours who improvise on rival themes, has not persisted in competition with the radio, juke box, and other types of music, both professional and mechanical.

Religious songs are widely sung, the *alabados* and *alabanzas.* The first are sacred hymns addressed to Jesus, the Blessed Sacrament, and to the Holy Family. Many of these are used by the fraternal order called *Los Hermanos de la Luz* (The Brothers of Light), better known as Penitentes. The second type are hymns addressed to the saints and in many cases are written by local *cantadores.* In Southwestern Catholic churches, where for generations the choir has been made up of village folk shut away from the development of music, traditional *alabados* are sung like the refrain heard in the Procession to the Cross of the Martyrs at Fiesta time in Santa Fe:

> O María, Madre mia
> O Consuelo al mortal,
> Amparadme y guiadme
> A la patria celestial.

Despite the number of *romances, décimas, corridos, alabados* and *alabanzos,* by far the greatest wealth of popular Spanish Southwestern song lies in the *canciones,* the popular lyric balladry suited to the moods of the heart, though some spring from wit and fancy as well. In musical form the Southwestern *canciones* derive from the lyric traditions of Andalucía, Estremadura, Castilla and other provinces of Spain, where distinctive Visigothic, Moorish, Arabic, and Jewish musical forms were introduced in the Medieval and Renaissance centuries and were supplemented by the music of troubadours from France, Italy, and Portugal. It is this mixture of musical strains that gives the richness to Spanish lyric balladry. In the Americas, some melodic and rhythmic materials have been added by Indian and Negro musical traditions.[16]

---

15. Perhaps the most astonishing expression of the custom of improvising is that practiced by the Cuban *calypso* singers who compose immediately before any audience on any subject given them.

16. The *indita* is a type of song in which Spanish and Indian elements unite. It originated in Mexico where in early nineteenth-century musical comedies (*tonedillas*) American elements were used to adapt the entertainment to New World audiences. See illustration in Campa, *Spanish Folk Poetry in New Mexico* (1946), p. 220.

The basic element in all Spanish songs may be traced to the simple pattern known as the *villancico* (rustic song, carol), which is essentially a stanza and a refrain.[17] The *villancico* in thirteenth-century Spain was a simple three- or four-line stanza in octosyllables with a one-line *estribillo* or refrain. The form was used by the common people in songs to the Virgin, songs of love, songs of proverbial wisdom. When the professional *trovadores* used the *villancico,* they shaped it with embellishments into madrigals, serenades, and other musical patterns with sophisticated literary texts. But the *villancico,* or rustic lyric song, is the basic pattern for such modern ballads as *Cielito Lindo* or *La Cucaracha.* "Cielito Lindo" is a love song by a woman who compares love to a dart in the air that wounds and to a child that is satisfied with very little when it is born but as it grows constantly demands more. The black eyes of her lover and a mark on his face both fascinate and anger her for

> El hombre que te quiera,
> Cielito lindo
> Si no te miente
> Llorar te hará algun día
> Cielito lindo
> Seguramente.
>
> If a man loves you truly,
> Cielito lindo,
> Does not deceive you
> To make you weep he will someday
> Cielito lindo
> Be succeeding.

"Cielito lindo" has been interpreted as a sweetheart, a mountain sprite, or just a beautiful day with a blue sky! The song is lilting in rhythm (*seguidilla* measure) and fanciful in text, and throughout Spain, Spanish America, and the United States it is heard on concert programs, in private and public gatherings sung by both professionals and amateurs. Frequently it is

---

17. The finest discussion of the musical tradition behind Southwestern Spanish songs is to be found in Vicente T. Mendoza's unpublished manuscript, *The Folk Music of New Mexico.* This work, in two volumes, discusses all available material in New Mexico in comparison with like materials in Mexico and Spain. The volumes may be made available by the University of New Mexico Library through inter-library loan.

played by dance bands. Yet it is just an elaborated *villancico,* stanzas followed by a simple refrain,

> Ay! ay! ay! ay!
> Canta y no llores,
> Porque cantando se alegran,
> Cielito lindo;
> Los corazones.

> Ay! Ay! Ay! Ay!
> Singing not weeping,
> For now, in singing, our hearts,
> Cielito lindo,
> Are always happy.

The Spanish *trovador* accompanied the army; he accompanied the trader. He was in demand for fiestas and weddings. Even at wakes, the minstrel's services were in demand.[18] He knew ballads of mourning, songs of successful as well as unrequited love, satires on men and morals. Glance at the titles of any collection of Spanish songs. They will show the range of sentiment covered by Spanish lyrics: *Los Altenitas* (A Gay Ranchero), *Cuatro Milpas* (Four Corn Fields), *Amapola* (The Poppy), *La Nocha Está Serena* (The Night is Calm), *Lupita, Adelita, Te Quiero Porque Te Quiero* (I Love You Because I Love You), *Recuerdos de Amistad* (Memories of Friendship), *La Borrachita* (The Fickle One), *Canción de La Luna* (Song of the Moon), *Allá en el rancho grande* (There on My Ranch).

"Ay! Caray!" the vaquero says to his *chaparrita,* "Don't weep for your Pancho, because, if he goes from the ranch, he will come back soon and bring you beautiful things and a kiss for your sorrows." *La Chaparrita* is a *canción popular,* and there are new ones and old ones, like the lyrics popular in English. Guitars are always popular in Mexican homes and a song like "La Firolera," which was originally in an eight-

18. A. L. Campa, "Spanish Folksong in the Southwest," University of New Mexico *Bulletin,* Language Series, Vol. IV, No. 1 (November 15, 1933), p. 10. *La Paloma* and *La Golondrina,* heard throughout Europe and the Americas, are more of the concert stage than of folksong. Yet each is loved for its sentiment. *La Paloma,* composed by Yradier, a nineteenth-century professional Cuban writer, has become folk music in much the way "Home, Sweet Home" has become a folk song throughout the English-speaking world.

eenth-century Italian comic opera will be sung along with "Un Viejo Amor" which sounds like a medieval lyric from Provence.

Everyone sings the Spanish *canciones* at Fiesta time, because they are beautiful; and they carry the romance, the pathos, the humor common to every folk. When boys stroll by the doorstep singing "La Paloma," or when a Spanish dance lyric is played by a Típica orchestra over the radio, the words and music may be those of some forgotten troubadour, but they will still describe the blue of Southwestern skies, the enchantment of moonlit nights, the idle beauty of a butterfly. It is the same world of experience in every century, a world more persistent than state lines or even national boundaries.

FOLKTALES

The art of story telling in the Southwest has been largely a verbal one. There were no printing presses until early in the nineteenth century, and story telling, had it depended upon a reading public, would have been largely nonexistent. The region was rich in story tellers and their products. In the Rio Grande villages traditional *cuentos* are still told carrying on the lore of folktales known in Spain and other European countries. These stories have been collected in modern times by such scholars as Aurelio Espinosa, Elsie Clews Parsons, Franz Boas, José M. Espinosa, and others. Their work has not only preserved the classic form of these tales but it has shown the influence of European *motifs* upon Indian story traditions. In turn the collections of Spanish tales reflect some Indian elements.[19]

Spanish folktales in the Southwest deal with magic, religion, rogery, romance, and animal lore. Typical are the themes of poor youths seeking their fortunes aided by God and the Virgin and opposed by giants, witches, or the Devil; rejected suitors winning their sweethearts by bravery and

19. Aurelio Espinosa, "Spanish Folk-Lore in New Mexico," *New Mexico Historical Review,* I (1936), 135-55; Elsie Clews Parsons, "Pueblo Indian Folk-Tales Probably of Spanish Provenience," *Journal of American Folklore,* XXXI (1918), 216-55; Elsie Clews Parsons and Franz Boas, "Spanish Tales from Laguna and Zuñi, New Mexico," *Journal of American Folklore,* XXXIII (1920), 47-72; Franz Boas, "Tales of Spanish Provenience from *Publications* of the Texas Folk-Lore Society, XII (1935), 77-79. In Riley Willis DeHuff, "Pueblo Versions of Old World Tales," *Publications* of the Texas Folk-Lore Society, XIV (1938), 104-26.

enchanted objects; Cinderellas rewarded for their virtues; innocent princesses wronged by wicked rivals. One of the most popular of all the themes is that of "Juan Oso." This story tells how a girl is stolen by a bear and gives birth to a child, half man and half bear. In his marvelous career this bear-man, Juan, meets three companions with whom he seeks fortune. When three daughters of the king are stolen by a giant, Juan descends into a pit and rescues them. He kills the giant by hitting him in the forehead with an egg given to him by a witch. Then his faithless companions carry off the princesses, leaving Juan in the pit. Finally through the help of the witch Juan reaches the king's palace and exposes his false companions. He marries the youngest daughter and forgives his companions, two of whom also marry princesses. The story of Juan Oso is known not only in its European form but in new versions characteristic of the American Southwest. In the Mexican version, Juan Oso dresses in a *charro* suit, rides in a saddle embroidered with silver, carries an iron walking cane and has for companions a man who runs like an antelope, a hunter who can kill game at such a distance he has no strength to run and get it, and two others who can pull up anything on the earth or suck in air or water enough to cause whirlwinds and a flood. Juan and his men are imprisoned by a wicked king who assigns them such tasks that only miracles can save them from death. These tasks they perform, including one in which Juan Oso descends into a pit after a black devil. He finds there four beautiful maidens whom his companions draw up, abandoning Juan, who has to save himself from the pit. After Juan Oso comes out of the pit, the king gives him his daughter to wed. Juan's companions marry the four beautiful maidens who were rescued from the black devil and the pit.[20] Such traditional *cuentos* have become the roots from which Southwestern story lore in Spanish has grown.

More readily adapted to the region have been the saints tales in the Southwest and stories of lost mines and hidden

---

20. J. Frank Dobie, *Tongues of the Monte* (1935), pp. 212-26. Cf. a simpler version in Riley Aiken, "A Pack Load of Mexican Tales," *Puro Mexicano, Publications* of the Texas Folk-Lore Society, XII (1935), 77-79. In Riley Aiken's version Juan's companions are two mighty fellows who flatten out or knock down anything in their path. With their aid, Juan takes a city and becomes powerful without rescuing any maidens or marrying the king's daughter.

treasure. The ruins of old churches, such as those at Gran
Quivira in New Mexico, have been honeycombed by treasure
hunters who believe that when the priests fled, during the
Pueblo Indian Rebellion in 1680, they buried the silver and
gold altar vessels and other treasures of the church in a pit dug
outside the walls. Then they carved a map on a stone and
placed it in the sanctuary of the church beneath the altar. The
friars are supposed to have carried away with them tracings on
paper of the stone map, and these maps or copies of them have
reappeared for more than three centuries. There is a pattern
to all these Spanish treasure stories: an early document appears
or is reported to have appeared and facts (or the representation of them) relating to concealed treasure become known;
then links in the story are broken, usually by murder or Indian
attack or the disappearance of central figures; search for the
lost locations produce apparently reliable signs confirming the
stories, such as relics of previous searchers, traces of ore or
coins; the story keeps rebuilding itself by new reports of signs
of the treasure and new rumors of those who have talked with
someone who knew persons who had heard about it or hunted
for it.

The raw material of folktales are these word-of-mouth
accounts, such as the lore called *brujería,* witchcraft. Everyone knows, in certain Southwestern communities, of individuals
with the power of the evil eye, who must be warded off by
crosses, or by tieing knots on a rope and saying certain prayers;
or, if your name is Juan, by drawing a circle, taking off your
shirt, then turning it inside out and throwing it in the circle.
Witches will either avoid such charms or be caught by them in
a knot or imprisoned within circles. There have been folktales of witches, charms, magic, and magical circles in the
Southwest since the days of the Spanish occupation.

Stories of clever rascals are more familiar in the Spanish
language than in any other European tongue. These are the
themes dealing with the *picaro.* The best known character of
this type in Southwestern stories is Pedro Rimales, who appears in clever tricks with merchants, companions, priests, and
others. Pedro is shiftless, rascally, and immoral but he is
always witty and amusing. A favorite tale of Pedro Rimales is
that in which he sells the hogs of his master to the butcher.

Then he cuts off their ears and sticks them in a mud puddle where he leads the owner convincing him that the hogs have been lost in the mire. Pedro lives by his wits, and whatever his moral character, he has a tremendous following among listeners.

The Spanish Southwest is a prolific source of folktales, many of which have been recorded from the oral versions. Some of these tales have become the basis for professional writers who have turned them into artistic forms of both literary folktales[21] and passages in novels. Yet even in their simplest versions they illustrate what Tolstoy meant when he remarked of the folktale: "The region of this art of the simplest feelings accessible to all is enormous and it is as yet almost untouched."[22]

---

21. See Part Three, Ch. IV, Literary Folktales.
22. Leo Tolstoy, "What is Art?" quoted in "Preface" to *Twenty-Three Tales,* translated by Louise and Aylmer Maude for *The World's Classics* (1906, 1921).

PART TWO

LITERATURE OF ANGLO-AMERICAN
ADVENTURERS AND SETTLERS
1800—c.1918

I

CHRONICLES, TRAVEL BOOKS, AND JOURNALS

As ECONOMIC and social life on each frontier repeats the pattern of all frontiers, so the literature recapitulates the development of the written cultural expression of the older settlements. The first literature of an old culture in a new land, as we have seen in the case of the Spanish explorers, is not primarily belles lettres but observations, records of this strange world—plants, animals, climate, primitive people, and the minutiae of pioneer living. Often these early records are preserved in diaries and letters. Sometimes the motive of the writer is to promote settlement in a new Canaan. Many of the books are to further geographical and scientific knowledge; others are for the entertainment of people back home who take their dangers and travel vicariously. These narratives and descriptions are in a few cases produced by professional writers who travel seeking "copy," but more often they are records by true explorers, adventurers, and pioneer settlers.

The early writings of the Anglo-American settlers naturally belong to the tradition of the Virginia and New England colonists instead of to that of the Spanish explorers. The first Englishman of whom we have any record as journeying into the Southwest seems to have been one M. John Chilton. Richard Hakluyt in *The Principal Voyages of the English Nation* (1589-1600) tells of Chilton's adventures as he traveled from Mexico City through the Southwest to California in the year 1570, and mentions the rumors Chilton heard of the Spanish search for the Seven Cities of Cíbola.[1] In 1625 Samuel Purchas in his famous *Pilgrimages* gave to the English-reading public a brief but rather accurate account of Friar Marcos, Stephen the Negro, and Coronado's search for the fabled cities.[2]

1. *Everyman Edition*, VI, 267, 283-84; see also Hakluyt's account in the first edition of *The Principal Voyages*, etc. (1589), pp. 557-62, of the journey of three Englishmen across Texas in the year 1568. Carl Hertzog reprinted this account from Hakluyt, with an introductory essay by E. DeGolyer, for the Peripatetic Press, in El Paso, 1947.
2. *Purchas His Pilgrimage* (Glasgow: James MacLehose & Sons, 1906), XVIII, 61-68.

It was not, however, until the early nineteenth century that Anglo-Americans began in earnest to make explorations into the Southwest. Zebulon Pike was among the first (1805-07) but only a small part of his record deals with this section of the country.[3] Of the three narratives that resulted from explorations in Arkansas Territory in 1819 Thomas Nuttall's is the most vivid in details of flora and fauna and appearance and habits of Indian tribes.[4]

One of these early travelers in the Southwest to show real literary talent was a cousin of Stephen F. Austin, Mary Austin Holley, who came to Texas on a visit in 1831. The widow of a former president of Transylvania University, she had a background of books and literary talk. The twelve letters which make up Mrs. Holley's *Texas* (1833) were frankly designed to encourage immigration to the new territory. As the first available book on Texas it attracted so much notice that it was enlarged into a *History of Texas* in 1836.[5]

The most distinguished writer who traveled in the early Southwest was Washington Irving. When he came in 1832 into what is now Oklahoma and Arkansas, he was already famous as a writer in America and England. In his Introduction to *A Tour of the Prairies* (1835) he says that the public expected him to write about the West; so he came avowedly seeking copy, as he had previously traveled in England, Germany, and Spain. From Fort Gibson, accompanied by General M. Arbuckle and Samuel Houston,[6] for one month he roved the Indian country.[7] He saw in the Indians not a dangerous cruel enemy to be exterminated, but the "noble savage" of the romantic tradition who was leading a "sunshiny life . . . on

---

3. *The Expedition of Zebulon Montgomery Pike to Head Waters of the Mississippi, through Louisiana Territory, and in New Spain, during the years 1805-6-7* (1895).
4. *A Journal of Travels into the Arkansas Territory during the year 1819* . . . (First edition, 1821). Reuben Gold Thwaites, ed., *Early Western Travels* (1904-07), Vol. XIII. The other two well-known accounts are: Edwin James, *Account of an Expedition from Pittsburgh to the Rocky Mountains* . . . *under the Command of Major S. H. Long.* Thwaites, *op. cit.,* Vol. XIV; and Timothy Flint, *History of the Mississippi Valley* (1827).
5. See *Mary Austin Holley, Her Life and Her Works,* 1784-1846. Edited by Mary Austin Hatcher (1933).
6. See Marquis James, *The Raven,* pp. 185-86.
7. For the route taken and a map of the tour, see J. B. Thoburn, "Irving's Tour on the Prairie," *Chronicles of Oklahoma,* X (September, 1932), 426-33. See also Henry Leavitt Ellsworth, *Washington Irving on the Prairie.* Edited by Stanley T. Williams and Barbara D. Simison (1937). From letters of Ellsworth to his wife written in 1832.

vast flowery prairies and under cloudless skies." He recorded
Indian legends as told him by a half-breed. He admired the
French trappers and hunters and listened to their tales.

Another variant of the findings of an observer in the early
Southwest is Frederick Law Olmsted's *A Journey Through
Texas* (1857). Olmsted's appraisal was more severe, less
glowing than those of Mrs. Holley or Washington Irving. A
Yale student, widely traveled in the United States and
abroad, he came to Texas in 1853 to observe economic and
social conditions. He deplored the way of life in East Texas
under the slave system. He found the Spaniards in and around
San Antonio dirty and shiftless. Texas food was bad, the
coffee "revolting," grammar "execrable." But he was charmed
by the prairies. All west of Austin he called "West Texas."
The book is valuable as a realistic, sophisticated criticism of
life on the frontier from a writer who was the product of the
"Golden Age" of New England culture. It links the Southwest
with contemporary Eastern urban standards.[8]

More sympathetic with Texas life was Sidney Lanier who
came to San Antonio in the 1870's, broken in health from his
service in the Confederate Army. He saw the striking contrasts in architecture, language, and customs of the American,
German, and Mexican peoples, and recorded his impressions
in a charming essay, "San Antonio de Bexar."[9] He was heart-
ened and enriched by the German musical culture there. It is
highly probable that his performances as guest flutist for the
San Antonio Männerchor influenced his decision to devote his
life not to law but to music and literature.

Writing with more of a sense of participation, a succession
of men and women came to the early Southwest not on a visit
or a tour but to be part of the life about which they wrote.
Many of these participants recorded straight fact with vary-
ing degrees of writing skill: James O. Pattie, Albert Pike,
George Kendall, Josiah Gregg, Lewis Garrard, Kit Carson,
Colonel Ellis Bean,[10] Susan Magoffin, Elizabeth Custer, Susan
Wallace, and Sister Blandina Segale.

---

8. F. L. Olmsted later became famous for planning Central Park, New York
   City, Forest Park, St. Louis; and the grounds of Chicago World's Fair, 1893.
9. Lanier in *Retrospects and Prospects* (1899). See also John S. Mayfield,
   "Lanier in Lastekas," *Southwest Review*, XVII (October, 1931), 20-44.
10. Bean's *Memoirs,* which first appeared in Yoakum's *History of Texas* (1856),
    deals with prison life in Mexico. New edition, Book Club of Texas (1936).

One of the earliest of these to leave a record was the young Kentuckian James O. Pattie who, with his father, came to the Southwest in 1824. In Arizona and parts of New Mexico, where Caucasian civilization had not yet penetrated, he hunted, trapped, fought Indians, and was taken captive. For six years he lived this dangerous life. He set down his adventures with a simple, straightforward style in *The Personal Narrative of James O. Pattie of Kentucky* (1831).

In the spring of 1831 Albert Pike, a Bostonian, started West. He walked much of the way, journeying as far as the Navajo country, exploring, trading, living among the Indians. He met Aaron B. Lewis and recorded his expedition in "Journey in the Prairie." "Narrative of Second Journey in the Prairie" and "The Inroad of the Nabajo" are primarily of his own travels.[11] Pike described the Governor's Palace in Santa Fe as a "mud building 15 feet high, with a mud-covered portico, supported by rough pine pillars." He wrote of both Indians and Spaniards with realism. In 1833 Albert Pike settled in Little Rock, gained renown as a poet, an editor, and a lawyer, and built a colonial mansion which is still the show place of the city. He served in the Confederate Army as a brigadier general.[12]

George W. Kendall, of the New Orleans *Picayune,* had mixed motives for joining the ill-advised Texas-Santa Fé Expedition in 1841. His health was bad. He had a desire to see the Indians and take part in a buffalo hunt. He was looking for material for writing. The party set out from Austin on June 18, Kendall in a wagon, on account of a broken ankle. Not until they were well on their way did Kendall learn the real object of what purported to be a trading expedition, but was in fact an attempt to annex New Mexico to the Republic of Texas. Kendall recorded, with a journalist's eye, the blunders, hardships, and inevitable failure of the expedition.[13] The ac-

11. These three accounts were published in *Prose Sketches and Poems* (1834).
12. See biographical introduction to William L. Boyden, *Bibliography of the Writings of Albert Pike* (1931).
13. George W. Kendall, *Narratives of an Expedition Across the Great Southwestern Prairies from Texas to Santa Fé; with an Account of the Disasters which befell the Expedition from Want of Food and the Attacks of Hostile Indians; the Final Capture of the Texans and their Sufferings on a March of Two Thousand Miles as Prisoners of War, and in the Prisons and Lazarettos of Mexico* (1844).

count of the long, tragic march to Mexico City, the imprison-
ment, and final release of the survivors is particularly moving.[14]

Kendall in his Preface acknowledges help from "Mr.
Gregg, an intelligent merchant who has been for many years
engaged in the Santa Fé trade and also from Albert Pike . . .
a poet and writer of great distinction" who had gone to Santa
Fé in 1832. Josiah Gregg, in turn, in the Preface to his *Commerce of the Prairies, The Journal of a Santa Fé Trader*
(1844), apologizes for adding another book where Irving
"and more recently" Kendall have written. Like Kendall he
went to the prairies for his health. From 1831 to 1840 he was
a trader. Later he drew on his carefully kept journals for
articles to periodicals and for his volume which soon came to be
a sort of handbook for travelers over the Santa Fé Trail.

Lewis Hector Garrard gives credit not to Gregg but to
Fremont's Report of his 1842-43 expedition to the Rocky
Mountains for turning his fancy West. The year before, when
only sixteen, he had "thrown away his schoolbooks" and on a
river steamer from his home in Cincinnati had gone to Louisiana and Texas. Now in the summer of 1846 at Westport
Landing he joined the caravan of Céran St. Vrain of Taos,
member of the famous trading firm of Bent and St. Vrain.
Upon his return to Ohio after ten months' absence he recorded
in *Wah-To-Yah* [15] *and the Taos Trail* (1850) with boyish
gusto and humor his experiences on the Trail, and in and near
Bent's Fort and Taos. For several months of this time he lived
with the Cheyennes, delighting in their free life. The news of
the insurrection at Taos during which Charles Bent was killed
brought these carefree days to an end for Garrard. His account of the hanging of the eighty and more rebels at Taos is
realistic tragedy. Three modern editions of *Wah-To-Yah* attest to the lasting interest of Garrard's book.[16]

Susan Shelby Magoffin, said by some to be the first American lady to cross the plains, refers several times in her diary
Down the Santa Fé Trail and into Mexico, 1846-1847 to
the books of Kendall and Gregg. These she had evidently

---

14. For Kendall's *Narrative* as a source for Hervey Allen's *Anthony Adverse,*
see *Saturday Review of Literature,* January 13, 1934.
15. The name meaning "Breasts of the World" given by the Indians to the
Spanish Peaks in southern Colorado.
16. See Selected Bibliography, First and Second Editions.

studied preparatory for her journey with her trader husband. Well educated, the daughter of an illustrious Kentucky family, she showed an intelligent interest in everything she saw and heard. She kept a detailed and, except for periods of illness or imminent danger, a day by day record of events. This expedition, like the one Kendall accompanied, was no usual trading trip, but had the secret purpose of paving the way "for General Kearny's bloodless conquest of the Southwest." This diary is a significant record of the courage and graciousness of a gently bred lady in the Southwest during the dangerous years of the Mexican War.

Not until after the Civil War did another woman, coming into the Southwest with her husband, write of historic events, people, and places. Elizabeth Custer in 1865 was in Texas with her husband the boy general, George A. Custer, and the government troops. Her lively accounts of army life in the turbulent post-war days in what seemed at first to her to be "the stepping off place" still make good reading.[17]

Early in 1879 another army wife, Susan Wallace, came to the Southwest to join her husband, General Lew Wallace, newly appointed Governor of New Mexico Territory. In Santa Fe she presided over the Governor's Palace. She visited pueblos, turquoise and silver mines, and the ruins of Casa Grande and Montezuma's Palace. Always she was excited by the long distances and the antiquity of Indian and Spanish civilization. While the governor was writing *Ben Hur,* she was recording the Southwest scene, the people, their history and legends. These articles were published in magazines, among them *The Atlantic,* and later, in 1889, collected and republished in *The Land of the Pueblos.*

A year before the Wallaces came to live in *El Palacio,* a lone, Italian-born Sister of Charity from Ohio, Sister Blandina Segale, started her work in the Catholic Orphan Asylum and Hospital in Santa Fe. For twelve years in Santa Fe and Albuquerque, with rare courage and endurance, she taught Spanish

17. Elizabeth Custer, *Tenting on the Plains: or General Custer in Kansas and Texas* (1887).

children, tended the sick, promoted building expansion, often making adobe bricks and plastering walls herself. She nursed the aging Archbishop Lamy with whom she had formed a tender friendship. For weeks she visited daily a wounded bandit of Billy the Kid's gang and in return received the Kid's protection on lonely coach trips. Once alone with a cross held before her she walked through the desert toward a menacing Apache band and persuaded them to negotiate with the whites. All of this and much more she recorded with realism and humor in a journal to her own sister in the Order, Sister Justina, then in Ohio. Without revision in 1932 it was published in book form. *At the End of the Santa Fe Trail* stands as a rare chronicle of the courage of a selfless woman.

Another group of early participants in Southwestern life spiced fact with fiction. It is often impossible to distinguish between the actual and the fabricated. The borderline is very thin. Legends, tall tales, episodes expanded with fictionized dialogue, composite and imaginary type-characters embellish these narratives. In this group belong David Crockett,[18] George Ruxton, Frederick Gerstaecker, and John Crittenden Duval.

One of the earliest of the fictionized narratives was by George Frederick Ruxton, an English sportsman and explorer. After varied experiences in the West he wrote for *Blackwood's Magazine* of 1848 a serial, *Life in the Far West,* later published in book form with the title *In the Old West, As It Was in the Days of Kit Carson and the "Mountain Men"* (1920).[19] The characters and most of the incidents are real, though some of the names of people are changed; the plot is fictionized. There is much use of dialect and Western idiom. Old Killbuck, the veteran trapper, is a Cooperesque character. The book is made up of swift action, romance, and an almost unbelievable coincidence that happened to be true. It contains all the elements of a good Western movie.

Probably less fictionized but employing more legends and

---

18. Discussed in Part Two, Ch. II, Humor and Tall Tales.
19. Of the numerous contemporary books about Kit Carson none are of literary value, although useful for source material. One of these is *Kit Carson's Own Story of His Life,* as dictated to Colonel and Mrs. D. C. Peters about 1856-57. Edited by Blanche Grant (1926). See also Henry Nash Smith, "Kit Carson Books," *Southwest Review,* XXVIII (1942-43), 164-89.

tall tales to spice the plain truth is Frederick Gerstaecker's *Wild Sports in the Far West* (1860). Gerstaecker, a German writer, came to America in 1837 to hunt big game. Disappointed at finding no bear tracks around New York City, he started on foot for Arkansas, the paradise of hunters. For four years he hunted and trapped and listened to the tales of the veteran bear killers. Like Irving, Gerstaecker found frontier life and characters picturesque and romantic.

John Crittenden Duval, whom J. Frank Dobie calls the Father of Texas Literature, grew up under the Irving influence.[20] Indeed, his father William Pope Duval, the first governor of the Territory of Florida, was the hero of Irving's *The Early Experiences of Ralph Ringwood* (1855). Young John C., aged nineteen, came to Texas in 1836 with a company of Bardstown, Kentucky, men under the captaincy of his older brother, Burr. Like David Crockett they longed to help Texas in the struggle for independence from Mexico. John C. was one of the few survivors of the massacre of Goliad. He encountered almost unbelievable privations and dangers, living for months by his wits in the cane brakes.

In 1867-68 his narrative of these experiences ran under the title of *Jack Dobell; Or, A Boy's Adventures in Texas* as a serial, in *Burke's Weekly*, published in Macon, Georgia. In 1892, with only minor changes, the story appeared in book form as *Early Times in Texas; or the Adventures of Jack Dobell* by J. C. Dobell. The amount of fiction is probably slight. He called himself Jack Dobell and perhaps amplified the Robinson Crusoe nature of his experience. William Corner writing in 1897 said, "Some day this will be a Texas classic. . . ."[21]

Duval's better-known book, *The Adventures of Big-Foot Wallace* (1870), based on the life of his friend and comrade in Jack Hay's company of Texas Rangers, is probably more fictionized in certain parts.[22] The ill-fated Mier Expedition, however, of which Wallace was a survivor, is recounted in straight chronicle manner and is the most valuable account of that tragic episode of Texas history. Duval's book on Big-Foot

20. See Introductions to Major and Smith editions of *The Adventures of Big-Foot Wallace* and *Early Times in Texas* (1936).
21. *Quarterly of Texas State Historical Association*, No. 1.
22. For humorous elements of *The Adventures of Big-Foot Wallace*, see Part Two, Ch. II, Humor and Tall Tales.

still stands as the liveliest and most interesting of the accounts of this early hero.[23]

The faithful, vivid record of their adventures left by the intrepid men and women who established Anglo-American culture in the Southwest is a worthy chapter of our literature.

---

23. A. J. Sowell's *Life of Big-Foot Wallace* (1899), although a valuable record, is without literary merit. Stanley Vestal's *Big-Foot Wallace* (1942), while following closely ascertainable facts, falls short of the spirit of the man. For other accounts of the Mier Expedition, see General Thomas J. Green, *Journal of the Texian Expedition Against Mier* (1845); William Preston Stapp, *The Prisoners of Perote* (1845); and Frederick Chabot, *The Perote Prisoners* (1934).

II

HUMOR AND TALL TALES

The American frontier produced a characteristic humor based upon the experiences of pioneer life. Lonely people tell tales for their own pleasure: adventures, anecdotes of eccentric characters in the neighborhood, and traditions bordering on the supernatural. The tellers exaggerate or understate to furnish that surprise element and incongruity which underlie all simple humor. Thus, a backwoodsman would recount how he had out-witted a greenhorn or killed a "bar" of prodigious size or how some mighty man of his acquaintance once waded the Missis-sippi with a tree stump for a walking stick—all the while keep-ing a solemn face and a leisurely manner. The formula of such tales is easily recognized. A homespun narrator vouches for the truth of his yarn; he has seen it or heard if from a reliable witness. Slowly the stage is set with a frontier background; then the tall hero or clumsy victim—or both—are introduced, and the action begins. The hero does mighty deeds and the victim is discomfited. Often the setting includes stupendous natural phenomena with episodes of super-snakes or wind-storms or grasshoppers, which can develop into independent tales.[1]

This humor of character in action, of violent contrast, is fundamentally related to humor in all ages; but it takes deep root on the American frontier and spreads westward with it. Humor is the American folkway of passing judgment on the contemporary scene. A people not addicted to open compli-ments can best express their admiration of Davy Crockett or Kit Carson or Sam Houston by preserving tales of his prowess compounded equally of hero-worship and burlesque. If the frontier loves a man, it "joshes" him. Or, with equal swiftness, the pioneer community uses humor to deflate and crush those

---

1. Consult Walter Blair, *Native American Humor* (1937) and *Tall Tale Amer-ica* (1944); Franklin Meine, *Tall Tales of the Southwest* (1930); Constance Rourke, *American Humor* (1930); J. Frank Dobie's Preface to Mody Boat-right, *Tall Tales from Texas Cow Camps* (1934); Mody Boatright, "Frontier Humor: Despairing or Buoyant," *Southwest Review*, XXVII (Spring, 1942), 320-34.

who do not fit into its way of life. It laughs into insignificance
and impotence the cowardly, the pompous, the eccentric, the
specialized persons in its midst.

This tradition of humor came to the Southwest with the
Anglo-American settlers, both as a habit of living and as a
literary tradition. For the half century following 1830, humorous books, magazines, newspaper columns, and lectures added
to the joy of the nation and shouted to the world the social
judgments of the frontier. Mark Twain, son of the Great Valley, elevated Western humor into literature.[2] In all this the
Southwest shared, but inevitably it added new materials and
humorists to the tradition, keeping the familiar patterns and
techniques.

One of the famous tales of the Trans-Mississippi frontier
is T. B. Thorpe's "The Big Bear of Arkansas."[3] The author
is making a trip on a Mississippi River steamboat, and in di-
gressive style relates the tales he hears from the passengers
regarding wild turkeys and mosquitoes in the vicinity. Then the
"man from Arkansaw" begins his yarn of the big bear. "Stranger," he said, "in bar hunts *I am numerous . . .*" and we are
involved in the pursuit of a bear as weird and supernatural as
Moby Dick the Whale or the White Stallion of the Plains.

David Crockett, of Tennessee, was the first frontier humorist to whom the new Southwest could lay legitimate claim. As
a redoubtable hunter and coonskin politician in his native state,
Crockett had written or at least had inspired two considerable
books of his adventures, *A Narrative of the Life of David
Crockett* (1834) and *An Account of Colonel Crockett's Tour
to the North and Down East* (1835) before he decided to leave
politics in Tennessee to Andrew Jackson and "lend the Texians
a helping hand." *Colonel Crockett's Exploits and Adventures
in Texas* (1836) was written, of course, entirely or partially
by someone else, but it is in the same general style as the others.[4]
In all three the manner is that of the frontier humorist.
Crockett is relating his own adventures throughout and so must
be his own hero, but he burlesques his achievements and joshes
about himself in the salty pioneer way. He digresses to include

2. Consult Bernard De Voto, *Mark Twain's America* (1931).
3. Meine, *op. cit.,* pp. 7-21. For Ozark folk beliefs, many of which are humorous,
   see Vance Randolph's *Ozark Superstitions* (1947).
4. Constance Rourke, *Davy Crockett* (1930), pp. 247-76.

minor anecdotes such as his trading a coonskin over and over for whiskey and the familiar yarn of the fellow rehearsing a fight all by himself.[5] Crockett's stories use dialect and homely aphorisms to give them flavor, a device consciously cultivated by the humorous journalist-lecturers.

Crockett's books illustrate the fact that in the early days the humor of the Southwest was an adjunct to other kinds of writing. Many adventure and travel accounts were cast in that form or enlivened by it. For example, the narrative of George Frederick Ruxton, originally published as *Life in the Far West* (1848), presents a mountain man, Killbuck, who draws a long bow in relating his travels, especially his getting lost in the "putrified forest," a true tall tale, that is to say, a gorgeous lie, worthy of Sir John Mandeville or Baron Munchausen. An Englishman, Ruxton unerringly perceived the humorous anecdote to be characteristic of the new country.

Another excellent travel record, Lewis Garrard's *Wah-to-Yah* (1850), is rich in humor, especially in dialect and the rhythm of tale-telling. His best character creation is Hatcher, one time foreman at Bent's Fort, who has "an inexhaustible fund of anecdotes and humor, which kept his camp circle in a continual roar." The long inset story of his descent into hell is one of the best of all pioneer devil legends.[6] Somewhat later in date but of the same brand is the humor of John C. Duval, which pervades most of his account of *The Adventures of Big-Foot Wallace* (1870). The anecdotes of fights with wolves, Indians, and cattle stealers, while serious in action, are told with the exaggeration and nonchalance that mark the frontier yarn-swapper, and even the tragic Mier Expedition is enlivened by homely details and understatement. The ridicule of a tenderfoot author touring Texas in search of material seems bookish; but it is well to recall that Duval and many other frontier writers were possessed of a literary background. In Part III of the *Adventures* Big-Foot goes back to the settlements to take the measure of town men and ways. He sees the sights of New Orleans, and entertains the girls in Virginia with

---

5. This episode in Chap. III of the *Exploits* parallels almost *verbatim* a similar scene in A. B. Longstreet's *Georgia Scenes* (1835), quoted in Meine, *op. cit.*, as "Georgia Theatrics," pp. 337-39.
6. Compare with Frank Goodwyn, *The Devil in Texas* (1936).

tall tales of Texas. In any company he turns out to be a first-rate man.

The professional journalists who made humor their staple were at the height of their vogue when the Southwest was being settled. As early as 1858, S. A. Hammett found the Southwest apt material to include in one of his popular Sam Slick series, *In Piney Woods Tavern; or Sam Slick in Texas.* In Austin in the early 1880's Alexander Sweet and J. Armory Knox issued *Texas Siftings,* a weekly journal of "cheerful statistics, hilarious facts, and solemn truths." In this tradition young Will Porter (O. Henry) wrote funny pieces for *The Rolling Stone* in Austin a few years later. The last great frontier humorist was Will Rogers of Oklahoma, cowboy philosopher, whose newspaper column and radio programs epitomized the common sense of the American people in the two decades following the first World War.

The most indigenous of all Southwestern tall tales is the legend of the folk hero. On a frontier made unusually violent by climate and long distances and mounted Indians, literally anything might happen and a strong, resourceful man was looked up to by all. His fame grew apace. The typical hero of the region is some historical person about whom legends gather. We have noted the exaggeration of David Crockett into a legendary figure; and to a less degree the same phenomenon took place with Kit Carson and Sam Houston. An early clear-cut example of the metamorphosis of real man into folk hero is Captain Aylett C. Buckner, of the Old Three Hundred, who settled with Austin in Texas in 1821, who became Strap Buckner, the hero of terrific encounters with black bulls and the devil.[7] Equally interesting is Mabry C. Gray, a San Jacinto and Mexican War fighter, who became Mustang Gray, outlaw hero of a novel, a ballad, and countless tales, oral and written.[8]

The lawbreaker has often seemed a hero on the frontier, a Robin Hood defying range laws and asserting his freedom. Among the Southwest's "bad men," the most feared and re-

7. Consult H. F. McDanield and N. A. Taylor, *The Coming Empire or Two Thousand Miles in Texas on Horseback* (1877), pp. 49-73; N. A. Taylor, "The Devil and Strap Buckner," *Publications* of the Texas Folk-Lore Society, III (1924), 118-30, Florence E. Barns, "Strap Buckner of the Texas Frontier," *Publications* of the Texas Folk-Lore Society, VIII (1930), 129-51.
8. J. Frank Dobie, "Mustang Gray: Fact, Tradition, and Song," *Publications* of the Texas Folk-Lore Society, X (1932), 109-23.

membered is the boy bandit, Billy the Kid. Killed in 1881 after an amazing career of horse-stealing and murder, Billy became a legend with good men vying for the honor of having known him or killed him.[9] More glamorous still is the young train robber, Sam Bass, who first came out to Texas, "a cowboy for to be," but who soon thought he had "the world by the tail, with a downhill pull." He not only gave gold to the poor, but, so the folk still believe, he buried it in caves all over the state. Almost immediately after his death, a paper-back life of him appeared; he is still commemorated by scholars and popular singers alike.[10] But the outlaws were not alone the heroes of the frontier. The enforcers of the law likewise loomed large. For example, Judge Roy Bean, who was "Law West of the Pecos," lived a rich life in all truth and has steadily become a legend not only in the Southwest but on the screen.[11]

Gib Morgan of oil field fame, was a real person, too, born in Western Pennsylvania in 1842. Like David Crockett and Big-Foot Wallace he was himself a teller of tall tales, often of places where he had never been as Russia and Texas. His stories of his fantastic deeds have spread and grown with the oil industry. Though the records say he died in 1909, he is still laying pipe line under the ocean and bringing in wells in Texas with a needle and thread.[12]

Less indigenous to the Southwest than the historical heroes but equally colorful are the mythical doers-of-great-deeds. Paul Bunyan has intermittently deserted his logging camp to become an oil man here;[13] and John Henry, that "hammer-swingin', cotton-snatchin', natchal man," must have ridden the Cotton Belt sometime or other into this region.[14] The tallest folk hero in the Southwest is a late comer, Pecos Bill, who did not break into print apparently until about twenty-five years ago. The superlative cowboy is Pecos Bill; all the adventures are his,

9. An early account of Billy the Kid is Charles A. Siringo, *A Texas Cowboy* (1886), pp. 196-230; 269-84. See also Walter Noble Burns, *Saga of Billy the Kid* (1926) ; Pat Garrett, *The Life of Billy the Kid* (1927) ; George W. Coe, *Frontier Fighter* (1934).
10. Wayne Gard, *Sam Bass* (1936).
11. Everett Lloyd, *Law West of the Pecos* (1931) ; C. L. Sonnichsen, *Roy Bean, Law West of the Pecos* (1943).
12. Mody Boatright, *Gib Morgan, Minstrel of the Oil Fields* (1945).
13. John Lee Brooks, "Paul Bunyan: Oil Man," *Publications* of the Texas Folk-Lore Society, VII (1929), 45-54.
14. Roark Bradford, *John Henry* (1931).

even courting the ladies, a field into which heroes rarely adventure in the tradition of Southwestern humor. If Davy Crockett of legend, with the sunrise in his pocket, is the first of our true folk heroes, the last may well be Pecos Bill, "a-settin' on that tornado and a-spurrin' it in the withers." [15]

15. Edward O'Reilly, "Saga of Pecos Bill," *Century Magazine*, CVI (1923), 827-33; Mody Boatright, *op. cit.*, pp. 68-100; James C. Bowman, *Pecos Bill: The Greatest Cowboy of All Time* (1937); Leigh Peck, *Pecos Bill and Lightning* (1940).

III

FOLK BALLADS

The rivals of the raconteur of tall tales as an entertainer on the frontier were the ballad singer and fiddler. Whether the gathering was a house-warming to which hundreds came in wagons or on horseback or just the family before the fireplace in winter, the person who could sing or play a tune took the place of modern radio and dance orchestra. And this music was something that all could take part in, adding stanzas to the ballads, joining in on the chorus, or swinging one's partner and "do-se-do-ing" to the fiddler's tunes. Life was made happier by the old British ballads, the traditional tunes, the more newly improvised cowboy songs, and, wherever there were Negroes, by the haunting spirituals and rhythmic work songs.[1]

Tracing earlier American versions of the British ballads sung in the Southwest results in a population chart of the origins of the inhabitants. A few of these ballads came from the North and a few direct from Great Britain. But most of them came in by the Southern route from the mountains of Virginia, Kentucky, Tennessee, Arkansas.

The most cherished of the British ballads were the love songs, mostly tragic. The mournful tales of cruel Barbara Allan and Sweet William, and of bloodthirsty Lord Thomas and Fair Eleanor were sung as the pioneers walked beside their wagon trains or mothers hushed their babies. At frontier gatherings they were even used for play-party games. Thus the ballad and dance were reunited after a long separation.[2] Most of the ancient ballads of the supernatural lost their mystical elements and became mere love ballads with local place names

1. For discussions of theories of ballad origin, see: Francis James Child, *English and Scottish Popular Ballads* (1882-89); Francis Barton Gummere, *The Popular Ballad* (1907); Gordon Hall Gerould, *The Ballad of Tradition* (1932); "Making of Ballads," *Modern Philology* XXI (August, 1923), 15 ff.; Louise Pound, *Poetic Origins of the Ballad* (1921), "A Recent Theory of Ballad Making," *Publications of Modern Language Association,* XLIV (June, 1929), 622 ff.
2. Mabel Major, "British Ballads in Texas," *Publications* of the Texas Folk-Lore Society, X (1932), 131-38; and Vance Randolph, *Ozark Mountain Folks* (1932).

instead of the British ones. A few sea ballads survived their
long overland trek from the Atlantic seaboard; a few came in
by the Gulf. Humorous ballads survived mostly for the children. Many people living in the Southwest today grew up
entertained by their own family version of "The Frog's Courting." [3]

A gifted singer would often make up new ballads relating
the tragic happenings of the community—an Indian raid, a
fatal shooting, a mine cave-in, or the exploits of a bad man such
as Sam Bass.[4] But to a great extent the old songs were more
popular, and, together with the walnut bureau and fragile blue
china brought in the covered wagon, gave a sense of the continuity of life in a strange environment.

Although a few of the narrative songs were used for play-
party games, the play-party song is a type in itself. The narrative element is unimportant, repetition is prevalent, nonsense
refrains are usual, and directions for the dancers are a part of
the song, making the presence of a "caller" unnecessary.[5] In
fact, the distinction between play-party games and square
dances is chiefly that in the former the players sing and follow
the directions in the song; in the latter, which can be more lively, a fiddler plays and a "caller" chants the directions for the
figures. He may be the fiddler or even one of the dancers who
is "long on breath."

Many people in the Southwest still sing ballads and play-
party songs. In some communities square dances have survived
or been revived, as the famous Cowboy's Christmas Ball at
Anson, Texas. For a time it looked as if these traditional ways
of entertainment would give place to the movie, the radio, the
phonograph, and the swing orchestra. However, the radio
singers and recordings are aiding in keeping alive and even
spreading interest in folk music. Now, just as the latest Broadway and Hollywood hits, grand operas and symphonies are
heard in the most remote sections of the country, the folk songs
and tunes have their audiences in the metropolitan areas.

---

3. L. W. Payne, Jr., "Some Texas Versions of the Frog's Courting," *Publications of the Texas Folk-Lore Society*, V (1926), 5 ff.
4. Charles Finger, *Frontier Outlaw Ballads* (1927).
5. W. A. Owens, *Swing and Turn* (1936). B. A. Botkin, "Play-Party in Oklahoma," *Publications* of the Texas Folk-Lore Society, VII (1928), 7 ff.

Although the cowboy songs [6] are the most nearly indigenous of Southwest ballads, some of these derive from old English songs. "The Dying Cowboy," the most widely known of them all, is a sort of parody and adaptation of the English sea chanty, "The Ocean Burial," [7] and "The Cowboy's Dream" is sung to the tune of "My Bonnie Lies Over the Ocean." Both of these are night herding songs. Many of the range ballads, however, are entirely original and sprang out of the cattle industry itself, such as the trail drivers' "Whoopee Ti Yi Yo"— with the crack of a whip at a lagging dogie's heels for its refrain. "Old Paint," a song of the homeward trail after driving a herd north to market, came to be the "Home Sweet Home" of cowboy dances.

Who composed many of these songs no one knows though only a few decades have passed. It would be almost as impossible to trace their inception as to find the origin of "Sir Patrick Spens" or "The Wife of Usher's Well." John Lomax sees in these songs of the range evidences of group authorship that he advances as support of the communal authorship theory of medieval European ballads as held by Gummere, Child, Wendell, Kittredge, and others.[8] Louise Pound, on the other hand, interprets what can be learned of the origin of cowboy ballads to uphold her adherence to the individual authorship theory of ballad origin.[9] With most of these songs, as with the British, there are as many variants as there are singers. Multiple composition has been achieved in fact, if not according to the group authorship theory.

One true cowboy ballad-maker was Howard N. (Jack) Thorp, the author of "Little Joe the Wrangler" and some twenty-five lesser known ballads.[10] Born in 1867, the son of a New York lawyer, he came West as a youth to visit his brother's cattle ranch in Nebraska. Thorp became a rancher himself in the San Andrés Mountains of New Mexico in the '80's. He

---

6. See the collections by Jack Thorp and John Lomax.
7. Ernest E. Leisy, "O Bury Me Not," *Publications* of the Texas Folk-Lore Society, IX (1931), 183 ff.
8. *Journal of American Folk-Lore,* XXVIII (January-March, 1915), 1 ff. Also Introduction to *Cowboy Songs* (1910).
9. See Note 1, p. 64.
10. Howard N. (Jack) Thorp died June 4, 1940, a few months before his article, "Banjo in the Cow Camps," telling of his collecting cowboy songs, appeared in *The Atlantic Monthly*. It is reprinted in Thorp's posthumous book in collaboration with Neil McCullough Clark, *Pardner of the Wind* (1945).

pioneered in collecting ballads in the West, riding from cow camp to cow camp on his first song hunt in 1889. At Estancia, New Mexico, in 1908 he published his first collection, a small paper-backed volume of twenty-three ballads, five of which he had composed himself.[11] Unfortunately not until 1921 in *Songs of the Cowboys,* a volume expanded to one hundred and one songs, did he acknowledge authorship of his own ballads.

The most extensive collections of cowboy songs have been made by John A. Lomax. Born the same year as Jack Thorp, he grew up on a bottom land farm in Bosque County, Texas. As a boy he learned to sing cowboy songs and wrote down all he heard. Not until he was a graduate student at Harvard in 1907 did he find anyone in the academic world interested in his roll of Western ballads. The great folklorists Barrett Wendell and George Lyman Kittredge aided him in securing a Sheldon Fellowship for ballad collecting. Since then he has had many fellowships and grants for this purpose. His first volume, *Cowboy Songs and Other Frontier Ballads,* with music for eighteen of the ballads, appeared in 1910 with an introduction by Professor Wendell. It contained, too, a letter from Theodore Roosevelt making the interesting observation, "There is something very curious in the reproduction here on this new continent of essentially the conditions of ballad-growth which obtained in medieval England. . . ." In 1918 Mr. Lomax published "an overflow book," *Songs of the Cattle Trail and Cow Camp.* In *Adventures of a Ballad Hunter* (1947) John Lomax with a genius for recreating places, singers, and moods sets down the record of his more than half a century of folk song collecting.[12]

Some of the Negro folk songs in the Southwest have grown up here, but a large group came in from plantations of the Old South. The ballad of "The Boll Weevil" originated somewhere in Texas with the coming of the pest about the turn of the century.[13] Since then the pest and the song have spread to every cotton-growing state in the nation. The origin of

---

11. Despite Thorp's statement in the "Preface"—"I plead ignorant of the authorship of them"—he really knew a good deal about these songs both as to authorship and circumstance. In his 1921 volume, he annotates all of the songs, including those in his original collection.
12. John A. Lomax died January 27, 1948, in Greenville, Mississippi, while on a lecture tour.
13. Dorothy Scarborough, *On the Trail of the Negro Folk Song* (1925).

"Frankie and Johnnie" is disputed; some say it tells of a Negro shooting craps at Paris, Texas. Many of these Negro songs survive from slave days. One of the most interesting is "Foller de Drinkin' Gou'd" (the Big Dipper) in which directions were given in song form by a peg-legged Northern Negro for slaves to follow a certain route North to freedom.[14] It is still bad luck for a Negro to let a white man hear him sing this song. "What Is Dis?" with its haunting, weird melody is said to have been made by a dying slave woman whose cruel mistress had choked her nearly to death.[15]

The most beautiful of the Negro songs, the spirituals, deal with Biblical stories and religious exaltation. Some of them even have haunting suggestions of Africa and paganism. "Swing Low Sweet Chariot," "Glory Road," "God's Heben," "Nobody Knows the Trouble I've Seen," sung by the richly emotional Negro voices, thrill blacks and whites alike.

So great is the power of song over Negroes that employers often hire gifted Negroes at double wages to lead the workers in singing as they drive railroad spikes or work on the levee. Work songs, usually with a large amount of repetition, have grown up to the rhythm of the special work the singers are doing.

Among the collectors of Negro folk songs of the Southwest are Dorothy Scarborough and John A. and Alan Lomax. Miss Scarborough's *On the Trail of the Negro Folk Song* (1925) shows a rare understanding of the Negro on farm and plantation. The Lomaxes—father and son—recorded chiefly the moving, often brutal songs from convicts in penitentiaries and on prison farms.[16]

In spite of mechanical music, the people of the Southwest are still more a singing people than those of more urbanized sections of the country. The outdoor season is long; the open country is never far away; summer evenings are made for picnics and song and long rides into the westering moon.

---

14. *Publications* of the Texas Folk-Lore Society, VII (1928), 81 ff.
15. In the collection of Virginia Bales, *ibid.*, p. 109.
16. *American Ballads and Folk Songs* (1934), *Negro Folk Songs as Sung by Lead Belly* (1937), and *Our Singing Country* (1941). John Lomax states in *Adventures of a Ballad Hunter* (p. 296) that along with Alan Lomax he has contributed more than ten thousand songs on records to the Archive of American Folk Song of the Library of Congress. A great many of these were collected in the Southwest.

IV

HISTORICAL WRITING

The first historians of any new region are the writers of travel books and journals. These chronicles in the early Southwest have already been discussed; but it is worth while to note that the region is still new enough to impel authors today to record pioneer adventures.

In Colonial America nearly three centuries ago the first chroniclers wrote personal, informal, simple narratives. After the establishment of a political government and the waging of wars to defend it, formal political histories were produced, flavored with strong patriotic sentiment. As culture increased, private individuals and libraries and colleges collected historical documents; scholars were trained to study and edit them. With these resources at hand, the scientific historians of the late nineteenth and early twentieth centuries have thoroughly re-examined the evidence of the national past, and have interpreted it in the light of modern social and economic theories.[1]

Much this same sequence, on a smaller scale, has appeared in the Anglo-American historical writing of the Southwest.[2] In the wake of the first type of writing, the travels and adventures, appeared the more formal political state histories, with a patriotic bias. It was shortly following the Texas War for Independence that William Kennedy's *Texas* (1841) and Henderson Yoakum's *History of Texas* (1856) were published, works which established the beginnings of the republic-state on a sound basis of idealism and democratic policy. These histories, dignified in tone and concerned with public events, followed the great example of Bancroft's *American Annals,*

---

1. See *Cambridge History of American Literature* (1921), Vol. I, Chs. I-II; Vol. II, Ch. XVII; Vol. III, Ch. XV; and Michael Kraus, *A History of American History* (1938).
2. Somewhat arbitrarily we discuss here those histories of the Southwest which have been written by authors working in the region, thereby omitting many noteworthy scholarly studies originating elsewhere, such as George P. Winship's *The Coronado Expedition, 1540-1542* (1896) and Justin H. Smith, *The Annexation of Texas* (1911).

and were in turn followed by many other conventional Texas histories—H. S. Thrall's *History of Texas* (1879), John Henry Brown's *History of Texas* (1893), Dudley G. Wooten's *Comprehensive History of Texas* (1898), and others.

Arkansas, rich in early travel literature, spent its initial historical impulse in chronicling the Civil War rather than its own story. However, John Hallum's *Biographical and Pictorial History of Arkansas* (1887) furnished a survey of the life of the state, and was enriched by a dozen sketches contributed by Albert Pike. First place among early state historians of New Mexico is generally conceded to W. W. H. Davis, whose *El Gringo* (1857) and *The Spanish Conquest of New Mexico* (1869) made accessible in a clear, pleasant style the materials in the early Spanish narratives. Historians in New Mexico, which included Arizona until 1863, naturally have emphasized the colorful early events of that region.[3] Since Oklahoma was not officially opened to white American settlers until 1889, little formal historical writing was done until early in the next century. A distinguished pioneer in the Oklahoma field is Edward Everett Dale, of the University of Oklahoma, author of *Territorial Acquisitions of the United States* (1912), *History of Oklahoma* (with J. S. Buchanan, 1924), whose scholarship places him with the modern school of historians.

"The Southwest is best covered by the various volumes of Hubert Howe Bancroft's *Works*," writes Herbert E. Bolton, himself an authority in the field.[4] "All . . . writers on the Southwest," says F. L. Paxson, historian of the American frontier, "owe a debt to the great collector and preserver of local records, Hubert Howe Bancroft of San Francisco, who wrote, edited, or signed nearly forty great volumes of Pacific Coast history between 1874 and 1890. From his collections, now owned by the University of California, there come frequent volumes of scholarly writings. . . ."[5] With H. H. Bancroft, historical writing in the Southwest attained scholarly maturity, for he gathered and utilized vast original source materials,

3. See Charles F. Lummis, *Spanish Pioneers* (1893); Frank W. Blackmar, *Spanish Institutions in the Southwest* (1891); R. E. Twitchell, *Leading Facts of New Mexican History* (1911-12); C. F. Coan, *A Shorter History of New Mexico* (1925).
4. *The Spanish Borderlands* (1921), bibliographical note, p. 298.
5. F. L. Paxson, *History of the American Frontier* (1924), p. 351 footnote.

documented his narratives with copious notes and bibliographies. For the purposes of this study the most valuable of his volumes are the two titled *History of the North Mexican States and Texas* (1889) and *History of Arizona and New Mexico* (1889). In spite of their rich documentation and great length, these histories are not heavy or dull, for Bancroft writes fluently and interestingly. The first chapter, for example, of the work on Arizona and New Mexico, with its discussion of the Northern Mystery and Cabeza de Vaca, is a model introduction to the subject.

After scholarship has accumulated and recorded sources, the next step in historical writing is sound, modern interpretation. That step in the Southwest was first taken by George P. Garrison, of the University of Texas. In *Texas, A Contest of Civilization* (1903), and other studies, as well as in his long career as a teacher,[6] he integrated the colonization of Texas and the Mexican War with the main currents of settlement on the widespread American frontier. He showed that much more than the issue of slavery was involved, and thereby rescued the history of Texas from the unfavorable interpretations given to it by Northern historians writing in the prejudice of Civil War issues. It may well be said that the writing of history in the Southwest took on a national significance with the work of Garrison.

During the first century of Anglo-American occupation of the Southwest, the historical writings have been rich and valuable. We have considered here the older types of work: the formal state histories which follow early travel accounts. Many of them are conventional in style, somewhat rhetorical, and, in some cases, chauvinistic; but few frontier regions can match them for variety, interest, and color. Later on we shall discuss the more recent scholarly editing and modern interpretation of historical materials in the region.

6. Among the distinguished historians who were trained under Garrison are Eugene C. Barker, Herbert Bolton, Charles Ramsdell, Walter P. Webb, and Charles Hackett.

V

ARCHAEOLOGICAL AND ANTHROPOLOGICAL
WRITINGS

History treats of man's past and present as a political creature; anthropology treats of man's span of existence as a social creature. Paralleling the early scientific investigation by regional historians were the explorations and reports by the pioneer archaeologists, workers in that branch of anthropology which deals with man's prehistory as revealed in his ancient artifacts and monuments. It is the archaeologists who have shown that America has an early history and that American culture has in it indigenous as well as European elements. Too many American scholars in history, literature, and the arts have assumed that all elements in American civilization are of relatively recent date and of European derivation entirely. It is in the American Southwest that the most extensive recovery of the Indian past has been made; and from the scientific writings dealing with this prehistoric period, America has gained a past, a beginning, and the matrix for an important type of literature.[1]

In 1879, Frank Cushing at the age of twenty-two years accompanied the Powell archaeological expedition to New Mexico. At his own request he was left at the Indian pueblo of Zuñi, where he remained for six years, learning the language, becoming a member of the inner ceremonial group called the Priests-of-the-Bow. From this experience grew his studies of Zuñi creation myths and folk beliefs. It was not, however, until 1931 that his book, *Zuñi Folk Tales,* was published, an acknowledged classic in the treasury of American mythology.

In 1881, an Army surgeon came into the West and in connection with his medical work began the study of the habits and customs of the Navajo Indians. From this avocational

---

1. Henry Rowe Schoolcraft anticipated the cultural and literary outlook of the Southwestern anthropologists. As an Indian agent in Michigan from 1822 to 1841, he was a pioneer in the study of Indian myths and folktales. In his volumes on the Indian tribes of the United States he contributed important background material for such writers as Henry Wadsworth Longfellow and Margaret Fuller.

interest Dr. Washington Matthews carried on broader and deeper investigations into Navajo ceremonies, symbolism, legends and folktales. Much of his work is preserved in the Bureau of Ethnology Reports, but the American Folklore Society published *Navajo Legends* in 1897.

These men of science were not men of letters by initial training, but they became men of letters because of the irresistable pull of the imaginative material with which they were dealing. Their work in such scientific periodicals as the *Journal of American Folklore* and the publications of the Smithsonian Institution have supplied the folklore and culture history for innumerable popular books. Frequently the debt is acknowledged. Sometimes it is not; but those who browse in the massive tomes of text and drawing prepared by Jesse Fewkes, Alice Fletcher, Matilda Coxe Stevenson, and Washington Matthews recognize how much of the material in short stories and novels treating of Southwestern Indian life comes from these pioneer investigators. Publications by these early anthropologists describing the culture of Pueblo, Navajo, and Plains Indians began in the 1880's and '90's. Fifty years ago they laid the foundations for the best grounded literature upon the Indian written in America.

C. F. Lummis is one of the great names in early Southwestern writing that deals with archaeological sites, historic monuments, ethnology and sociology as these fields are susceptible of literary treatment. Lummis was a New Englander, who, like many other New Englanders, had the zeal of investigation and the flame of imagination kindled at Harvard. But he never graduated there, and after a year or two of newspaper work in Ohio pushed farther west on foot and on horseback. He lived at Isleta Pueblo from 1888 to 1892, married an Indian woman who bore him a daughter. From the prolific pen of Charles Lummis came *A New Mexico David* (1891), *The Land of Poco Tiempo* (1893), *Pueblo Indian Folk Tales* (1894), and eleven other books dealing with the nature of life in the Indian-Spanish Southwest. In 1915, Lummis was knighted by the King of Spain for his research in Spanish-American history. The career of Lummis was crowned by the founding of the Southwest Museum in Los Angeles in 1907.

Adolph Bandelier, like Lummis, is difficult to classify as

archaeologist, historian, or ethnologist, because he was all three at one time or another, a man of broad interests, but no jack-of-all-trades. He was thorough-going in all that he did. In 1890, he and Charles F. Lummis discovered the ruins of Frijoles Canyon, now named the Bandelier National Monument. Earlier Bandelier had written on the social organization of ancient Mexico, and accounts of the archaeological wonders of that country. Proof of the imaginative grasp he had on the details of ancient life is his *Delight Makers* (1890), a novel dealing with the clan life of the Cliff Dwellers of Frijoles Canyon. Properly, this work belongs in Belles Lettres, where it will be discussed. Reference to it here is further evidence of the relationships between research and creative writing in this region to which the anthropologists so largely contributed.

Edgar Lee Hewett began his work in the Southwest as an educator in Greeley, Colorado, and Las Vegas, New Mexico. As a teacher first in literature of ancient Egypt and Greece, he felt a kinship to the living past of aboriginal life in the Southwest. Beginning his field work on the Pajarito Plateau in 1896, Dr. Hewett went on to explore other sites in this area including work at Chaco Canyon. A bibliography of his articles and books runs into more than two hundred titles covering notable scientific reports and observations upon the relationship of science to humanity. In several fine books Dr. Hewett has converted scientific lore into descriptions that make dead civilizations live. The most important of these works are *Ancient Life in the American Southwest* (1930), *Indians of the Rio Grande Valley* (1937), *Landmarks of New Mexico* (co-authored with Wayne L. Mauzy, 1940), *Mission Monuments of New Mexico* (co-authored with Reginald G. Fisher, 1943). His books *Ancient Life in Mexico and Central America* (1936) and *Ancient Indian Life* (1939), though not Southwestern works, are of interest to those who wish to trace the culture stream of Indian life through its various stages. Among the last words which Dr. Hewett wrote were these:

If archaeology had to do only with the rescue of dead things and their exhibition in museum halls, I could take little interest in it. But it is the science of things that live; that through the ages do not grow old; of things that disasters cannot kill; works of the spirit that, buried for millennia, rise again to new life and potency; the science which demonstrates that in races that have survived from a far past, powers lie dormant which may be energized anew.[2]

So Edgar Lee Hewett justified his interest in the aesthetic and religious nature of the American Indian from whose harmonious social order he felt modern society might learn valuable lessons.

Archaeologists with whom Dr. Hewett was associated in these early days of anthropology of the Southwest were Lewis H. Morgan, John Wesley Powell, Daniel Brinton, Alice C. Fletcher, William H. Holmes, and J. Walter Fewkes. When the Committee for the Archaeological Institute of America selected Santa Fe for the home of the School of American Research, Dr. Hewett became its first Director. His service in this office began on January 1, 1907. For more than forty years this School in its association with the Museum of New Mexico has been a center for many of the scientific and creative activities connected with past and present culture in the Southwest.

Hartley Burr Alexander is of the same humanistic school in the study of archaeology and its related disciplines as Dr. Hewett. His work was concerned primarily with the aesthetic elements of the Indian dance, paintings and myth, and appeared between 1910 and 1927. *God's Drum and Other Cycles From Indian Lore* (1927) and *Pueblo Indian Painting* (1932) are his best known works.

Frederick Webb Hodge, who became curator of the Southwest Museum in Los Angeles in 1932, has written with authority upon many aspects of Southwestern social history. In articles for The American Antiquarian Society and for the *Masterkey* of the Southwestern Museum, Dr. Hodge has published on pueblo pottery, rites, and ceremonials. His *Handbook of American Indians North of Mexico* (1907, 1910) is an invaluable reference work to the Indians of the Southwest. In greater detail he has written of the Zuñis, the Navajos, and the Apaches.

The younger school of anthropologists have more and more tended to convert materials of their research into articles for a wider reading public. They are men and women whose research is sound and who have in addition a gift for expres-

2. *El Palacio,* 54 (January, 1947), 3.

sion. In this group are such names as Gladys Reichard, Clyde Kluckhohn, Ruth M. Underhill, W. W. Hill, Florence Hawley, Emil Haury, Edward Spicer, and Harold S. Colton. Their work will be treated in History and Interpretation, Chapter I of Part Three.

El Palacio, the magazine of the School of American Research in Santa Fe, has for thirty years presented articles on the varied aspects of the arts and sciences in the Southwest. The *Tree Ring Bulletin* of the Museum of Northern Arizona, the *Masterkey* of the Southwest Museum in Los Angeles, and the *Southwestern Journal of Anthropology* of the University of New Mexico, are other magazines which publish well-written articles by Southwestern anthropologists.
anthropologists.

VI

BELLES LETTRES

POETRY

The belles lettres of a new frontier are likely to be inferior to the fact writing and folktales: chronicles, archaeology, history, legend, and song. These belles lettres are usually imitative and thin, at best new wine in old bottles. And they are often imitative not of current literature of the older settlements but of the literature of the past generation. It is not until a transplanted culture, such as the Anglo-American in the Southwest, fuses with the life of the new region that a sophisticated and professional literature flowers, rooted in history, folklore, and the land itself.

The art poetry of the Southwest before 1880 is mostly romantic, frequently sentimental. Often it is finished in technique and musical. It is largely imitative of Byron, Shelley, and the early Tennyson among the English poets, and N. P. Willis, G. P. Morris, and Longfellow of the Americans.[1] The earliest Southwest poetry in English came from the Woodland section, Arkansas and East Texas, and was in the tradition of the lyric South. Southwest poetry even today is primarily lyric.

Albert Pike—pioneer, soldier, scholar—in 1834 published his *Prose Sketches and Poems, Written in the Western Country.* Four years later, when he sent "Hymns to the Gods" to *Blackwood's Magazine,* he was hailed by the crotchety Christopher North as "the coming poet of America." North added: "These fine hymns entitle their author to take his place in the highest order of his country's poets. . . . His massive genius marks him to be a poet of the Titans."[2] In addition to highly literary verse, more neo-classic than romantic, Pike wrote a few very original poems of the Western land. "A Dirge: Over a Companion Killed by Comanches and Buried on the Prairie" is one of the best.

1. See "Introduction" to Sam H. Dixon, *The Poets and Poetry of Texas* (1885).
2. For a complete list of Pike's works, see William L. Boyden, *Bibliography of the Writings of Albert Pike* (1921) ; for selections from his writings, see *Library of Southern Literature.*

In Texas[3] another soldier-statesman, Mirabeau B. Lamar, was the state's first poet.[4] His *Verse Memorials* (1857) shows him to be a facile romantic writer.[5] His best known poem, "The Daughter of Mendoza," written to a Spanish-American beauty was found after his death. It is one of the few poems of the early Southwest that employ a Spanish theme. R. M. Potter's *Ode to Texas,* translated from the Spanish, is another. Potter was also the author of a fine patriotic song, "Hymn of the Alamo." Lamar Fontaine, who had been secretary to Mirabeau Lamar as President of the Republic, claimed, and his claim appears well established, to have written the widely known Civil War poem, "All Quiet Along the Potomac."

The best known of the Civil War poets of the Southwest was Mollie E. Moore Davis, who wrote extensively in behalf of the South. "Lee at the Wilderness" and "Minding the Gap" are widely reprinted in collections. However, her poetry is less original, more sentimental and moralizing than her novels and stories.

During Civil War days Charles D. Poston, called "the Father of Arizona," was Superintendent of Indian Affairs of that territory. "Apache-Land," a long narrative poem, came out of this experience.[6] But with a few such scattered exceptions, poetry in the Southwest until the end of the century continued in the romantic, mild manner of the Old South. The cowboy and the hard-riding life of the plains were late in getting into Southwest art poetry.

The Bret Harte-Joaquin Miller [7] tradition of adventure in the "broad open spaces," with humor, often pathos, sometimes dialect, became the chief force in Southwest poetry in the 1890's and the early years of the new century. Much of this poetry has the flavor of the cowboy folk ballad. Larry Chittenden, a New Yorker, came to Texas as a newspaper correspondent in 1883, bought a ranch with fifty borrowed dollars, turned poet-ranchman. His *Ranch Verse* (1893) contains "The

---

3. For selections from early Texas poets, see Sam H. Dixon, *The Poets and Poetry of Texas* (1885); also Hilton Ross Greer, *Voices of the Southwest* (1923).
4. Hugh Kerr's *A Poetical Description of Texas and Narrative of Many Interesting Events,* etc. (1838), said to be the first book of poems produced in the state, is little more than doggerel.
5. See Philip Graham, *Life and Poems of Mirabeau B. Lamar* (1937).
6. See Mary Boyer, *Arizona in Literature* (1934), pp. 261 ff.
7. Note Miller's *Kit Carson's Ride* (1871).

Cowboy's Christmas Ball," "The Ranchman's Ride," "The Dying Scout," and others of perennial popularity. Frank Desprez's "Lasca" was declaimed with gusto by school boys; newspapers copied Arthur Chapman's "Out Where the West Begins."

John Rollins Ridge (1827-67), a quarter-breed Cherokee, was in the Southwest for a time. He wrote in the romantic, Byronic vein.[8] Alexander Posey, an educated Creek Indian of Oklahoma, in the early 1900's wrote, in an English-Indian dialect, satirical poems purporting to be conversations between Wolf Warrior, Hotgun, Kono Hayo, and Tookpofko Micco about the treatment the Indians got from the white men. They were widely reprinted.[9] Marquis James in *The Cherokee Strip* (1945) says, "Posey's imagery was altogether Indian; every sound of nature was music to his ears. . . . No other Oklahoman has written anything so worthy of preservation." His early tragic death was a great loss to Southwest literature.

Sharlot Hall, bred in Arizona, published *Cactus and Pine* (1910), a volume of swift moving, straight shooting narrative poems. Robert V. Carr published *Cowboy Lyrics* (1912), largely sentimental but with touches of realism. Yet he is always writing from the viewpoint of an outsider.

Badger Clark, in *Sun and Saddle Leather* (1915), wrote in dialect with an attempt to reveal the psychology of the cowboy and not merely his outward life. Author of *High Chin Bob,* he wrote, too, of the land itself, desert, plains and sky.

These two currents in Southwest poetry — the romantic lyric stream—poems of nature, religion, patriotism—and the bolder, more narrative, objective poetry that we think of as Western—have persisted into the present.

FICTION

The fiction of the Southwest before the Civil War belongs to the Scott-Cooper tradition. It abounds in picturesque descriptions, heroic deeds, type characters, and a plot dependent largely on coincidence. A number of these novels were written, in fact, while Scott was yet alive. *L'Heroine du Texas* by M.

8. See Maurice Kelley's article in *Folk-Say*, II, 396 ff.
9. *The Poems of Alexander Lawrence Posey,* collected and arranged by Mrs. Minnie H. Posey, with a Memoir by William Elsey Connelley (1910).

G——n F——n was published in Paris in 1819 but translated into English only in recent years.[10] Timothy Flint, a Congregational missionary in the West in 1826, wrote a romantic novel that touches on Texas, *Francis Berrien or the Mexican Patriot*. About Arkansas and New Mexico, Albert Pike, better known for his poetry than prose, was writing narrative sketches, published in *Prose Sketches and Poems* (1834). A. T. Myrthe, probably a pen name for Anthony Ganilk, claimed that his story of the Texas War for Independence, *Mexico Versus Texas* (1838), was the first Texian novel. It is quite likely that he did not know of *L'Heroine du Texas*. These early writers of fiction were not above borrowing from the records of real adventurers. George Kendall complained that Captain Frederick Marryat had "stolen" from his "series of rough sketches in the *New Orleans Picayune*" for the *Narratives of Travel and Adventures of Monsieur Violet in California, Sonora and Western Texas* (1843).[11] Karl Postl,[12] who, in America after his break with a religious order in his native Austria, used the name of Charles Sealsfield, wrote to a thesis in his *Cabin Book; or National Characteristics* (1844).[13] He saw the frontier as a place where bold men, even bad men, could redeem their misdeeds by heroic adventures, sometimes by death for a cause. The hero of the *Cabin Book,* Bob, a rough fellow who had killed a man, dies a hero's death at San Jacinto. Edward Morse, the narrator, after exploits in Texas, where he knew Bob, ends his career amid the beauties of nature in a cabin in Louisiana. Karl Postl wrote a number of other novels in both English and German and came to be known as the "Writer of Two Hemispheres."[14]

In the later 1840's and 1850's there were dozens of novels and books of short stories, many of the nature of juveniles, recounting the exploits of guides, hunters, rangers, and desper-

---

10. See translation by Donald Joseph in *The Story of Champ d'Asile* (1937). For a useful discussion of early Texas fiction, see L. W. Payne, Jr., *A Survey of Texas Literature* (1928), pp. 10-17.
11. See Preface to *Narrative of an Expedition Across the Great Southwestern Prairies from Texas to Santa Fe* (1844).
12. See Selman M. Raunick, "A Survey of German Literature in Texas," *Southwestern Historical Quarterly,* XXX, 142-44.
13. Written in German under the title *Das Kajutenbuch oder National Charakteristiken.* Translated into English and published in London in 1852.
14. Another early Southwestern novelist who wrote in German was A. Siemering. *The Hermit of the Cavern* (1876) was first translated into English in 1932.

adoes of this new frontier. Charles Wilkins Webber, at one time a ranger, wrote *Old Hicks the Guide* (1848), *The Hunter Naturalist* (1851), *Tales of the Southern Border* (1853); Alfred W. Arrington (Charles Summerfield), *Desperadoes of the Southwest* (1849), and *The Rangers and Regulators of Tanaha . . . a Tale of the Republic of Texas* (1856); Gustave Aimard (Oliver Gloux), *The Trappers of Arkansas* (1858) set in Arkansas and eastern Oklahoma, and *The Freebooters, a Story of the Texas War* (c. 1860). Jeremiah R. Clemens in his novel, *Mustang Gray* (1857), is said to have narrated Mabry Gray's exploits "on the short side rather than the long side of facts."[15] Clemens, like Gray, had fought in the Mexican War and knew the scenes and situations about which he wrote. Captain Mayne Reid alone wrote almost a dozen novels of Southwestern adventures. His books, while not significant as literature, were widely read and important in forming the concept of the Southwest in the East and in Europe.

The love motif was of minor importance in these early man-written novels. The main conflicts were of man against man, and man against nature. One of the few romantic love stories was *Inez, A Tale of the Alamo* (1855) by Augusta E. Wilson. Set in San Antonio, the complicated plot, strongly anti-Catholic, develops against the backdrop of the Texas War for Independence. It belongs to the line of sentimental fiction of the "weeping fifties."[16] A somewhat later and much superior example of the romantic historic novel with the Alamo as background is Amelia Barr's *Remember the Alamo* (c. 1888). Yet this is still pure romance with little real relation to Texas life.

After the Civil War, arose the local color movement in American fiction (c. 1870-1900). Scenes were definitely recognizable, costumes and dialect of a specific locale were faithfully reported, and characters and plot fitted the setting. Writing was objective and usually "smiling." Sentiment was all pervasive except with the very best men, Mark Twain and Howells and James; yet the tendency was toward realism. The Old South was a favorite section for fiction. As a consequence, in Arkansas and East Texas, where the Woodland culture had

15. See J. Frank Dobie, "Mustang Gray: Fact, Tradition and Song," *Publications of the Texas Folk-Lore Society*, X, 108-23.
16. See Carl Van Doren, *The American Novel* (1921), p. 125.

been transplanted, local color fiction first developed in the Southwest. Short stories became popular.

In Arkansas in the eighties and nineties Alice French (Octave Thanet), Ruth McEnery Stuart, and Opie Read were writing local color stories. Alice French, a Middle Western woman, who lived for a time in Arkansas, showed a good deal of realism in *Knitters in the Sun* (1891) and *Stories of a Western Town* (1892). More sentimental are the stories of Ruth McEnery Stuart, *In Simpkinsville* (1899). Opie Read in *An Arkansas Planter* (1896) wrote in the Southern plantation tradition.

Mollie E. Moore Davis is the most significant of these post-war writers in the Old South local color manner. Her sketches titled *In War-times at La Rose Blanche* (1888) are written with emphasis on character delineation and dialect. Like the stories of Thomas Nelson Page, they mix humor, pathos, and tenderness. Of even more merit is the novel *Under the Man-Fig* (1895). Set in Columbia, Texas, on the Brazos from about 1857 to 1872, the story, rather improbable in itself, makes admirable use of the legend of the man-fig tree. Non-partisan, save for a tender regard for the South, there is a detachment from all of the great events and an almost realistic concern with the details of average daily life. It is more rooted than any preceding novel of Southwestern life.

Belles lettres of the far Southwest are represented by such titles as *A Fortune Hunter; or The Old Stone Corral* (1888) by John Dunloe Carteret, which announces itself further in a second title, "A Tale of the Santa Fé Trail." The book treats of the lost treasure of "Montezuma," a web of mystery, the course of true love, and the cattle king's daughter. Newspapers in New Mexico and Arizona during the second half of the nineteenth century printed stories from papers farther east with such titles as: "The Eton Boy," "A Coon Hunt in Fency County," and "Duty and Kindness," which treats of the efforts of Deacon Browning to reform his prodigal boy.[17] An extraordinary saint's tale called "La Cambioda" appeared in a New Mexico paper in 1863, written by someone who signed himself An Obscure Author. It concerns a devil-may-care Juan, saved from his riotous living by the intervention of St. Francis, who

17. Albuquerque: *Rio Abajo Weekly Press,* April 21, 1863.

transforms Juan's sister into the likeness of a man and allows her to go to El Paso to rescue him.[18] Though the setting is local, the time is placed in the previous century. Of contemporary life little was written of belles lettres quality.

In 1878 General Lew Wallace came to New Mexico as governor of the Territory. In the Old Palace at Santa Fe he wrote the final chapters of his classic, *Ben Hur* (1880). The book treats of a distant soil and a distant time, and illustrates, as well as any other work, the cultural expatriation of writers at this time in the Southwest. A few years before General Wallace came to New Mexico, he embarked on his admirable literary work *The Fair God* (1873), selecting the soil and tradition of Mexico for this notable historical romance. *The Fair God* deserves attention as one of the earliest American novels to consider aboriginal life on the continent. It treats of life in the plateau of Mexico at the time of the Spanish conquest.

One of the earliest, if not the first, novels of aboriginal life in the area now of the United States is Adolph Bandelier's *The Delight Makers* (1890). Written by a Swiss schoolmaster, turned investigator for the Smithsonian Institution of Washington, *The Delight Makers* will remain without rival among the nineteenth-century creative works dealing with the American Indian. Bandelier lived among the Southwestern Indians whose prehistory he recreated in his novel. Using the location of the cliff dwellings in Frijoles Canyon, now the Bandelier National Monument, he brought to life events which, with more than ordinary historical illusion, could have occurred in America's medieval past. Bandelier's novel was prophetic of a literary appreciation for the Southwest scene which was to grow among writers and to flower some twenty-five years later.

In the first quarter of the new century Marah Ellis Ryan, a prolific writer, published a number of novels about the Southwest. The most significant of these is *The Flute of the Gods* (1909), a story dealing with the Hopi people of Arizona. Her books of Indian life were written, like Bandelier's work, to introduce American readers to the true cultural values among the earliest citizens of this land. These values have lasted,

18. *Ibid.*

with the ceremonies which objectify them, until the present day. "Only the death of the elders and the breaking up of the clans can eradicate them," writes Mrs. Ryan. "When that is done, the Latin and the Anglo-Saxon will have swept from the heart of the land, primitive, conservative cults ancient as the Druids."[19] Among her other novels of the Southwest are *For the Soul of Rafael* (1906) and *The Treasure Trove* (1918). *The Dancer of Tuluum* (1924) is a story of ancient Yucatan. Marah Ellis Ryan like most writers of fiction in the Southwest before 1918 was prevailingly romantic, yet with others she points the way to a fuller understanding of the land and the peoples.

19. Preface to *The Flute of the Gods,* VI.

VII

NARRATIVES OF THE CATTLE COUNTRY

The most original stories that the Southwest has told have come from the cattle country. The half century after the Civil War, that saw the cattle industry rise to power on the open range, before barbed wire and settlers closed in on it, was a unique episode in American history, one not likely to be repeated.[1] The English-speaking cowboy learned quickly from the *vaquero* how to herd cattle on horseback and, with characteristic audacity, evolved the long drive to market across the plains. His costume, picturesque to the rest of the world, is practical for hard riding. His language, his brands, his songs, his amusements are as natural to him as a sailor's lingo and rolling walk.[2] His tales of adventure are simply the high points of his routine life — sometimes thrilling exploits, sometimes ludicrous mishaps, sometimes tributes to the loyalty of comrades.

The first of the cowboy tale tellers was Charlie Siringo, a native Texan, who rode the range for nearly half a century after 1867. In 1886 he decided to turn author and produced a history of his own "short but rugged life" titled *A Texas Cowboy*.[3] His book, which circulated widely among plain readers at the time, was overlooked by literary circles; but now, rewritten, it is recognized as an early authority. Its value lies not in literary grace, to which it makes no claim, but in sincerity and firsthand information.[4]

By the turn of the century the cowboy had ridden into liter-

1. See Walter P. Webb, *The Great Plains* (1931), Ch. X; *Prose and Poetry of the Live Stock Industry of the United States* (1904, 1905); Douglas Branch, *The Cowboy and His Interpreters* (1926).
2. Ramon Adams, *Cowboy Lingo* (1936); *Western Words* (1944).
3. *A Texas Cowboy; or, Fifteen Years on the Hurricane Deck of a Spanish Pony. Taken from Real Life. By Chas. A. Siringo, an Old Stove Up "Cow Puncher," Who Has Spent Nearly Twenty Years on the Great Western Cattle Ranges* (1886). See also his *The Lone Star Cowboy* (1919), and *Riata and Spurs* (1912, 1927). Will Rogers once said that *A Texas Cowboy* was "the Cowboys' Bible when I was growing up."
4. *The Trail Drivers of Texas* (1924) contains some 200 sketches of reminiscences by old timers who rode the trail. Many volumes of such tales have appeared since Siringo's in 1886.

ature in Charles Hoyt's successful drama, *A Texas Steer* (1890), and Owen Wister's *Red Men and White* (1896) and *The Virginian* (1902). But whereas Wister and Hoyt were tenderfeet spinning literary plots of the range, a real cowboy wrote *The Log of a Cowboy* (1903), the best of all the realistic tales of the range. Andy Adams was typical of thousands of cowhands. An Indiana farm boy of good stock, he came to Texas in 1882, drove horses and cattle, rode the trail to Abilene, made some money and lost it in business, then drifted to Colorado to try mining and finally writing. The *Log* is a plain chronicle, unplotted and accurate in technical details, of a young fellow's experiences on a long drive. It deserves comparison with tales of sea life such as Richard Henry Dana's *Two Years Before the Mast* (1840). Adams' first book was so well received that its author continued writing stories of the West for the rest of his life, undaunted by the fact that no later book of his ever approached *The Log of a Cowboy* in popularity. The fiction of Andy Adams reveals the strength and weakness of range life. It is vigorous, full of action and suspense, vivid, and convincing; it is also purely objective, emphasizing material prosperity and success, and it faithfully excludes women and the love motif.

To outsiders life on the cattle range has always seemed romantic, that is, exciting, glamorous, different from ordinary farm or urban existence. In a measure, this opinion is true; but most of the professional writers of western romance have erred in at least two ways in their portrayals. First, they have selected a few of the most thrilling, "different" phases of ranch life, such as the cattle thieves, the stranger cowhand, the round-up, the drive to market, and combined them over and over in set formulas. In the next place, they have brought in the ready-made "cowboy meets girl" plot and overworked it. Nevertheless, romantic tales of the cattle country, from the best type to the "pulps," have been continuously popular for more than a quarter of a century; today every newsstand carries a dozen or more magazines devoted to the deeds of the cowboy hero.[5]

5. See Edmund Pearson, *Dime Novels* (1929) for the literary ancestors of the current "westerns." Also Webb, *op. cit.*, for a discussion of western magazines. Among the better known of the numerous writers of popular books of the range are: Robert Ames Bennet, Hal. G. Evarts, Jackson Gregory, Oscar J. Friend, W. D. Hoffman, Clarence E. Mulford, Edwin L. Sabin, William P. White.

The moving pictures have nowhere found more thrilling material than in romantic "westerns." Hollywood has made the settings more elaborately real than in the published versions, but the movie plots are even more sentimental and conventional.

From a literary point of view nine-tenths of these range romances are negligible because of their stereotyped style, unconvincing characters, and exaggerated plots; but it is a mistake to think that all adventure stories of the region are poor literature. Good fictional treatments of life in the cattle country, with complicated plots and an emphasis on thrilling experiences, are fairly numerous, although it must be added that they are best when they are tied close to realism with a short stake-rope. For several decades a few excellent craftsmen, who have themselves rounded up the dogies, have published western novels and stories. In the Southwest Alfred Henry Lewis pioneered with his *Wolfville* (1897), episodes in the life of an Arizona cowtown. O. Henry experienced Texas ranch life near San Antonio, and utilized it in some of his best writing. *The Heart of the West* (1907) contains many of his Southwestern tales. O. Henry owed much to the Bret Harte tradition, as do most of the adventure writers of the cattle country, especially the combining of picturesque setting, frontier humor, exaggerated character types, and theatrical plot.

One of the best of the romantic western novels was also one of the earliest, Emerson Hough's *Heart's Desire* (1903). Soon after completing his college study in Iowa, Hough came to White Oaks, New Mexico, to practice law. He must have given more time to sharing the life of a little western town than to law, if the portraits of the old-fashioned cowboy, the Jewish storekeeper, the young Georgia cowboy with a drawl, the girls west of the Pecos who always came from Kansas along with the butter and hay, and the wandering osteopath whose only patient was a cross-eyed horse, are evidence of his affection for the community. "Your Anglo-Saxon, craving ever savagery, has no sooner found it than he seeks to civilize it; there being for him in his aeon of the world no real content or peace," Hough remarks in this novel. His *North of 36* (1923) deserves its popularity, on the screen as well as in story form, for its vigorous portrayal of an epic theme, the early trail drive from South Texas to the railroad. Readers who prefer un-varnished tales like those of Andy Adams may object to a drive that took along a young heroine with her Negro mammy and considerable luggage, but the general public has approved Hough's romance. Stewart Edward White's *Arizona Nights* (1904) is a volume of stories true to the cattle kingdom. "The Rawhide" is one of the classics of early western range fiction.

Probably the most significant of the realistic romancers of the plains was Eugene Manlove Rhodes, prolific and successful author for more than a quarter of a century. As a young man, Rhodes rode the range in New Mexico; then he moved to the East, married, settled down, and began to write his western stories, finding publication in the better popular magazines. Later he bought a ranch in the San Andrés Mountains but his health compelled him to spend the last years of his life in California. "New Mexico's incurable romantic," as Gene Rhodes has been called, loved the old West, and maintained to the end that highly civilized society could offer no full compensation for the loss of "the arms that mocked at weariness, the feet that trod on fear."

Rhodes was widely read and esteemed highly his profession as a novelist. "He wrote a story in his mind, from beginning to end," says Henry Herbert Knibbs, "before he even put a word on paper. . . . Often he has told me, word for word (as the printed story eventually proved), a yarn he contemplated writing, even including gestures, postures, attitudes, dialogue, and background." [6] This preparation doubtless accounts for the intricate plots and carefully shaded characters of his novels.

Eugene Manlove Rhodes' best known story is *Pasó Por Aquí* which tells of a cowboy-bandit who stops to aid a Mexican family stricken with diphtheria. When the sheriff sent in pursuit of him learns of the man's humanity, he discovers that his crime looms less important in the eyes of the law, and allows the cowboy to make his way free out of the region. The story appears in the book *Once in the Saddle* (1927).

Other worthwhile stories by Rhodes are *Good Men and True* (1911), *Desire of the Moth* (1916), *Trusty Knaves*

6. Henry Herbert Knibbs, Introduction to Eugene Manlove Rhodes, *The Proud Sheriff* (1935), p. vii. See also Eddy Orcutt, "Passed by Here. A Memorial to Gene Rhodes," *Saturday Evening Post*, August 20, 1938.

(1933), and *Beyond the Desert* (1934). Rhodes was faithful to the facts of the early days in New Mexico, so much so that a governor of the state once declared "that certain characters have threatened to shoot him on sight." He avoided excessive love interest and likewise glamorous bad men, believing that they were not typical of the cattle country. He found his frontier good—better than life elsewhere. "What I remember is generosity, laughter, courage, and kindness," he has written. Since his death in 1934, recognition of Eugene Manlove Rhodes has been increasing. Such critics as Bernard De Voto,[7] and such writers of western fiction as Knibbs agree in declaring his novels "the finest ever written about that strange and violent and beautiful era in American life, the years of the cattle trade."

Omar Barker, Westmoreland Gray, H. H. Knibbs, Eugene Cunningham, Owen P. White, William McLeod Raine, and many others write excellent romances, short and long, of love and adventure against the background of ranch life. There is also an enormous body of short fiction in the popular periodicals or "pulps" devoted to western themes. While these last stories are usually superficial, many competent writers add to their incomes by supplying the insatiable demand of the public for cowboy tales.

7. Editorial, *Saturday Review of Literature,* October 17, 1936. J. Frank Dobie has written an appraisal of Rhodes' wit, vivacity, and idealism as "Introduction" to *The Little World Waddies,* a collection of Rhodes' stories and poems, arranged by William Hutchinson of Cohasset Stage, Chico, California, and printed by Carl Hertzog of El Paso, Texas (1946).

PART THREE

LITERATURE FROM c. 1918—1948

I

HISTORY AND INTERPRETATION

O𝒥T IS NOT possible to divide historical writings in the Southwest into two distinct periods, to say that before 1918 the past was recorded in one way and after 1918 in another. One of the most fascinating phases of our study is the way in which all the types of writing of a pioneer civilization in the various stages of development are present here today. In the literature of the Southwest early materials and techniques are counterpointed against works which belong to contemporary trends of our national letters. This is certainly true of historical writing.

After the chronicles and formal state histories, which we have already considered, came more earnest collecting of documents, journals, letters in English and other languages, state papers and other records of the past. Simultaneously, collections were made of belles lettres and scholarly sources in other languages, and likewise of historical objects, such as branding irons, portraits, costumes, furniture.[1] By the end of the nineteenth century the task of making these rare and important documents available to the public began to attract the attention of scholars in the Southwest. An early labor was performed by Adolph and Fanny Bandelier in translating the *Journey of Cabeza de Vaca* in 1905. Eugene C. Barker laid the foundations for much early Texas history as well as for his own biography of Stephen F. Austin by editing the *Papers* of Moses and Stephen F. Austin. R. E. Twitchell's *The Spanish Archives of New Mexico* (1914), and H. E. Bolton's *Spanish Explora-*

---

1. Some of the chief collections of Southwestern historical documents are: Texas State Library, University of Texas Library, Rosenberg Library of Galveston, Oklahoma Historical Society Collection, University of Oklahoma Library, University of Arkansas Library, Coronado and Van de Velde Collections of University of New Mexico.

Among the private collectors of Southwestern books have been E. De-Golyer, Dr. Alexander Dienst, J. Frank Dobie, J. Marvin Hunter, Charles J. Finger, Howard Roosa, W. A. Keleher, Clinton Anderson, Luis Armijo, F. C. Lockwood. Herman Schweizer, of the Fred Harvey Company, was an expert upon Southwestern art objects and made a private collection of unusual interest and value.

Typical of the collections of world literatures are the Browning Collection of Baylor University, and the Wrenn Library of the University of Texas.

tion in the Southwest, 1542-1706 (1916) contain many early sources. The Quivira Society was organized in 1929 with George P. Hammond as managing editor for the translating, editing, and publishing of old and inaccessible Spanish and other records. From 1929 until 1942 a series of volumes were published first at the University of Southern California and later at the University of New Mexico, with Agapito Rey, Margaret Eyer Wilbur, Irving A. Leonard, Frederick Webb Hodge, Fritz Leo Hoffman, Carlos Eduardo Castañeda, Henry R. Wagner, H. Bailey Carroll, J. Villasana Haggard, and George P. Hammond as editors. In 1940, Dr. Hammond began the editing of the Coronado Historical Series, a group of twelve volumes presented by the Coronado Cuarto Centennial Commission as part of the celebration to commemorate the Spanish exploration of the entire Southwest. Six of these volumes have been published, and the others will appear under the sponsorship of the University of New Mexico Historical Publications Fund. France V. Scholes, who became Dean of the Graduate School at the University of New Mexico in 1946, has worked upon archival materials in Spain and Central America as a staff member of the Carnegie Institution since 1931. Dean Scholes has done much to fill the gaps in seventeenth-century Southwestern history, especially relating to the activities of the Inquisition in New Mexico.

A. B. Thomas, a younger scholar working under the guidance of Bolton, Dale, and others, has translated and amply edited the original papers of an eighteenth-century governor of New Mexico. "Stanley Vestal" (Professor Walter S. Campbell of the University of Oklahoma) has blazed his own trail in source material for studies in the Plains Indians by collecting not only many published and unpublished documents but by working out a technique for recording oral narrations of events delivered by trustworthy Indians.[2] Other vast resources of untouched materials in Government files in Washington, D. C., relating to the Indians, especially the Five Civilized Tribes, have been tapped by Grant Foreman. His *Indians and Pioneers, The Story of the American Southwest Before 1830* (1930), *Indian Removals* (1932), and *The Five*

2. See his *New Sources of Indian History* (1934), Prefatory Note, Part II, pp. 121-30.

Civilized Tribes (1934), for example, utilize the old files of many offices of the United States War Department as well as those in the departments of State, the Interior, and the Post Office.[3] Angie Debo in *The Rise and Fall of the Choctaw Republic* (1934), and Marion L. Starkey in *The Cherokee Nation* (1946) likewise have made use of official records in preparing scholarly and highly readable histories. Mary J. Atkinson's *Texas Indians* (1936), a book of sound research, is the most comprehensive treatment of the many tribes that once inhabited the vast state. Alice Marriott in *The Ten Grandmothers* (1945) has combined painstaking research with certain of the techniques of the novelist in presenting the tribal history of the Kiowas in the story of sacred medicine bundles handed down from the past.

Out of this careful historical search have come at least two excellent modern state histories, Grant Foreman's *A History of Oklahoma* (1942) and R. N. Richardson's *Texas, the Lone Star State* (1943). *Pioneer Days in Arizona* (1932), by Frank C. Lockwood, while not covering the entire span of history of a state, narrates in an orderly and graphic way the chief incidents that took place in Arizona from the coming of the Spaniards in 1539 to the achievement of Statehood in 1912.

Three periods of Texas history have received careful study. Julia Kathryn Garrett in *Green Flag Over Texas* (1939) writes of the establishment of the almost forgotten and short lived First Republic of 1813. William Ransom Hogan in *The Texas Republic, A Social and Economic History* (1946) recreates Texas between 1836 and 1845. He sees life dominated by robust individualism in politics, religion, entertainment, and money-making. Twenty-seven pages of bibliography in fine print attest to the scholarship behind this portrait of frontier life. Lt. Colonel James Farber in *Texas C. S. A.* (1947), from a military point of view, records the important part that Texas played in the War between the States.

In many instances, however, recent historical writing in the Southwest adds the exemplification of a theme or even a thesis to this scholarly use of firsthand sources and excellent literary style. The search in past records for some law, some pattern, is the achievement of historical scholarship of the last half

---

3. See *Indians and Pioneers* (1930), Bibliography, pp. 315-27.

century under the tutelage of science. Henry Adams and others led the way in America. Today some of the most fruitful reinterpretation of the American past is emanating from the Southwest.

A notable example is Walter P. Webb's *The Great Plains* (1931), which makes clear to the general reader as well as to the student the unity and uniqueness of that area, more or less arid, treeless, and level, which is the Great Plains of the North American continent. Most vividly Webb shows how living in this area is conditioned by physical environment — in short, "what happened in American civilization when in its westward progress it emerged from the woods and essayed life on the plains . . . east of the Mississippi civilization stood on three legs—land, water, and timber; west of the Mississippi not one but two of these legs were withdrawn—water and timber— and civilization was left on one leg—land." As a social scientist, the author expands history to include geography, economics, sociology, literary criticism; and in his wide survey of the Plains environment he not only finds it a geographic unity but contends that it has produced "a new phase of Aryan civilization." *The Texas Rangers* (1935) relates the history of this unique organization to frontier life and needs. *Divided We Stand* (1937) is written to the thesis of the economic exploitation of the South and West by the North and East.

Two books written in 1930 represent special studies of peoples of the past in terms of social movements rather than the political histories of territories and states. *The Santa Fe Trail* by R. L. Duffus is a picturesque narrative in terms of human values, enriched with details from contemporary diaries. We rock with the wagons on the trail and enter old Santa Fe, brushing the dust from our clothes and staring wide-eyed at the Mexican men in their bright *serapes*. Accuracy and a good bibliography do not hinder the colorful style of this book. The "Recessional" with which it closes is a poetic farewell to the Trail. "The Trail was but a single thread in that vast roaring loom on which was woven the fabric of modern America. Yet there it shines, if we bend to look, like a pattern of untarnishable gold." W. C. Holden's *Alkali Trails* is a presentation of economic and social problems without a narrative thread or picturesque coloring. Some of the chapter headings indicate the trend: The Buffalo Slaughter, The Cattle Kingdom, Frontier Journalism, Drouths, Mirages.

Stanley Vestal in *The Old Santa Fe Trail* (1939) employs the techniques of the novelist to make live again the most exciting events along the thousand miles from Westport to Santa Fe. For these tales he drew on Gregg, Ruxton, Garrard, and the memories of still living old-timers. He threads them on the journey of a mythical caravan. Stanley Vestal sees in the adventures along the Trail, with all of the tragedies, a better and larger life than the present offers.

Following in the wake of these re-creators of the days of the covered wagons and cattle trails, James Marshall writes of the iron trail in *Santa Fe, The Railroad that Built an Empire* (1945). His is the viewpoint and style of the modern journalist.

Among the early surveys of great ranches and the part these single units played in the history of the Southwest are *The XIT Ranch of Texas* (1929), by Evetts Haley, and *The 101 Ranch* (1927), by Ellsworth Collings and Alma Miller England. Like empires in themselves (the X I T Ranch covered a large part of the Panhandle of Texas), these establishments had an administration that included governing, judicial, banking, and overall supply functions. W. F. Keleher has written a similar study in his *Maxwell Land Grant* (1942), devoted to the political and economic fortunes during the nineteenth century of an area covering 1,714,764 acres of land in northern New Mexico and southern Colorado.

Although J. Frank Dobie's *The Longhorns* (1941) is not the study of one ranch, it treats of all of Central, South, and West Texas in terms of one great ranch where the cow camps and cowtowns were outposts to produce and market a breed of cattle as rugged, sagacious, and individualistic as any range land ever produced. Winifred Kupper's *The Golden Hoof* (1945) does for the sheep industry in the Southwest what these writers have done for the world of cattle—dignified its traditions, traced its growth, described its feuds and warfare, presented its folklore and personal history along with the political and economic story.

A little more flexibility in defining history will permit the inclusion of a typical Southwestern study by Paul B. Sears,

Deserts on the March (1935), which has been aptly termed "at once an historical survey, a scientific exposition—and a warning." Impersonally, from the point of view of the ecologist, Sears tells the story, not of certain men, but of man on the North American continent struggling with soil and wind and rain.

Heaven's Tableland (1947) by Vance Johnson records the history of the Dust Bowl of Oklahoma and Texas from the thirteenth century to the present; from an early irrigation system of vanished Indians through the days of the buffalo, the era of ranching, back to farming. The book is at once a record of periods of drouth and plentiful rainfall and a warning to present day wheat farmers.

Interpretation from the pen of the scientist or historian in search of new patterns and laws is one thing; from the pen of an artist seeking to express himself in terms of beauty, or a philosopher striving to find a *modus vivendi,* it is another form of literature. One of the most interesting types of writing being produced today in the Southwest is the historical-descriptive interpretation by sensitive men and women who seek to record their personal impressions of the land, the peoples on it, its history. This sort of book comes most often from New Mexico and Arizona, which have in late years captured the imagination of many artists, from Mary Austin to J. B. Priestley, and compelled them, as it were, to pay tribute to the land.

These interpretations, as we shall loosely apply the term, cannot be neatly defined; for they represent highly personal impressions. On the whole, however, they emphasize one or more of these themes: the pageant of the past, especially of the primitive dwellers; the customs of the present dwellers; or the land, beautiful and harsh, and its power over those who dwell on it. The author nearly always reveals an individualist point of view, often frankly relating a narrative of his own experiences. The stuff of his book is his impressions. No matter if he is repeating experiences long familiar to others if he can only tell them vividly. Vividness of experience and beauty of style, these are hallmarks of the type; but the deepest significance lies in the philosophy of the author. So, in Mary Austin's *The Land of Little Rain* (1903) a certain chapter on scavengers may seem to deal only with three kinds of buzzards, but it is essentially an expression of her reverence for the endless processes of nature.

It is hard to indicate any dividing line between history proper and what we have called historical-descriptive interpretation; but the difference is apparent to a thoughtful reader. Thus the earliest work of the great observer and student of Indian life, Charles F. Lummis, such as *Spanish Pioneers* (1893), belongs to conventional history. But many of his later works—*The Land of Poco Tiempo* (1921) and *Mesa, Canyon and Pueblo* (1925)—belong to the contemporary group of interpretations. From his own point of view as a white man deeply sympathetic with the Indian but never primitivistic, Lummis describes the land, the customs, the occupations of the Southwestern Indians in a style so readable that his books have been a large factor in acquainting the general public with the region. In a more formal style George Wharton James has done much the same thing for Arizona and New Mexico in *Indians of the Painted Desert Region* (1903), *Arizona, the Wonderland* (1917), and other volumes. More informal, on the other hand, even than Lummis is Leo Crane's *Desert Drums* (1928), a book of personal experiences as Indian Agent for the New Mexico Pueblos, in which much history is interwoven.

The pageant of the past appears in many of these historical-descriptive interpretations, but a clear example of the emphasis on interpretation is Harvey Fergusson's *Rio Grande* (1933), a superbly written exposition of his theory that the upper valley of the Rio Grande is the best locale in America to study the primitive and the modern side by side. In this valley which is so peculiarly resistant to change and where only the few large towns fully know the "modern life of money and machines," Fergusson reads a significant story, one that "has more than local significance. It describes the aboriginal America, which is typical of all primitive life. It recounts the last thrust of religious empire on this continent and the decay of a lost and isolated fragment of the world. It pictures the modern man in the sharp contrast of conflict with these older cultures, first as a fighting hunter, then as a trader and explorer and finally as the master and slave of his machines." At the end of his survey of past and present, the author, a native of New Mexico, can declare: "I say no more of New Mexico as it is today, except that here surely is a place where many kinds of men live and work, where one may dig or dream, make poems, bricks, or love, or merely sit in the sun, and find some tolerance and some companionship. Here handicraft as well as the machine has some place in life, the primitive persists beside the civilized, the changeless mountains offer refuge to the weary sons of change."

Other interpretations using the same materials in part are Ruth Laughlin Alexander's *Caballeros* (1931), a vivid re-creation of the Spanish conquerors; D. J. Hall's *Enchanted Sand* (1933), a romantic pilgrimage through Indian country; Anna Wilmarth Ickes' *Mesa Land* (1933), devoted to the Pueblo and Navajo world; Blanche C. Grant's *When Old Trails Were New* (1934), the story of the mountain men and Taos country; Mabel Dodge Luhan's *Winter in Taos* (1935), a picture of the season and its tasks and pleasures; Dorothy Hogner's *South to Padre* (1936), describing the life of the present and past along the Gulf shore of Texas; Nina Otero Warren's *Old Spain in Our Southwest* (1936), recapturing the charm of colonial New Mexico.

The nation-wide interest in an interpretation of the land and peoples of the Southwest is attested to by four highly readable volumes in the American Folkways series: Edwin Corle's *Desert Country* (1941), Haniel Long's *Piñon Country* (1941), Stanley Vestal's *Short Grass Country* (1941), and Donald Day's *Big Country Texas* (1947).[4] In these volumes history, geography, folktales, and folkways are combined to produce books both informative and entertaining. George Sessions Perry in *Texas a World in Itself* (1942) employs the same materials with equal success. His concern is more with the present than with the past. Edwin Corle's *Listen, Bright Angel* (1946) takes its title from a famous trail of the Grand Canyon of the Colorado. The book combines geology, description, and stories of explorations of the Canyon, with special details of the trips by the Kolb brothers.

Two books that treat altogether of folkways are Erna Fergusson's *Dancing Gods* (1931) and Alice Corbin Henderson's *Brothers of Light* (1937). Native of the region, Miss Fergusson makes the Indian dance ceremonials an unforgettable pic-

4. Edited by Erskine Caldwell for Duell, Sloan and Pearce.

ture; she misses nothing of the pageantry and tenseness of the participants. Yet she frankly and humbly admits that the white race is alien to the Indian world, even though she perceives that their "religon is of the earth and the things of the earth . . . and they pray for real things: for sun and rain and corn. For growth. For life." Such sympathetic understanding is rare and valuable. Mrs. Henderson is equally sensitive in her small, rich account of the Penitentes of the Southwest. Holy Week at Abiquiu revealed to her the sincerity and meaning of the ancient rites of penance. To her account of this experience she adds a scholarly discussion of the origins of the ceremony, transcripts of some of the *alabados* or hymns, and beautiful descriptions of the isolated village and the rhythmic processions.

No such humility and aloofness mark the interpretations of land and people by Mary Austin, explorer, scholar, artist, mystic. From 1888 when she came as a young woman to the West, she felt herself *en rapport* with the deserts and valleys and mountains of her adopted country. She declared that "there was a part for her in the Indian life." By her many books, beginning as early as 1903, she compelled attention to the region, its arts and peoples, and its object lesson in simple values for a modern world. In *The Land of Little Rain* she is guided by the romantic American concept of nature that prevailed in the Golden Day. As Thoreau records the struggle of the ants and the daily history of Walden Pond, so she writes of water trails and coyotes. Indeed, it is odd that so little notice has been taken of the likeness both in content and style between Thoreau and Mary Austin. The Concord naturalist-philosopher might almost have written the chapter titled "My Neighbor's Field," and such a passage as this from Mary Austin will chime with many passages in *Walden* to the ear of any sensitive reader.

Choose a hill country for storms. There all the business of the weather is carried on above your horizon and loses its terror in familiarity. When you come to think about it, the disastrous storms are on the levels, sea or sand or plains. . . . You are lapped in them like uprooted grass; suspect them of a personal grudge. But the storms of hill countries have other business. They scoop water-courses, manure the pines, twist them to finer fibre, fit the firs to be masts and spars, and, if you keep reasonably out of the track of their affairs, do you no harm.[5]

Later volumes by Mary Austin are more colorful and flowing in style, as *The Land of Journey's Ending* (1924), or more explicit in setting forth Mary's philosophy, as the great autobiography, *Earth Horizon* (1932); but there is a clarity and freshness about *The Land of Little Rain* that belong to her youth.

Another woman interpreter with a turn for mysticism is Laura Adams Armer, well-known author of books for children and also of *Southwest* (1935), in which she outlines the pattern of life that she sees in the region. "The earth in process becomes a symbol of mutability in the Southwest, understandable and obvious. . . . The earth in process challenges ideas of stability, forcing men to invent harbors of thought. . . ."

Roy Bedichek shows himself to be not only a naturalist but a philosopher and something of a mystic in *Adventures with a Texas Naturalist* (1947). He is Wordsworthian in his reverence for the Divine plan as manifested in the harmony of nature—a harmony too often interfered with by civilized man. A quarter of a century of travel and study of flora and fauna went into the making of this fine book. In *Arkansas* (1947), the poet John Gould Fletcher has written a state history that reads like a novel as the author describes life in his native state as "different from life everywhere else in the United States." It is with this difference that he is concerned as with vivid details he tells the story of the state, from De Soto's seeking for gold to the people of the farms and cities of the present.

Ross Calvin, a clergyman yet hardly a mystic in his writings, approaches the problem from a different angle in his *Sky Determines, An Interpretation of the Southwest* (1934). He is the ecologist, anthropologist, economist, pointing out what forms of life can exist and upon what terms in the arid and semi-arid lands or in the rich valleys and high altitudes. He states his thesis in the Foreword.

But there hovers over many of the pages a shadowy ulterior purpose of pointing out to a bedevilled humanity that in the world of roots and clouds and wings and leaves there exists no Depression; that in its

5. *The Land of Little Rain* (1903), pp. 245-46.

beauties and simplicities rather than from divers bewildered senates and parliaments is man's peace most likely to be derived; that as life progressively adapts itself to its background of sun and soil, it gains in wholesomeness and sincerity.

River of the Sun: Stories of the Storied Gila (1946), also by Dr. Calvin, is written with the framework of his world of nature-determinism, but in this book more emphasis is placed upon man as the shaper of his environment. Perhaps a deciding factor was the intrepidity of such characters as Spanish Coronado and Anglo Kit Carson with whom two of the most interesting chapters deal.

Without a particular thesis but with modern techniques of appraisal, a new type of social scientist has made an important contribution to the literature of interpretation in the Southwest. Reference is made to such books as *First Penthouse Dwellers of America* (1938) written by an anthropologist and linguist, Ruth M. Underhill; *Latin Americans in Texas* (1946) written by a sociologist and journalist, Pauline R. Kibbe; *The Navaho* (1946), written by two authors, an anthropologist and a psychiatrist, Clyde Kluckhohn and Dorothea Leighton, respectively. These books view the people and the land from all the angles at which culture patterns may combine or clash. They strive to analyze the conditions of peoples upon the land in given situations and then from an understanding of the values appraise both in terms which make for harmony and social welfare or for discord and impoverishment. From such studies the reader learns that in the broad areas of the Southwest where there are both majority and minority cultural groups that each can contribute something to the other in terms of living for group satisfactions and for individual self-assurance.

A modern social scientist whose interest in Southwestern society has been largely confined to the period before 10,000 B. C. is Frank C. Hibben, whose book *The Lost Americans* (1946) makes the dawn-people in the region quite as absorbing as the people upon whom the light of history has shown clearly. Tracing the story of man on the continent back to Ice Age America when Wyoming was green and verdant, Dr. Hibben has proved the existence of homes of a cave dwelling group twenty-five thousand years ago in the Sandia Mountains northeast of Albuquerque. Folsom Man, labelled "The First Texan," Mohave Man, called "The First Californian," now have a rival in Sandia Man, named by Dr. Hibben as "The First New Mexican."

The technique of appraisal as employed by Erna Fergusson in *Our Southwest* (1940) is both a matter of definition and description. Miss Fergusson, the granddaughter of Southwestern pioneers, views the region from the perspective of its history, its economic development, its scientific, artistic, and recreational interests. El Paso as a "crossroads," Tucson as a resort, Albuquerque as a health mecca, Santa Fe and Taos as art colonies, and Ft. Worth "where cattle began"—so the Southwest is described in terms of its centers of interest and significance.

No more delightful study of adaptations to surroundings has been written about the Southwest and its neighborhood than D. H. Lawrence's *Mornings in Mexico*. Life is less primitive north of the Rio Grande but the mood of man and nature may be much the same—the patio, tree-shadowed with its familiar associations, or the wide sweep of outer world, impersonal, awe-inspiring. Parrots, Aztec gods, a market day, Indian dances of New Mexico make up this book, not just in colorful descriptive details but in the creative world of Lawrence's mind, where as in the first chapter of the green parrot calling the little curly dog, Corasmin, the world in its evolutionary cycles comes surging up from time. Nowhere is Lawrence's genius more apparent. It is this gift of seeing beneath what Lawrence calls "the mucous-paper wrapping of civilization" that leads him in his essay "New Mexico" (1929) to write:

But the moment I saw the brilliant, proud morning shine high up over the deserts of Santa Fe, something stood still in my soul, and I started to attend. . . . In the magnificent fierce morning of New Mexico one sprang awake, a new part of the soul woke up suddenly, and the old world gave way to a new.[6]

Philosophical comment upon the land and its way of life

6. From *Survey Graphic* (1929); also in *Phoenix, The Posthumous Papers of D. H. Lawrence,* edited by Edward D. McDonald (1936), pp. 141-47. Reprinted in *Southwesterners Write* (1946), edited by T. M. Pearce and A. P. Thomason.

has not been wholly confined to Arizona and New Mexico, despite the preponderance of it there. In the older Anglo sections of the Southwest, in the woods and hills and rich farmlands of Arkansas and East Texas, a few writers have paused to contemplate nature and to meditate on patterns of living. We may note at least three. Charles J. Finger, whose home in the Arkansas Ozarks was a literary center, carried on the vigorous tradition of late nineteenth-century nature writers associated with John Muir. In *Ozark Fantasia* (1927), for example, he climbs "sun-flooded hills to see haze-hung mountains" and hears old wisdom from an aged mountaineer. Finger declares that the primitive folks are "the salt of the earth." Another nature essayist is Karle Wilson Baker, also a poet and a novelist, who attentively watches the birds in her tall East Texas pines. If Finger carried on the traditions of Muir, Mrs. Baker belongs to the company of John Burroughs. *The Birds of Tanglewood* (1930), light but excellent in style, tells again the experiences of a lover of nature who finds "no end to her surprises . . . always some uncaptured marvel."

Only recently with growing urbanization have Southwesterners turned to recording the histories of towns and cities, attempting to distill their spirit. Colonel John W. Thomason, soldier, artist, writer, grew up in South Texas, and returned to it spiritually in his memorable little essay "Huntsville."[7] With a hint of nostalgia for the little town's Confederate memories, he sums up its history, past and present, in a pregnant sentence or two: "It has, I think, that rare and lovely thing called the sense of proportion. It pursues the common round, with only an academic eye cocked at the dubious future; which is, I consider, no bad law for living."

Samuel Wood Geiser in "Ghost-Towns and Lost-Towns of Texas, 1840-1880" preserved the names and partial history of once busy communities and pointed the way for further studies.[8] *Maverick Town, the Story of Old Tascosa* (1946) by John L. McCarty records the history and spirit of a Texas Panhandle community that became a ghost town until it was recently converted into Boys' Ranch. *Old Fort Davis* (1947)

7. *Southwest Review,* XIX (Spring, 1934), 233-44.
8. *The Texas Geographic Magazine,* Vol. VIII, No. I, (Spring, 1944).

by Barry Scobee traces the history of this once important but deserted ghost fort.

Shine Philips, a druggist, with a long memory, in *Big Spring, The Casual Biography of a Prairie Town* (1944) records vividly the tales of early and present days in West Texas. His fictionized device of recounting these stories to a stranger is at times strained. Boyce House, a nationally known raconteur of tall tales, found little need to stretch the truth in his histories of oil boom towns, *Were You In Ranger?* (1935) and *Oil Boom; The Story of Spindletop, Burkburnett, Mexia, Smackover, Desdemona, and Ranger* (1941).

Angie Debo in *Tulsa: From Creek Town to Oil Capital* (1943) traces the genesis and rapid growth of a thriving Oklahoma city. In *Prairie City* (1944) Miss Debo mixes imagination with history to write the story of a typical Oklahoma town from its founding on the Cherokee Strip in 1889 to World War II.

Green Peyton with *San Antonio, City in the Sun* won the 1946 book award of The Texas Institute of Letters. Mr. Peyton, formerly of the editorial staffs of *Fortune* and *Time,* is a newcomer to Texas, but he reminds us that "some of the best people in Texas have been Newcomers, including those men who died in the Alamo." He is conscious of the unamalgamated elements of the city: the cattle and oil Anglos, the German merchants and brewers, the Latins—foreigners in their native city—and always the Army of old Fort Sam Houston and Randolph and Kelly Fields. Of all of this he writes with journalistic realism, with no glamorizing of the past or white-washing of the present. He sees the Mexican slums as well as the Texas flag in the sunshine over the Alamo.

George Sessions Perry has chosen from the Southwest for his *Cities of America* (1947) Dallas-Fort Worth, linked by a continuous half-humorous feud; San Antonio "cosmopolitan and manifold"; and his home town, Rockdale, Texas (pop. 2,000). Mr. Perry has traveled the nation savoring expertly the taste of her cities, but he writes best of Saturday afternoon in his own farm town.

Albuquerque (1947) by Erna Fergusson is an informal portrait of an informal city. Miss Fergusson, a native daughter and a far traveler, has combined description, history, and anecdote into a readable and informative book. Her appraisal of her home town with its three races avoids both the sentimental and the harshly critical, picturing Albuquerque as no Utopia, but yet a pleasant place to live.

History and interpretation, as we have applied the terms, cover a wide range. Indeed, if we include biography, a kindred type, the group is the richest of all literary expression in the Southwest, past and present. The impulse back of all such writing is to record and explain. Now, what one esteems worth recording varies greatly. It may be one's own physical adventures on the frontier, or the development of a region, a state, or a city, or the working out of a social change, or, again, one's own spiritual and psychological adventures. The earlier Southwestern recorders set down the objective facts; the moderns try to explain why. This same trend toward accuracy, psychological subtlety, introspection marks the development of Southwestern biography and autobiography as well.

II

BIOGRAPHY AND AUTOBIOGRAPHY

Artless stories of personal adventures recounted by pioneers, such as those in *The Trail Drivers of Texas* and Kit Carson's story of his own life, are very simple forms of biography. But it is not until the central interest of the teller shifts from something done by a person to the person himself that we arrive at the essential quality of autobiography and biography. Not what Doctor Johnson did but Johnson the man is Boswell's subject in the greatest of all life stories. Much of the early Southwestern writing classed as travel and adventure is biographical in so far as it tells the personal experiences of Kendall or Irving or Gregg, but it contains no full length characterizations, no delineations of personality. It was that same impetus toward scholarship and motivation which we have noted in historical writing that changed biographical writing into the modern type—the impulse toward more complete and intense realization of experience.

The Southwest produced few of the sound, conventional biographies characteristic of mid-nineteenth-century America, but A. B. Paine's *Captain Bill McDonald, Texas Ranger* (1909) is a sturdy example. Intensive scholarship, however, is the hallmark of the best of the contemporary biographies. Eugene C. Barker employs all available sources in his definitive *Life of Stephen F. Austin* (1926). The slender figure of Austin, cut off in his prime, was in danger of being relegated to the realm of sentiment and tradition until Dr. Barker painstakingly subjected the copious Austin manuscripts to examination. Stephen F. Austin, lonely, iron-willed, intellectual, stands forth in this biography, a New England idealist who, had he settled in Boston instead of colonizing in Texas, might have shared the friendship of Emerson and Ticknor and Sumner.

Frank C. Lockwood has presented in *Arizona Characters* (1928), a series of studies of men who have made history in the state. In the group are Father Kino; Bill Williams (for whom the town of Williams is named, as well as a mountain and a river); Charles D. Poston, poet, mining engineer, and Arizona's first congressman; Pete Kitchen, early rancher who defied Apache raiders; Cochise, leader of Apaches for whom an Arizona county is named; General Crook; Ed Schieffelen; Governor Hunt, six times governor; and Dr. J. A. Munk, Arizona rancher and collector of Arizoniana, which he presented to the Southwest Museum in Los Angeles.

Thoroughness marks Evetts Haley's fine *Charles Goodnight* (1936). Goodnight, the dominant ranchman of the North Texas plains, is a harder man to track than Austin, who left written records at every step. Haley has trailed his man on cattle drives, and in the midst of Indian parleys at the bottom of Palo Duro Canyon. Skillfully, with no straining for effect, he weaves into the life of Goodnight the historical, economic, and social life of Texas during the heyday of the range cattle industry. In 1943 Mr. Haley added another full length portrait in *George Littlefield, Texan.* Littlefield in addition to being a cattleman was a soldier, banker, and philanthropist. Evetts Haley with his years of historical research in this period of the recent past, his own experience in ranching, and his knowledge of Texas politics and education was ideally suited to write this biography. Littlefield's paternalism is emphasized throughout the book as he amassed wealth and distributed it.

The same careful scholarship is shown in *Captain Lee Hall of Texas* (1940) by Dora Neill Raymond, a West Texan, now professor of history at Sweet Briar College. The greatest value of the book is perhaps as a history of the "smoking seventies" in Texas and Oklahoma rather than as a biography of one man. The six-feet-four red-headed ranger captain is often crowded off the pages by better known characters: Shanghai Pierce, Sam Bass, Quanah Parker, O. Henry, and Rough Rider Theodore Roosevelt with his "vigorous and dental smile." The book received the Texas Institute of Letters award as the best Texas book of 1940.

In *Kendall of the Picayune* (1943), another Texas Institute of Letters award book, Fayette Copeland after painstaking research in diaries, letters, and newspaper files traces the contributions of this pioneer adventurer, soldier, and newspaperman to the history of Texas and Louisiana. The work which is thoroughly documented and stays close to facts is highly readable. A clearer picture than was previously available emerges of the founder of the New Orleans *Picayune* and the author of *The Texas-Santa Fe Expedition*.

Carl Coke Rister, a research professor of history at the University of Oklahoma, has written a number of books treating of Indian wars, and Anglos pioneering in the Southwest. Among these works in which the thin line between history and biography practically disappears are *Southern Plainsmen* (1938), *Border Captives* (1940), and *Land Hunger* (1942). In *Robert E. Lee in Texas* (1946) Mr. Rister focuses his attention upon one man. Texas between 1856 and 1861 with Indian raids, Border incidents, frontier hardships is the proving ground for a West Point Lieutenant Colonel who emerges, in the words of General Winfield Scott, as "America's very best soldier." The reader comes to appreciate more fully than before, too, Lee the man, the kind, solicitous father and husband, the considerate friend, the troubled patriot forced to choose between two strong allegiances, the Union and his native state, Virginia.

Other biographies admirable in scholarship and style are Althea Bass's *Cherokee Messenger* (1936), the life of Samuel Austin Worcester, pioneer missionary to the Oklahoma Indians; Grant Foreman's *Sequoyah* (1938); Herbert Gambrell's *Mirabeau B. Lamar* (1934); and *Anson Jones, The Last President of Texas* (1948). Samuel Geiser's *Naturalist of the Frontier* (1937) is a series of sketches of those intelligent early naturalists, many of them foreign born, who first brought the scientific spirit to the Southwest: Boll, Berlandier, Drummond, Von Roemer, Lincecum, and others.

"After the opening of the new century," writes F. L. Pattee in his discussion of the "new biography" of our time, "biographical methods changed rapidly."[1] The "new" school not only utilizes scholarship but also folklore, folkways, and social traditions. This rich content is amalgamated with formal sources and analyzed in the light of modern psychology to determine motives and states of mind. This is what Gamaliel Bradford has termed the psychographic treatment. Likewise

---

1. See his excellent chapter, "The New Biography," in *The New American Literature* (1930).

the new biographer has developed a technique of writing. He employs literary devices familiar to the novelist: dramatization of scene by dialogue; conflict and suspense; description of background and personal appearance. The effect is much the same as that of fiction except for the careful documentation employed by the biographer. Where fiction creates imaginatively, biography now re-creates experience out of the knowledgeable past. Because life in the Southwest has been diverse and colorful, Southwestern biography is rich in content, offering a tempting field for the new technique.

A brilliant modern biography is Marquis James's *The Raven, A Life Story of Sam Houston* (1929), awarded the Pulitzer Prize for that year. Houston's career has always fascinated writers, both because of his political genius and his violent adventures. James makes the most of the inherent drama in his subject. Thus we read in *The Raven* how in 1813, when Sam enlisted in the Volunteers of Tennessee, his mother gave him a plain gold ring, on the inside of which "was engraved a single word epitomizing the creed that Elizabeth Houston said must forever shine in the conduct of her son." But we do not learn until the ring is taken from his dead finger on a July day in 1863 what that word was. It was Honor. Such writing might seem to border on melodrama were it not buttressed with scholarship. Almost every important statement is accounted for, a score of footnotes to each chapter. Yet Sam Houston the man emerges, life size and alive, moving in his own *milieu* and speaking his own words.

Stanley Vestal's interpretation of a great Sioux chief in *Sitting Bull* (1932) is hardly so dramatic as *The Raven,* but it represents a more difficult piece of research. Stanley Vestal works with his own knowledge of Plains tribes, forces of the land, traditions and oral history of the Indians, in order to create flesh and blood to clothe the bare bones of recorded fact. The narrative of the Sioux lad's happy childhood and novitiate as a warrior belongs with those beautiful early chapters of *The Education of Henry Adams* and of Lincoln Steffens' *Autobiography*. A companion study to *Sitting Bull,* yet less effective, is *Warpath, The True Story of the Fighting Sioux in a Biography of Chief White Bull* (1934).

Although Stanley Vestal's *Big-Foot Wallace* (1942) in

liveliness falls short of Duval's story of his comrade in *The Adventures of Big-Foot Wallace* (1870), yet it supplies a contrast between the modern and the nineteenth-century methods of combining fact and legend. This modern biography, too, has raised Big-Foot from a regional hero into the class of the all-American tall men of the frontier: Daniel Boone, Kit Carson, and David Crockett.

Constance Rourke, an authority on folklore, has completed the portrait of Crockett in her fascinating *Davy Crockett* (1934) by incorporating the legends and humor that reveal him as a folk hero as well as a defender of the Alamo. She uses all the literary devices as well as the skill of the frontier tall-tale teller, and confirms her picture with a useful bibliographical chapter.

These volumes are typical of the scholarly biographies which, however vivid the style, are carefully documented for the student. More informal are other recent Southwestern life stories which, although based upon research, are cast in popular form. Their authors prefer not to exhibit the blueprints from which they built their structures.

Julia Keleher and Elsie Ruth Chant in *The Padre of Isleta* (1940) write sympathetically of the French priest, Father Docher, and his thirty-seven years of service at Isleta. Father Padilla, stirring in his coffin where he lies buried in the church by the altar, is recorded as a legend. Adolph Bandelier and Charles Lummis, friends of the Padre relive through the pages. The book achieves something of the quiet charm of *Death Comes for the Archbishop*.

Stanley Vestal's *Kit Carson* (1928) takes a long step in the direction of fiction—it enters into the mind of the hero. See the boy Kit riding into Santa Fe for the first time with the Bent caravan.

Kit Carson sat on his mule, his quirt dangling, his tired body propped on the horn of the saddle, his curious eyes ranging over the pillars of the Governor's Palace, the facades of the Cathedral, the shop fronts and mud walls of the houses. So this was Santy Fee?

The scenes are often completely dramatized. The dialogue is cast in a drawling frontier dialect that rings true and doubtless owes much to the author's study of Garrard and the early travel writers.

Now as in their own time the early bad men and women of the Southwest have their biographers. Fact, legend, and the tall tale are blended into exciting reading. Walter Noble Burns retells *The Saga of Billy the Kid* (1925); Wayne Gard makes the train and bank robber ride again in *Sam Bass* (1936); Burton Rascoe adds a woman bandit, glamorized by time, in *Belle Starr* (1941); Kyle S. Crichton finds little need to employ legend in writing of the desperado turned sheriff in *Law and Order Limited, The Life of Elfego Baca* (1928); C. L. Sonnichsen, in *Roy Bean, Law West of the Pecos* (1943), gathers together the best of the tall tales of the Judge.

A successful variant of biographical writing is *A Vaquero of the Brush Country, Partly from the Reminiscences of John Young* (1929) by J. Frank Dobie. Old John Young, a pioneer brush rider of Southwest Texas, was a man of imagination who had in his youth dreamed of breaking the biggest monte bank in Mexico and in his old age of writing his own life. He found the ideal collaborator in Frank Dobie, bred on a Nueces River ranch and a gifted tale teller. Together they produced a narrative that has in it "the genius of the unfenced world . . . the open range before barbed wire revolutionized it." Dobie has never written a better book than *A Vaquero*.

Further instances of collaboration are George M. Coe's *Frontier Fighter* (1934), Jim (Lane) Cook's *Lane of the Llano* (1936), and W. S. Bartlett's *My Foot's in the Stirrup* (1936). Nan Hillary Harrison recorded Coe's reminiscences of the Lincoln County War. Jim Cook, once a wandering cowboy in the Southwest, told his experiences to T. M. Pearce, the best episodes of which are "The Days of the Longhorn" about his life in Texas from 1880 to 1900. Bartlett's story of his days as a scout with Mackenzie was rewritten by Mabel Major and Rebecca W. Smith. Many interesting informal biographies represent similar coöperation between author and subject: C. L. Douglas's *The Gentlemen in the White Hats* (1934), sketches of famous Texas Rangers; Dane Coolidge's *Texas Cowboys* (1937) and *Arizona Cowboys* (1938). C. L. Sonnichsen used the reminiscences of Billy King, one time cowboy, gambler, saloonkeeper, and peace officer, to write the biography of a man and a town in *Billy King's Tombstone* (1942). Fred Gipson listened to Colonel Zack Miller's tales of the famous 101 Ranch and, retaining much of the idiom of the old timer, set them down in *Fabulous Empire* (1946).

Miguel Otero's story, *My Life on the Frontier* (1936), gives an unvarnished account of Las Vegas, Trinidad, Santa Fe, and Taos when celebrities like Clay Allison, "Uncle Dick" Wootton, Kit Carson, and Billy the Kid were in those "diggin's." Otero, at one time Governor of New Mexico, recalls all classes of society from the Grand Duke Alexis of Russia, whom he helped to conduct on one of the last buffalo hunts, to Wild Bill Hickok, the prodigious killer, marshal of Fort Hays, Kansas, and later of Abilene, Texas.

Spin a Silver Dollar (1946) by Alberta Hannum is a delightful account of the four years that her friends Sally and Bill Lippincott spent running a trading post at Wide Ruins on the Navajo Indian Reservation in Arizona and of their discovery and encouragement of the art talent of Beatien Yazz, a shy Indian boy. The sensitive, lovely illustrations by the boy artist add greatly to the charm of the book.

Women played a larger part in frontier and range life than early chroniclers make clear and certainly a different role from the sentimental episodes featured by the western moving pictures. Within the past few years some of these women have written honest autobiographies, straightforward narrations of their own share in building a civilization alongside their husbands. Mary Rak, who ranches in the southeast part of Arizona, tells a homespun story in *A Cowman's Wife* (1934); her sense of humor and her fluency give the book real charm. Hilda Faunce is more introspective and tense—one might say, more modern—in *Desert Wife* (1934) as she tells how she and her husband, a desert-bred man, left towns and machinery to drive a wagon into the heart of the Navajo Reservation to take over a trading post. She runs the gamut of loneliness and primitive conditions, battling with illness and poverty and fatigue but winning full compensations in friendship and peace under the wide sky. Other women, too, have written good autobiographies recently. Louisa Wade Wetherell, with the aid of Frances Gillmor, relates in *Traders to the Navajos* (1934), the archaeological and ethnological explorations of the Wetherells at Mesa Verde. L. Walden Smith's *Saddles Up* (1937) is the experience of two city-bred Texans, man and wife, who discover the verities of existence on a McMullen County ranch.

Agnes Morley Cleaveland's *No Life for a Lady* (1941) begins with a woman's wedding journey to Cimarron, New Mexico, in a stagecoach under armed escort in 1872. It ends with that woman's daughter watching a new generation of ranchers occupying the baronial homesteads of an earlier day in the Datil Mountain region. In between the first and last chapters of *No Life for a Lady,* the reader learns of the wit, wisdom, and all round resourcefulness of a pioneer family in which the woman's role was as basic as the man's. It seems that the old saying about the cattle country being good for men but "hell on women and horses" is distinctly qualified by these candid, unassuming autobiographies of courageous women.

One of the chapters in *No Life for a Lady* is entitled "Gene Rhodes." Here Mrs. Cleaveland tells of the encouragement given to her first writing efforts by a reader, named Eugene Manlove Rhodes, who was then living at Engle, New Mexico. She pays tribute to the lively humor and generosity in the character of this man, who became her friend and one of the West's outstanding writers. A full length biography of Rhodes has been written by his wife, May Davidson Rhodes. The book is called *The Hired Man on Horseback* (1938) and takes its title from a poem Gene wrote in reply to an editorial in a midwestern newspaper using the phrase in disparagement of range life. This fine poem, along with Rhodes' famous epitaph, is printed in the volume. Mrs. Rhodes explained, in measure, the remarkable phenomenon of a man who wrote seven novels and some twenty stories about a land two thousand miles away from his pen but ever present in his memory. The biography brings Rhodes back to New Mexico and California for the writing of more novels, stories, articles and poems. The end is a mountain grave where two shapely junipers form the tapers, and a headstone bears the inscription, "Pasó Por Aquí," "He passed by here."

Autobiography in the modern introspective manner has outstanding examples in recent Southwestern literature. *Life Is My Song* (1937), by John Gould Fletcher, poet and citizen of the world, is as frank, as devoid of reticence as a novel. It is a strange bodily and spiritual odyssey that took him from the pre-Civil War mansion that was his boyhood home in Little Rock back and forth across this continent, back and forth across Europe, and home at fifty to Arkansas. The motif of Fletcher's "song" is that a writer must create in his own section of the country where he has roots. "American culture," he writes, "must be primarily regional, not metropolitan."

Harvey Fergusson in *Home in the West: An Inquiry into My Origins* (1945) announces that his purpose is "to write social history in terms of individual experience and observation." He probes into his own antecedents, childhood and youth in Albuquerque, Old Town, and the East for his answers. The biography ends with his formal education in Washington. The best chapters are of his grandparents, his own childhood home, and his boyhood on horseback or beside the river for which he had a passionate love.

Oliver La Farge states that in *Raw Material* (1945) he makes "no attempt at coherent autobiography." It is an honest effort to put down what has made him as he is, hence the kind of writer he is. The work is of interest to the student of Southwest literature, however, primarily for an account of Mr. La Farge's maturing attitude toward the Indian, his advance from the romantic escapism of *Laughing Boy* to an appreciation of the complex problems of the Indian in modern America.

At least two nationally known Oklahoma authors have written autobiographically. Burton Rascoe in *Before I Forget* (1937) has recorded a series of vivid recollections including those of his youth in Oklahoma. Sensitive and discerning, he evaluates the people and places he has known; yet he shows nothing of the bitterness and rebellion that appear in many such narratives. This volume takes the author through his twenty-eighth year and to 1919. *We Were Interrupted* (1947) is primarily of the "Roaring Twenties" as Mr. Rascoe knew them. Only briefly in this decade was he in Oklahoma, but long enough to see his father catapulted from "dirt farmer to oil baron." In Chicago and New York as a journalist he knew many important writers—Conrad, Galsworthy, Dreiser, Willa Cather, Somerset Maugham, T. S. Eliot. Marquis James has remembered his Oklahoma boyhood in *The Cherokee Strip*

(1946). He tells his own story with the same skill in selecting and recounting incidents that he employed in *The Raven* and *Andrew Jackson,* both Pulitizer Prize biographies.

Mr. James' account of the run on the Cherokee Strip is from his father's story. Mrs. Tom B. Ferguson in *They Carried the Torch* (1937) tells of the run from her own experience. She tells, too, of newspaper pioneering in Indian Territory and Oklahoma. Her life story furnished Edna Ferber suggestions for the popular novel and movie *Cimarron.*

The most significant autobiography that the Southwest has produced is undoubtedly Mary Austin's *Earth Horizon* (1932). At heart a philosopher—a rare attitude in a woman —Mrs. Austin tells the truth unflinchingly about "everything that matters" in her life. That is, about the little girl who found God by the walnut tree at the bottom of the orchard, the I-Mary as child and woman who was always "more solid and satisfying than Mary-by-herself." The book lays relatively little stress on those emotional relationships which women usually count to be the important events of their lives. It deals, instead, with I-Mary's relations with the Earth Horizon, "the incalculable blue ring of sky meeting earth, which is the source of experience." There emerges from the close-packed, somewhat disorderly story the very quality and function of Mary Austin's mind. It was her destiny, as she herself has phrased it, to "write imaginatively, not only of people, but of the scene, the totality which is called Nature . . . and the quality of experience called Folk and the frame of behavior known as Mystical." There is no other autobiography by a woman like *Earth Horizon* and few in the world's literature of its stature. Six years after Mary Austin's death, *The Beloved House* (1940), a study of her life and work was written by T. M. Pearce. The title of the book is a translation of the Spanish by which Mrs. Austin identified her home in Santa Fe, *Casa Querida.* Mr. Pearce interprets the phrase in terms of the nature world of America and Mary Austin's insight into the genius of minority as well as majority groups who people it.

The English essayist, poet, and novelist D. H. Lawrence came to New Mexico from Italy in the fall of 1922, and stayed in Taos until spring, journeying then to Mexico and later in that year returning to England. In the spring of 1924, Lawrence was again in Taos, again in Mexico in the summer, and back to Taos in the fall where he remained until April of 1925. The record of Lawrence in the Southwest has been preserved in a series of books, notable among them being *Lorenzo in Taos* (1932) by Mabel Dodge Luhan, *Lawrence and Brett* (1933) by Dorothy Eugenie Brett, and *"Not I, But the Wind . . ."* (1934) by Frieda Lawrence, his wife.[2]

Mrs. Luhan writes her book to Robinson Jeffers, offering it as a biographical interpretation of Lawrence. She recounts the circumstances of his trip to America, his desire to find in Taos and its Red Indian world a new creative center of living and sincere human relationships. His letters and conversation, as presented by Mabel Luhan tell of Lawrence's desire to write a novel in the Southwest that would express the life and the spirit of America. This he failed to do in Taos, partly because of the tension which developed between the Lawrences and Mrs. Luhan, the Honorable Brett sharing in both harmony and discord. "How ruthless we are when we live on the surface of life," observes Mrs. Luhan.[3] Dorothy Brett tells the story of her friendship with Lawrence, using "the facts and events as they happened, good or bad, for they were the framework upon which our days were built." Brett is tolerant, sympathetic, and understanding of the tortured moods in Lawrence.

Frieda Lawrence's autobiographical and biographical memoirs of her life with Lawrence begin in 1912 when she first met the young school-teacher writer who came to lunch to discuss with her husband a lectureship at a German university. Six weeks later she and Lawrence determined to make destined sacrifices and not long afterward they began their lives together in the Bavarian Alps. Italy, Germany, England, Sicily, Ceylon, Australia were to feed Lawrence's mind and slake his thirst for life, before he and Frieda arrived at Taos. *"Not I, But the Wind . . ."* (1934) reveals better than any of the other writings about Lawrence how terrifically he fought to solve the problem of personal relationships and yet how, possessed

2. The masculine view of Lawrence may be found in Knud Merrild, *A Poet and Two Painters* (1938) and in Aldous Huxley, "Introduction" to *The Letters of D. H. Lawrence* (1932). There are, of course, the books by Horace Gregory, Hugh Kingsmill, J. Middleton Murry, and W. Y. Tindall (to list only a few) which fill in the picture. The best bibliography is E. W. Tedlock's *The Frieda Lawrence Collection of D. H. Lawrence Manuscripts* (1948).
3. *Lorenzo in Taos* (1932), p. 141.

by his own impressions of rightness and truth, he continually provoked antagonism or aroused devotion in others.

Two months before Lawrence died at Vence in the French Alps, on March 2, 1930, he wrote of returning to the Southwest. "I believe I should get strong if I could get back but I am not well enough to travel yet." [4] Although the work Lawrence did in the Southwest does not loom large in his total achievement,[5] his stay in this part of America was crucial to his artistic evolution and to his developing thought. On his second return to New Mexico, he asked his friends in England to follow him there and establish a new way of life.[6] In one of his last letters he echoes this thought.[7] For D. H. Lawrence, the artist and prophet, and for Frieda, who returned to Taos in 1933 and lived there until her death, the American Southwest opened up new vistas of beauty in land and sky and of creative expression in the arts and living. The story of the Lawrences is a record of a great love, crossed by currents of friendships, positive as well as adverse. America is written into the heart of it and the American Southwest became no little part of its soul.

Mabel Luhan had begun her lengthy autobiographical memoirs while the Lawrences were living in Taos. "My total ego needed to pass off into words," [8] she says of her urge to unburden the impressions she had been storing through a lifetime of artistic activities and literary associations. Only the last volume of the memoirs, strictly speaking, belongs to her life in the Southwest.[9] This is *Edge of Taos Desert* (1937), where she testifies that life in Taos transformed her former world of values derived from Buffalo, New York, and Florence. The gift of the Taos country is a mystical one to Mrs. Luhan: there from the great mountain with the hidden Blue Lake she draws inspiration to which the beliefs of Indians and the creative way of artists contribute. For her knowledge of the Indian world, the author of *Edge of Taos Desert* is largely indebted

4. *Ibid.,* pp. 350.
5. See Part Three, Ch. I, History and Interpretation.
6. Catherine Carswell, *The Savage Pilgrimage* (1932), pp. 209-13.
7. M. Luhan, *Lorenzo in Taos* (1932), p. 351.
8. *Lorenzo in Taos* (1932), p. 63.
9. *Intimate Memories*: Vol. I, *Background* (1933); Vol. II, *European Experiences* (1935); Vol. III, *Movers and Shakers* (1936); Vol. IV, *Edge of Taos Desert* (1937).

to her husband Tony Luhan, a full-blood Taos Pueblo Indian. *Winter in Taos* (1935), a companion piece to the last volume of the memoirs, transcribes the quality of New Mexico which has caught the imagination of many people, and if, in Mrs. Luhan's version, it is not always convincing, it is always thought provoking and entertaining.[10]

A contemporary journalistic note is struck in Maury Maverick's *A Maverick American* (1937). The author, who has served as a United States Congressman from Texas, is a member of a distinguished American family known in the Southwest as cattle ranchers. He is a militant and somewhat theatrical reformer whose account of his genesis and development makes a chapter in the New Deal era of our national life. *A Maverick American* is the sort of bold, half-humorous autobiography that one would expect the Southwest to produce.

Another maverick American is J. Frank Dobie, who for the first time has written autobiographically in *A Texan in England* (1945). The fifteen racy, intense essays are from a war year spent lecturing on American History at Cambridge. He sees England both as a lover of English literature and as an ardent Southwesterner: England and the Southwest in juxtaposition page after page. Big-Foot Wallace and George Ruxton rub elbows with Shelley and Shakespeare. Back in Texas finishing the book, Mr. Dobie concludes: "I prefer to live in a country that is still developing, that has plenty of outlet, but for travel I'll choose a country with a past. . . ."

---

10. Mrs. Luhan's latest work is an interpretation of Taos in terms of the painters who live there: *Taos and Its Artists* (1947).

III

FICTION

The serious fiction of the contemporary Southwest reveals two strong tendencies: a desire to recapture the form and meaning of the past, and an urge to record and criticize the present scene. The first is, on the whole, the temper of idealism and of sentiment; the second is a part of the scientific trend of our age. These two tendencies are apparent in all modern American fiction, but their presence concurrently in the Southwest is particularly striking.

One of the few contemporary novels on the prehistoric Indian is John Louw Nelson's *Rhythm for Rain* (1937). It is a story of a Hopi community, written in the tradition of Bandelier's *The Delight Makers*. The early Spanish and Anglo-American eras have received more attention.

Anthony Adverse (1933), by Hervey Allen, one of the most widely read novels of that period, uses the early nineteenth-century Southwest for the setting of most of the final book. History and scenes are portrayed with care for exact details. In Santa Fe the long arm of coincidence reaches out, and the hero's lifetime enemy, Don Luis, causes his arrest and tortuous march to the prison of St. Lazarus in Mexico City. In the end, though, Anthony finds the happiness he has sought during his odyssey on three continents, in the simple life of the New Mexico mountain village, La Luz.[1]

The finest novel that has come from the Southwest—and one of the finest novels of America—is Willa Cather's *Death Comes for the Archbishop* (1927), a quiet, gracious character portrayal of two mid-nineteenth-century French priests, Jean Marie Latour and Joseph Vaillant, as they come in contact with

---

1. In *The Saturday Review of Literature* for January 13, 1934, Hervey Allen gives the Southwestern sources for material in *Anthony Adverse* from Chapter Sixty-five on. Notable among them are Kendall's *Narrative of the Texas-Santa Fe Expedition* (1884) and Gregg's *Commerce of the Prairies* (1844). He concludes his acknowledgments to people and to books with the statement ". . . It must be remembered of all this southwestern section depicted in the later pages of *Anthony Adverse* that I am personally familiar with it from my army experience on the Mexican border in 1916. I actually walked over much of the trail covered by Anthony."

the old Spanish and older Pueblo cultures of New Mexico. The building of the cathedral at Santa Fe is the core of the slight plot, but Indian and Spanish legends link the story with a more remote past. History is used candidly but without pedantry. Miss Cather has succeeded in a most difficult task, the portrayal of Spanish and Indian life from the viewpoint of the French priests.[2]

As would be expected, most Southwestern historical novels are written from the Anglo-American point of view. They concern the Anglos in contact, usually in conflict, with the Mexicans, the Indians, and sometimes with each other. Laura Krey in *On the Long Tide* (1940) and Karle Wilson Baker in *Star of the Wilderness* (1942) have both written romantically of Anglo attempts before 1836 to settle Texas and wrest the land from Mexico. Mrs. Baker's book continues into 1836 but her main story is of Dr. Grant, the "Beloved Scot" and his unsuccessful filibuster. Pendleton Hogan in *The Dark Comes Early* (1934), J. Frank Davis in *The Road to San Jacinto* (1936), and Monte Barrett in *The Tempered Blade* (1946) all focus attention on the Texas Revolution. *The Tempered Blade* is a biographical romance of Jim Bowie, the almost legendary hero of the Alamo.

Of the books centering around Taos and Bent's Fort in the 1830's and 1840's, Harvey Fergusson's *Wolf Song* (1927) alone creates characters.[3] His people matter: Sam Lash, the Kentucky "blond buck in hickory and homespun," Lola Salazar, spoiled daughter of a Spanish *rico,* and Black Wolf, the Cheyenne who hunts a scalp to gain favor with his sweetheart's father. Three ways of life and of thought are made vivid. The author is equally sympathetic toward the Anglo, the Spanish-American, the Indian. There are no villains. Stanley Vestal in *'Dobe Walls* (1929) and *Revolt on the Border* (1938) is also sympathetic toward the three races. His stories are frankly romances, with the interest in swift moving action. His people are far less memorable than his scenes.

2. In her autobiography, Mary Austin takes exception to Miss Cather's allegiance to the French tradition of Archbishop Lamy instead of to the Spanish tradition of the region. See comments in Mary Austin, *Earth Horizon* (1932), p. 459, and in T. M. Pearce, *The Beloved House* (1940), pp. 176-78.
3. The first in the trilogy of the Santa Fe Trail called *Followers of the Sun* (1936). The other two are *In Those Days* and *The Blood of the Conquerors.*

Mr. Fergusson's *In Those Days* (1929) covers the adult life of the central figure, Robert Jayson, during the swift changes of the Anglo-American conquest of New Mexico: trading, fighting, town building, the decay of Spanish wealth. Main Street supplants the plaza in an old town—Albuquerque this time rather than the more written about Santa Fe and Taos. Jack Connor's *Conquest* (1930) is of the same Anglo-American domination in Arizona. The plot resembles the pattern of *In Those Days*. The book is clearly intended to be anti-sentimental, anti-romantic.

A recent treatment of the Indian-Mexican-Anglo wars in the Southwest is *Blood Brother* (1947) by Elliott Arnold. From histories, unpublished manuscripts and diaries, Arnold has written the life stories of Mangas Coloradas and Cochise, the two great leaders of the Chiricahua Apache tribe, who held the peace and broke it in accord with fair dealing or treachery by the Americans. Tom Jeffords, the chief white character in the book, was as real a historical personage as Cochise with whom he seals a pact of blood brotherhood. The book presents in a fairer light than many frontier novels the case of the Southwestern Indians against American conquest and settlement.

Conrad Richter's *Early Americana* (1936) is a group of sharp-cut stories of Southwest Texas and New Mexico during the sixties, seventies, and eighties. Many of them are of young women courageously facing toil and childbirth and death. *The Sea of Grass* (1937) is a novelette of a slightly later period. The main conflict is between Jim Brewton, a domineering cattleman on a ranch "larger than Massachusetts with Connecticut thrown in" and the nesters who are trying to turn the grass lands into farms. Lutie, his wife, is the Irene Forsyte of this man of property. She brings beauty and tragedy to the ranch house of the Brewton men. Richter's *Tacey Cromwell* (1942) is also the study of a woman, but from another level of society. The story is told by Nugget Oldaker, who runs away from Kansas to Arizona to join his brother, Gaye. He finds him in a gambling place where he lives with Tacey, a being of strange conflicting forces. Before the story ends, Richter has written a study not only of Tacey, Gaye, and Nugget, but of frontier community and the individuals who gave it character.

Edna Ferber's *Cimarron* (1930) and Noll Houston's *The*

Great Promise (1946) are romances beginning with the run on the Cherokee Strip in 1889 and the establishment of the white man in Indian Territory. Miss Ferber's story continues into the present, with the finding of oil in Oklamoma. Its objective qualities made it a good movie. *The Wind Blew West* (1935) by Edwin Lanham, a young Texan, is of the same period in West Texas; Weatherford is the town. In this novel Lanham is a realist who records much that was not pretty in ranch and pioneer town life.

Brothers Three (1935) by John M. Oskison could be a sequel to *Brothers in the West* (1931) by Robert Raynolds. Not that descendants of Charles and David, if they had left them, would have resembled Timmy, Henry, and Roger Odell, brothers in Oskison's book. But brothers, held by the fine ties of companionship, are a like plot in any time. Charles and David, of Raynolds' novel on their pilgrimage through the old West, finding security in the mountain ranch-home with wives, friends, children, separated from them by death, adversity, are like the three Odells in a later age, on a pilgrimage which traverses an Oklahoma farm, the bargaining on the cattle plains, and the new type of American bargaining, the New York stock exchange. Those early brothers in the West end in a symbolic transfiguration of friendship after the loss of Karin, David's wife. They die in the wilderness where the lonely mountain peak looks down upon the spot they guess to be their birthplace. The later brothers return to Under-Ridge farm, their birthplace, which one of them calls a "living organism . . . nourished by the lives that are fed into it."

Other writers have rediscovered the Southwest for Civil War and Reconstruction novels. From the time of his boyhood in South Texas, John W. Thomason—later Colonel Thomason of the United States Marines—had loved stories of the Civil War as told to him by old soldiers. For his biography *Jeb Stuart* he did historical research on the conflict. His first novel to come out of this background was *Gone to Texas* (1937), a swashbuckling romance in which a handsome Yankee officer falls in love with a pretty Rebel hell-cat and wins her after thrilling gun play on both sides of the Rio Grande. Colonel Thomason's *Lone Star Preacher* (1941) is nearer biography and history than romance. The Reverend Praxiteles Swan, M. E. Church South, who serves as a chaplain in Hood's Texas Brigade is, the author tells us, "a combination of two distinguished early Methodist saints in Texas." The major events and many of the characters are historical. In giving the reader a sense of actual participation in the conflict this novel is comparable to Stephen Crane's *The Red Badge of Courage*. But unlike Crane's memorable tale, *The Lone Star Preacher* is rich in frontier humor.

And Tell of Time (1938) by Laura Krey is a full-bodied pageant of Reconstruction days in South Texas. Cavin Darcy, a boyish Confederate veteran, limping homeward from Appomattox, woos a cousin for a bride and brings her to his plantation on the Brazos. They live amply—loving, working, rearing children, suffering much in the body but little in the spirit—and the house they build endures. Mrs. Krey, like Colonel Thomason, learned history not "cold and dead, shut up in books," but from the men and women who had lived it.

Most of the historical fiction of the Southwest is of men and women who were equal to the hardships of the land and times. Little has been written of the failures. Dorothy Scarborough's *The Wind* (1925) is a striking exception. It is Hardy-esque in theme. Letty Mason, a sensitive Virginia girl living on a West Texas ranch, is driven to desperation, murder, and suicide. "The wind was the cause of it all," writes Miss Scarborough in the Foreword. "The sand too had a part in it, and human beings were involved, but the wind was the primal force." Maude E. Cole's *Wind Against Stone* (1941) is a more "smiling" but less convincing story of the same region and period.

In contrast to the fiction about the past, which is prevailingly romantic, that which treats the contemporary scene is inclined to be realistic.[4] The portrayals of farm and village life are often either preachments against the present system or disillusioned studies of narrowness, greed, and hypocrisy. Dorothy Scarborough, in *The Land of Cotton* (1923), *Can't Get a Redbird* (1929), *The Stretchberry Smile* (1932), and

---

4. The fiction of the range continues to be romantic, as has been pointed out in a previous section. Surprisingly little has been done in Southwestern fiction on the Negro. Probably Barry Benefield's "Ole Mistis" in *Short Turns* (1927), a sentimental character sketch of an old Negro man, is the best example.

such short stories as "The Drought,"[5] protest against the one crop, tenant farmer system of the cotton country. Ruth Cross makes the same protest in *The Golden Cocoon* (1924) and *The Big Road* (1931) as does Edward Everett Davis in *The White Scourge* (1940).

The novels of George Sessions Perry strike a rich mid-channel between the idealized romantic stream and stark, caustic realism. In *Hold Autumn in Your Hand* (1941), he deals with the people living on Texas bottom lands. Sam Tucker is more than an East Texas tenant farmer. He is Every Farmer who in spite of drought and flood and pests wins a living for himself and his family during the round of the seasons. The starkness of the conflict with unfriendly nature is relieved by racy country humor. This novel won both the National booksellers' award and the Texas Institute of Letters award for the year in which it appeared. In *Hackberry Cavalier* (1944), some of the same characters reappear in a series of stories loosely strung together by Edgar Selfridge, the cavalier, who plays a role in most, and is merely a listener in others. All are delicious humor of the American tall-tale variety, recounted with an easy drawl.

Jewell Gibson's *Joshua Beene and God* (1946) likewise combines realism and country humor. The story tells of the Reverend Joshua Beene, preacher, fanatic, charlatan, and the fighting of rival church people in a backwoods East Texas cotton farming community. This robust novel falls short of Mr. Perry's *Hold Autumn in Your Hand* in universality of theme and firmness of plot structure.

Sigman Byrd's *The Redlander* (1939), also of Southeast Texas farm and small town setting, is realistic in portrayal of people, but is weakened by a melodramatic conclusion. Mr. Byrd's short stories of the same region in *Tall Grew the Pines* (1936) show no such flaw.

In 1939, a book about "the red country and part of the gray country of Oklahoma" aroused all of America to the plight of families living upon marginal land in areas of the West where the richness of the earth had disappeared. This book was John Steinbeck's *The Grapes of Wrath,* a prose epic of man's fight against unyielding forces in nature and society.

5. *Best Short Stories of the Southwest* (1928), edited by Hilton Ross Greer.

The Joad family made their overland trek from their lost farmland in Oklahoma through the Panhandle of Texas, across New Mexico and the desert of eastern California to the vineyards of the coast. There are more than a dozen characters in *The Grapes of Wrath,* but the important unit is the family to which all are related or attached, and in the center is Ma Joad, "the citadel of the family, the strong place that could not be shaken." In 1940, a novel of less stature, but of somewhat similar theme was written by Lorraine Carr. It was called *Mother of the Smiths* and dealt with a migratory family from Texas, that came into Taos penniless, hoping to find new roots there. The central figure is Sabe Smith, who gives herself unselfishly to her family and even to her antagonistic neighbors, and brings up six sons with little help from their worthless father, Si. Three years later, John Sinclair wrote *In Time of Harvest,* the story of another family from Oklahoma. The McClungs settled in the Estancia Valley of New Mexico. They are just as hardy as the Smiths and just as vulgar as the Joads. The chief figures in the McClung family are the males, Tod McClung and his father-in-law, a unique creation who calls himself a "he-rounder" and is a derivative of Davy Crockett and Grandpa Joad. There are interesting parallels among the Joads of Steinbeck, the Smiths of Lorraine Carr, the McClungs of John Sinclair.

Hart Stilwell in *The Uncovered Wagon* (1947) tells the story of a family of the Texas Rio Grande Valley who are constantly on the move. Wife and children are dominated and terrorized by the father, "My Old Man," who rages at people and animals but has a way with things that grow from the soil. Less forceful but certainly more pleasant novels of pioneering in the same region are Margaret Bell Houston's *Magic Valley* (1934) and Cleo Dawson's *She Came to the Valley* (1943).

Whether these people are on the red earth of Oklahoma, the sandy loam of New Mexico, the irrigated soil of Texas or California, or on the bottom lands of Texas, they have in common the love of whatever soil they own and the attempt to hold it and make it yield to them the nourishment for life.

An increasing number of novelists are writing of contemporary town and city life. George Milburn in the short stories of *Oklahoma Town* (1931) and *No More Trumpets* (1933) and in the novel *Catalogue* (1936) writes of the sunburnt, frame-built town of the Plains, ugly, crude, complacent. There are a few Indians, a few Negroes; the white people are mostly poor. There is not even the glamour of new-found oil in Milburn's little towns. The "folk" to Milburn are not "children of nature," but lusty, cruel creatures, whose activities are relaxed by moments of sardonic humor. In the short novel *Flannigan's Folly* (1947) Mr. Milburn has mixed sentiment and country lore with realism. Quick wit has taken the place of the sardonic humor of such short stories as "The Fight at Hendryx's."[6]

No such humor relieves Frank Elser's bitter memories of the Plains town of his youth, Fort Worth, as he sets them down in *The Keen Desire* (1926). In *The Inheritors* (1940) Philip Atlee (James Phillips) of a later generation in Fort Worth blames the decadent escapades of the country club younger-set on their having grown up overly privileged and undisciplined. Both Frank Elser and James Phillips have continued writing novels but not of the Southwest.

Anne Pence Davis writes neither bitterly nor sentimentally in *The Customer Is Always Right* (1940), a novel of Stracy's Department Store in Plainstown, Texas. The town is obviously Wichita Falls. The yellow brick walls of the store and the change of the seasons through a year bind together the comedies and tragedies of many lives.

The Ring and the Cross (1947) by Robert Rylee has its setting during World War II in a Texas seaport city, obviously Houston. Mr. Rylee perhaps turned to his native Mississippi for his main character, Senator Adam Denbow. This controversial novel, while overly lurid and melodramatic, is indicative of the trend in Southwest fiction to grapple with present day evils.

Not too long ago fiction writers discovered oil. Many excellent short stories and novels have been published. "Windfall" by Winifred Sanford pictures the confusion of an overworked farm woman when an oil well comes in on her land.[7] *Family Style, We Inheritors, Oklahoma Wildcat,*

---

6. *The American Mercury*, XXV (February , 1932), 152-59.
7. *Best Short Stories from the Southwest* (1928), edited by Hilton Ross Greer.

all by women, appeared in 1937 and 1938. Karle Wilson Baker in *Family Style* shows the effect of sudden oil wealth on the various ramifications of the Priest family in the East Texas field. Mrs. Baker, who is primarily a poet and essayist, makes places real; her people and plot are unconvincing. Mary Stuart Chamberlain's *We Inheritors* is a psychological study of second-generation oil money in Houston. *Oklahoma Wildcat* by Augusta Weaver shows the insatiable spirit of gambling which motivates the oil game. In *Thunder in the Earth* (1941), Edwin Lanham draws upon similar motivation and settings for his story of Cobb Walters, who begins with nothing, becomes a millionaire, fights the bankers and the government controls, is broken in the fight, and starts again with the same devil-may-care grit and nonchalance that once carried him to the top. Mary King's *Quincie Bolliver,* published in the same year, is written from the viewpoint of the child of a mule driver as she comes to know oil men in a shabby boarding house and a shanty in a Texas boom town. In her more recent novel *These Other People* (1946) Miss King turned to the French Quarter of New Orleans for her characters and setting. Popular magazines publish serial stories with oil fields as settings. "Derrick Town" by Norma Patterson and Crate Dalton, which appeared in *Holland's Magazine,* and "Never Another Moon" by Helen Topping Miller in the *Ladies Home Journal* are typical of these.[8]

The Indian has been a stock figure in American fiction since Cooper. Only recently has there been a serious attempt to enter into the redman's psychology and present his problems. Oliver La Farge, who has lived much with the Navajos, has done two full length studies of young Indian men and women in *Laughing Boy,* the Pulitzer Prize novel for 1929, and *Enemy Gods* (1937). Both books are neo-romantic in portraying the primitive life as the good life. It is only by turning away from the white man's civilization back to the order and rhythm of the Trail of Beauty that the Indian boy or girl finds satisfaction. In *Laughing Boy* the hero meets the white man's ways through Slim Girl, a product of the Government School; in *Enemy*

8. See *Holland's Magazine,* Vol. 56 (July, 1937-August, 1938); *Ladies Home Journal,* Vol. 55 (April-August, 1938). *Never Another Moon* was published in book form later in the same year.

Gods the boy goes to school, tries the Christian-White way, hopes to become a leader of his people, but finally returns to the Navajo prayers and the hogans of "The People." "If we want to save ourselves," he says, "we have to learn to use the white man's knowledge, his weapons, his machines—and—still be Navajos."

There have been other Southwestern studies of Indians. In *Sundown* (1934) by J. J. Mathews the Oklahoma Indian boy who goes to college, fights as an aviator in World War I, gets oil money, drinks, and drives fast cars, finds in the end that he can live happily neither with Indians nor white men. The book closes on a note of frustration. Not so Edwin Corle's *People on the Earth* (1937), in which the Navajo youth smashes through the white man's codes to achieve freedom with his own people. Corle's book, sensitive and restrained, compares favorably with La Farge's treatment of a similar plot in *Enemy Gods*.

Frances Gillmor in *Windsinger* (1930) writes of a Navajo medicine man in his relationship with his own people and tribal religion. The white men are only the traders and herders that he meets at post and windmill. During a drouth the Windsinger prays for the wind to bring rain, and fails. He leaves the reservation ashamed; later he returns, sings, and the rain comes. The mood and style are that of the Old Testament prophets. Stanley Vestal in an unforgettable short story, "The Listeners Under-the-Ground," makes his reader feel the tragedy of the failure of the stoical Arapaho whose wife dies after he has caused sixty-four pieces of skin to be cut from his body that she might live.[9]

In *The Man Who Killed the Deer* (1942), Frank Waters has wrestled with the same problem as La Farge, Mathews, and Corle: "Can the Indian adjust himself to a world not of his making?" Martiniano, the Taos Indian, who has been six years in a Government School, runs afoul of the Game Laws, the rules of the Indian Council, and the customs of the Spanish natives before he finds his way back to the friendship of his people and to the power of their tribal faith.

9. *Best Short Stories of the Southwest,* Second Series (1931), edited by Hilton Ross Greer.

Discussion of the peyote cult is an important feature of the book; the Indian trader, Byers, is an outstanding character.

Until 1941, the Spanish-American in the Southwest had been less written about than the Indian. Harvey Fergusson's *Blood of the Conquerors* (1921) was one of the early novels to deal with Spanish-American life. This book is the story of Ramon Delcasar, the last scion of a once powerful New Mexico family. In an effort to win as his wife a wealthy Anglo "subdeb," he violates every principle of honor. Failing he sinks into idle half-contentment on a small farm that had been part of the large holdings of his grandfather.

About 1941 a surge of writing interest developed about the culture of the native Spanish. Between 1941 and 1947 there were six novels published whose themes centered upon the life of the Spanish in New Mexican communities. The novels with their authors and themes are as follows: *People of the Valley* (1941), by Frank Waters, the struggle between Spanish and Anglos for land and power in the Mora Valley near Las Vegas; *In the Night Did I Sing* (1942), by O'Kane Foster, the spiritual unrest in a group of villagers in the Sangre de Cristo Mountains near Taos; *The Life and Death of Little Joe* (1944), by Robert Bright, the struggle against ignorance and poverty of an isolated community as symbolized by a boy whose father was serving a penitentiary sentence for murder; *The Proud People* (1944), by Kyle Crichton, the decline in prestige and wealth of an aristocratic Spanish family in the business metropolis of the state, Albuquerque; *Dayspring* (1945), by Harry Sylvester, the search of an eastern anthropologist for a personal philosophy or the hope of religion among the Penitentes, a fraternity practicing flagellation during its pre-Easter rites: *The Turquoise* (1946), by Anya Seton, the survival, through experiences that carry her from poverty to wealth and power in New York, of the gift of healing and insight in the life of a Santa Fe girl born of a Spanish mother and a Scottish father. The writers of these novels have opened channels for understanding the Spanish traditions and character. They have brought appreciation and sympathy for the problems facing rural communities whose economy and culture have been dislocated by the invasion of industrialism, war, and scientific advance. Best of all, they have shown appreciation for the qualities in the Spanish genius which can add to the variety and worth of life in America.

Two Texas novels protest against the injustices to Mexicans in the Rio Grande Valley. Hart Stilwell's *Border City* (1945) is of the uneven conflict between Anglos and Mexicans in business, social life, and politics. Claud Garner's *Wetback* (1947) reveals convincingly the pitiable plight of the Mexican workman who has entered the United States illegally, usually by swimming the River. Mr. Garner, who has employed hundreds of wetbacks, writes with force and sincerity about conditions that he knows well. Frank Waters' novel, *The Yogi of Cockroach Court* (1947), also deals with border life, shocking the reader with its portrayal of social conditions. Against a background of sordid vice, Mr. Waters places a Chinese philosopher whose Oriental wisdom transcends but little changes the environment.

A number of sophisticated, psychological novels and short stories have been written in the Southwest. They treat the individual problems of sensitive Anglo-Americans in a modern world. In many instances the heroes are such introspective young men as the writers themselves. The Southwest settings and characters enrich the stories but often are not an integral part of them. There is much attention to pattern and style. Donald Joseph's *October's Child* (1930) and *Four Blind Mice* (1932) are of this school. Experiences are presented not directly but through the consciousness of adolescents and young men. The mood is that of disillusion.

Stark Young in *The Street of the Islands* (1930) includes a number of sympathetic sketches of Southwest scenes and characters. He is aware of nuances of light and shade. His stories are exquisitely done little pictures.

Katherine Anne Porter, who grew up near San Antonio and has lived in Dallas and Fort Worth, is recognized as one of America's most distinguished writers of the shorter forms of fiction. Many of her finest short stories and novelettes in the three volumes *Flowering Judas* (1930), *Pale Horse, Pale Rider* (1939), and *The Leaning Tower* (1944) are of Southwest people and places. For perfect artistry in portraying moods and impressions on a small canvas Miss Porter is com-

parable to Katherine Mansfield. In the stark realism of a few
of her stories she is more like John Steinbeck.[10]

Mary Austin's canvas for *Starry Adventure* (1931) is
crowded with details of New Mexico folklore and native customs. Gard Sitwell's adventure does not rise significantly above
its setting. A story of somewhat similar setting is Myron
Brinig's *All of Their Lives* (1941). Florence Gresham becomes the symbol of a group in the Southwest who seek the
exotic aspects of the region as an explanation of their own
failures to make emotional and social adjustments, Florence
comes to Taos after the disappointment of three marriages
and her life spent in the East and Europe. Brinig's drama of
characters in the studios and salons of Taos is drawn to life.

Paul Horgan's two novels of a projected trilogy, *Main
Line West* (1936) and *A Lamp on the Plains* (1937), carry
the story of the hero, Milford, to his graduation from a military school in southern New Mexico. Life assumes a serious
aspect for him after the death of his mother, who is stoned at
a pacifist meeting, and the death of a companion at military
school. He is a prematurely thoughtful and earnest youth
when Mr. Horgan leaves him at the end of the second novel.
The characters in *Far from Cibola,* which Horgan wrote in
1938, are of the same region as those in *Main Line West* and
A Lamp on the Plains, but the time is that of economic depression, government relief, the imprint of insecurity upon ranch
families, clerks, truck drivers, road workers, and hitch-hikers.

Fire in the Night (1934) and *No Quarter Given* (1935)
are novels whose locale is Santa Fe, and the life conflicts stimulated by artistic temperament. Raymond Otis, author of the
first, has used the Volunteer Fire Department of Santa Fe for
an introduction to his unique group of characters, but there is
symbolism implied for the emotional discontent which smoul-
ders in a triangle involving an American couple and a romantic
Spaniard. Paul Horgan's *No Quarter Given* has a central
character, Edmund Abbey, whose career in the East as a musi-
cian-composer is cut short by an illness that directs him to the
Southwest. There he meets Maggie Michaelis, an actress flee-

---

10. For a discerning critical review, see Vernon A. Young, "The Art of Kath-
    erine Anne Porter," *New Mexico Quarterly Review,* XV (Autumn, 1945),
    326-41.

ing from the frustration of a love affair. What would be unalleviated tragedy in the ending of Abbey's life finds a measure of fulfillment in the worthy and creative love he and Maggie share, which enables him to write a last symphonic work of triumph.

Dorothy Belle Hughes, who established herself as a first rank mystery writer with plots laid in New York, California, Spain, and elsewhere, places the action of *The Blackbirder* (1943) and *Ride the Pink Horse* (1946) in Santa Fe and Albuquerque, where she made her home for many years. In the first novel, Mrs. Hughes builds an exciting story from a new type of slave trade, the traffic in refugees from war torn Europe. In *Ride the Pink Horse,* a Chicago political murder is solved during the annual Santa Fe Fiesta, where the old fashioned merry-go-round called "Tio Vivo" whirls the pink horse as a mount for laughing children. Writer Hughes captures the mood of the place while sustaining suspense and suspicion.

Three novels written during and immediately following the World War II period sound a note that has not been conventional among Southwestern novelists— the satisfactions of the home place. As one looks back over the many novels, significant in interpreting traditions, peoples, and events, the number devoted to love of places and their associations are in the minority. Such novels tax the powers of writers to make readers share particular loyalties through universal experiences of love and friendship or their opposites in typical community living. Paul Horgan's *The Common Heart* (1942) draws upon his early memories of Albuquerque for scenes of the physician, Peter Rush, and his long service in an arid country to which healthseekers came and in which they found new meaning as well as new vitality in living. Curtis Martin's *The Hills of Home* (1943) describes the youth of an ordinary American boy, but it is not a commonplace youth, because John Fellows is alive in his imagination to the vibrations he feels from the characters, both strong and weak, both loving and unloving, who make up his home town in the canyon of the Cimarron.

Loula Grace Erdman's *The Years of the Locust* (1947) has its setting in rural Missouri, but its theme of the importance of the individual and family and community tradition is equally valid for Texas, the author's adopted state. Between Old Dade's death on Thursday and his funeral on Saturday, "the years that the locust hath eaten" are restored to many through their memories of the influence the dead man exercised upon the lives of the living.[11]

This world of steadfast values is one which the reader of Southwestern fiction comes to treasure as a sign that novelists have discovered the final inexhaustible vein of ore for their work in the personal associations indefinably yet inseparably fixed on the hillside, plain, or river bottom of the home place.[12]

---

11. Miss Erdman's book won the Dodd-Mead $10,000 novel contest for 1947.
12. Although the limitations of this chapter exclude such a fine sea tale as *Wake of the Red Witch* (1946) by Garland Roark, this Texan, whose first novel was a "Literary Guild" selection, is a name to be watched.

IV

LITERARY FOLKTALES

The literary folktale based on popular material is a narrative, usually short, with a loose plot that has dramatic situations, suspense, and a climax frequently pointed in a witty or homely saying. Sometimes there is characterization. It is consciously well written; indeed, the craftsmanship is often of a high order. This type of narrative has the same relation to the literally translated or transcribed story of the folk that such an art ballad as Scott's "Lochinvar" bears to the old Scottish "Katharine Jaffray" or David Guion's concert piece "Turkey in the Straw" to the old folk tune as strummed by a Negro. Washington Irving set a first precedent in America for transmuting folk material into literature. In the Southwest Frank Applegate, J. Frank Dobie, Mary Austin, and many others have practiced the art.

Frank Applegate left two books: *Indian Stories from the Pueblos* (1929) and *Native Tales of New Mexico* (1932), memories of his life among Indians as a friend and trader. He wrote not for a ready fiction market, but to record what he had learned of the history of pueblos and individuals. His stories do not lack taste and artistry, though they are not the work of a professional man of letters. "Ancestral Eagles," one of the best stories in the first book, tells of the difficulties that Hopi Tabo had in getting the Government Agent to recover an eagle stolen by a Navajo. The feathers were necessary to Tabo for a ceremonial dance, and the nest which had been robbed was clearly on the Hopi Reservation. Tired of waiting for the law to help him, Tabo disappears in the direction of a Navajo sheepherder's camp. The next morning Tabo's eagle is released at the proper time to carry its message to the gods, and about the same time a Navajo is waking up at his sheep camp with a large lump on his head. In one hand he grasps the tail feathers of a golden eagle.

Native Tales has the same quiet, forceful wisdom and humor. The account of how Juan Mora recovered his lost

burro Miguelito and got drunk with him down in the abandoned well is one of the priceless literary folktales of the country. "The salient characteristic of all of them is that they
could not have happened anywhere else, which is the unassail-
able hallmark of regionalism in literature," was Mary Austin's
comment on Applegate's work in her Introduction to the
volume.

Mary Austin's *Lost Borders* (1909) is a masterpiece of
story telling. The setting is the Mojave desert; the cast a
health-seeking Englishman who becomes a squaw man, a
sheepherder who befriends an antelope, a clerk who leaves
his family to hunt gold, a prostitute, and others who play
their parts within the destiny of that dim, hot valley marked by
misty ranges which are the borderline between society and
nature. *One-Smoke Stories* (1934), another book of folktales by Mrs. Austin, is a less unified group but equally final
in the perfect artistry with which each little tale unfolds its
significance.

The most influential volume of American literary folktales
is J. Frank Dobie's *Coronado's Children* (1930), widely circulated as the choice of one of the book-of-the-month clubs.
Search for lost mines and buried treasure, an age-old lure, is
the theme of a score of exciting and convincing tales. Actually,
after the appearance of the book, hunting for silver and gold
in the hills and caves of Texas began anew. *Tongues of the
Monte* (1935) is the framework for a series of richly colored
stories from Mexico. Such wisdom as Innocencio's is of the
tradition of Sancho Panza. In 1939, Dobie wrote *Apache Gold
and Yaqui Silver,* a second volume of treasure legends, including the Lost Adams Diggings in New Mexico.

Many other skillful craftsmen have written literary folktales. Elizabeth Willis DeHuff, student and teacher among
the Indians of New Mexico, shows humor and sympathetic
understanding in "The Grinding Stones."[1] Ruth Laughlin
Alexander, who has lived all her life along the upper Rio
Grande, is aware of the overtones and undertones of Spanish-
American life, and captures them in such a story as "The

1. *New Mexico Quarterly*, II (November, 1932), 299-311; also in Pearce
and Hendon, *America in the Southwest* (1933), 228-42.

House of the Wall Door."[2] Nina Otero Warren, herself of aristocratic Spanish descent, tells charming saints tales and folk stories, warm in emotional values.[3]

Frank Goodwyn, cousin of J. Frank Dobie, has followed the Dobie tradition in his novel-length folktale, *The Magic of Limping John* (1944). This is a story of rare humor, telling the experiences of a charlatan who comes to believe in the truth of his own faking and imposture. The Franciscan Fray Angelico Chavez, native born Spanish-American, has reached a fullness of tradition and artistry in the stories of *New Mexico Triptych* (1945). "Hunchback Madonna," one panel in the triptych, is a folktale told with more than the groping language of the simple informant, enriched by the insight of creative imagination and framed by the language of the artist in letters.

The numerous volumes of the *Publications* of the Texas Folk-Lore Society and *Folk-Say* preserve a rich, miscellaneous body of narratives, ranging from homespun hearsay to carefully wrought literary folktales. J. Frank Dobie, editor of the Texas Folk-Lore Society from 1922 to 1943, and Mody Boatright, his assistant and successor as editor, have welcomed contributions close to everyday living. They have included much valuable source material, and from time to time have discovered tales touched with creative imagination. Some of them are: Riley Aiken, "A Pack Load of Mexican Tales"; Ruth Laughlin Barker, "New Mexico Witch Tales"; Julia Beasley, "The Uneasy Ghost of Jean LaFitte"; J. Mason Brewer, "Juneteenth"; John R. Craddock, "The Legend of Stampede Mesa"; Martha Emmons, "Dyin' Easy" and "Walk Around My Bedside"; Everardo Gámiz and Bertha McKee Dobie, "Legends from Durango"; Jovita Gonzales, "Among My People" and "The Bullet-Swallower"; Charles L. Sonnichsen, "Mexican Spooks from El Paso"; N. A. Taylor, "The Devil and Strap Buckner."[4]

B. A. Botkin, guiding hand in the four issues of *Folk-Say; A Regional Miscellany,* published by the Oklahoma Folk-Lore Society from 1929 to 1932, began by collecting folk materials;

2. *Space,* I (September, 1934).
3. *Old Spain in Our Southwest* (1936).
4. All of these are in the *Publications,* Vol. III (1923), Vol. X (1932), Vol. XII (1935), and Vol. XIII (1937).

but after the first number he sought vivid, conscious writing
and modern craftsmanship. In the handsome volume for 1930,
for example, are to be found such instances of the literary folktale as Maurice G. Fulton's "Apocrypha of Billy the Kid,"
Daniel M. Garrison's "A Song of the Pipeline," Charles Morrow Wilson's "Folk Beliefs in the Ozark Hills," Paul Horgan's "The Witch," and Della I. Young's "The Pioneer
Dance." In some of these the transition from folk recording to
literary tale is so clear that the volume makes a good study of
the problem. The third and fourth issues of *Folk-Say* are
devoted chiefly to literature about the folk.

In June of 1947, the New Mexico Folklore Society published its first volume of folklore material, *The New Mexico
Folklore Record*. Materials ranged from the recorded narratives of folklore informants to articles about folk crafts and
the production of folk dramas. "The Devil, Saint Michael,
and the Hermit's Bottle" by Margaret Page Hood is a story
of the production of "Los Pastores" by the people in a village
of southern New Mexico. The text and characters in the play
carry on a folk tradition, but the story is an interpretation of
the village people and their background from the sympathetic
point of view of the author. Such is the milieu of the literary
folktale, i. e. folk materials handled by a skilled interpreter.

An area rich in the streams of folklore and one where collecting of folk materials is actively pursued will see more and
more of this transmutation of traditional subject matter into
conscious literature. The supreme achievement in the form
comes when writers grow up in the folk traditions and
then, in a sense, grow beyond it through sophistication of mind
and taste by education and literary experience.

V

POETRY

Nowhere is the outdoorness of Southwest life more reflected than in the poetry, whether the poet is an Omar Barker making hard riding range ballads, a Karle Wilson Baker writing delicate lyrics of star and pine, a John Gould Fletcher etching sharp images, a Witter Bynner or a Haniel Long searching for significance in experience. The visitors, too, write of the far horizons, of the immense bowl of the sky, and of man dwarfed by Nature. Each in this land of sun and wind and space experiences "a visitation of the divine excitement" and in accordance with his gifts makes it into a poem.[1]

The western tradition of vigorous ballad poetry and the gentler strain of romantic lyrics are still vital in the Southwest, but each has become within recent years truly rooted. To these two streams of influence has been added a third, difficult to define. When we call it modern, we recognize that it has the qualities of contemporary European and American poetry. It is experimental in technique, experiential and psychological in subject matter. There is a striving for intensity and uniqueness. It is sophisticated, disillusioned, yet not unrarely metaphysical. Often it is neo-primitive, influenced by the songs and dance rhythms of the Indians and exalting the folkways of pueblo and hogan. Beneath the cadence of *vers libre* can be heard the drum beat. Above the preoccupation with turn of phrase is the searching for the primitive harmony with the universe.

Not so much poetry has been written in the range tradition in recent years as one would expect, though the quality is high. Omar Barker has published the greatest number of these poems of the cattle country. *Buckaroo Ballads* (1928) preserves the stories and psychology of the cowboy, his need for elbow room and a horse, his hatred of cities and cars. There

---

1. Most of the individual poems mentioned in this section may be found in one of the following: Beaty, Payne, Smith, and Vann, *Texas Poems;* Botkin, *The Southwest Scene;* Bushby, *The Golden Stallion;* Greer, *Voices of the Southwest;* Greer and Barns, *New Voices of the Southwest;* Henderson, *The Turquoise Trail;* Major and Smith, *The Southwest in Literature; Kaleidograph; Folk-Say; New Mexico Quarterly Review; Southwest Review; Arizona Quarterly.* For titles of volumes by individual poets, see the bibliography.

have been many other good poems in this near heroic manner:
Berta Hart Nance's "Cattle"; Whitney Montgomery's "Death
Rode a Pinto Pony"; Vaida Montgomery's "Stampede"; E. E.
Dale's "The Prairie Schooner"; Karle Wilson Baker's "Song
of the Forerunners"; Kenneth Kaufman's "The Passing
Herd"; Badger Clark's "High-Chin-Bob"; Henry Herbert
Knibbs' "The Lone Red Rock"; Eugene Manlove Rhodes'
"The Hired Man on Horseback"; Everett Gillis' "Hello the
House!"; to name a few of the more original. These poems are,
on the whole, of the past, a past that seems to the writers
larger and better than the present.

A very few poets have written of this past with humor,
a touch of braggadocio, a note of the tall tale. Stanley Vestal
with his tongue in his cheek in several poems of the volume
Fandango; Lynn Riggs plainly grinning in such poems as "The
Old Timer"; Carlos Ashley with a smile and a heart-tug in
These Texas Hills. These poems are to the serious, romantic
verse narratives as Charles Russell's and Mary Bonner's exaggerated, almost burlesque pictures of the cowboy are to
Frederic Remington's idealized paintings.

John Houghton Allen in *Song to Randado* is unlike any
other Southwestern poet. He writes of a Mexican Texas ranch
with a love of the old and a bitterness toward the new. His
songs are psychological, harsh, moving.

Most of this new western poetry has the authentic ring.
The writers are usually native. They know their history first
or second hand and their geography first hand. Many of the
poems are from the author's own experiences. The life portrayed whether of the past or the present is a good life. The
poetic form and style are traditional. The ballad stanza is
often used.

By far the largest number of volumes of poetry published
by Southwesterners in recent years are lyrics, primarily of
Nature, though the other lyrical strings are plucked—love,
death, war, religion. In the Southwest people live much in the
open and if not actually in the country at least with patios and
gardens as outdoor living rooms. Karle Wilson Baker and
Grace Noll Crowell stand out among these nature poets. Each
has published a number of volumes and has received national
recognition. They are both skilled craftswomen and possess
the lyrical gift in a high degree. Mrs. Baker is almost Words-

worthian in her reverence for Nature. The pine tree and the star are her poetic symbols. Her volumes are *Blue Smoke* (1919), *The Burning Bush* (1922), and *Dreamers on Horseback* (1931). Grace Noll Crowell's intense love for her adopted land is sung in many volumes, among which are *Silver in the Sun* (1928) and *Flame in the Wind* (1934). Yet she may have made her most lasting gift to Southwest poetry in her religious verse in *The Light of the Years* (1936) and *Songs of Courage* (1930). It has been a long time since such fine religious poetry has been written in the United States, not since the period of Whittier and Bryant.

Lexie Dean Robertson and Margaret Bell Houston add a touch of lightness and whimsicality to the usual romantic sweetness in such poems as "My Sins and I," and "If You Leave Your Door Ajar." But Lexie Dean Robertson's strongest and most original poems are of the Texas oil fields. No pretty lyrics these. She casts aside regular rhythms and writes starkly in free verse and polyphonic prose. Another romantic poet who writes realistically of oil is Violet McDougal of Oklahoma.

Margaret Bell Houston's most quoted lyric is "Song from Traffic." This theme of nostalgia, homesickness for the Plains, for the Gulf, the hills, for childhood, has produced many tender and beautiful lyrics in the Southwest: Kenneth Kaufman's "Blanket Flowers"; John McClure's "In Bourbon Street"; Hazel Harper Harris' "A Blue Bonnet Picture"; C. T. Davis' "Hills of Home"; Clyde Walton Hill's "The Little Towns of Texas"; Carey Holbrook's "Little Houses."

Hilton Ross Greer, founder and for many years president of the Texas Poetry Society, is one of the few Southwest poets who writes of city life as often as of country. "Bird on a Downtown Wire" from *Ten and Twenty Aprils* (1935) is characteristic with its philosophical twist. His most copied poem from the same collection is a majestic backward look, "The Road of Midnight Pageants." A. E. Browning in "Tulsa, Oklahoma" and Ann McClure in "Roofs" cut sharp city images in free verse. Boyce House usually writes of the city harshly, in *Texas Rhythm* (1936), but in "Beauty is Elsewhere" with freshness and a sense of awe.

David Russell, who succeeded Mr. Greer as president of

the Texas Poetry Society, is primarily a writer of lyrics, though he has successfully assayed the narrative. "Crescent Moon" from his volume *Sing With Me Now* (1946) cuts an incisive image and is philosophical in its implications. Ruth Averitt, too, writes of nature interpretively. "Melody in Crystal" is one of her most successful poems in employing nature as a symbol.[2]

Patrick Moreland, while handling the usual lyrical themes, writes astringently and with a touch of irony, even grim humor as in "Mice" and "The Black Cat." He is not afraid of the unlovely. Tom H. McNeal in brief poems in *Motley's the Only Wear* (1942) smiles wryly at life. He writes sensitively, often whimsically of youth, April, and death. Fray Angelico Chavez writes of man and beast, reptile and fly, with philosophical humor in "Adventures in Cibola," "Saints and Dogs," "To A Fly," and "Rattlesnake."

Siddie Joe Johnson discovers the beauty she ever seeks in the sounds and sights of the city in "Southwest City" from *Gallant the Hour* (1946). But it is of her own Gulf coast that she writes with the most intensity in "The Land I Know" from the volume called *Agarita Berry* (1933). In addition to her lyrical gift Miss Johnson tells a story in verse with sustained interest and emotional appeal. "The Ballad of the Old Woman" and "The Ballad of Dolores" read well aloud, and "Norther," a sonnet sequence, grips the attention like a well-told short story. Stanley Babb, another poet of the Gulf, in *The Death of a Buccaneer* (1927) finds an escape to Cathay or the haunts of the pirates in lyric and ballad. Like his fore-runner John Sjolander he sees poems in the folktales of the coast. He is not inclined to moralize, however, like Sjolander in his well-known poem "O Steerman."

Glenn Ward Dresbach writes feelingly of land and cliff and sky in *The Colors of the West* (1922) and *Star Dust and Stone* (1928), but he is even more concerned with the individual. "Water Finder" creates a character as definite as Robert Frost's "Hired Hand." His poem "The Golden Stallion" gives the title to D. Maitland Bushby's useful anthology of Southwestern verse. Arthur Sampley, too, is more often a portrait than a landscape painter in the brief, discerning character

---

2. Included by Ted Malone in *Adventures in Poetry* (1946).

studies in *This Is Our Time* (1943) and *Of the Strong and the Fleet* (1947).

In the far Southwest poets write with the same intensity of the desert, the turquoise sky, the too infrequent rain, and the lights on the mountains. Harvena, talented daughter of Conrad Richter, shows this feeling for her country in "Accents of the West" and "Shadows on the Sandias"; Ethel Cheney in "Turquoise Spring" and "Revanant"; Maude Davis Crosno in "Autumn at Taos"; and Norman Macleod in "Yet Autumn Mournfully," and "Coniferous," a poem of the Petrified Forest. Arthur Davison Ficke has written the hills above the sunset, the golden yellow of aspen groves into lyrics.

Most Southwest poetry portrays country life as the good life in spite of drouth and storm. The pictorial aspects are exalted. Fay Yauger is in revolt against this idealistic school of rural poetry. "Planter's Charm," in the volume to which it gives the title, is a strong, fine poem of tenant farm life which received the first award of the Poetry Society of America in 1935. "Desert Born" and "County Fair," too, are fine poems.

Irene Carlyle, in *Music by Lamplight* (1945), also writes realistically of the country, usually Ozark rural life. The dazed farmer in "Country Auction" who watches "his provident years . . . carted away in bits" is a portrait of Everyman in his first moment of incomprehensible defeat. "Sonnets to Strength" retells the age-old conflict between the farmer and the farmer's wife and the contrariness of the weather. As a riveter in a war plant in the dark and din under her hood, Mrs. Carlyle continued to make poems, one called "The Welder."

Fania Kruger writes out of the agonies of her race, the Russian Jews. *Cossack Laughter* (1937) contains poems of the Czarist Russia she knew in her youth, and of the Jew in America. Her verse has a more agonizing cry than Southwest poetry has before known. Like Fay Yauger she belongs to the active Wichita Falls Manuscript Club. She, too, received a first award (1946) of the Poetry Society of America. "Passover Eve," her award poem, is of a Jewish family in this land of refuge revisited at their feast table by their sons who have "fallen in an alien land . . . that men be free . . . the air be sweet with peace."

There has been very little poetry in the Southwest about

the Negro. A few romantic poems by Whitney Montgomery as "The Cotton Picker's Song," a slight volume by a Texas Negro, Mason Brewer, called *Negrito,* and a volume *Free Steppin'* by Kate McAlpin Crady. Mrs. Crady, who grew up on a Mississippi Delta plantation, knows her Negro psychology and idiom and writes with pathos and humor.

In the mid-nineteenth century in England and America, poetry came to be used primarily as a social and moral instrument. This social earnestness in poetry has been almost skipped in the Southwest. Marina Wister Dasburgh, the daughter of Owen Wister, has employed certain social themes in *Fantasy and Fugue* (1937), as has Margaret Page Hood in such poems as "Knitting." Thomas Wood Stevens in a long dramatic poem *Westward Under Vega* (1938) in combination blank verse and lyrics recounts the trip of a young couple, John and April, across the continent from Washington, D. C., to Santa Fe in a topless Ford. The love of the two and their reaction to the socio-economic scene are the themes. Witter Bynner, primarily a lyricist, in *Take Away the Darkness* (1947) speaks "Words on Public Affairs" with a new awareness of political, economic, and social evils. More poetry of this type will probably come. But with a few exceptions in the Southwest today we have the old romanticism, a glorification of the past and of Nature, in traditional patterns; and twentieth-century neo-romanticism, which largely takes the form of sharp appeal to the senses and neo-primitivism, in new experimental rhythms.

John Gould Fletcher, a native of Little Rock, through experience a cosmopolite, who in his maturity has returned home in body and soul, is an example of the neo-romantic.[3] He was one of the original group of Imagists when the school was born in London before World War I under the tutelage of Amy Lowell. They espoused freedom of form, *vers libre,* and the concrete and sensory. Intellectual concepts were conveyed chiefly by implication. Moralizing was taboo. In his poems about the Southwest, many of which are included in his *Selected Poems* (1938), Mr. Fletcher utilizes the powerful appeal to the senses of the modern. "Down the Mississippi" is made up of unforgettable images that etch themselves into the mind. "Mexican Quarter" gets its effects from sharp contrasts, the

---

3. See his autobiography, *Life is My Song* (1937).

smell of a dead horse mingled with the smell of tamales frying, a mangy dog, a girl in a black shawl, the explosion of the stars, and Juan stringing a brown guitar—realism and romanticism. In "Burning Mountain," a legend of the Santa Fe Trail, the red sandstone pyramid "reaching to the sky" is the constant before which move the kaleidoscope of Comanche and buffalo, creaking wagon trains, longhorns and cowboys. This poem gives the title to Mr. Fletcher's 1946 volume.

Witter Bynner, too, is a citizen of the world. A native of New York, he finds refuge from urban, standardized civilization in an adobe house in Santa Fe fitted with Indian and Oriental objects of art. Their easy juxtaposition suggests to one without the aid of ethnologists that the two came from a common art world. Witter Bynner writes of many things, and well. His "Dance for Rain at Cochiti" is one of the most effective poems in theme and expression the Southwest has produced. Significant for the region is his feeling for the movement of Indian and Mexican life in their psychology, dancing, and religion. *Indian Earth* (1929) ranks among his best poetry.

Spud Johnson recreates the world of the primitive worship of nature in poems like "Taos Dance" and "Morning of the First Spring" in his book *Horizontal Yellow* (1935). But he shows, also, contrasts between the worlds of Indian and white man in such poems as "Patricio Came" and "Poppies." There are fine personal observations in "Half Bracelet," "Mountain Parting," and a rhapsody of memories and impressions in the longer poem "Yellow."

In Arizona, Edward Doro in *The Boar and Shibboleth* employs "fantastic symbolism and music that is unforgettable." The subject matter is not of the Southwest nor any other place.

Mary Austin treats Indian life in the cadences of Indian verse in what she called "re-expressions" in her *American Rhythm* (1923). How much is Indian and how much the mystic "I-Mary" is impossible to tell. Indeed, how much is Mary, wise in folkways, and how much the children who are purported to have made the poems in *The Children Sing in the Far West* (1928)? Ina Cassidy, also, has translated Indian poetry successfully in *The House of the Sky*.[4] Herbert Joseph

---

4. For other effective translations of Indian poetry that have intrinsic poetic merit, see Natalie Curtis Burlin's *The Indians' Book* and the references in the section of this book on "Myth, Legend, and Song of the Indian."

Spinden has prefaced his *Songs of the Tewa* with an illuminating essay on the aesthetic point of view of the Indian. Ruth Underhill in *Singing for Power* (1938) has translated as literally as possible "the song magic of the Papago Indians." A dominant theme of these Indian poems of the arid lands is a prayer for rain "to make the corn and children grow."

"Gray Roadster" by Paul Eldridge of Oklahoma stands out as one of the few poems of the ironic tragedy of the Indian in contact with the white man's machine civilization. D. Maitland Bushby of Arizona also pictures this incongruity in "Indian Side Show" and "Yo-Tan-E-Ke." In addition to his poems on Indian life, Bushby, the best known poet of Arizona, writes of the desert in bold colors.

The Spanish-American has influenced Southwest poetry in English less than has the Indian. Alice Corbin in her two books of poetry, *Red Earth* and *The Sun Turns West,* has a number of sympathetic interpretations of Spanish life, among them "Old Juan Quintana," the picture of a goat-herd; "Cundiyo," the sketch of three black-shawled women each holding a sorrow to her breast; "El Coyotito," a poem of love and prison, rephrased from the Spanish. Mrs. Henderson (Alice Corbin) as co-founder of *Poetry, A Magazine of Verse,* in 1918, has known most of the major figures in modern American poetry. Coming to New Mexico in 1921, she established a Poets' Round-Up which was held annually in Santa Fe for a number of years each spring. Ina Sizer Cassidy also writes sympathetically of the native people in her Penitente poem "Crosses." Charles Bechtol in "Old Tucson" sings a love poem to a Spanish girl within a 'dobe wall.

Fray Angelico Chavez, himself a Spanish-American, writes with simple effectiveness about his own people in "Southwestern Night," "Who Pass by the Way" and "Peña Blanca," his town. He is reminiscent of William Blake with Biblical images employed unexpectedly, often whimsically, in "Cherub," "Trees," "Stigmata of Saint Francis." Often in his poems Palestine and New Mexico are as one. His first volume was entitled *Clothed with the Sun* (1939). The later books, *Eleven Lady-Lyrics* (1945) and *The Single Rose* (1948) are in the vein of the great mystical writers of Spain, yet the language is English, and thus are fused the elements of more than one literary tradition.

A recurring motif in the poetry of the far Southwest is the timelessness of Nature, the antiquity of Indian and Spanish civilization in the region, and the recentness of the white man in this old land, together with the briefness of individual life. The poet looks at a rock covered with inscriptions, a piece of ancient pottery, the dim painting of hands in a cave, a circle of trees where a house has been and no house is, an age-old road and writes of the twin deities, Permanence and Evanescence. Such poems are the terse "Pasó Por Aquí" and "Bowl on a Shelf" by William Haskell Simpson; Margaret Pond Church's "Los Santos"; Alice Corbin Henderson's "El Rito de Santa Fe" and "Indian Earth"; and Mary Austin's "Campo Santo at San Juan."

Haniel Long is not content merely to put into sharp contrast the beautiful and the ugly or the ancient and the new as details seize on the ear, the eye, the nostrils. All of these must first be sifted through the poet's mind, not merely screened on his senses. He gropes for significances, reaches beyond physical perception into the metaphysical. His narrative poem *Malinche* (1939) is a study of the gifts which a woman from the New World made to a leader of men from the Old World, gifts which made possible a conquest, a civilizing, an enslavement. The shorter poems in his earlier volume *Atlantides* (1933) are as clear in their imagery and as sure in their phrasing as the lyric-epigrams by Chinese poets whom he has widely read.

Many of the best known contemporary American writers and a few British have come to the Southwest to visit or for a longer sojourn and written poems in response to the dramatic quality of its scenery and history. Amy Lowell in "Texas" in jingling rimes writes of "cowboys perched on forty-dollar saddles." Carl Sandburg in "Santa Fe Sketches" does more than "sniff with the tourists" in the Museum; he senses that "when a city picks a valley—and a valley picks a city—it is a marriage —and there are children." In "The Santa Fe Trail" Vachel Lindsay shouts of the automobiles racing with strident horns along Highway 50 and whispers the sweet voice of the Rachel Jane singing of "love and glory, stars and rain." When he sees the Indians "dancing for a Babbitt Jamboree" his anger rises "like high tide in the sea." Alfred Kreymborg in "Indian Sky" sees the old squaw, her bowl, and the earth in perfect harmony.

Harriet Monroe in "At O'Neill's Point" salutes Cardenas, the
buccaneering Spaniard, who "three centuries before the next
white man" stood on the "rim of the world" and looked down
into the Grand Canyon. Edna St. Vincent Millay in "Pueblo
Pot" bending mournfully over lovely broken shards is solaced
by the beauty of living birds. Robinson Jeffers in his unforgettable poem "Hands" writes of the prehistoric handpaintings
on cave walls: "We also were human, we had hands not
paws." Thomas Hornsby Ferril pens stirring words for New
Mexico in "Nocturne at Noon—1605." Katherine Garrison
Chapin in her volume *Plain Chant for America* in five poems
commemorates the New Mexican landscape. Edgar Lee Masters weaves the colonial history of the Southwest into his long
poem *The New World*. In the last lines he asks:

> To what good end has the New World come
> Superior to the good that Indians kept unchanged?

Willa Cather, in Santa Fe writing *Death Comes for the
Archbishop*, makes a ballad "Spanish Johnny." The English
novelist John Galsworthy upon entering Santa Fe puts his
longing for the scent and the drip of rain into "Desert Song."
Jan Struther, of *Mrs. Miniver* fame, in *Travelling America*
journeying through New England, the Old South, the Middle
West is ever reminded of her English hills, meadows, and
streams. Reaching the Southwest she says,

> But here, in the Southwest, opening my eyes on
> Vermilion mesas rising from painted sands,
> I have found at last a land with a new horizon,
> A land which holds no echoes of other lands. . . .
>
> Silence, and sun, and sand. The lizards flicker.
> Ghostly and restless rolls the tumbleweed.
> The eyes that gaze from the scattered huts of wicker
> Are the secret eyes of an ancient and secret breed.
>
> This is a country of dream, a world enchanted,
> Improbable, fantastic, a wild release.
> Here, and here alone, I can walk unhaunted.
> I shall stay here long. Strangeness, at last, brings peace.[5]

---

5. *Atlantic Monthly*, CLXX (October, 1942), 56-57. Reprinted in *A Pocketful
of Pebbles* (1946), by Jan Struther, pp. 5-6.

VI

DRAMA

Civilization from its outset in the Southwest had a place for dramatic entertainments. Religion here among Indian tribes was associated with pageantry and ceremony. The Spanish brought with them feast days and fiestas and even folk plays of the religious type. Such a dance as *El Jarabe Tapatía,* the most popular Spanish dance in the region, is really a little dance drama in itself, telling the story of the courtship of the rooster and the hen, the *charro* and his sweetheart. Simple isolated societies make their own drama as they fashion their own garments—out of the materials at hand to suit their own needs.[1] Later on, as folk cultures are merged in a specialized civilization, professionals write the plays and professional producers stage them in commercial theatres. There are records of Mexican puppet shows in New Mexico during the nineteenth century.[2] The peoples in the region with Spanish background were thoroughly receptive to the theatre, yet aside from the pure materials that go to make up theatre, such as the ceremonial dances and fiesta shows, professional plays and acting were almost non-existent in the Southwest before the Anglo-American occupation.

Inevitably Anglo-American dramatic activity has been influenced by the American theatre, that is, by New York and the eastern cities. From early times show companies followed the routes of travel to the frontier.[3] Magicians, minstrels, and circuses vied with the drama proper for support. For example, during the Republic of Texas traveling entertainers appeared in Houston, Galveston, Corpus Christi, and other towns. "Houston's first dramatic season was launched on the eleventh of June, 1838, with . . . the presentation of Sheridan Knowles's comedy *The Hunchback.* . . . The performance came to an end

---

1. See sections on "Indian Myth, Legend, and Song," and "Spanish Folk Dramas, Songs, and Narratives."
2. "Los Titeres," *Spanish Folk Ways.* Federal Writers' Project, Vol. I, No. 2.
3. W. G. B. Carson, *The Theatre on the Frontier* (1932).

with a popular farce, *The Dumb Belle, or I'm Perfection*." [4]
Many ambitious actors barnstormed in Texas before the Civil
War, among them seventeen-year-old Joseph Jefferson and
his mother. An equally precocious dramatic activity manifested
itself fifty years later when the frontier pushed farther west.
Tombstone, Arizona, a typical mining center in the eighties,
was a good show town, supporting the famous Bird Cage Variety Theatre where semicomic singers, Irish comedians, acrobats
and jugglers were presented as well as full-blown comedies. At
Schiefflin Hall, where more serious drama was offered, a partial
list of productions given between 1881 and 1918 shows nearly
three hundred titles, beginning with *Kathleen Mavourneen* and
ending with *As You Like It*.[5] In approximately the same period,
that is, from 1880 to 1910, towns in New Mexico like Santa
Fe, Albuquerque, and Roswell had playhouses in which traveling troupes of actors produced such plays as "Leah the Forsaken" and "Fanchon the Cricket." [6]

In addition to professional performances of drama, amateur actors have been active in the Southwest from early times.
By 1840, Texas newspapers were praising the efforts of "Thes-
pian Societies" at Matagorda and Houston,[7] and within a
generation San Antonio nourished a group of local actors directed by the mayor. Later frontier theatres such as the ones
in Tombstone were supported by a strong amateur tradition.

Conventional amateur productions, however, interest only
a small portion of any frontier community. The people amuse
themselves with robust, out-of-doors entertainments. In much
of the Southwest these have been riding matches, tournaments,
and "bull-tailings." "In the rodeo, the Wild West show, and the
'Frontier Day' celebrations now presented annually throughout
the West," asserts Winifred Johnston, "America has made a
unique contribution to the major entertainments of the world."[8]
The rodeo, she explains, is primarily a contest; the Wild West
show is a commercial organization for the display of frontier

4. W. R. Hogan, "The Theatre in the Republic of Texas," *Southwest Review,*
   XIX (July, 1934), 383-84.
5. Clair E. Willson, *Mimes and Miners, A Historical Study of the Theatre in
   Tombstone,* University of Arizona *Bulletin,* VI (October, 1935).
6. Hazel Vineyard, "Trails of the Trouper." Unpublished M. A. Thesis, University of New Mexico, 1941.
7. Hogan, *op. cit.,* p. 375.
8. "Cow-Country Theatre," *Southwest Review,* XVIII (Autumn, 1932), 10.

activities; the "Frontier Days" is distinctly an entertainment. All three are marked by the speed and syncopation characteristic of our nation. These developments of the people's drama, together with the "western" movie, interpret one phase of American life to the rest of the world.

In the years immediately following World War I, the economic, social, and artistic pace of the Southwest was greatly accelerated. The region, long remote from the Atlantic seaboard, was caught up into the rhythm of modern life. An example of this synchronizing is the Little Theatre Movement which flourished from about 1918 to 1931. In most of the urban centers and many small towns, eager amateurs produced plays for which they supplied the scenery and costumes as well as the actors and direction. Beginning with one-act plays, they undertook current Broadway hits, foreign masterpieces, costume revivals, and occasionally original compositions. Among the hardiest of the Southwestern little theatres have been those at Dallas (the Little Theatre of Dallas and the Oak Cliff Little Theatre), Albuquerque, Amarillo, San Antonio, Tulsa, Oklahoma City, Fort Worth, Carlsbad, Phoenix, Tucson, El Paso, the Green Mask Players of Houston, and the Santa Fe Players. Robert Nail with his original Christmas plays and annual historical *Fandangle* has made the little West Texas town Albany a dramatic center for a large ranching area. His play *Black Is the Color* was given its premiere at Hardin-Simmons University in the spring of 1948. Important work has been accomplished at all of the state universities and at many of the other colleges and universities.[9]

A little theatre should discover and foster local playwrights as well as actors and scene-shifters, but it does so much more rarely. The Southwest has produced a creditable number of native dramas for its local players, but, being remote from New York, has contributed few successful vehicles to Broadway.

Judge Lynch, by John William Rogers, Texas dramatic critic, won the first Belasco Cup Prize in 1925 when it was

9. See "Points of View," *Southwest Review,* XVII (Summer, 1932), 483-89; V. S. Albertson, "The Green Mask Players," *Southwest Review,* XVI (Winter, 1931), 164-77; John Rosenfeld, "The Southwest Amuses Itself," *Southwest Review,* XVI (Spring, 1931), 277-89; John W. Rogers, "Little Theatres and Indigenous Plays," *Southwest Review,* XVII (Summer, 1932), 477-82; Norris Houghton, "Drama at the Crossroads," *Atlantic Monthly,* 168 (November, 1941), 596-604.

presented by the Dallas Little Theatre under the direction of
Oliver Hinsdell. It is a bold arraignment of racial injustices
to the Negro, almost too powerful for a little theatre one-act
play. Rogers has also written *Bumblepuppy, Westward People,*
and other plays. The Belasco Cup for the next year was
awarded to Margaret Larkin's *El Cristo,* based on the Penitente rites of Spanish New Mexicans. This moving one-act play
is the tragedy of José, chosen to be El Cristo, who defies his
destiny. In 1942 a volume called *Three Southwest Plays* was
published with an introduction by John Rosenfield. It contains
Sam Acheson's *We Are Besieged,* a tense dramatization of the
defense and fall of the Alamo; John William Rogers' *Where
the Dear Antelope Play,* an amusing satire on women culture-
seekers; and Kathleen Witherspoon's *Jute,*[10] an indictment
of social cruelty to the Negro. Each of these is a three-act play.

Perhaps the most important play to choose the Southwest
as a setting and Southwestern events for a plot is Maxwell
Anderson's *Night over Taos* (1932). This well-written poetic
drama deals with the conflict between two civilizations during
the American occupation. The central figure in the play is
Pablo Montoya, a leader in the Taos rebellion of 1847. During
the action of the play, Montoya battles against the American
troops only to discover that at home both his sons have betrayed him. The older son has made a deal with the Americans
and the younger has fallen in love with a young maiden in the
household, whom the father had selected for his own bride.
In the tragic downfall of the personal empire of Montoya, the
hardy virtues of feudalism disappear along with the iron-clad
paternalism and slavery. *Night over Taos* was first presented
by the Group Theatre in New York, but between 1932 and
1947 the play has been produced by community playhouses
and university groups all over the country. In the Southwest,
there have been productions at the University of New Mexico
and at Texas Christian University.

The most successful Southwestern playwright on Broadway is Lynn Riggs of Oklahoma and New Mexico. In 1925
his one-act *Knives from Syria* was presented by the Santa Fe
Players, and in 1927 the American Laboratory Theatre gave

---

10. *Jute* and *We Are Besieged* had first appeared in *Southwest Review,* XVI
(Spring, 1931), 385-436; XXVII (Autumn, 1941), 1-95, respectively.

Big Lake. His first nationally known drama was *Green Grow the Lilacs,* produced in 1931 by the Theatre Guild, which took it on tour. This full length play of Oklahoma rural life is enhanced by the songs of a cowboy chorus which link the acts in a rhythmic continuity. *Green Grow the Lilacs* became the basis for the musical play, *Oklahoma,* with lyrics by Oscar Hammerstein and music by Richard Rodgers and dances by Agnes de Mille. *Russet Mantle,* also by Lynn Riggs, was produced in New York in 1936. It deals with a group of sophisticates in Santa Fe. Amid the comedy of their strivings, a youth and a girl, symbols of freedom, break through artificial conventions to seek a new world. "An odd and strangely haunting beauty permeates Riggs' work," according to Barrett H. Clark, who counts him a significant dramatist of folk materials.[11]

Pauline Williams, who began her playwriting at Rodey Theatre of the University of New Mexico, has seen three of her plays in production at East and West playhouses. "Accidentally Yours" completed a successful run in the spring and summer of 1947, with Billie Burke as the feminine lead.

Several Southwestern writers, already well known in other fields, have essayed drama. Paul Horgan, New Mexico novelist, who was at one time on the production staff of the Rochester (N. Y.) Opera Company, wrote the libretto for a folk opera entitled *A Tree on the Plains.*[12] The music is by Ernst Bacon. This work was given its premiere on May 2, 1942, at Spartanburg, South Carolina. On May 5, 1943, it was produced in New York by the Columbia Theatre Associates and the University's Department of Music with the same soloist who had created the leading role the year before. Philip Stevenson, another New Mexico author, who won the Theatre Union's nation-wide contest in 1934 with *God's in His Heaven,* has published and presented several other plays, including one on Billy the Kid.

Recent years have seen an increasing number of successful Southwestern novels made into films by Hollywood. A complete list would be lengthy and the result of long investigation. A partial list is suggestive and will point to fields of interest which American audiences have viewed from the writing of

11. See also Henry Roth, "Lynn Riggs and the Individual," *Folk-Say,* Vol. II (1930).
12. The libretto was published in *Southwest Review,* XXVIII (Summer, 1943), 345-76.

novelists in this area: Conrad Richter's "The Sea of Grass," from the novel by that title; George Sessions Perry's "The Southerner" from *Hold Autumn in Your Hand;* Eugene Manlove Rhodes' "Four Faces West," from the novelette *Pasó Por Aquí;* Dorothy B. Hughes' "Ride the Pink Horse" from the mystery novel by the same name.

Dramatic activity in the Southwest, then, is of many kinds and springs from many sources. The Indians dance for rain and the Spanish-Americans celebrate Christmas with *Los Pastores*. Histrionic cowboys in red silk shirts ride the broncs of the sawdust ring. Little theatres produce plays and playwrights. Meanwhile thriving cities support one-night stands of last year's Pulitzer Prize plays and even opera, while the ubiquitous movies flash in glowing signs the names of the newest Hollywood stars. Whether for worship or entertainment, for fashion or creative expression, the Southwest likes a good show.

VII

LITERATURE FOR CHILDREN

There was a close relationship between the work of folk-lorists and the first writing of juveniles in the Southwest. A reading audience among children developed for fiction with Southwestern themes and background before it developed among older readers. The writers of juveniles explored the Indian and Spanish backgrounds to provide stories for eastern as well as western readers in the early 1900's, whereas the novel as a form for older minds did not truly flourish until after 1925. A survey of the children's books, therefore, has an added significance for this region. Much of the finest material for creative writing in the Southwest was first assayed by the writers of juveniles.

A kind of pioneer in the field was Mary Austin's *The Basket Woman* (1904), a book of Indian tales written especially for children and incorporating the lore of the Indians of California. The Basket Woman is an old Indian who does the washing for a white family. She carries wood for fires in a big basket, the size of which terrifies the little boy of the household whose mind is filled with vague ideas of Indian secrecy and cruelty. He finally is won by the kindness of the Basket Woman, who saves his life when he wanders off into the desert in search of a merry-go-round in the air, really buzzards wheeling over a dead animal. Mrs. Austin's *The Trail Book* (1918) is a juvenile in the manner of Rudyard Kipling's *The Jungle Book*. In her plot, she brings alive the stuffed animals in a museum. The two children of the caretaker hear stories about a coyote, a puma, a chaparral cock called "the road runner," a condor, and others.

Although Ernest Thompson Seton did not make his permanent home in the Southwest until 1930, he had lived here in the 1890's and one of his early stories concerns a giant leader of a pack of gray wolves that ravaged a valley in northern New Mexico. It was five years before the old outlaw succumbed to the traps and lassos of the cowboys. This story,

"Lobo, King of the Currumpaw" appears in Seton's *Wild Animals I Have Known* (1898, 1942) which was reissued a number of times, the last while the author was living at Seton Village near Santa Fe. Here Ernest Thompson Seton established headquarters for his Woodcraft League of America and his School of Indian Wisdom. Hundreds of boys visited this center of Indian and American folklore before Mr. Seton died in 1946. As a writer of books for young America, Ernest Thompson Seton will be long remembered.

The Indian world, with its colorful ceremonies, outdoor life, and nature lore has always had a strong appeal for young people, since their minds more readily accept the wonder and miracle of nature than do the minds of adults. The child is not a skeptic; the world is still a place full of puzzles to him, and the Indians' explanations and reactions are full of charm and color, not to be scoffed at.

Elizabeth Willis DeHuff was one of a group of writers in the 1920's who introduced Indian lore and customs to young readers. In her preface to *Taytay's Tales* (1922), she tells how she collected the stories for her own daughter. The first tales were gotten by chance from a young Indian boy who turned out to be an artist as well. He was Fred Kabotie, a Hopi lad who drew the pictures and colored them in accord with Indian conceptions and in the Indian style of painting. Mrs. De-Huff refers to earlier collections of Pueblo tales, such as those made by John M. Gunn in *Schat-Chen* (1904) and Charles F. Lummis in *Pueblo Indian Folk-Stories* (1894, 1910). As a writer trained to adapt material to the child's point of view, Elizabeth DeHuff was notably successful in this volume, and in those she wrote in succeeding years: *Taytay's Memories* (1924), *Five Little Katchinas* (1930), *Two Little Hopi* (1936), *Hoppity Bunny's Hop* (1939), and *Little-Boy-Dance* (1946).

A number of the books for children portray the life of Indian young people as well as give the stories told to them by their elders. Such are Grace Moon's *Chi-Wee* (1925), *Chi-Wee and Loki of the Desert,* and later books; James Schultz's *A Son of the Navajos* (1926); Deric Nusbaum's *Deric With the Indians* (1927); Ahlee James' *Tewa Firelight Tales* (1927); Alida Sims Malkus' *The Dragon Fly of*

Zuñi (1928); and Florence C. Coolidge's *Little Ugly Face and Other Indian Tales* (1929). A group of volumes to make Indian crafts and songs available to young Anglos are *Sign Talk* (1918) by Ernest Thompson Seton; *Boys' Games among the North American Indians* (1924) by Edith Stow; *The Book of Indian Crafts and Indian Lore* (1928) by Julian H. Salomon. Very few of the books deal with the prehistoric past of the Indians. One such title is *Lolami, The Little Cliff Dweller* (1901) by Clara Kern Bayliss.

Probably unique, because it is the work both of an Indian writer and of Indian illustrators, is Louise Abeita's *I Am a Pueblo Indian Girl* (1939). This book of poems and sketches about Indian life was called by Oliver La Farge "a first tentative step" of literature about Indian culture written by Indians: "It crosses a threshold till now deemed forever closed."

Books on modern Southwest Indians stress the theme of understanding the Indian and overcoming the prejudices drawn from the past relations between Indians and Whites. Such books as Laura Adams Armer's *Waterless Mountain* (1931) and *Dark Circle of Branches* (1933) show how Navajo boys are taught dignity and reverence along with the normal Indian games and sports of youth. Mrs. Armer's story is the only book about the Southwest to win the Newberry Award as "the most distinguished" children's book of the year. Dorothy Childs Hogner's *Navajo Winter Nights* (1935) is one of the best books containing legends and folktales because of its variety and clear style. Mrs. Hogner's *The Education of a Burro* (1936) is also distinguished for its readable quality, plus wisdom and humor. Mary and Conrad Buff's *Dancing Cloud* (1937) tells how, years ago, Kit Carson captured the Navajos and how the United States allowed them to return to their old home. Eva L. Butler's *Two Little Navajos Dip Their Sheep* (1937) is a well-written story, using a very simple vocabulary in telling of the fears of a little Navajo girl as she watches her pet sheep being dipped. Isis L. Harrington, for many years a teacher in Indian schools, has written stories of both Pueblo and Navajo children. In *Nah-le Kah-de (He Herds Sheep)* (1937), she gives a short glossary of Navajo words. *Told in the Twilight* (1938), includes a group of poems called "Navajo Mother Goose Rhymes" with stories.

A number of the books about Indian children treat of the reluctance of Indian parents to send the children away to American schools and of the difficulties of the boys and girls when they arrive at school and after they return to their homes. In Eda Lou Walton's *Turquoise Boy and White Shell Girl* (1933) the mother and father hide the twins whenever the school officials appear, telling them they have no children. The little girl, Carrie, in Rutherford Montgomery's *The Mystery of the Turquoise Frog* (1946) was scorned by her uncle because he did not like her ways after she returned from school. In Anna Nolan Clark's *The Little Navajo Bluebird* (1943), the family dreads the evil of school so much that they hold a big chant accompanied by a sand-painting ceremony to keep Hobah, who is going away to school, from evil.

This theme, however, is absent from several of the recent books of Indian life. Ann Nolan Clark says of her book *In My Mother's House* (1941) that it was "written to answer the need for books with the Indian point of view. . . . Indian children helped make the book, helped write the short sentences that read like free verse." A Cochiti Pueblo Indian boy, Velino Herrera, illustrated the book. Her *Little Navajo Bluebird* (1943) is tenderly charming without being sentimental. *Dusty Desert Tales* (1941) by Richard Summers emphasizes the different Indian tribes and their various customs. Many Americans do not recognize that Indians differ as much as do Englishmen and Frenchmen or other European groups.

Few books, unfortunately, have been written to acquaint children with the Woodland and Plains Tribes of the Southwest. In 1941 Margaret Alison Johansen told the story of a Tejas Indian boy in *Hawk of Hawk Clan*. In 1947 Alice Marriott, author of *The Ten Grandmothers,* a history of the Kiowas for grown-ups, put her knowledge of the life and legends of this tribe into an entertaining book for the young reader. *Winter-Telling Stories* (1947), illustrated skillfully by a Kiowa, Roland Whitehorse, tells the sometimes heroic, sometimes humorous, exploits of Saynday, a demigod.

Children's books portraying the Spanish way of life in the Southwest have not been so numerous as the stories about Indians. Such books as Covelle Newcomb's *Cortez, the Conqueror* (1947); Camilla Campbell's *Galleons Sail Westward*

(1939), the tale of Cabeza de Vaca; and Cornelia James Cannon's *The Pueblo Boy; A Story of Coronado's Search for the Seven Cities of Cibola* (1926); and *The Fight for the Pueblo; The Story of Oñate's Expedition and the Founding of Santa Fe* combine the history of European exploration and conquest with the Indian life that the Spanish found. Margaret Ann Hubbard in *Seraphina Todd* (1941) makes San Antonio, a Spanish town in an Indian territory, live again in the 1770's. James Willard Schultz deals with these early Spanish adventures in *The Trail of the Spanish Horse* (1922).

Stories employing Spanish-American folklore and customs make a strong appeal to children, whether of Spanish or Anglo heritage. The young readers of Nina Otero's *Old Spain in Our Southwest* (1936) learn what early schools were like in the Spanish Southwest, how young couples carried on courtship and at last were married with ceremony, feasting, and a *baile*. They learn of treasure hunting and the miracles of the saints. In Camilla Campbell's *Star Mountain* (1946) they read the beautiful Mexican legends of the "Virgin of Guadalupe," the "Sleeping Woman of the Snows," "El Niño de la Panelita," and many others.

Florence C. Means in *Adella Mary in Old New Mexico* (1930) introduces the reader and the little English girl of the story to the fascination of a land with scenery and customs like Spain. Charlotte Baker in *Necessary Nellie* (1946) and *Nellie and the Mayor's Hat* (1947) tells stories of small Mexicans.

Animal stories always delight children. For the small child there is Loyd Tireman's Mesaland Series, called "a child's library of the wild life of the mesa." Characters in the books are jackrabbits, prairie dogs, road runners, and their animal neighbors. So far, the following titles have appeared: *Baby Jack and Jumping Jack Rabbit* (1943), *Hop-A-Long* (1944), *Dumbee* (1945), *Cocky* (1946), and *Big Fat* (1947). *The Little Valley Quail* (1945) by Emilie and F. A. Toepperwein pleases both the child and the adult who reads it to him. A favorite animal with children in the Southwest is the burro. He is a patient, sleepy-eyed little beast who can be made to carry wood for the fireplace or children to a fiesta. In 1936, Margaret Pond Church wrote *The Burro of Angelitos,* a charming story of the pet owned by a little Spanish boy in a village near

Santa Fe. Barbara Latham's book, *Pedro, Nina and Perrita* (1939), illustrated by the author, concerns the same world of pets and children's values in a Spanish village of the upper Rio Grande. Many of the poems in Mary Austin's *The Children Sing in the Far West* (1928) draw upon animal lore for themes.

Juveniles about Anglo-American life in the Southwest take the pioneer figures of forest and trail for their heroes. Some of these books are *Christopher Carson, Known as Kit Carson* (1901) by John S. C. Abbot; *The Boy's Life of Kit Carson* (1929) by Flora Warren Seymour; *General Crook and the Fighting Apaches* (1918) and *Old Jim Bridger on the Moccasin Trail* (1928) by Edwin L. Sabin; *The Pony Express Goes Through; An American Saga Told by Its Heroes* (1935) by William A. Jackson. Many of the short tales of true adventures compiled by Oliver G. Swan in *Covered Wagon Days* (1928) are of the Southwest.

Texas is the scene for most Anglo literature for young people, as New Mexico and Arizona supplied settings for most of the juveniles about Indian and Spanish life. An interesting combination of all of the traditions is found in one of the earliest juveniles written about the region, a book published in 1878 and written by one Thomas Pilgrim. It was called *Live Boys: or Charley and Nasho in Texas, A Narrative Relating to Two Boys of Fourteen, One a Texan, the Other a Mexican: Showing Their Life on the Cattle Trail, and their Adventures in Indian Territory, Kansas, and Northern Texas: Embracing Many Thrilling Adventures*. The reference to Indian Territory brings Oklahoma into the field as a setting for juveniles. But Texas appears early and continues as the favorite locale for adventure books for boys. J. C. Duval's *Early Times in Texas or the Adventures of Jack Dobell* (1892), which has been discussed earlier, was written for young readers, as Duval announces in his preface. It concerns the Fannin Expedition that ended in 1836 at Goliad. The hero is the nineteen-year-old Duval, himself, who escapes the massacre and wanders across the deserted countryside, dodging the enemy and living by his wits. Duval also wrote a sequel, *The Young Explorers: or, Continuation of the Adventures of Jack Dobell* (1892), Duval's better known book is *Big-Foot Wallace* (1870) about his friend, the noted Indian fighter and Texas Ranger, and the hero of many a tall tale. This, too, the author considered a juvenile on the basis of its lack of "style or literary merit." Duval's books are good reading for adults as well as older-age boys.

Tall tales of folk heroes, animal and human, continue to delight boys and girls. Leigh Peck in *Don Coyote* (1942) tells of the wily animal hero of Southwestern lore, and in *Pecos Bill and Lightning* (1940) of the mythical cowboy and his pony. Irwin Shapiro in *John Henry and the Double Jointed Steam Drill* (1945) adapts the lusty stories of the mighty Negro for juvenile readers.

A small avalanche of "series" books appeared on the Texas prairies between 1910 and 1915. Two *Little Colonel* books by Annie Fellows Johnson had the Southwest for their settings, *Mary Ware in Texas* being one of them. The other was *Little Colonel in Arizona*. The *Bluebonnet* series came into being in 1910. Stratmeyer did a boy's series on Texas. And Joseph Altsheler wrote *Texan Star, Texan Triumph,* and *Texan Scout* for publication dates in 1912 and 1913. These three Altsheler books are still on standard lists. Andy Adams wrote two juveniles, *Wells Brothers* (1911) and *Ranch on the Beaver* (1927). Three recent books of ranch life are *I Want to Be a Cowboy* (1947) by Emilie and Fritz Toepperwein for small would-be-cowboys of both sexes; and *Let the Coyote Howl* (1946) by Samuel D. Bogan, and *Sancho of the Long, Long Horns* (1947) by Allan Bosworth for older boys.

Two excellent children's books came out as a prelude to the Texas Centennial. The first was Bessie James's *Six-Feet-Six* (1931), a children's version of Marquis James's *The Raven*. Frances Clarke Sayers' *Bluebonnets for Lucinda* (1934) is one of the first really artistic Texas books in the juvenile field. Many of the books the Texas Centennial brought forth for children were of textbook type.

In 1940, five children's books out of Texas made their way from national publishers' presses, won favorable critical appraisal in national magazines, and made a place for themselves in permanent lists of recommended books. These books realize fully the scope of the material in reading interest and values for young people. They are Gertrude Crownfield's

Lone Star Rising, Le Grand Henderson's *Augustus Goes South,* Eric P. Kelly's *On the Staked Plain,* Siddie Joe Johnson's *Debby,* and Janette Sebring Lowrey's *Silver Dollar.*

Two books published in 1943 brought to children the history and geography of Texas in story and pictures. *Texas, the Land of the Tejas* by Siddie Joe Johnson, illustrated by Fanita Lanier, is easy, pleasurable history. *Seeing Texas* by Ileta Kerr Ladd takes a child on a happy trip through the big state. In 1947 Leah Carter Johnson chose the most colorful city of Texas for a story-history guide-book called *San Antonio, St. Anthony's Town.*

After the success of *Debby* drawn from her own childhood on the Gulf, Miss Johnson wrote *New Town in Texas* (1942) from the stories of her father and aunts. In *Cathy* (1945) she returned to the scenes of her own growing-up, and of the two wars that she had known. These books are for what Miss Johnson calls "middle-aged" girls, the girls who are of the age for *Little Women.*

Miss Johnson, who reviews the children's books for the *Dallas Morning News,* considers Janette Sebring Lowrey of San Antonio the finest children's writer of Texas. Mrs. Lowrey creates stories of fantasy for the imaginative child, the type of child who likes Hans Christian Andersen. Among her long list of books, besides the *Silver Dollar,* which are of special interest to Southwestern children are *Annunciata and the Shepherds* (1938) and *The Bird* (1947).

Nancy Paschal, pseudonym for Grace Trotter of Dallas, writes novels for a slightly older age group. *Clover Creek* (1946) with its lore of flowers, and *Magnolia Heights* (1947) with lore of pets, both have their settings in Dallas County and both were Junior Literary Guild selections.

One other Southwestern state has produced excellent writing for children, differing somewhat in the kind of theme and in quantity. Arkansas early contributed the notable fantasy by Albert B. Paine, *Arkansas Bear* (1898). Charles Finger won the coveted Newberry Award for his collection of South American stories, *Tales from Silver Lands* (1924). Charlie May Simon, one of the best known writers of juveniles, lives at Johnswood, Little Rock, Arkansas. Her books tell of the excitement at home for young lads and girls who are discovering the woods, wild life, and people, kindly and harsh, who are nearby. Some of these titles are *Robin on the Mountain* (1934), *Lost Corner* (1935), *Teeny Gay* (1936), *Bright Morning* (1939), and *Faraway Trail* (1940).

The many peoples of the Southwest—each with its distinctive folklore, customs, and proud history—have provided writers with materials that make an appeal to boys and girls of varying ages and tastes. There are books for all—from the little fellow with his love of small animals and birds and flowers to the big girl longing for romance, and the tall boy dreaming of heroic adventure. Never in the history of culture have as well-written and beautifully made books for children been published as are coming off our presses in America today. It is gratifying that so many of these are of the Southwest.

PART FOUR

LITERATURE FROM 1948-1970

I

HISTORY AND INTERPRETATION

ODAY IN THE Southwest, as in the pre-atomic, pre-space years, fact writing is dominant. Well-written books range from the objective, scientific to the interpretive, philosophical, even poetic. Although the past is at times viewed with nostalgia, little of the iconoclastic has appeared.

In the past twenty years at least two Southwesterners have considered their native region in important works that treat areas of vaster scope. Walter Prescott Webb in *The Great Frontier* (1952) after twenty years of research and contemplation advanced the original interpretation of European history of the past five hundred years as being conditioned by the existence of free land in the New World. On the North American continent the Great Plains offered almost the last of this free, or at least very cheap, viable land. With land frontiers ended, peoples must with the aid of science discover new frontiers. An automobile accident in 1963 cut off the life of this distinguished historian before science enabled the Houston-trained space men to walk on the moon, presaging other great frontiers of the future.

Henry Nash Smith, Dallas-born-and-bred scholar, treats the American West as symbol and myth in *Virgin Land* (1950). As a specialist in American civilization, he concerns himself with the American West as portrayed in fiction as well as in history and folklore. He interprets each United States land frontier as a result of dual ideals of the good life: the one stemming from the concept of transplanting various stages of European culture to the New World; the other stemming from the romantic concept of the independent primitive or neo-primitive life close to nature. These two diametrically opposed attitudes are most evident in the Anglo-American treatment, both in fact and in fiction, of the American Indian.

Odie B. Faulk limits his concern with the frontier to the Southwest as composed, by his definition, of New Mexico, Arizona, southern California, much of Texas, and parts of

Utah, Colorado, Nevada, and Oklahoma. The several frontiers he writes about in *Land of Many Frontiers, A History of the American Southwest* (1968) succeed each other in time as they were experienced by the native Indians, the Spanish explorers and colonizers, and the Anglo-American ranchers and farmers. Learning to live and to make a living in a land where aridity is the arch enemy has been the dominant factor from prehistoric times to the present. Although Mr. Faulk shifts his presentation of his thesis from the narrative style, in the first two-thirds of this book, to the analytical, in the last third, the book is highly readable and provocative.

Paul I. Wellman, novelist and historian, categorizes his *Glory, God, and Gold* (1954) as "a narrative history of the Southwest . . . the story of five different peoples: Indians, Spaniards, French, Mexicans, and Americans." He includes in his terrain "Texas, New Mexico, Arizona, and parts of Oklahoma, Colorado, Nevada, and even Mexico," with a brief excursion into California. The swift-moving narrative is for the general reader rather than the scholar.

Walter Prescott Webb in a bitterly contested article, "The American West, Perpetual Mirage,"[1] contended that the American West is basically desert with oases of greenery along the banks of the few rivers, in the high areas, and on the fringes, such as the plains to the east and certain coastal lands in the far West. His plan to expand this thesis into a book was abandoned a few years before his death. He had come to covet the time demanded by research and writing, for leisure to enjoy living. Could it have been, also, that he came to question the validity of his sweeping generalizations? Dr. Webb's thesis, however, was taken up and developed by W. Eugene Hollon in *The Great American Desert, Then and Now* (1966). Hollon had dedicated to Webb his earlier book *The Southwest, Old and New* (1961). In this study he limits the region to Texas, Oklahoma, New Mexico, and Arizona, with apologies to southern California. The emphasis is upon the cultural, social, and political history of the region, beginning with the cliff dwellers and advancing to the present. Hollon handles controversial economic and political issues, leaving no doubt as to the side he favors.

---

1. *Harper's Magazine,* Vol. 214, No. 1284 (May, 1957), pp. 25-31.

Approaching Mary Austin most nearly as an interpreter of the arid lands of the far Southwest is Joseph Wood Krutch, who late in life deserted his native New England for Arizona. *The Voice of the Desert, A Naturalist's Interpretation* (1955) adds to his established reputation as an essayist on places, people, and books. In the quiet land of little rain he finds the same mystical closeness to the eternal that D. H. Lawrence and Mary Austin had experienced. Other Southwest books of naturalist Krutch are *The Desert Year* (1952), *The Best of Two Worlds* (1953), and *Grand Canyon, Today and All Its Yesterdays* (1958). Krutch is a Thoreau scholar and disciple as evidenced by his pre-Arizona book *Henry David Thoreau* (1948).

A number of individual state histories of the Southwest region written in the last twenty-odd years merit attention. Erna Fergusson, who in 1940 published the widely read *Our Southwest,* followed it in 1951 with *New Mexico.* Miss Fergusson wrote books about many places, but she was at her best in writing about her native, much loved state. In *Land of the Conquistadores* (1950), Cleve Hallenbeck, a meteorologist of the United States Weather Bureau, produced a much needed history of New Mexico written for the general reader. He acknowledges the specialized researches of a number of scholars in the archives of Madrid, Seville, Mexico City, and Santa Fe. The seventeenth century in the Southwest has now been documented almost as fully as that period in New England and the Eastern Seaboard. Conquistadors, brown-garbed Franciscans, painted Indians, and venturesome colonists appeared in the pageant of the early Southwest.

Before his death in 1967, Professor Frank D. Reeve had almost completed a manuscript surveying the spectrum of life in the state where he had studied and taught for more than forty years. A collaborator finished his manuscript, and the book *New Mexico, Land of Many Cultures* appeared in 1969. Students as well as other readers will find it a most useful introduction to both the pre-history and the history of the state. More limited in time, but more intensive in treatment, is Robert W. Larson's *New Mexico's Quest for Statehood, 1846-1912* (1969). Mr. Larson probes deeply into the regional and national causes for the length of this finally successful quest.

A state history for the general reader and for one who needs a ready reference book is Madeline Ferren Pare's *Arizona Pageant, A Short History of the 48th State* (1965). Odie B. Faulk in *Arizona, A Short History* (1970) has produced a book for students as well as for the general reader. After a survey of the Spanish Colonial period Faulk presents in detail the territorial years 1863-1912 as being of prime importance in the development of the state as it is today.

Oklahoma, A Guide (1957), edited by Ruth Kent and the staff of the University of Oklahoma Press, is an authoritative and useful reference work, though it lacks historical interpretations that many readers desire. Edward Everett Dale and Morris L. Wardell's *History of Oklahoma* (1948) remains the standard history of the state for students and the general public.

Texas, as the largest and perhaps the most state-conscious of the political divisions of the Southwest, accounts for the greatest number of histories. Newspaper men are the authors of several. Among them are Frank X. Tolbert with his easily read *An Informal History of Texas* (1961); Stanley Walker with *Texas*, published a few weeks before his death in 1962; Lewis Nordyke with *The Truth about Texas* (1957); and George Fuermann with a different type of history, *Reluctant Empire* (1957). In the Preface to his somewhat dated book Fuermann stated: "This is a book about Texas now. It could be called *The Mind of Texas, 1946-65,* for in it the last decade is tracked and the next one is guessed."

Under the able editorship of Seymour V. Connor, *The Saga of Texas Series* was published in 1965 in six small volumes each prepared by a trained historian. The earlier periods are more adequately treated than is the twentieth century.[2]

Herbert and Virginia Gambrell's *A Pictorial History of Texas* (1960) is a book to enjoy visually and to trust for accuracy. A comprehensive and handsomely illustrated work is *Lone Star, A History of Texas and the Texans* (1968) by T. R. Fehrenbach. The standard one-volume Texas history for students remains *Texas, The Lone Star State* by Rupert N. Richardson, first published in 1943, revised in 1958 and again in

2. For authors and titles of volumes, see S. V. Connor, *The Saga of Texas Series* in Bibliography, Third Edition.

1970 in collaboration with Ernest Wallace and Adrian Anderson.

Perhaps of greater interest to the general reader than the state histories are the expanded accounts of selected historical events encompassing a brief, or relatively brief, time span. Sue Flanagan's *Sam Houston's Texas* (1964) is a handsome pictorial volume with explanatory text of Houston's arrival from Oklahoma in 1835 until his death at Steamboat House in Huntsville, Texas, twenty-eight years later. After the death of Houston, who had remained loyal to the Union, a band of defeated Texas Confederates sought safety and new land in Mexico. This attempt ended in failure and tragedy. The episode is related in a well-documented work by W. C. Nunn entitled *Escape from Reconstruction* (1956).

Lon Tinkle chose a period of only a few days for his *13 Days to Glory, Siege of the Alamo* (1958). Although the book reads with the suspense of a novel, except for one admittedly fictionized scene, it is history with flashbacks into the lives of the famous men who fought and died in the old mission fortress. Frank X. Tolbert in *The Day of San Jacinto* (1959) writes, with the journalist's sense of immediacy, of the victory of General Sam Houston over General Santa Anna on April 21, 1836, which resulted in Texas' independence from Mexico.

James M. Day in *Black Beans and Goose Quills, Literature of the Texas Mier Expedition* (1970) surveys and expertly analyzes works dealing with the ill-fated 1842 expedition in which the Texas forces were taken prisoners in Mexico, their ranks decimated by the drawing of black beans, and the survivors imprisoned for two years in Mexico City.

The punitive expedition of U.S. Army forces led by General John J. Pershing into Mexico in 1916-17 in pursuit of Pancho Villa and his bandits, who had been raiding north of the border, is dramatically recounted by Herbert Molloy Mason, Jr., in *Great Pursuit* (1970). Although the Mexican bandits eluded capture in the mountains of Chihuahua, American soldiers were given experiences that many of them soon needed in Europe in World War I.

John Edward Weems in *Weekend in September* (1957) recreates, with sensory details gathered from both printed and oral accounts, the Galveston storm of 1900, which was termed "the worst disaster ever to strike the North American continent." One of the most tragic days for Texas and the entire nation was November 22, 1963. *The Day Kennedy Died* (1964) by Dan Wise and Marietta Maxfield chronicles those fateful hours. This book has been followed by others. It may be years before the ultimate work on this national and world tragedy can be written.

A somewhat different type of Southwest history employs an ethnic group as its basis. Of these the Indian has been the most studied and written about, sometimes in reference book form, at others in descriptive narratives.

In title, *Indians of the Southwest* (1963) by Mary Jourdan Atkinson promises more than it fulfills. Primarily it is a rearrangement and enlargement of material published by her in *Texas Indians* (1935). Mildred P. Mayhall deals in considerable detail with one aspect of pioneer life in *Indian Wars in Texas* (1965). The Indians involved are chiefly the Kiowas and Comanches, who most fiercely resisted being restricted to reservations in Oklahoma. *The Treaty of Medicine Lodge* (1966) by Douglas C. Jones is about a famous truce, rather than a treaty, arrived at by representatives of Plains Indians and United States officials in October, 1867. The meeting was southwest of Wichita, Kansas, and two of the Kiowa chiefs present, Santanta and Satank, later caused trouble in Texas. W. W. Newcomb, Jr., writes of this trouble in his scholarly work *The Indians of Texas* (1961). Some years earlier, *Guide to Indian Tribes of Oklahoma* (1951) by Muriel H. Wright had supplied a usable and dependable reference work about the many Plains and Woodland Indians located in that state. Miss Wright is a Choctaw.

Before 1949 a number of Indian tribes of the Southwest had been treated in separate books. Among them are volumes on the Choctaws, Kiowas, and Navajos. Several of these historical and folklore studies were published by the University of Oklahoma Press in its Civilization of the American Indian Series, established in 1932. In recent years certain of the older books have been reissued and an impressive number added to the series. Among the more recent works, which are history primarily as distinguished from biography and folklore, are *The Navajos* (1956) by Ruth M. Underhill; *The Seminoles*

(1957) by Edwin C. McReynolds; *The Mescalero Apaches* (1958) by C. L. Sonnichsen; *The Osages, Children of the Middle Waters* (1961) by John Joseph Mathews; *The Kiowas* (1962) by Mildred P. Mayhall; and *The Cherokees* (1963) by Grace Steele Woodward.[3]

Some other recent well-researched and well-presented books on Indians of the Southwest are *Cochiti, A New Mexico Pueblo, Past and Present* (1959, 1968) by Charles H. Lange; *Warpath and Council Fire, the Plains Indians' Struggle for Survival in War and in Diplomacy* (1948) by Stanley Vestal; *Plains Indian Raiders* (1968) by Wilbur Sturtevant Nye, with original photographs by William S. Soule; and Aline Rothe's *Kalita's People* (1963), a history of the Alabama-Coushatta Tribe formed by the union of two tribes, and the only reservation Indians in Texas. Kalita was the honored chief who aided the Texans in their war for independence.

Pueblo Warrior and Spanish Conquest (1966) by Oakah L. Jones focuses on certain warriors who unintentionally aided the Spanish in the reestablishment of Spanish rule after the Rebellion of 1680. These Pueblo warriors opposed the continuation of Pueblo unity after the Spanish had withdrawn from Santa Fe. Oral history is written dramatically by Eve Ball as she records the story of James Kaywaykla, her informant for *In the Days of Victorio* (1970). Kaywaykla, a full-blood Apache, tells of the Indian campaigns against both Mexican and United States cavalry in 1889. He speaks for the Apache nation, for the women and children as well as the chieftains, when their lands were invaded. Lozen, the woman warrior, becomes a central figure in the account, as she fights like a man and uses her outstretched arms, palms held upward, to find the direction and the distance the Apaches were from their foes. Mrs. Ball has written a book that will confront historians with facts not available in written documents, facts which reveal the human aspects of Apache religion and life.

Of the many books on the Spanish explorations and conquests in the New World, Paul Horgan's *Conquistadors* (1963) is eminent both as history and as literature. With the

---

3. In this series also appeared Mrs. Woodward's book *Pocahontas* (1969), which has found readers both in the United States and England, where Pocahontas died at age twenty-one.

technique of the novelist in employing sensory details, dramatizing episodes, and telescoping uneventful months and years, author Horgan carries the reader through two centuries of adventure beginning with Columbus sighting land and ending with the last of the gentlemen conquerors, who reentered Santa Fe without bloodshed twelve years after the 1680 Pueblo Indian Rebellion.

An almost forgotten religious controversy in Spain that held up for months the northward march of these Spanish generals and their forces from Mexico was recounted in English by the Spanish history scholar Lewis U. Hanke. The work, with the astonishing title *Aristotle and the American Indian* (1959), focuses on two sessions of "The Council of Fourteen" called by Charles V in August, 1550 and April-May, 1551 at Valladolid, Spain, to hear and judge arguments on the question: "Is it lawful for the King of Spain to wage war on the Indians before preaching the faith to them in order to subject them to his rule, so that afterwards they may be more easily instructed in the faith?" The Aristotelian concept was evoked by one side which thought that some men are born superior and some are born inferior and to be slaves; hence the Spanish had the right to subjugate the Indians by force. The other side advocated peaceful conversion of the Indians as mentally capable of receiving Christian instruction. The Council failed to come to a "collective decision." However, the results seem to have been that in so far as feasible the lands north of Mexico were to be acquired peacefully.

Perhaps the least written about of the important ethnic groups in the Southwest is the German. Chester Williams Geue and Ethel Hander Geue help to supply this gap in *A New Land Beckoned, German Immigration to Texas, 1844-1847* (1967). During these years two still prospering German communities were established in Southeast Texas: New Braunfels, by a group led by Prince Carl of Solms-Braunfels; and Fredericksburg, founded by Baron Ottfried Hans Meuseback and his fellow immigrants. While retaining many of their Old World customs and traditions, these German-Americans of today are loyal Americans as were the founders of the communities.

Along the Rio Grande, the Gila, and the Colorado wherever the Spanish influence extended, farms and ranches developed, employing both Indian and Spanish methods and languages. Into this world in the nineteenth century came the Anglo-American farm and river pioneers, as well as settlers from Germany and France and other European countries.

In South Texas an ex-riverboat captain, Richard King, developed what has been called the greatest ranch in the world. Much of a somewhat popular nature has been written about this vast domain. Tom Lea, painter and novelist, with the aid of researcher Holland McCombs, produced a top-ranking literary work, *The King Ranch* (1957). Volume One is primarily a biography of remarkable Richard King; Volume Two traces the history of the ranch from Captain King's death in 1885 to the mid-fifties, with especial attention to the Santa Gertrudis breed of cattle, said to be the only new breed developed in the New World. *The King Ranch* is a satisfaction and joy to read, and with the author's illustration and Carl Hertzog's typography, a pleasure to look at and to handle.

Frank Goodwyn, who grew up on the King Ranch as the son of a foreman, in *Life on the King Ranch* (1951) writes with the spotlight on the Spanish-speaking workers and their families. The book, richly anecdotal, reflects the skill of the bilingual author in translating into English, flavored with Spanish words and idiom, the tales of his Mexican ranch friends. Goodwyn's *Lone Star Land* (1955) is less personal, more instructional, with the stated purpose "to describe Texas as it is today" in order to disabuse both outsiders and Texans of misconceptions.

A ranch that rivals the South Texas King domain in area and also in words written about it is the XIT Ranch in the Texas Panhandle. The scholarly book on this spread remains historian J. Evetts Haley's *XIT Ranch of Texas* (1929, new edition 1953). *Cattle Empire* (1949) by Lewis Nordyke presents the material in more popular style and at the same time emphasizes the political involvement.

New Mexico ranches have received less attention in books and articles than have those of Texas, yet a number of interesting studies have been published. One of these is by Wilbur Coe, *Ranch on the Ruidoso, The Story of a Pioneer Family in New Mexico 1871-1968* (1968). The ranch was established by Frank Coe, a participant in the Lincoln County War and father of the author. In defiance of crippling paralysis, Wilbur

Coe operated the ranch successfully and wrote its history, published shortly before his death. *Ranch on the Ruidoso,* with Introduction by neighbor Peter Hurd and illustrations by Peter and Henriette Hurd, is of much more than local interest.

Writers have usually concentrated on the past of cattle raising, especially the glamorized days of the open range and long drives to market. Henry D. and Frances T. McCallum have focused their attention on the invention that was a large factor in ending the era. *The Wire That Fenced the West* (1965) pays tribute to this thorny metal.

C. L. Sonnichsen, authority on Western badmen and sheriffs and much else of the past, in *Cowboys and Cattle Kings* (1950) turns from yesterday to write of the living and working conditions on present-day ranches. The book was needed.

E. E. Dale, Oklahoma pioneer, historian, and poet, reaches back to the end of the Civil War for the first events in his *Ranching on the Great Plains, 1865-1925* (1960), and brings his descriptive account up to the time when oil began to supplant cattle in certain parts of the short grass land. The author's own memories enrich this volume.

Wayne Gard, newspaper man, who began his book-writing career with a study of Sam Bass, badman folk hero, has continued with careful research to write other Western books, at times of broad scope as *Rawhide Texas* (1965); at others, more limited in content, as *The Great Buffalo Hunt* (1959) and *Fabulous Quarter Horse, Steel Dust* (1958); and the work most frequently referred to, *The Chisholm Trail* (1954). *Great Roundup* (1955) by Lewis Nordyke is written in a popular, journalistic style.

Ben K. Green, cowman and taleteller, entered the bookwriter's corral with *Horse Trading* (1967). "The Shield Mares," one of the yarns in that book, is highly praised by readers who are knowledgeable about horses. *Wild Cow Tales* (1969) adds to Mr. Green's renown as a raconteur.

A book that limits itself to facts is Malcolm D. McLean's *Fine Texas Horses, Their Pedigrees and Performance, 1830-1845* (1966). This scholarly treatise is of interest to horse lovers and of practical value to horse breeders.

Burs Under the Saddle, A Second Look at Books and Histories of the West (1964) by Ramon F. Adams is much more than a bibliography, though it is that, too. Adams examines each work listed for factual accuracy, points out errors, and in most instances supplies corrections. The book was compiled with the same care as were his earlier highly useful Western dictionaries: *Cowboy Lingo* (1936) and *Western Words* (1944). Manfred R. Wolfenstine's comprehensive *The Manual of Brands and Marks* (1970) was meticulously edited with an introduction by Adams.

J. Frank Dobie, of national and international renown as a Southwest writer, felt sympathy with all animals of the woods and plains. Besides dozens of articles, he wrote five books about these wild creatures, beginning with *Tales of the Mustang* (1936) and continuing through *The Longhorns* (1941), *The Voice of the Coyote* (1949), and *The Mustangs* (1952) to *Rattlesnakes* (1965), which was published in the year following his death. Into *The Mustangs* went the most of Dobie the man, in spirit. He spent an unusual amount of time in research for this volume. In the Introduction, he says, "Like the wild West Wind that Shelley yearned to be, the mustangs, the best ones at least, were 'tameless, and swift, and proud.' Their essence was the spirit of freedom." Such was the essence of J. Frank Dobie, who above all else valued freedom of life and thought. In recognition of his distinguished contribution to American literature and the quality of American life, Dobie was awarded the Medal of Freedom on September 13, 1964, by President Lyndon B. Johnson.

Another writer who holds the mustangs in high esteem is Hope Ryden, whose book *America's Last Wild Horses* (1970) is a plea for the preservation of this rapidly diminishing species. Beautiful photographs add to the eloquence of the author's plea.

Although the region of West Texas that lies in the big bend of the Rio Grande is marginal as a mining- and cattle-producing area, it is the most scenic part of the state. The Big Bend National Park was created in 1943, and since then writers, as well as tourists, have discovered this sparsely inhabited, rugged land. Two books that treat of historic as well as scenic features are J. Oscar Langford's *Big Bend* (1953) and Virginia Madison's *The Big Bend Country of Texas* (1955).

Roy Bedichek, naturalist and conservationist, focused attention on the wildlife preserve on the Texas coast of the Gulf of Mexico. In *Karankaway Country* (1950), he reconstructs the scene as it was when the only humans in the area were the cannibalistic Karankaways, and brings its human and wildlife ecological history up to mid-twentieth century. Although this work of Bedicheck and his book *The Sense of Smell* (1960) fall short of the charm of his earlier *Adventures with a Texas Naturalist* (1947), all are books to be read with profit and pleasure.

Frank X. Tolbert in *The Staked Plains* (1958) combines geography, history, and folklore in writing of a high arid West Texas area known to the Spanish as Llano Estacado. He is the somewhat detached reporter.

A. C. Greene, former reporter on the *Abilene (Texas) Reporter News* and former book editor of *The Dallas Times Herald,* writes subjectively about a section of his native state. *A Personal Country* (1969) is geography, history, autobiography. It is good reading whether the reader knows Abilene and the environs or is a stranger to this unspectacular region.

Second only to the cattle industry in the Southwest in inspiring books, articles, and movies is oil. The thoroughly researched, invaluable reference book for the entire region is Carl Coke Rister's *Oil, Titan of the Southwest* (1949), with a Foreword by E. DeGolyer. *The Houston Post* called it "the bible of the industry."

Tales from the Derrick Floor (1970) by Mody C. Boatright and William A. Owens preserves the human history of Texas oil fields as told to the authors and recorded on tape for them by oil field workers. Each chapter is introduced by the two authors, thus providing a background for the tales. The book also includes a list of dates, proration laws, a selected bibliography, and photographs.

Of the number of books about individual fields, two on Spindletop and one on Ranger merit special mention: James Anthony Clark and Michel T. Halbouty's *Spindletop* (1952) and John S. Spratt's *The Road to Spindletop* (1955) and Boyce House's *Roaring Ranger* (1951).

For three-and-a-half centuries European explorers, soldiers, missionaries, traders, colonizers came by water and land routes into the Indian Southwest. Many recorded their adventures in journals and official reports. In the twentieth century, writers studying these records and the terrain have recreated and interpreted this history. In the second half of our century, a number of distinguished books have come from this early material.

Many have written of the life on and along the Rio Grande, the chief waterway of the Southwest that flows eighteen hundred miles from the San Juan Mountains of southwest Colorado to the Gulf of Mexico. Laura Gilpin emphasizes the historical importance of the life-giving stream in *The Rio Grande, River of Destiny* (1949).

Paul Horgan employed all his talents as historian, novelist, poet, painter, and musician in *Great River, The Rio Grande in North American History* (1954). Volume One deals with Indians and Spain; Volume Two, with Mexico and the United States. Music inspired by the book was composed by Ernst Bacon for orchestra and narrator, and premiered by the Dallas Symphony Orchestra in 1957. For at least one performance Mr. Horgan was the narrator. The work is a literary masterpiece although historians have missed documentation and discovered some factual errors. For a 1970 volume titled *The Heroic Triad,* Horgan selected from *Great River* a group of essays about the three dominant Southwest cultures: the Indian, the Latin, and the Anglo-American. These essays he arranged chronologically to give the reader a sense of time and introduced them with a Prologue to give him a sense of place. The result is a stimulating and pleasing book.

More informal in style, though no less effective, is John Graves' *Goodbye to a River* (1960). His "river"—the Brazos —is not even a whole stream, but a mere hundred and fifty to two hundred miles known to the author from boyhood and "re-canoed" in farewell before dams changed its nature. His sentimental journey with only Passenger, a dachshund pup, as companion, covers three blustery November weeks of 1957. As the author paddles the stream, camps on the banks, and tramps inland into the hills, he recreates from memory and research life along this river from the struggles between Indians and whites until the present. His own trip serves as a frame-plot for historical events. The result is a naturalist-historical classic—a minor classic perhaps— but as surely a classic in content and style as are Thoreau's *Walden* and Mark Twain's *Life on the Mississippi.*

Robert Brewster Stanton, engineer and nature lover, in 1889 and 1890 explored the Colorado River for a railroad company. His unpublished report with photographs and drawings, in 1965 was edited with an Introduction by Dwight L. Smith for The American Exploration and Travel Series of the University of Oklahoma Press. Titled *Down the Colorado,* the work is of literary as well as scientific interest.

Two books published by the University of Oklahoma Press in 1967 make readily available early material on overland trails to Santa Fe: *Pedro Vial and the Roads to Santa Fe* by Noel M. Loomis and Abraham P. Nasatir; and *Soldiers on the Santa Fe Trail* by Leo E. Oliva. The Loomis-Nasatir work serves to refute the usual concept that aside from Camino Real via Chihuahua and El Paso, the only trail to Santa Fe led from Westport, Missouri, through Kansas into Colorado and down to Santa Fe. The records of the three trails to Santa Fe established by Pedro Vial, a Frenchman employed by the Spanish, were buried for a hundred and forty years in archives in Mexico City, Havana, Seville, Madrid, and Santa Fe before being ferreted out and translated by Loomis and arranged by Nasatir for publication in The American Exploration and Travel Series. The three trails established by Vial beginning in 1786 linked Santa Fe with New Orleans and San Antonio, Natchez, and St. Louis. Oliva's *Soldiers on the Santa Fe Trail* deals with the protection given and attempted by the United States military to travelers from Westport to Santa Fe between the first military escort in 1829 to the arrival of the Atchison, Topeka, and Santa Fe Railroad in 1880. Insight is given into the lives of soldiers and their families who lived in the forts built along the 770-mile trail.

Frontier Forts of Texas (1966), a portfolio-size volume, deals with thirty forts established either by the Republic of Texas or the Federal government as protection against South-of-the-Border Mexicans or the Plains Indians. Eight of these forts are treated in individual chapters, each by a different established historian. The others are presented in capsule form in a lengthy Introduction by Rupert N. Richardson. On the site of a few of these frontier forts, cities or towns have grown; several have been partially restored; one, Fort Sam Houston, has continued in active service; but most were abandoned after a few years, decayed into ghost forts, then into rubble.

Hundreds, perhaps thousands, of books have been written on violence in the Southwest. A number of the factual works published since 1948 record events of the area and also stylistically may be classified as literature. *Frontier Justice* (1949) by Wayne Gard records examples of crime and swift punishment from East Texas to the Pacific between 1836 and 1900. Lynch-law, feud-law gradually gave way to court-law. But before that evolved, fighting and feuding took many lives. C. L. Sonnichsen has established himself as an authority on Texas feuds with books that are sound history and at the same time exciting reading. The first of these, *I'll Die Before I'll Run* (1951), was followed by *Ten Texas Feuds* (1957) and *The El Paso Salt War, 1877* (1961). *Outlaw* (1965) is the story of how Billy Mitchell, alias Baldy Russell, evaded capture for twenty-six years following his revenge murder of James Truitt in Timpson, Texas. In *Tularosa, Last of the Frontier West* (1960), Sonnichsen stepped over into New Mexico for material. *Tularosa* is a feud book in that it deals largely with rivalries that erupted into murder and revenge during territorial days in the rugged cattle country of the Tularosa Valley. However, this is more than another feud book. It offers an exposition, in some respects a justification, of the cattleman's code of conduct on the frontier. Novelist-poet Eugene Manlove Rhodes is frequently quoted in support of a point.

The Lincoln County War of New Mexico Territory, in the late 1870's and early 1880's is the subject of scores of books, many of which focus on Henry McCarty, alias William Bonney, known as Billy the Kid. In most of these books, fact, legend, and fiction are mixed, with fact the least of the ingredients.

The comprehensive volume *History of The Lincoln County War* (1968) by Maurice Garland Fulton, edited by Robert N. Mullin, is the product of years of research and writing by the author before his death in 1955 and the careful editing of the uncompleted manuscript by his literary executor. The book corrects a number of errors in facts and interpretations by earlier writers.

Another persevering historian, attorney William A. Keleher, after years of research and judicial weighing of evidence, presents the facts in readable, layman's language in *Violence in Lincoln County, 1869-1881* (1957). The frontispiece is by distinguished artist Ernest L. Blumenschein. In an earlier book, *Turmoil in New Mexico* (1952), Mr. Keleher describes such critical periods as the American occupation in 1846; the Confederate invasion in 1861; the march of the California column in 1862; and the return in 1865 of Apaches and Navajos from a concentration camp near Ft. Sumner to their previous homes in Arizona and New Mexico. The impact of the Civil War on New Mexico is told in detail for the first time.

Stories of crime and punishment, some involving vigilantes, are recounted in *Murder and Mystery in New Mexico* (1948) by Erna Fergusson. Gifted as a writer of travel books, Miss Fergusson demonstrates considerable skill as a court reporter and judge of the evidence in crimes ranging from individual shootings to mass confrontations such as the workers' violence during a coal strike in Gallup. She plays the detective with sufficient skill to unravel some of the unsolved crimes in her native state, and despite leaning to the parties she considers the underdogs, her judgments enlighten and entertain the reader. However, with Billy the Kid, she accepted as factual, accounts that now have been shown to be fabrications.

New Mexico's Troubled Years, The Story of the Territorial Governors (1963) by Calvin Horn has a Foreword contributed by President John F. Kennedy, who calls the history of New Mexico "a distillation of the American experience." Historian Horn could have entitled his book "Lessons in Democracy," for the ten governors whose administrations he scans had to deal with Indians governed by caciques; rural Hispanos dominated by their local *patrones;* and Anglos who had inherited the prejudices of both Northern and Southern states from which they had emigrated. The last of the governors surveyed is Lew Wallace, who did not allow his administrative problems to prevent him from finishing his novel *Ben Hur*. The reader can absorb politics as well as history from this valuable study of governors and legislators building a democratic structure from a society part tribal, part feudal, and almost totally unlettered.

Apache Vengeance (1954) by Jess G. Hayes is a well-told factual account of how Apaches in Arizona turned to reprisals in

1886 after the surrender of Geronimo and his being sent to far away Florida with twenty-eight of his followers. Haskay, known as Apache Kid, was one of the leaders in the acts of vengeance. Many whites and Indians, including the Kid, met violent deaths before peace was restored.

Mining towns were often the scenes of violence in the late nineteenth century. These towns mushroomed with the discovery of gold or silver, lived feverishly for a few years and, as the ore played out, were left to the coyotes, the wind, and the sand. Abandoned mining towns of New Mexico and Arizona are memorialized in three modern books: *Ghost Towns of New Mexico* (1967) by Michael Jenkinson, with photographs by Karl Kernberger; *Haunted Highways* (1968) by Ralph Looney; and *Ghost Towns of Arizona* (1969) by James E. and Barbara H. Sherman. Jenkinson's book traces the history of mining in New Mexico from the earliest Spanish expeditions through the late nineteenth century, with detailed treatment of a number of towns that grew up near the mines. Looney, with a more personal approach, takes the reader with him along the highways and lanes of New Mexico to the remains of once flourishing sites. The famous towns of Real de Dolores, Golden, Cerrillos, San Pedro, and E-Town appear in both books. Photographs and maps add interest. *Ghost Towns of Arizona* with its numerous illustrations and maps enables the vacationer to locate 130 abandoned towns, and the stay-at-home reader to enjoy a pleasant mental adventure.

One Texas Panhandle ghost cowtown, Tascosa, has a happy sequel as told in the new and enlarged edition of John L. Mc-Carty's *Maverick Town, The Story of Old Tascosa* (1946, 1968). The one-time ghost town has been converted into a busy Boys' Ranch where several hundred disadvantaged boys are given a chance to grow into useful men.

The myriads of books about Southwest cities published since 1948 attest to the shift, especially in Texas, from a rural toward an industrial urban culture. A few of these books concentrate on city beginnings but most stress the present and recent past. There is little glamorizing of pioneer days.

Kenneth Wheeler in *To Wear a City's Crown, The Beginnings of Urban Growth in Texas* (1968) deals with four South Texas cities in the years between the Texas Revolution and the

Civil War: Houston and Galveston, the rival seaports; and San Antonio and Austin, inland cultural, governmental, and commercial centers. The book is more descriptive, less analytical, than the title suggests.

Houston, the largest of Southwest cities has been presented in a number of books, the most comprehensive of which is *Houston, the Bayou City* (1969) by David G. McComb. In his Introduction the author proposes to answer the question: Why and how has Houston grown? This he does in an information-packed, thoroughly researched, documented, and indexed volume. In addition the style is clear and pleasing.

Journalist George Fuermann has supplied the text for three books on the Bayou City. Two of these, *Houston, the Feast Years* (1962) and *The Face of Houston* (1963), are handsome, slender volumes in which photographs and drawings share interest with the lively text. Fuermann's earlier book, *Houston, Land of the Big Rich* (1952), deals chiefly with the eccentricities and extravagancies of the newly rich, with little attention paid to the initiative and hard work that had produced this wealth and the resulting philanthropic and cultural contributions to the community.

Sigman Byrd in *Sig Byrd's Houston* (1955) reports on the opposite face of Houston, the poorest, most crime-infested areas. He writes with realism, humor, and compassion. The book is made up of sketches of people, places, and incidents. Many of the pieces had appeared in slightly different form in Houston newspapers.

The Galveston Era, The Texas Crescent on the Eve of Secession (1961) by Earl Wesley Fornell focuses on the political and economic issues in this cosmopolitan Gulf area between 1845-61 and the people in control. The work is designed for the scholar rather than the general reader.

San Antonio, the most richly historical of Texas cities, is treated in a number of books which merit attention since Green Peyton's widely read *San Antonio, City in the Sun* (1946). Robert S. Weddle in *San Juan Bautista, Gateway to Spanish Texas* (1968) traces the inception of San Antonio to San Juan Bautista Mission, now in ruins on the Coahuila-Texas border. The book is a rich source of information about the many Texas missions that earned for San Juan Bautista the title, Mother of Texas Missions. Ray F. Broussard's *San Antonio During the Texas Republic, A City in Transition* (1967) is a study of the changes in the old Spanish city caused by the influx of Anglos. The result was an important bicultural center, which the city has continued to be. Two books are essentially of a guide or promotional nature. *City of Flaming Adventure, The Chronicle of San Antonio* (1949) by Boyce House, poet and raconteur, is a pleasant preparation for a relaxed visit to the city. *San Antonio, A Historical and Pictorial Guide* (1960) by Charles Ramsdell, with photographs by Fred Schmidt and others, is for the serious tourist who appreciates detailed descriptions of places and accounts of historical happenings. Neither House nor Ramsdell calls attention to the problems arising from the biracial components of the city. Julia Nott Waugh in *The Silver Cradle* (1955), a group of narrative-descriptive sketches, voices her appreciation of the traditional customs of Mexican-Americans of San Antonio. The title essay is about Graciana Reyes, "patroness in her neighborhood of Las Posadas," and of her most treasured possession, a delicately made silver cradle, or crèche, for a tiny waxen infant.

Dallas, the rival of Houston as a commercial and industrial city, has inspired books by three writers, each of whom had previously distinguished himself in types of writing other than history: John William Rogers, dramatist and columnist; Stanley Walker, journalist; and Warren Leslie, novelist and advertiser. Rogers in *The Lusty Texans of Dallas* (1951) is a native son who writes pridefully of the early days, the years of steady progress, and the economic and cultural achievements of his city. He stresses the educational and artistic aspects of Dallas. "Fortunate" would be a more appropriate title-adjective for Rogers' book than "lusty." Stanley Walker, who had recently come home to Texas from New York and a distinguished newspaper career, in a slender volume, *The Dallas Story* (1956), portrays the city in the post-World War II years as a good place to work, to be a civic servant, and to enjoy material and cultural advantages.

Warren Leslie, a New Yorker, with seventeen years of residence in Dallas as journalist and business executive, in *Dallas, Public and Private, Aspects of an American City,*

(1964) agrees with Rogers and Walker that men—not any natural advantages, of which there is a lack—have built a great city. Leslie, writing a year after the assassination of President Kennedy, analyzes what he considers a climate of "absolutistic thinking" in Dallas. He deals little with the great tragedy itself, rather with the various aspects of the life of the city in the years just before and the months following the black day of November 22, 1963. Leslie writes of business, culture, poverty, crime, and racial strife. In the Epilogue he reflects: "Americans were told long ago what the American dream was all about . . . people could rise from nothing to power and great riches . . . now they are told that it was a bad dream, that because they have made money, they are un-American. . . . If they lash back, one can understand."

Dallas is where the East ends; Fort Worth is where the West begins. Oliver Knight in *Fort Worth, Outpost on the Trinity* (1953) emphasizes this essential difference between two North Central Texas neighbors. Knight writes with gusto of the early days of an army post that evolved into a cowtown, a railroad center, and later into an oil-boom city. He rather slights the years of industrial and cultural development. The book appropriately is dedicated to his pioneering grandmother.

Two histories of Oklahoma City are different in purpose, content-emphasis, and in style of presentation. *And Satan Came Also, an Inside Story of a City's Social and Political History* (1955) by Albert McRill emphasizes the dramatic conflict between good and evil in a locale that during one lifetime grew from a speck on the Atchison, Topeka, and Santa Fe Railroad to a metropolis of more than half a million. From 1902 when McRill came from Kansas to Oklahoma City, he fought crime. He fought it as a newspaper editor, as City Manager, as practicing attorney, as Professor of Law at Oklahoma City University, and as teacher of a Men's Bible Class of a thousand members. McRill concludes his book with a plea that the state capital, which is also an industrial and cultural center, not be destroyed by vice. Two years after McRill's impassioned plea for righteousness, the Oklahoma City Board of Education in order to combat ignorance of the city's history among the young and to provide a library and home reference work sponsored *Oklahoma City, Capital of Soonerland* (1957) by Lucyl Shirk. The volume with carefully prepared text and numerous photographs fulfills its purpose.

Dodge City, Queen of Cowtowns (1952) by Stanley Vestal belongs in the present study on two counts: the Kansas town's growth and character were derived chiefly from Texas cattle drives; and the author, an Oklahoman, was one of the Southwest's most distinguished writers. From 1872 to 1886, the years covered by the book, Dodge City was called the leading cattle market of the world and the "wickedest little city in America." Stanley Vestal, with his gift as a storyteller, re-creates the excitement and violence of these years, and also supplies facts and figures of the cattle market.

Land of the High Sky (1959) by John Howard Griffin recounts the history of a West Texas ranch and oil field region with emphasis on the city of Midland, which lies in the heart of the oil-rich Permian Basin. The skillfully written book transcends the occasion, the opening of a bank building, for which it was commissioned. Nearby Odessa, which like Midland exploded from a ranching town into an industrial oil metropolis, is commemorated in a less ambitious book, *Odessa, City of Dreams* (1952) by Velma Barrett and Hazel Oliver. Ozona likewise owes its prosperity to oil but has remained a small town. Allan R. Bosworth, a native son, in *Ozona Country* (1964) recalls the town and drought-stricken ranch country of his boyhood and portrays the dramatic change that oil has brought. Ozona today, he says, is known as a millionaires' town, with three cars, many of them Cadillacs, in every driveway.

Post City, another West Texas town, has a quite different history. It was founded by C. W. Post, of cereal foods wealth, as a demonstration of his belief that individual ownership and hard work can produce prosperity. Although the farming community and town that he planned and promoted have never experienced great wealth, they continue to thrive after more than half a century. Charles Dudley Eaves and C. A. Hutchinson tell the story of the community and its founder in *Post City, Texas* (1952).

The City Moves West (1969) by Robert L. Martin is an

economic study and a warning. The cities involved are West Texas ranch and industrial centers: Lamesa, Snyder, Sweetwater, Big Spring, Midland, and Odessa. In concluding, the author stresses the water problem. Unless this is solved, the limited life of oil will "leave in its wake a series of ghost towns on the prairies."

Pass of the North, Four Centuries on the Rio Grande (1968) by C. L. Sonnichsen is a well-planned and executed history of life on both banks of the river as it turns through the mountain pass. Perhaps the most salient aspects of the volume deal with the two cities, El Paso and Juarez, and the encouraging signs the author observes of the developing of a great bicultural future for the cities and the entire area.

Two Southwest towns, Nacogdoches, Texas, and Chimayo, New Mexico, were chosen by editor Thomas C. Wheeler for inclusion in *A Vanishing America, The Life and Times of the Small Town* (1964). Wallace Stegner, literary critic, supplied an introduction to the volume, which includes many photographs. John Edward Weems writes of Nacogdoches on the Louisiana border as a gateway to the West in the eighteenth and nineteenth centuries, and as a pleasant college town in the present century, neither glamorizing its adventuresome past nor striving to be a hurrying city. Winfield Townley Scott sees the adobe village of Chimayo, strung along a narrow valley north of Santa Fe, as part of nature's beauty. It is true that many buildings are in decay and some men have to go on the highway to Santa Fe or Los Alamos to work, but they live in their own village with weavers and produce raisers as neighbors. In the twelve towns portrayed in the book, there is no revolt from the village, more nearly a revolt against the industrialized city.

A town with a contrasting history is written about by Eve Ball in *Ruidoso, The Last Frontier* (1963), a slight volume calculated to interest both old-time residents, who remember early turbulent days, and modern vacationers. The story ends with the opening of the racetrack and ski runs that have turned a quiet town into a crowded resort.

Hot Springs, Arkansas, and Hot Springs National Park (1966) by Dr. Francis J. Scully, and *Tucson* (1953) by Bernice Cosulich are histories of two Southwest cities that attract vacationers, and are well known as health resorts. Dr. Scully first planned a medical history of the city and park, but as his research progressed he decided to include other aspects. Although fullest treatment is accorded to health facilities, details about hotels, transportation, businesses, education and religious institutions, and entertainment add up to a full portrait of the area. Mrs. Cosulich, a newspaper woman, delved into records of early Tucson for a series of articles for *The Arizona Desert Star*. Twenty of these articles that were published through the years, with some added sketches, make up her book. It should have been titled *Old Tucson,* as were the articles, since the book ends in the 1890's with the coming of the railroads. The best health advice during the times she wrote about was given by an old frontiersman to newcomers, "When yer see signs of Apaches, be keerful. When yer don' see signs, be more keerful." Dances, church socials, the theatre, and horse races supplied entertainment in old Tucson.

El Rio Abajo (1966) by two attorneys, Gilberto Espinosa and Tibo J. Chavez, recounts the history of a region in the Rio Grande Valley around the town of Belen, south of Albuquerque. The book has the character of personal memoirs, since both its authors are lifetime residents in the general area, and they interpolate anecdotes, *corridos* or ballads, and family records to illustrate the Hispanic way of life. Photographs of people and places enliven the text, which deals with the fortunes of the people in this locality from Spanish times until the beginning of the present century.

A work on Santa Fe is a fitting conclusion to a discussion of books on Southwest towns and cities, since in this old town mingle now as in past centuries the three dominant cultures of the region. The city has defied a comprehensive history. Paul Horgan, perhaps in frustration, turned to fictionizing in *The Centuries of Santa Fe* (1956).[4] Oliver La Farge in *Santa Fe: The Autobiography of a Southwestern Town* (1959), with the assistance of Arthur N. Morgan, chose to present the past 110 years of the city's life through selections of news stories and editorials from the *New Mexican,* the leading newspaper of Santa Fe and the area since 1849. La Farge provided the continuity and necessary explanation for the se-

4. For a discussion, see Part Four, Ch. III.

lections, and Paul Horgan supplied a critical Foreword. The resulting book reveals what was important to the people of the area during these years, whether it was wars and assassinations of Presidents or the threatened invasion of local culture by an out-of-state culture colony, or the erection in the town of the Bryant Baker statue "The Pioneer Woman." The days and years of the town parade by as reflected on the pages of a periodical that, like the town, has preserved its individuality.

The foregoing examination of historical writings in the Southwest between 1948 and 1970 indicates certain tendencies. In the first place an increasing number of books have been written for the general reader, and by others than professional historians. Writers have tended to follow principles of selection and presentation of material besides the strictly chronological, stressing ethnic, economic, and geographic factors, at times within a small area during a short time span. Books on cities and expanding towns have multiplied, giving evidence of the shift of certain areas from a rural to an urban culture. However, books on small towns that cherish their quiet ways have been written and well received. Whatever their subject matter, most of the writers employ sensory details and interpret as well as record events. A number of the books treated as history in this chapter are frankly autobiographical. The writers, on the whole, have revealed the Southwest as a good place to remember the past, to live in the present, and to view the future with optimism.

II

BIOGRAPHY AND AUTOBIOGRAPHY

The line between history and biography is often so thin as to be indistinguishable. In this chapter books are treated in which the emphasis is upon the individual as revealed in actions and words, spoken or written. The person chosen for an in-depth portrait may be of recognized historical importance, or he may be obscure. The biographer must be so intensely interested in his subject that he will search out the facts of his life and attempt to analyze the wells of his being. The biographer, too, must desire to communicate his findings and interpretations to his readers.

A hasty perusal might lead one to catalogue *Coronado, Knight of Pueblos and Plains* (1949) as history rather than as biography. The author, Herbert E. Bolton, is a most distinguished historian. The book begins with the "Spanish occupation of mainland America." Not until well into chapter three does the titular character or his family appear. Gradually, however, the reader realizes that a portrait is emerging other than that of the swashbuckling adventurer of tradition. Coronado is revealed as a man of substance in Mexico before being appointed by Viceroy Mendoza to head an expedition to seek the fabled wealth of Cibola and Quivira. Coronado proved himself to be an efficient and courageous leader who, in spite of finding no gold or silver, and no precious stones, rescued the expedition from disaster. Through his insistence on careful maps and records of the journey being kept, lands new to Europeans were opened up for further exploration and settlement.

John Edward Weems in *Men Without Countries* (1969) turns to the late eighteenth and early nineteenth centuries for three adventures in the Southwest. General James Wilkinson, veteran of the American Revolution, is portrayed as an out-and-out villain. While in command of United States troops on the frontier, he was a spy for Spain. How much his protégé, Philip Nolan, and seventeen-year-old Peter Ellis Bean knew or suspected about the secret tasks they were assigned is not clear. An interesting aspect of this book is detective Weems' separation of the little-known Philip Nolan of his study from the well-known fictitious Philip Nolan of Edward Everett Hale's *A Man Without a Country*.

Rarely has a man of affairs during his life and in the century following his death been more glorified and more vilified than has Sam Houston, successively Governor of Tennessee, self-exile among the Cherokees, hero of the Battle of San Jacinto, first President of the Republic of Texas, United States Senator from Texas, Governor of Texas. Around him legends have accumulated. Scholar Llerena Friend assembles and presents facts, labels rumors and conjectures as such, and unemotionally arrives at her portrait in *Sam Houston, The Great Designer* (1954). The emphasis is on Houston as a dynamic statesman.

Jack Gregory and Rennard Strickland, in *Sam Houston with the Cherokees* (1967), contribute to clarifying the years 1829 to 1833 spent by the ex-governor of Tennessee before he appeared in Texas. While at times he was the "Big Drunk" of tradition, more of the time he was instituting reforms in the Indian Agency system, and was helping with treaties and agreements to improve Indian-white relations on the frontier. Jack Gregory, a Cherokee himself, had unusual opportunities to gather information. *Sam Houston and His Twelve Women* (1966) by Martha Anne Turner provides interesting sidelights on a man whose public life is well documented. The chapters begin with his mother, Elizabeth Paxton Houston of Tennessee, and end with his Texas-born wife, Margaret Lea. Among the other women portrayed are Houston's pretty bride, Eliza Allen, and the dignified Tiana Rogers, his Cherokee wife. Houston's separation from Eliza when he was Governor of Tennessee changed the pages of history. Had Miss Turner chosen to add another sketch to this series, the subject might well have been Jane Long, beautiful wife and widow of Texas filibuster, Major James Long. Miss Turner chose to tell Mrs. Long's story in *The Life and Times of Jane Long* (1969), in which Houston often appears. Scores of photographs enhance the two volumes.

Although Gail Borden was not of major importance in

public life in Texas during the formation of the Republic, his surname is familiar to present-day Americans. Joe B. Frantz in *Gail Borden, Dairyman to a Nation* (1951), after giving Borden his rightful place in Texas history as land surveyor and newspaper editor, details his development of a process of preserving milk. Thus began a national industry. Gail Borden won no battles, but he benefitted millions.

The first history of Texas written in English is *Texas* (1833) by Mary Austin Holley, cousin to Stephen F. Austin, often called "The Father of Texas." As a frequent visitor to early Texas, and a landowner, Mrs. Holley, a widow, knew most of the important figures of the time: Sam Houston, David G. Burnet, Mirabeau Lamar, and Gail Borden among others. She appears briefly in the biographies of all these men. The life of this intrepid woman traveler and writer receives full treatment in Rebecca Smith Lee's *Mary Austin Holley* (1962). The biography, while sufficiently documented to satisfy the most exacting scholar, is of interest to the general reader. The romance between Mrs. Holley and her bachelor cousin, only hinted at by previous writers, is discussed by Mrs. Lee who had access to family letters and mementos.

Mary Whatley Clarke in *David G. Burnet, First President of Texas* (1969) rescues the all but forgotten president of the ad interim government of Texas (March to September, 1836) and shows him to have been a man of ability much maligned by Houston worshippers. Of considerable interest is Burnet's side of the rivalry that grew into a lifetime enmity between the two men. Quotations from newspapers and letters display the vicious nature of frontier politics. *David G. Burnet* is volume one of the Texas Presidents and Governors Series being published by the Pemberton Press.

Another political enemy of Houston's was John H. Reagan, whose activities and personal qualities are fully presented by Ben H. Procter in *Not Without Honor* (1962). Reagan opposed Governor Sam Houston in his attempts to prevent Texas from seceding from the Union, became a member of the cabinet of President Jefferson Davis of the Confederacy, stayed with him after Appomattox, and was taken prisoner. On his release and return to Texas, Reagan was reviled as a traitor to the Southern cause because of letters he had written from his prison cell advising Texans to accept their defeat and try to work with the Union. Reagan's integrity and devotion to public welfare, however, won back their respect. He served his state well as congressman, U.S. senator, and railroad commissioner.

A frontier hero who has come down in legend as a man without blot is Kit Carson—mountain man, explorer, guide, trapper, and a man with a way with women, white and red. Scores of books about his exploits have been written, ranging from the bare memoirs through Stanley Vestal's fine but somewhat fictionized biography in 1928 and from lurid Westerns to two scholarly works of the 1960's. For most readers, *Kit Carson: A Portrait in Courage* (1962) by M. Morgan Estergreen is perhaps the more interesting of the two. Estergreen attempts to sift out the myths and to present the facts. The actual adventures of Carson are shown by Estergreen to need no embellishment. Harvey Lewis Carter's *"Dear Old Kit," The Historical Christopher Carson* (1968) is for the scholar who enjoys seeing the author explode the myth through documented research. The volume contains a new edition of the Carson *Memoirs*.

The courageous young Englishman whose murder sparked the war in Lincoln County (New Mexico) is treated in full for the first time in *John Henry Tunstall* (1965) by Frederick W. Nolan, an executive of Transworld Publisher of London. Nolan believes that Tunstall, merchant and rancher, had almost overthrown a New Mexican faction that was plundering the people when he was cut down by Sheriff Brady's posse. Billy the Kid, a young employee on the Tunstall ranch, was one of the pallbearers at the funeral. His seeking to revenge his benefactor's murder is credited with turning the boy into a ruthless outlaw. The book contains letters, photographs, a chronological chart, and a bibliography of the Lincoln County War.

Before the cattle war in Lincoln County a very different type of gunman, Dr. John Henry Holliday, appeared in the Southwest. His story is told by John Myers Myers in *Doc Holliday* (1955). Forced by lung disease to seek the dry climate of the West, Holliday of Georgia came to Dallas to practice dentistry, but his bent for playing cards led to a career as a gambler,

supplemented by fame he acquired as a killer. The count for
Holliday's victims varies from sixteen by evidence to thirty by
estimate, but the drama in the conflicts, as described by Myers, is
unsurpassed because of his ironically crisp and humorous style.
Wherever Holliday went, in Texas, Arizona, New Mexico,
Kansas, and South Dakota, his fame preceded him. He did
not end his life in a blaze of gunfire, however, but died in a
health resort at Glenwood Springs, Colorado, on November 8,
1887. He was thirty-five years of age.

While Holliday was rounding the Gambler's Circuit from
Dodge City to Tombstone, young Luke Brite in Texas was
building up a herd. *The Brites of Capote* (1950) by Noel L.
Keith tells of the varied activities of Mr. Brite and his ex-
schoolteacher wife in the ranching, business, religious, and
educational life of Texas. Their headquarters were their home
in Marfa and their Bar Cross Ranch at the foot of Capote
Mountain in the Big Bend country. Although written as a
memorial to Luke Brite, who died in 1941, *The Brites of
Capote* contains much of interest to others than the family and
friends of this remarkable couple. Keith's tales of the Bloys
Cowboy Camp Meetings, his stirring account of the 1917
Christmas morning raid by Villa's bandits on the ranch headquarters, and of Brite's leading the Texas Rangers in pursuit
make good reading for everyone. Seemingly, the only unsuccessful venture of Luke Brite's life was the drilling for oil on
his ranch.

A well-known name in the oil industry in the Southwest is
that of E. W. Marland. He was born in Pittsburgh but was
reared in the British tradition by his English- and Scottish-born
parents. His friend and biographer John Joseph Mathews, in
Life and Death of an Oilman (1951), calls the book a "personal impression," rather than a documented biography. He
tells how in the 1920's Marland used his oil money to build
Ponca City for his 6,000 employees and to erect a Gothic-
style family mansion where he introduced polo and "riding to
hounds" as a pastime for amazed associates. As the era of the
independent oil operator waned, Marland turned to politics,
serving his adopted state of Oklahoma as congressman and as
governor. Mathews, educated at an Indian reservation school,
the University of Oklahoma, and Oxford University, under-

stood Marland as few could, and with an analytical pen produced a believable portrait of an unbelievable character and era.

Kansas-born Everette Lee DeGolyer in 1904 entered the University of Oklahoma to study a new subject called petroleum geology. He was eighteen years of age. By the time he was forty, DeGolyer ("De" or "Mr. De" to friends and associates) came to be one of the most prominent scientific oil men and financiers of the nation. In addition, he was a science writer, lecturer, and collector of scientific and historical books. Before his death in 1956, he gave much of his fine science collection to his alma mater. According to the terms of his will his main library, known as the DeGolyer Foundation Library, is being administered "for the public good" by a board of trustees. DeGolyer was fortunate to have Lon Tinkle, a skillful writer and one knowledgeable about books, as his biographer. *Mr. De* was published in 1970 with a grateful Introduction by Norman Cousins, editor of *The Saturday Review,* a magazine which DeGolyer had rescued from financial disaster.[1]

In his Preface to *Savage Son* (1951), author Oren Arnold designates as "improbable" the life of Apache Carlos Montezuma. The fiction-style biography begins with a naked, mouse-eating six-year-old and takes him through his capture by the Pimas, his sale by them (at Florence, Arizona) to a gentle, white bachelor, a photographer, who adopted him, had him christened Carlos Montezuma, and reared and educated him to be a doctor. The handsome young Indian's years as a Chicago society physician follow until his abnegation of the luxury life and his return to the Pimas to arouse them to oppose the government in its mistreatment of the Indians. In this he was unsuccessful, but he remained to aid his former captors with his medical skill and was honored by them before his death. A writer of fiction would scarcely dare such a fantastic tale.

Hosteen Klah, Navaho Medicine Man and Sandpainter (1964) by Franc Johnson Newcomb tells quite a different story. Except for rare trips to cities, Hosteen Klah lived out his life on the Navajo Reservation. To the Newcombs of the

1. Awaiting a permanent home, the resources of the DeGolyer Foundation Library are available to scholars through the library of Southern Methodist University.

Trading Post he was the grand old Indian who wove ritualistic designs into blankets and collaborated with Mrs. Newcomb and Miss Mary Cabot Wheelwright in the reproduction of sand paintings and the recording of Navajo mythology. Many of the paintings and recordings from his store of knowledge are in the Museum of Navaho Ceremonial Art in Santa Fe. Mrs. Newcomb's book *Navaho Neighbors* (1966) introduces the reader sympathetically to a number of the men, women, and children who came to the Newcomb Trading Post to barter and buy or just to visit. She explains community rituals, games, beliefs, social customs. She became both counsellor and friend to the Navajos. Her chapter entitled "The Gift of a Child" tells how a Navajo girl planned to bear a child outside of marriage in order to give the baby to her aunt after the woman had lost all her children through sickness in a brief time. The narrative is a masterpiece of storytelling.

Maria, The Potter of San Ildefonso (1948) by anthropologist Alice Marriott is a quiet book about a great ceramist and the daily life in the pueblo. With its many illustrations the volume is a joy to peruse and to return to when nerves are taut. Pots and trays by Maria Martinez are valued possessions of many a visitor to this Rio Grande Pueblo.

In the spring of 1928 Edith Warner, a shy, former Pennsylvania high school teacher, rented from Maria and her husband Julian Martinez, a dilapidated house at Otowi Bridge near the narrow-gauge railroad station. With a talent for creating beauty and with the friendly aid of brown and white hands, she turned the ugly house into a haven for the tired of mind and body. The tea room was her own idea. Warm friendships developed with the Martinez' and many others of the nearby pueblo, and with boys and teachers from the Los Alamos Ranch School. Peggy Pond Church's *The House at Otowi Bridge* (1959) is a heart-warming memorial to Miss Warner, who died in 1951 and is buried in the San Ildefonso Pueblo burying ground. The book discloses how the Los Alamos School for boys was closed soon after the start of World War II, and secrecy enveloped the building of the scientific laboratory which was to construct the atomic bomb and to supervise detonation at the White Sands Missile Range on July 16, 1945. Both before and after this event, scientists at the laboratory began coming for dinner at Edith's house, but not until the war's end did she learn the real names of her guests—Niels Bohr, Robert Oppenheimer, and Enrico Fermi among others. As a pleasant bonus, the reader comes to know Mrs. Church—the daughter of the founder of Los Alamos School, the wife of a science teacher, and the author of three books of poems.

"Profile" is a term at times used for a relatively short biographical sketch which focuses on the personality of the subject. Such are the chapters in Ann Nolan Clark's *These Were the Valiant, A Collection of New Mexico Profiles* (1969). Within a time-and-space frame of a hundred years, chiefly in the 1800's, and a small area of New Mexico, which includes Las Vegas, Mora, Taos, Santa Fe, and Albuquerque, the author places her sketches of some famous, some obscure men and women. Across the pages march Kit Carson, St. Vrain, General Kearny, Archbishop Lamy; and such lesser knowns as Granny Brackett, Mother Magdalene, the Romeros of Romeroville, and the Sisters of Loretto. They were alike in youthfulness—scarcely one over thirty—and in dedication to a challenge so compelling that they dared to confront the unknown.

No Banners Waving (1966) by Sytha Motto is devoted entirely to pioneering Anglo women. Some came with their husbands: army officers, traders, missionaries, homesteaders. Some came alone as teachers and missionaries or in groups such as the Sisters of Loretto. One of the stirring chapters, called "Bienvenida Hermanas" or "Welcome Sisters," is of the Sisters of Charity from Loretto, Kentucky, who despite difficulties including illness and death, made their way by river voyage to St. Louis and by wagon train to Santa Fe in 1852. Later in the century, Sister Blandina of the Cincinnati Sisters of Charity traveled alone to join them. Sytha Motto had as a source for her account of this vigorous woman, Sister Blandina Segale's autobiography, *At the End of the Santa Fe Trail* (1932, 1948). Likewise, as her source for the account of Susan Magoffin, the first Anglo lady to travel the Trail, the author used Mrs. Magoffin's *Down the Santa Fe Trial Into Mexico, 1846-47* (1926).

Cow People (1964) is a book about cattlemen and cowboys

with an occasional chivalric reference to a wife. The author, J. Frank Dobie, received an advance copy of this, his eighteenth book, on September 18, 1964, just before he lay down to take a nap from which he did not awaken. He was particularly pleased with the jacket. On the front are pictures of seven of his cow people, one of whom is a Negro; on the back is his own portrait by an artist-writer friend Tom Lea. The material for the book was collected over a lifetime of experiencing and listening. Certain of the chapters are Dobie's careful revisions of articles he had previously published in periodicals. In so far as feasible, the people are presented in their own words. Dobie never wrote more interestingly or more wisely than in *Cow People*.

Shanghai Pierce, A Fair Likeness (1953) by Chris Emmett is a sprightly biography of Abel Head Pierce, who, according to Andy Adams, was "the most widely known cattleman between the Rio Grande and the British possessions." His nickname, which he liked, was from his boisterous, bragging voice reminding someone of a crowing Shanghai rooster. Even before his death, Pierce, with his humorous, crafty, often ruthless ways, had become the subject of many a tall tale.

Books about the Plains, both fact and fiction, are sprinkled with references to Negro chuckwagon cooks, horse wranglers, and cowboys. Philip Durham and Everett L. Jones, California English teachers, noting these references, usually casual, perceived the need for a book about neglected black men of the cattle industry. *The Negro Cowboys* (1965) resulted. Their material was drawn perforce from secondary sources. But they went to good sources: Howard Thorp, Charles Siringo, Jack Potter, Andy Adams, James Evetts Haley, Walter Prescott Webb, and J. Frank Dobie, among others. The book is a serious treatment of the Negroes' importance in the cattle world from the time of slavery to the present. The authors make their point: the lives of the Negroes were like "those of all other cowboys—hard and dangerous. . . . They had neither peculiar virtues nor vices to be glorified or condemned. But they should be remembered."

Bob Crosby, World Champion Cowboy (1966) by Thelma Crosby and Eve Ball is unique among cowboy books, as it is written from the female viewpoint. Thelma Crosby, widow of

Bob, is interviewed by Mrs. Ball, who lives in Ruidoso, New Mexico, and is the author of books on pioneer life. The story is almost as much about Mrs. Crosby as about her husband. She is just as independent as Bob, but is more conservative than the high-spirited, trophy-winning man she married. She struggled to send their daughter to Ward Belmont College in Nashville; he wanted to put their son on a horse before he could hold his head up, and to have him in cowboy boots before he could crawl. Thelma stood up to Bob when he was domineering. The conflicts are often amusing.

George Sessions Perry's *My Granny Van* (1949) is subtitled *Running Battle of Rockdale, Texas*. The battle began when grandson George was in diapers, and kept up until Granny died at eighty-two. She battled with others, too, always for their own good; but George was her favorite sparring partner. Occasionally he outmanuevered her as he did about her whiskey; she insisted that she was taking "medicine" and that she was a temperance woman. She was proud of her grandson being an author and always knew he would write a book about her. Naturally she didn't recognize herself disguised as cantankerous Granny Tucker in *Hold Autumn in Your Hand* (1941) and again in *Hackberry Cavalier* (1944). So great was George's love and fear of his Granny Van that he waited until after her death to write the humorous yet tender account of her. The book was made into a successful play.

The growing number of books, pamphlets, and articles about the lives and works of Southwest writers attests to the increased interest of the reading public in Southwest literature. A spate of books appeared during the fifties and sixties about the English novelist D. H. Lawrence, who lived from 1922 to 1925 in New Mexico. A number of these are of special interest to those who seek to relate Lawrence to America and the Southwest. Volume II (1918-25) of Edward Nehls' three-volume *D. H. Lawrence, A Composite Biography* (1957, 1958, 1959) is a mine of factual information about Lawrence's American years. "The World's Rejected Guest," Part III of Richard Aldington's *D. H. Lawrence, Portrait of a Genius, But . . .* (1950), is an analytical study by a distinguished poet-novelist of the behavior of his countryman and friend in foreign lands. Great as is Aldington's admiration of Lawrence the writer, he cannot condone his frequent antisocial behavior. "No society is going to adapt itself to an indvidual, especially such a porcupine of prejudices as Lawrence," Aldington observes. The entire book is pleasant reading even to the person only casually interested in D. H. Lawrence.

Of recent Lawrence books by literary critics, *The Art of D. H. Lawrence* (1966) by Keith Sagar and *D. H. Lawrence and the New World* (1969) by David Cavitch contribute to an appreciation of the importance of the American visit to the Lawrence canon. Chapter eight of Sagar's book supplies a chronological listing of Lawrence's life and writings in New Mexico. Sagar analyzes in depth "The Woman Who Rode Away" and "Saint Mawr," tales with a New Mexico setting, and *The Plumed Serpent,* a novel that grew out of Lawrence's Mexican summers. Cavitch, in addition to an analysis of Lawrence's fiction, discusses what he terms "expository counterparts to the fictions": "Indians and Entertainment," "The Dance of the Sprouting Corn," and "The Hopi Snake Dance." Cavitch's interpretation of Lawrence's symbolism is discerning. *D. H. Lawrence and the New World* for the first time gives full attention to Lawrence's American experiences in his lifelong search for a physical and spiritual Utopia.

Witter Bynner, poet, artist, scholar, joined the Lawrences in Mexico, at Lawrence's insistence, and spent the summer of 1923 with them. Poet Spud Johnson made a fourth. This trip forms the core of *Journey with Genius, Recollections and Reflections Concerning the D. H. Lawrences* (1951) in which Bynner tells of his experiences with the "genius" and his wife Frieda over a period of years, and includes his critical appraisal of Lawrence, the writer. The incidents Bynner relates of Lawrence add up to a sensitive, at times charming, at times spoiled-child man who inspired friendship and love in those who could put up with him. Bynner was one who could. Frieda Lawrence is the heroine of Bynner's account.

Mrs. Lawrence in 1934, four years after her husband's death, paid loving, but never blind, tribute to him in *"Not I, But the Wind. . . ."* At her death in 1956, Frieda Lawrence, then Mrs. Angelino Ravagli, left a number of unpublished sketches of incidents from different periods of her life, together with several versions of a planned introduction for them. In these sketches she calls herself Paula and uses fictitious names for most of the people important to her. Andrew, who appears often, is Lawrence. E. W. Tedlock, Jr., with imaginative scholarship, selected, arranged chronologically, and annotated these fragmentary pieces, added ten essays that Frieda had written (most of them about Lawrence), numerous photographs, and 224 pages of correspondence to produce the delightful and valuable book *Frieda Lawrence, The Memoirs and Correspondence* (1964).

In one of the essays, "Apropos of Harry T. Moore's Book, *The Intelligent Heart*," Frieda takes exception to Moore's portrayal of Lawrence's relationship with herself and his mother. "*The Intelligent Heart* reads almost like fiction," she wrote, "and a great deal is fiction to me." However, Moore's book, published in 1954, is the product of years of careful research and deserves serious consideration. *D. H. Lawrence: His Life and Works* (1951, 1964) by Moore deals primarily with Lawrence's writing, with only the necessary biographical material. *The Collected Letters of D. H. Lawrence* (1962) edited by Moore, with its 1,200 letters, is a valuable resource book for scholars.

Another genius whose temper frequently gave offence was Arkansas-born and -bred poet John Gould Fletcher, who after twenty years as an expatriate, chiefly in London, returned to the Southwest in body and spirit. Fletcher's second wife, Charlie May Simon, following his death in 1950, wrote of their life together in their woodland home near Little Rock. *Johnswood* (1953) is a beautiful and tragic love story enriched with poems that Fletcher wrote to her. This book concludes the life story of Fletcher that he had completed up to 1937 in his autobiography, *Life Is My Song*. Mrs. Fletcher treats with frankness and compassion her poet husband's recurring mental illness that ended in suicide. Charlie May Simon, a well-known writer of juveniles, has in recent years completed biographies of Albert Schweitzer, Toyohiko Kagawa, and Dag Hammarskjold.

John Gould Fletcher (1967) by Edna B. Stephens, of Twayne's United States Authors Series, is literary criticism with a minimum of what is usually termed biography. Much of the study traces Fletcher's intellectual and spiritual odyssey as reflected in his poetry. His Southwest life and poems are inadequately treated. Edna Stephens' book is not for the general reader. But neither was most of Fletcher's poetry.

T. M. Pearce in *Mary Hunter Austin* (1965), also a book in Twayne's United States Authors Series, devotes almost as much space to biography as to literary analysis. *Place* was always important to Mary. Although she and Fletcher were both in a sense mystics, Mrs. Austin's mystical experiences were oriented to nature and people; Fletcher's were chiefly related to his reading. Pearce's critical reviews of Mrs. Austin's books encourage the reader to go to the novels, tales, and poems themselves. His fuller study of Mary Hunter Austin is *The Beloved House* (1940). He knew her as a friend and inspiration.

Oliver La Farge (1971) is a second book written by Pearce for the Twayne series. He calls La Farge a crusader for minority groups, especially the Indians in the Southwest and the mestizos in Mexico. He relates La Farge's writing to areas in which he lived and studied: New York City, New Orleans, and Santa Fe. As a leading ethnologist, La Farge brought a scientific background to his writing of fiction, and this made his imaginative work distinctive. *The Door in the Wall* (1965), a posthumous collection of short stories which deal with social scientists in an imaginary Talvert University, opened a new field for serious fiction.

Pennsylvania-born Conrad Richter, a contemporary of Bynner, Austin, and La Farge in New Mexico, lived in Albuquerque from 1929 to 1950 and did some of his best writing about the state. (Frieda Lawrence was up at the ranch near Taos during much of that time; and the Fletchers were for a while at Tesuque.) The first book-length study of Richter is by Edwin W. Gaston, Jr., whose *Conrad Richter* (1965) is number eighty-one in Twayne's United States Authors Series. Gaston relates the biographical material to several of Richter's stories and non-fiction books. He gives ample treatment to the author's Southwest books with attention to their genesis. The comparisons of Richer's novels with other contemporary American fiction are of special interest.

Andy Adams and William Sidney Porter came to Texas in 1882, or thereabout, the one from an Indiana farm, the other from a small North Carolina town. They seemingly never met, though each stayed in Texas long enough and experienced and observed enough to write stories and novels that have contributed importantly to the world concept of the big state.

Andy Adams kept busy with cattle and horses while he was in Texas with no writing ideas under his wide-brimmed hat. A falsely absurd portrayal of Texas cowboys in Charles Hoyt's *Texas Steer,* which Adams saw in Colorado Springs where he lived after 1893, and the need to recuperate from mining losses started him writing plays. Unsuccessful with these he turned to writing fiction that reads like fact. Wilson Hudson in *Andy Adams, His Life and Writings* (1964), after tracing the life of the ex-cowboy writer, synopsizes and analyzes Adams' plays and novels. He concurs with J. Frank Dobie's estimate of *The Log of the Cowboy* as the best cowboy book ever written. Whereas others, even Dobie, had contented themselves with praising the verisimilitude of Adams' fiction, Hudson, while not minimizing this quality, analyzes Adams' creative skill in achieving his true-to-life effects.

William Sidney Porter, better known by his pen name O. Henry, did very little cowboying in Texas though he lived for a time on a ranch.[2] In Texas he made friends, wrote for newspapers, worked in a bank, and got into trouble. *O. Henry, The Man and His Work* (1949) by E. Hudson Long is a pleasant-reading, authoritative biography and critical study of the famous short-story writer, forty of whose 250 stories are laid in Texas. The controversial matter of the trial for bank embezzlement and the Ohio prison term of Porter is handled frankly and humanely. "But terrible as it was at the time," Long comments, "it is doubtful if we should have had O. Henry, the short-story writer, if Will Porter had not gone to prison." The O. Henry surprise ending, attacked by some critics, is defended by Long as "no trick," but "the valid and inevitable finish that the reader should have expected all along." Long's account of Witter Bynner's four-year association with Porter in New York furnishes an interesting footnote to Southwest literature.

Hudson Long's *O. Henry* was followed in the fifties and

---

2. After 1898, Porter, who was christened William Sidney Porter, spelled his middle name Sydney.

sixties by a number of book-length studies. Gerald Langford in *Alias O. Henry, A Biography of William Sidney Porter* (1957) contributed a scholarly, fully documented work. His research involved certain primary sources, not easily available. Eugene Current-Garcia's *O. Henry* (1965), of the Twayne's United States Authors Series, is a useful handbook for a study of the stories with sufficient biographical data for the average reader. Current-Garcia relied considerably on Langford's fuller work. Richard O'Connor's *O. Henry, The Legendary Life of William S. Porter* (1970) combines facts and hearsay into a readable if not scholarly book that dwells on the weaknesses and tragedies of the man. O'Connor's handling of the North Carolina and New York periods is more satisfactory than his somewhat cavalier treatment of the Texas years.

While Andy Adams and Will Porter were storing up experiences in Texas or on the trail, Eugene Manlove Rhodes was in south central New Mexico, helping his father homestead, saving enough money for two years at College of the Pacific, and returning to work on Bar Cross Ranch and other places, including his own small homestead. He likely read more than he worked. J. Frank Dobie in his Introduction to the *Best Novels and Stories by Eugene Manlove Rhodes* (1949), edited by Frank V. Dearing, said that he would like to contribute to a statue of "Gene reading a book on a gentle cow horse."[3] From 1906 until his death in 1934, Rhodes lived chiefly on a farm in New York, writing stories and novels about New Mexico ranch life.

A Bar Cross Man, The Life and Personal Writings of Eugene Manlove Rhodes (1956) by W. H. Hutchinson greatly augments the information about Rhodes in New Mexico supplied by his widow, a New York woman, May D. Rhodes in her biography *The Hired Man on Horseback* (1938). The plan of Hutchison's book, with each chapter consisting of his narrative followed by Rhodes' correspondence from the same period, results in a certain amount of repetition and interferes with easy continuity.

Rarely in the history of any region have three men more fortunately come together in time and place than did Roy

---

3. Flyleaf maps of New Mexico with geographical and Rhodes' fictitious place names add to the reader's pleasure in the stories.

Bedichek, Walter Prescott Webb, and J. Frank Dobie. The time was the late 1920's until their deaths—Bedichek's in 1959, Webb's in 1963, Dobie's in 1964. The place was Austin, Texas, and its nearby lakes and ranches. Their "manly friendship," based on respect, enjoyment of each other's society, and deep affection, enriched their lives and writings. By the fifties, Texans were calling them the Texas Triumvirate. No one disputed their eminence; no one was jealous of their position. It was only, however, after their deaths and the publication of *Three Men in Texas* (1967), edited by Ronnie Dugger, and *Three Friends, Bedichek, Dobie, Webb* (1969) by William A. Owens that others realized the scope of their friendship as the three met, cooked and ate together, talked and argued in Austin or at Webb's nearby Friday Mountain Ranch or at Dobie's Rancho Paisano, and when separated wrote long letters to each other. From time to time a few writer or publisher friends were invited to their get-togethers.

Three Men in Texas edited by Ronnie Dugger, consists, with a few additions, of short pieces written by friends for special issues of *The Texas Observer*.[4] The issues on Bedichek and Webb were published after their deaths, the one on Dobie while he was yet alive. Dobie and Webb wrote affectionately of Bedichek, and Dobie wrote admiringly of Webb. An amusing paper that Webb had read at a dinner honoring Dobie is included in the Dobie issue. A listing of the writers of these pieces reads like a roster of Texas folklorists and historians: Mody Boatright, John Henry Faulk, Joe B. Frantz, Wilson M. Hudson, William A. Owens, Harry Ransom, Rupert N. Richardson, Martin Shockley, Henry Nash Smith, Lon Tinkle, Frank Wardlaw, and others. Each essay contributes to the portrait of the man being honored and each is literature itself.

Some time before his death Bedichek gave William A. Owens a truckload of letters that he had saved from his years of correspondence with Webb and Dobie. Owens, a younger friend of the three, selected from and arranged these letters, introduced them with biographical sketches, and wrote linking paragraphs or sentences and notes where needed. *Three*

4. "Roy Bedicheck," July 27, 1959; "Walter Prescott Webb, 1888-1963," July 26, 1963; "J. Frank Dobie of Texas," July 24, 1964.

Friends, Bedichek, Dobie, Webb (1969) is the satisfying result.

A Portrait of Pancho, The Life of a Great Texan: J. Frank Dobie (1965) by Winston Bode grew out of a television tribute the Austin journalist was asked to write for KLRN-TV after Dobie's death. With the generous help of many friends and Mrs. Dobie, the book was produced. It is far from the ultimate biography that no doubt will come in time, but with Bode's clear prose and the dozens of photographs, the book is a pleasure to own. Dobie was highly photogenic. Even black-and-white stills convey his mental and physical vitality.

For years before his death Dobie was urged to write his autobiography. He would say, "I am not ready yet." However, in his books, articles, and papers prepared for listening audiences, he was weaving on the warp of his own life, his tales of animals, lost mines and buried treasures, wartime England, farm and ranch folk, and descriptions of the Southwest land and sky. His "Sunday Pieces," as he called his syndicated newspaper stories, are often frankly autobiographical. In his later years Dobie kept an "autobiographical box" into which he tossed his published and unpublished pieces and notes about himself. "Scraps," he called them. After his death, Bertha McKee Dobie, wife and wise literary counsellor, selected from and arranged autobiographical material not included in his books into *Some Part of Myself* (1967), by J. Frank Dobie, thus making easily available these uncollected and some unpublished pieces. This brings the number of Dobie's books to twenty. With the exception of *A Texan in England*, they are all of the American Southwest, yet often transcend time and place.

At one larger than usual gathering at Walter Prescott Webb's Friday Mountain Ranch, dynamic Maury Maverick came late, bearing San Antonio commemorative plates for each of the thirty or so guests. Joe Frantz records the evening in his lively Foreword to Richard B. Henderson's *Maury Maverick, A Political Biography* (1970). The subtitle is an understatement. The biography is of a complete person, as Henderson ferrets out details and presents them so vividly that the reader feels that he knows fun-loving, blunt, crusading Maury

Maverick. In San Antonio as mayor, in Washington as congressman, Maverick spoke and wrote in plain, clear, yet eloquent language.[5] Noted for his courage and independence, he was also successful in getting Federal funds for the beautification of the San Antonio River and La Villita, on the bank. Death in 1954 ended the career of this controversial political figure and colorful personality.

Published biographical material is fragmentary and at times contradictory concerning Katherine Anne Porter, one of the most eminent writers born and reared in the Southwest. Of the full-length books about Miss Porter only George Hendrick's *Katherine Anne Porter* (1965), of the Twayne's United States Authors Series, supplies a chronology and a brief biographical chapter. Hendrick gives credit to Donald Stalling's unpublished Texas Christian University M.A. thesis, *Katherine Anne Porter, Life and Literary Mirror* (1951), for bringing "together material of utmost value for any biographical study of Miss Porter." Hendrick discusses in Chapters II and III of his book most of the stories of Katherine Anne Porter that seemingly have their source in the writer's life. The earliest published are from her experiences as a young woman in Mexico. The more numerous are family stories from her childhood in South Central Texas in which she is Miranda; her father, Harrison, is Harry; and her grandmother, who reared the Porter's five children after their mother's death in 1892, is Sophia Jane Rhea, of Old South memories and ways.

William L. Nance in *Katherine Anne Porter and the Art of Rejection* (1963), a book-length work, includes only the barest of biographical facts as he develops the thesis of rejection from his study of the content and style of Miss Porter's fiction and essays. Two monograph studies, *The Fiction and Criticism of Katherine Anne Porter* (1957, 1962) by Harry John Mooney, Jr., and *Katherine Anne Porter* (1963) by Ray B. West, are interesting critical essays with only slight biographical material. Mooney devotes a chapter to the "Miranda Stories," generally accepted as basically autobiographical. Winfred S. Emmons in Pamphlet No. 6, the South-

5. Maury Maverick invented the word *gobbledygook* for pretentious government language. The name of his grandfather, Samuel Maverick, had added to the language *maverick* as a term for an unbranded animal, hence an independent person who holds aloof from the crowd.

west Writers Series, *Katherine Anne Porter* (1967), analyzes
those stories which he, admittedly with "an element of arbi-
trariness," selects as "regional stories with respect to the
Southwest." Emmons' use of biographical material is minimal.

A biography of Miss Porter will have to wait. She is reti-
cent about her own life and discourages the research of others
into her background. An autobiography is perhaps too much
to hope for. If she ever chooses to write of herself with the
veil of fiction lifted, the product will be art of a high level, as
her stories and novels are.

A Picture Gallery (1968) by Tom Lea is a bivalve production in both format and content. Within folio-size hard
covers are thirty-five plates of pictures by artist Lea, and in
an inside attached slipcase is a monograph of critiques of these
pictures by writer Lea. J. Frank Dobie, in his Introduction to
Tom Lea: A Portfolio of Six Paintings (1953), observed,
"The style of his writing is that of his art . . . economy, pre-
cision, logic. . . . He files to the bone." Lea had illustrated
three of Dobie's books. *A Thomason Sketchbook, Drawings*
(1969), edited by Arnold Rosenfeld and with an Introduction
by John Graves, recalls to public attention the too short career
of Colonel John William Thomason, marine officer, artist,
writer. Graves, who saw service in the Marines in World War
II, titled his perceptive biographical and critical Introduction
"The Old Breed."[6]

Peter Hurd, A Portrait Sketch from Life (1965) by Paul
Horgan, in addition to Horgan's biographical and critical
sketch of his friend, contains twenty-two plates of Hurd's
paintings. (Horgan also wields a paint brush.) This volume
and *Peter Hurd, Portfolio of Landscapes and Portraits*
(1950), of the New Mexico Artists Series, the two Tom Lea
portfolios, and *A Thomason Sketchbook* belong in all public
and private Southwest collections.

Southwest Writers Series of biographical and critical pamphlets, published under the energetic editorship of James W.
Lee, furnishes an introduction to more than thirty authors of
the region. The writers of a number of these studies are well
known to students of Southwest literature. Others are neo-

6. Graves' Introduction with two of Thomason's sketches had been published
in *Southwest Review*, LIV, No. 1 (Winter, 1969), pp. 36-46.

phytes trying their critical wings. As would be expected, therefore, the studies are somewhat uneven in quality, but all are useful in supplying not always easily available facts and bibliographies. One misses the names of many poets and authors of juveniles among the titles of the published pamphlets. Perhaps these omissions will be remedied before the series is finished.[7]

A number of books about interesting and significant people of the Southwest, published since 1948, are the joint product of the individuals themselves and the editors of their usually unpublished autobiographical writings or orally transmitted reminiscences. An important example is *My Life in the Mountains and on the Plains, A Newly Discovered Autobiography* by David Meriwether. In his eighty-sixth year, Meriwether dictated to a fifteen-year-old granddaughter the story of his life from his birth in Virginia in 1800 to 1856, the third year of his term as governor of the vast and little known Territory of New Mexico. Left uncompleted at his death in 1892, the manuscript was preserved in the family, "discovered" and carefully edited with an Introduction and Epilogue by Robert A. Griffen, and published in 1965. The volume is a valuable addition to the early annals of the Southwest.

J. Ross Browne: Letters, Journals, Writings (1969), edited by Lina Fergusson Browne, granddaughter-in-law of Browne, is practically a collaboration between the living and the dead. Mrs. Browne compiled the book from unpublished family materials and excerpts from Browne's published, out-of-print, and rare printed works. The result is a full chronicle of one of the most ubiquitous figures of the nineteenth century. Browne's adventures took him from Ireland, where he was born in 1820, to America at the age of thirteen; then on whaling expeditions, explorations into the American West, including the Apache country; to England as the promoter of American mining; and to China as United States Minister. Browne's personal accounts of whaling have been suggested as sources for Melville's *Moby Dick,* and his experiences in England for Mark Twain's *Innocents Abroad.*

Robert Maudslay, between his seventy-fifth and eightieth

---

7. For authors and titles of pamphlets, see Southwest Writers Series in Bibliography (Third Edition).

years, was requested by a niece to write down his memories as a Texas sheep man. He sent them to her in the form of seventeen "Dear Amy" letters. These letters, with certain emendations by Maudslay himself, were edited by another niece, Winifred Kupper, author of *The Golden Hoof* (1945), and then published in 1951 as *Texas Sheep Man, The Reminiscences of Robert Maudslay*. Maudslay was born in York, England, in 1855, came to Texas in 1882 with other members of his family, and settled near Bandera in the Texas Hill Country, which is better suited to sheep than cattle raising. Along with his brother, he became a sheep man and a sheep man he remained until 1905 when he sold his last flock. Maudslay's account of his sheep raising days is realistic and witty. He regards with humor rather than rancor the disdain of the cow people for the sheep men.

Autobiographies of pioneer cattlemen published in recent years include *Life in the Saddle* (1963) by Frank Collinson, edited by Mary Whatley Clarke; *Lucky 7, A Cowman's Autobiography* (1957) by Will Tom Carpenter, edited by Elton Miles; and *From the Pecos to the Powder, A Cowboy's Autobiography* (1967), as told to Ramon F. Adams by Bob Kennon.

Collinson was born in the same county and year as Maudslay —York, England, in 1855. When he came to Texas, he was only seventeen years old and, except for brief periods of buffalo hunting and Indian fighting, he was a cattleman for more than sixty years. At the age of seventy-nine, he started writing his experiences, with the encouragement of artist Harold D. Bugbee for whom he had often posed. Mrs. Clarke's interest in Collinson was aroused by the recurring figure in Bugbee's Western paintings of an old cowman sitting on "a good horse on the open range" or shown chasing buffalo. She used interviews, letters, and Collinson's writings to compile *Life in the Saddle*. Fittingly the illustrations for the book are by Bugbee.

Lucky 7, A Cowman's Autobiography came into print as the result of a wish expressed by Walter Prescott Webb for "a diary or a self-written account of an early Western cattleman who was more interested in his day-to-day work than in the Indian skirmishes that had happened nearby or the famous outlaws and marshals he had met." Elton Miles, who heard the wish, passed it on to his students at Sul Ross College. A pencil manuscript written by Carpenter was turned over to Professor Miles for editing. Carpenter called himself Lucky 7 because he was the seventh child in his family. He came to Texas from Missouri during the Civil War, and worked from youth until middle age with cattle belonging to his family or with larger herds of other owners. He was a product of the open range before barbed wire. His language is salty and unlettered, and Professor Miles wisely left it that way.

From the Pecos to the Powder, A Cowboy's Autobiography is the account of a wanderer who "repped and rode" for cow outfits from Texas, where he was born in 1876, to Montana. Ramon F. Adams, who had written *Charles M. Russell, The Cowboy Artist* (1948), became interested in Bob Kennon when he learned that the ex-cowboy was a friend of Russell. Correspondence and interviews resulted in a first-person account of the life of Kennon. Some of the stories about Russell, as told by Kennon, seemingly are not recorded elsewhere, such as the account of the artist's obtaining well-cured deer hides from an old Indian to use in the place of canvas for paintings that he gave to his friends.

Another fortunate coming-together of a person who had a tale to tell and a person who could put the tale into a book was that of C. C. White, East Texas Negro preacher, and Ada Morehead Holland, white Houston journalist. The result was *No Quittin' Sense* (1969), fashioned by Mrs. Holland from tape recordings made for her by White talking about his life experiences. Mrs. Holland selected, cut, rearranged tales, carefully preserving the language and philosophy of the Reverend White, who was then eighty years of age. "When God gives you a vision," he explained, "your whole body just kind of soaks up the message, like a biscuit soaks up red-eye gravy." In Jacksonville, where he has a church, "Brother White" is even better known for "God's Storehouse," the shack he built to dispense food which had been contributed or which he raised to feed the needy people of all races. The title of the book is the way his wife described her husband when he would not be scared away from his church by threats: "He just ain't got no quittin' sense."

Force Without Fanfare (1969) is an accurate title for the

autobiography of K. M. Van Zandt, dictated in 1929 in his ninety-third year to his daughter Mrs. A. C. Williams, and edited by historian Sandra L. Myres. The activities of the nonagenarian and his father Isaac spanned almost a century in the building of Texas. Isaac was minister to the United States from the Republic of Texas and a framer of the Texas State constitution. After the Civil War, young Major K. M. Van Zandt, disgusted with carpetbagger rule in East Texas, moved to Fort Worth and until his death in 1936 was a force for good in the business, civic, educational, and religious life of the community. The well-documented book is almost the history of Fort Worth for the seventy years during which a village grew into a city.

A number of men, most of them accustomed to writing for publication, have in their late years prepared autobiographies. Among them are George Curry, William A. Keleher, Louis H. Hubbard, Joseph Martin Dawson, and Colby D. Hall. George Curry began his varied careers as a messenger boy in a Dodge City mercantile establishment during the days that Dodge was the chief market for Texas cattle. Later in New Mexico Curry became prominent in politics. In *An Autobiography* (1958) he reveals a unique insight into contemporary happenings which are now history: the Battle of Adobe Walls, the Fountain case, the struggle for statehood, the "Bull Moose" bolt, and the Teapot Dome affair. Curry's life, which began in 1861 with the Civil War, extended into the first years of the atomic age.

William A. Keleher calls his autobiography *Memoirs, 1892-1969, A New Mexico Item* (1969). The subtitle indicates that the memoirs include the author's observations on the state where he has lived since he was four. He recalls the feud between Old Town and New Town over the use of the name "Albuquerque." Keleher's public career began as a messenger boy and key-pounder for Western Union. He advanced to being a reporter on the Albuquerque *Journal*. From 1915 on, he was an attorney in Albuquerque, a historical writer, and a consultant to many of the influential political figures of New Mexico. Keleher's accounts of the circumstances leading to the writing of his own books of history are among the valuable details of this memorable autobiography.

Another New Mexico lawyer, A. T. Hannett, wrote his memories under the title of *Sagebrush Lawyer* (1964). Chiefly anecdotal, the book portrays the almost unique character of trials in a state where Spanish, Mexican, Anglo-American, even Indian concepts of jurisprudence held sway, and racial plus political partisanship sometimes took precedence over the law. Successful in criminal cases, some of which were sensational, Attorney Hannett was also successful in politics, serving for two terms as mayor of Gallup, New Mexico, and for one term as governor of the state. With his resources as a raconteur, Hannett provides entertainment along with political history in his diverting book.

An autobiography of national as well as local significance is Clinton P. Anderson's *Outsider in the Senate* (1970). Senator Anderson not only tells a personal story, but he relates the events of the thirty years he has served in the Congress and Senate of the United States. He came to New Mexico in 1917 for his health. Then only twenty-two years old, he was suffering from tuberculosis produced by severe winters in South Dakota, where his grandfather had settled along with other Scandinavians migrating to the Midwest in the nineteenth century. Young Anderson had studied journalism, and when his health improved he became a reporter for an Albuquerque newspaper at the New Mexico state capital. With this introduction to politics, he became identified with influential figures in the Democratic party, and after serving in several appointive positions, he was elected to Congress in 1940 and to the United States Senate in 1948, where he still serves his state. As a writer, Senator Anderson has the ability to speak frankly without malice, and his views are always supported by clear statements and documentation. Consequently, the part he played in the Dixon-Yates controversy, his approval of the Wilderness Conservation Bill, his guidance of the Atomic Energy Commission, and his sponsorship of the Medicare Program are outlined in the spirit he felt and under the conditions in which he worked. From pen portraits of personalities at the luncheons of Presidents to stories of tensions and friendships among his colleagues and friends, Senator Anderson's book holds the reader's interest from cover to cover.

Louis H. Hubbard, who from 1926 to 1960 was president

of Texas State College for Women (now Texas Women's University), had a most unlikely heritage for his career as recorded in *Recollections of a Texas Educator* (1965). He was born in Puerto Rico in 1882 to a U.S. consul of New England stock and a Paris-educated mother of Spanish, French, and Jewish blood. When he was five, the family moved to El Paso. Following the death of his father, Louis combined school with working as a newsboy and Western Union messenger. He recalls delivering a telegram to John Wesley Hardin in the Acme Saloon and receiving a dime tip with the advice never to touch whiskey, just a few hours before Hardin died from a bullet hole in the back of his head. In 1899 the Hubbard family moved to Austin where Louis entered the University of Texas in the year he and the school were the same age—seventeen. From the time of his graduation in 1903 until 1964 when he retired for the second time—then from Texas Wesleyan College—Louis Hubbard was not only an educator in the usual sense, but the conveyor of culture to the state by bringing to the campus through lectures, concerts, and writers' conferences, people of renown in music, literature, drama, the social sciences, and the arts. Of these campus guests, Dr. Hubbard writes as entertainingly as he does of his own career.

At the same time Hubbard was writing his autobiography, churchman Joseph Martin Dawson was preparing his *A Thousand Months to Remember* (1964). The Reverend Dawson's background was as typical as Hubbard's was unique. Dawson's parents were Texas cotton growers from Missouri and Georgia. Young Joseph's decision to train for the Baptist ministry rather than for journalism was a difficult one. The ministry won out, but during a long career he combined the two—preaching, editing religious periodicals, and writing books on religion. Joseph Martin Dawson became a force in Texas and the nation for his fearless and eloquent advocacy of the separation of church and state and for freedom of the press.

The Kentucky-born educator and churchman Colby D. Hall was a boy of sixteen when he came to Waco, Texas, in 1891. In the late 1950's, as emeritus dean of Brite College of the Bible of Texas Christian University, he wrote his memories after choosing to include only the years of young manhood.

His book, published in 1961, he titled *The Gay Nineties* though it spills over a little into the new century. In Waco, near the converging of the Bosque and Brazos rivers, young Hall found life good. He worked as bookkeeper in a store, swam and fished and picnicked, attended church and lectures with young friends. He shared the excitement and even the terror caused by W. C. Brann, fiery editor of the *Iconoclast*. Three men were killed, including Brann, and a number wounded before Waco had peace again. A lecture by the agnostic Robert G. Ingersoll is credited by Hall with "nudging him" into the Christian ministry. In 1896 he entered Add-Ran Christian University, which had moved to Waco the year before. From that day until his retirement in 1947, Colby D. Hall's life and career were a vital part of the University which, with the name changed to Texas Christian University, moved to Fort Worth in 1910.[8]

Three autobiographical works about Southwest Indians are presented from three quite different viewpoints. The most revealing is *Me and Mine, The Life Story of Helen Sekaquaptewa* (1969), as told to Louise Udall. Helen, the narrator, was born in 1898 in Old Oraibi, a Hopi village in northeast Arizona. Her father was a "hostile," who resisted the whites and was jailed for refusing to accept Federal decrees. As a child, both in the pueblo and even more in the U.S. Government School, Helen was taunted and persecuted by the "friendlies." She wasn't even allowed to return home for vacations. At school she gradually learned to be a "friendly," and on her return to the pueblo was shunned by the "hostiles." She at last learned to make peace with herself and others and to accept the best in the Indian and white cultures.

Elizabeth Ward, a white, town-bred Texas girl, lived for a number of years in Navajo land. She arrived at the same conclusion as Helen Sekaquaptewa about the best path for the Indians to take in a white man's world. She and her husband came to the Indian reservation reluctantly. It was the only place Dan Ward could find a job during the Depression. As the wife of a lowly government range rider, Elizabeth was snubbed socially by the wives who lived near the trading post. She found friends among the Indians and began to study their

8. See *History of Texas Christian University* (1947) by Colby D. Hall.

way of life. Her husband, too, won the friendship of the independent Navajos. At last his title was upgraded from "rider" to "stock man" and life was easier for the Wards. In *No Dudes, Few Women* (1951), Elizabeth Ward tells of these years with realism, sprinkled with wit, bitterness, and compassion.

Anthropologist Alice Marriott lived by choice among American Indians in order to observe their daily lives and to learn their traditional beliefs and arts. In *Greener Fields* (1953), she writes of her attempts, as an adopted member of an Indian family, to live just as the Indians live. She also introduces the reader to some of the problems and practices of the anthropologist. Miss Marriott reveals that both Indians and anthropologists confront situations with much the same resourcefulness.

We Fed Them Cactus (1954), by Fabiola Cabeza de Baca, is as much family history as it is the autobiography of Fabiola Gilbert, who published her book under her maiden name. She writes of four generations lived by the De Bacas on the Llano Estacado of New Mexico. They hunted buffalo and fought Indians; they raised cattle in this land of prickly pear and bunch grass. In her father's and her own time, the family came to know Anglo farmers, miners, merchants, and railroaders. Much that had been free rangeland for the Spanish-Americans was acquired by these newcomers. Mrs. Gilbert's presentation of the older period has a special charm, and her account of the transitional period contributes significantly to this phase of the history of the region.

Two recently published books by Texas women deal largely with the Washington scene: *Washington Wife, Journal of Ellen Maury Slayden, 1897-1919* (1963), and *A White House Diary* (1970) by Lady Bird Johnson. Mrs. Slayden's unpublished manuscript could not have come after her death into better hands than those of Terrell and Walter Prescott Webb. Mrs. Webb, as the wife of the late Congressman Maury Maverick (who inherited the manuscript from his aunt) had been a Washington wife. Historian Webb wrote an Introduction to the book, and Terrell Webb contributed personal memories of "Aunt Ellen." During the twenty-two years that John Luther Slayden served the San Antonio district in Congress, his wife was known to many as "the congressional wife who wrote pieces for the papers." In these "pieces" she attempted to curb her dislikes and caustic wit. Not so in her notebooks, which piled up as the years passed and President succeeded President. She respected and liked McKinley, Taft, and Teddy Roosevelt. Wilson she disliked—had since she thought he was "too stuck on himself" when they were both young. *Washington Wife* gives a revealing and entertaining survey of social, and to a less extent political, life in the nation's capital during and between the Spanish-American War and World War I. There are also references to the local scene in San Antonio, where Mrs. Slayden vacationed and campaigned with her husband.

Lady Bird Johnson had been a "Washington wife" for twenty-five years before she began to tape recordings from which *A White House Diary* evolved. Although she had the background of experiences when her husband was congressman, senator, and vice-president, it took all her knowledge, intelligence, and physical energy to cope with the five troubled yet, for her, glorious years as First Lady. From the first entry in her diary headed "Dallas, Friday, November 22, 1963" to the last entry, "White House and LBJ Ranch, Monday, January 20 [1969]" her primary concern was for Lyndon, with the terrible burden that he bore, and how best she could help. Their daughters with the problems and joys of youth came next and then her own endeavors in beautification and conservation and in education. She writes with kindness and insight of a great variety of events and people. Some of her happiest entries are of vacations at what she calls "our forever home," the rambling white house on the LBJ Ranch on the Pedernales River. Liz Carpenter, longtime Texas friend of Mrs. Johnson, was her White House press secretary, and in *Ruffles and Flourishes* (1970) was her perceptive and affectionate Boswell.

Three contrasting personal books about Texas country life are *Tales of a Foolish Farmer* (1951) by George Sessions Perry; *This Stubborn Soil* (1966) by William A. Owens; and *Southwest* (1952) by John Houghton Allen. Perry was a successful writer of novels and articles when he decided he must own the East Texas farm which he had used a decade earlier as the setting for *Hold Autumn in Your Hand*. He put trusted

Negro Rush Arwine on the place as "foreman," and, except for weekends, Perry stayed in town writing articles to support the stock farm. Seemingly everyone—including friends—enjoyed the always-in-the-red adventure, except his wife Claire, who kept the books, and the Federal Income Tax officials, who were difficult to convince that "when the drought doesn't kill our grass, the clover kills our cattle." The experience was not a total financial loss, however. It provided Perry with material for five magazine articles, and these, with twenty-one added essays, make a robust and amusing book.

Farming for William A. Owens began as soon as he could snatch a cotton boll and drag a sack to help his mother and his three older brothers make a crop on their forty acres of Red River bottom land. Mother Owens—widowed the day William was born—is the heroine of her son's book as she struggles to feed and clothe her boys, her mother and grandmother, all living in a two-room cabin with a lean-to. But they had an organ and a few books, from better days in Arkansas. William was the reader and the singer of his grandmother's old songs. (These, with other folk songs, later became material for his doctoral dissertation.) With less than eight years of formal education, William passed entrance examinations at East Texas State Normal and got a job for room and board. *This Stubborn Soil* ends as college begins for a man who became a distinguished folklorist, novelist, and teacher.

About the time that William Owens was picking cotton on the small family farm in Northeast Texas, John Houghton Allen was riding tough horses and working cattle on his family's 60,000-acre ranch in far Southwest Texas. For young Allen work was all adventure, to pursue only as long as he enjoyed it. Education came easily for him in Texas, in Eastern schools, and in France, as he chose. In *Southwest,* a series of twenty sketches, Allen writes with poetic fervor of his growing-up years, his love of the harsh beauty of the land, the excitement of his hard, at times dangerous, activities, and the tales of the older men whose lives seemed to him to have been truly glamorous. The author's happy memories of his youth are set against his bitterness over what automobiles, oil derricks, and highways have done to the land where his roots are deep.

Happy, almost carefree childhoods are recorded in both

Life Was Simpler Then (1963) by novelist Loula Grace Erdman and *Gay as a Grig* (1963) by Ellen Bowie Holland. Miss Erdman never has written more effectively than in the nostalgic yet amusing account of her own young years in a western Missouri farming community. Sixteen backward-glance sketches are fittingly grouped according to seasons rather than by calendar years. Miss Erdman's second autobiographical book, *A Time to Write* (1969), overlaps her earlier work somewhat, but concentrates chiefly on her life as a Texas teacher, on her students, especially those in her creative writing classes, and on her own writing experiences, including those with fellow writers and publishers.

Gay as a Grig, subtitled *Memories of a North Texas Girlhood,* is Mrs. Holland's first book. She was aroused to write by the ignorance of her grandchildren of such, to her, common things as running boards and flypaper. Mrs. Holland wrote also, no doubt, to record for the children tales of their ancestors, and to share with them her own happy childhood in a large house on a wooded hill, a home that "guests flowed through like an effluent stream." Her Scottish father called her "his gay as a grig daughter." At the end of the book Mrs. Holland wrote, "I have now reached the delightful age where I am . . . pleased to sit in the shade of a chinaberry tree . . . devoid of get up and go." This mood was short-lived, for rather soon Ellen Holland went on a camera safari to Africa. Her record of the trip, entitled *Quiet Please!* (1968), was named from a white hunter's hissed warnings, "Quiet please; you might scare the elephants."

I Know Why the Caged Bird Sings (1970) by Maya Angelou tells of the troubled girlhood of a black girl who grew up in the home of her grandmother in Stamps, Arkansas. Then she moved to St. Louis to be with her mother, returned to her grandmother, and lived again with her mother, this time in California. The grandmother kept a store and taught Maya and her brother Bailey to be clean, to say their prayers, and how to behave with white people. St. Louis brought them into a neighborhood where crime was rampant; and in California the children were in and out of rooming houses, even taverns. During World War II, Maya lied about her age in order to become the first black woman in San Francisco to hold a job as a streetcar conductor. The frank and at times poetic sketches in the book end with the birth of a son out of wedlock, her loving the baby and keeping it. It is gratifying to note that, by the time her autobiography was published, Maya Angelou (whose real name was Marguerite Johnson) had attained fame as the star of *Porgy and Bess,* as well as success as a newswriter in both America and Africa. The title for her book came from a poem called "Sympathy" by Paul Lawrence Dunbar, a Negro poet who composed verse in both dialect and standard American speech.

Two books of the past decade record the experiences and observations of white writers who darkened their skins and passed for a time as Negroes: *Black Like Me* (1961) by John Howard Griffin and *Soul Sister* (1969) by Grace Halsell. From November 7, 1959, until near Christmas Griffin traveled and lived in the Deep South. He kept a journal of the misery and general sense of hopelessness that he encountered among the blacks and of their wild abandon to drink and sex. He recorded, too, the kindnesses of Negroes to each other and to him, a black stranger. In Birmingham he sensed the spirit of Martin Luther King and his plea for Christian understanding. In Atlanta, with the mayor and a newspaper working for the improvement of racial conditions, Griffin felt hope.

Grace Halsell, a Texas free-lance journalist, who had written her way around and up and down the world, was a White House staff writer when she read Griffin's book. She resigned from her job, had her skin darkened, and set out to find out what it was like to be a comely black woman in Harlem and the South. It was bad, even worse for a woman than for a man, especially in the South, where she was subjected to the frequent and at one time vicious attentions of white men. Like Griffin she experienced the kindness of Negroes for the black stranger who needed help and friendship. Miss Halsell during the six months she lived as a Negro met with fewer civic discriminations, such as whether she could choose a place to sit on a bus or be served food or use a rest room, than had Griffin ten years earlier, but she met with as many social and economic inequalities. Both writers returned to their own world with a deepened understanding of racial problems and a determination to do what each could to help solve them.

Two self-exiled Southwesterners, after more than a quarter of a century as successful New York writers, returned home, liked what they found, stayed, and wrote books about it. In *Home to Texas* (1956), Stanley Walker, editor and New York newspaper and magazine writer, remembers his youth in Texas and, as a returnee, his satisfaction in restoring the family ranch. He continued to write, but this time chiefly about his native state. His autobiographical book is urbane, non-chauvinistic. He disliked bragging Texans. A few years after Walker returned with the intent of staying in Texas, Mary Lasswell came on a visit to her hometown of Brownsville. She remained to rediscover the parts of the state that she knew and to discover the many areas that she had never known. *I'll Take Texas* (1958) is an amusing record of her findings. She reminisces nostalgically of her childhood and quotes in full the old Texas poem "Lasca" as recited with goose pimple effects by her Glasgow-born mother. She regrets that her mother was not familiar with Mabel Major's discovery that the author, Frank Desprez, was a Britisher.[9]

North Toward Home (1967) by Willie Morris represents almost a reversal of the circumstances that produced *Home to Texas* and *I'll Take Texas*. Morris' autobiographical work was published the year he became, at thirty-two, the youngest editor-in-chief of the 117-year-old *Harper's* magazine. His book is divided into three parts: "Mississippi," "Texas" (the longest section), and "New York." Willie Morris' accounts of his boyhood in a Mississippi town are reminiscent of Mark Twain, except there is no Nigger Jim. Negroes lived among them, but, with the exception of a few servants, Willie had little contact with or concern for the dark-skinned people. Willie's father, wanting his son to know another part of the world, put the seventeen-year-old boy on a bus for Texas and the University of Texas. Young Morris plunged into campus life, then into state politics as a reformer. With a degree from the University of Texas and four years at Oxford, he returned as editor of *The Texas Observor, A Journal of Free Voices*. Writing and editing opportunities opened in New York, and from there Morris looked back on the road he had traveled.

9. See Mabel Major, "The Man Who Wrote 'Lasca,'" *Southwest Review*, XXXVI, No. 4 (Autumn, 1951), pp. 298-305.

Physically and emotionally he felt an alien in New York, but intellectually, he felt at home.

A few generalizations may be made about the books in this chapter, both those which concern major political, military, and economic figures and those which deal with eventful if somewhat less dramatic personalities. Each of the volumes displays a variety of excellence. The books about Southwest writers, often by the writers themselves, are notable, as are the accounts of figures representative of minority groups. Individualism and independence are outstanding in these life stories, revealing elements characteristic of society in the region.

III

FICTION

In the second edition of *Southwest Heritage* (1948), novels are grouped in two categories: those which attempt to recapture the form and meaning of the past and those which record with criticism the contemporary scene. Novels written since 1948 seem to be interpreting the past in terms of the present, or reading the present in terms of the past. Not only are time barriers ignored, but literary forms seem to be combined. Fantasy may be introduced in realistic settings, or mysticism may emerge from a scientific environment.

Narratives are still being written in the form called romance, which draws on heroic adventures in which the leading figures seem to be of more than ordinary stature. Such stories, usually told of older periods, become the first category considered in this chapter. A second kind of narrative consists of books that treat less of physical encounters and the hazards of nature than they do of community life and family environment. Novels of this type concentrate on the harshness or warmth of personal relationships in both urban and rural scenes. Conflicts equally dangerous to personal safety can occur, but they differ in locale and outline, and therefore can be considered a domestic type of narrative writing.

In the last two decades, much satire has been written, satire intermixed with fantasy. The tall tale or yarn was the product of nineteenth-century storytelling, but the new forms of fantasy emphasize ideas and philosophy. Even the semi-historical narratives today can sometimes be suspected of caricature or jesting. Another type of narrative which has grown in popularity is the confessional story, which has a plot relying on personal analysis and revelation. Stories of this type can release not only individual memories but entire family concepts of guilt and inadequacy or obligation. There remains the mystery and detective story, but it can be classified according to subject matter or method of treatment. Throughout much recent fiction, a tendency is apparent to assail the citadels of Southwestern culture and to use storytelling as a medium to record changes in social and literary scenes. Thus, fiction like drama becomes a mirror in which man can view himself, as he is, as he was, and perhaps as he may be.[1]

Within a few months of the publication of the second edition of *Southwest Heritage*, Ruth Laughlin's *The Wind Leaves No Shadow* (1948) added fiction to history about the American occupation of the Southwest outside the boundaries of Texas. She weaves a thread of creative imagination through the twenty-five-year period preceding the Mexican War, a period when peaceful penetration of the Southwest through trade and visitation opened the way to military conquest. The central figure in her story is Maria Gertrudis Barcelo, better known as Doña Tules, famous for her flaming red hair and skill as a monte dealer. She was friendly to the Americans and preferred American victory to the regime of native politicians or the sway of Mexico. This same period serves as the setting for *The Time of the Gringo* (1953) by Elliott Arnold. The book contains dramatic episodes in which the hero Esquipulas Caballero, a Spanish aristocrat, opposes the Mexican governor's military power and his love for the daughter of a Spanish official. Lurid accounts of torture and mutilation practiced by pagans and Christians alike introduce a new degree of brutality in the writing of Southwestern fiction. Shirley Seiffert's *The Turquoise Trail* (1950) dramatizes the diary of Susan Shelby Magoffin, written in 1846-47. The novelist supplies imaginary dialogue for the illustrous Kentucky lady, riding in her coach with a Negro servant and trunks of gowns with matching accessories. The day in which her coach overturned on an arroyo bank, spilling its occupants as well as its contents in the sandy draw, was only one of the hazards Mrs. Magoffin survived with courage and aplomb.

The events in Edna Ferber's *Giant* (1952) occur between 1925 and 1950, when the vast ranchlands of Texas were becoming dotted by oil derricks. The central figure, Jordan (Bick) Benedict, is heir to Reata Ranch, one of the largest holdings in the cattle kingdom. He marries Leslie Lynnton, of Virginia plantation background, who encourages her son and

---

1. See Northrop Frye's "The Four Forms of Fiction" in *Discussions of the Novel*, edited by Roger Sale (1960), pp. 3-11.

daughter to break with a dynastic inheritance in order to introduce community clinics and educational reforms. The book
more often caricatures than it characterizes and was written
from an all too brief acquaintance with the region.

Dramatic changes in society along the Gulf Coast are described by William A. Owens in his novel *Fever in the Earth*
(1958). The location is Beaumont and the time is 1901 when
the oil boom brought gamblers, thieves, rowdies, and spurious
stock promoters to the city along with honest financiers and
thrifty workers. The main characters in the novel are Bo
Carrington, from the farmlands of East Texas, and Gaither
Ware, a school teacher, who was discharged from her position
in Louisiana because she played dance music on her piano and
seemed more interested in music than books. She arrives in
Beaumont where she meets Carrington and their fortunes ebb
and flow as the novelist describes both failures and successes in
the oil field.

Tom Pendleton transfers the scene in *The Iron Orchard*
(1966) to a West Texas "oil patch," where his hero Jim
McNeely is strong enough to survive in a fiercely competitive industry. From his own experience and that of friends
and acquaintances, the author constructed a convincing portrayal of the West Texas oil boom era of the twenties and
thirties. Winfield, the city of the novel, is readily recognized as
Fort Worth. "Tom Pendleton" is a pseudonym for a writer
whose later novels, *Husak* (1969) and *The Seventh Girl*
(1970), are adventure tales of love and war. In *Husak,* a U.S.
marine and a Tulsa oil heiress become involved in a Latin-
American revolution. The time is contemporary. The time of
The Seventh Girl is the Civil War and the chief locale, West
Texas. The hero's problem is doubled by loving a girl he does
not want to love and fighting a war he does not want to fight.

Harvey Fergusson wrote two novels in the 1950's which
treated anew the romantic appeal of his early Southwestern
books. *Grant of Kingdom* (1950) is the story of a large area
which comes into the control of an Anglo through his marriage
to the granddaughter of the original owner. Four men dominate the land grant in successive periods, and the land brings
wealth or fame to all, but only at the price of suffering and
bloodshed. *The Conquest of Don Pedro* (1954) is an account

of wealth as it grows from commerce. Leo Mendes, the chief character, is a Jewish peddler who adjusts to the religion and patriarchal way of Spanish life. Fergusson emphasizes the importance of an individual in the success of any institution—commercial, political, or religious.

Irwin R. Blacker's novel, *Taos* (1959), animates the period of Spanish rule in the Southwest from colonization in 1598 until the Pueblo Rebellion in 1680. Very little is known about family life during this interval, because all the documents and reports were written by military figures or custodians of the missions. Blacker's story is history with special liberties to emphasize the ruthless nature of colonial administration and the reaction of the Indians. He creates an imaginary pueblo called Santa Flora, where a brother and sister from Mexico City dominate the Indians and the missionary priest with the help of vicious bulldogs. The lives of these characters, as presented in this pueblo, offer sufficient motivation for Indian revolt, but they are admittedly fictitious and the morals as well as the cruelty challenge probability. An idyllic romance between a Taos Indian and the daughter of a Spanish count brightens an otherwise harsh story.

Fort Discovery, as created by Paul Horgan, in the Apache country of southern Arizona, is the chief setting for his novel *A Distant Trumpet* (1960). The unusual character of General Alexander Upton Quait, a soldier with a Latin quotation to fit every military situation, highlights the military background. The general's niece becomes the bride of Mathew Hazard, hero of the story, who leads his troop of cavalry into Mexico and persuades the Apaches to return as prisoners of war. The story takes a non-military turn when Lieutenant Hazard rejects the Medal of Honor and retires from the service when the Secretary of War permits a loyal Indian scout to be imprisoned with a captured renegade. The background of detail in *A Distant Trumpet* is tremendous, and the book is a major achievement in the literary career of the author. Horgan's device of presenting history through narrative sketches is used for *The Centuries of Santa Fe* (1956), which expanded those in an earlier group called *From the Royal City*. *Humble Powers* (1954) is a collection of three long stories, each of which illustrates the power of one of the virtues: faith, love, and sacrifice. Their titles are "The Devil in the Desert," "One Red Rose for Christmas," and "To the Castle." "The Devil in the Desert," which grew from fact, is a modern morality, dramatizing the eternal conflict between good and evil.

Mexico is the locale for Tom Lea's *The Brave Bulls* (1949), a story which deals with every man's fear of death. The glamour and terror of the bullring cannot be experienced within the territorial limits of the United States, but Tom Lea brings them as a vicarious experience for readers on both sides of the Mexican border. In *The Wonderful Country* (1952), he deals with another kind of suspense, the exploit of a man who as a boy killed his father and fled from the United States to Mexico to escape the law. After growing to manhood, he returns to the country of his birth, but is never free to enjoy peace of mind. The story moves between the two countries as he tries to escape discovery. *The Hands of Cantu* (1964) is written with an austere elegance of style which is matched by the splendid ink-drawn illustrations provided by the author. The story tells of the days in New Spain when Cantu trails and recaptures a rare breed of Spanish horses which have been stolen by Indians.

Two novels of romance with historical settings that are not loaded with sociological import are Walter O'Meara's *The Spanish Bride* (1954) and Jack Y. Bryan's *Come to the Bower* (1963). O'Meara gives imagination free play as his "bride," a glamorous dancer, finds love and adventure in Santa Fe, where she has been brought by Governor Antonio Valverde. In his Author's Note to *Come to the Bower,* Bryan writes that history is less the subject of his story than the choice of his young hero to fight for freedom with the Texans instead of seeking love and security at home. When the Texans triumph, he manages to win both. A novel which offers a similar choice in a contemporary period is *The Blind Bull* (1952), by George Guion Williams, but the fight for freedom is transferred from a Texas Gulf farm to a battlefield on the island of Saipan. The search for meaning in the contest against Japan is more difficult for Major Sweeney than it was for participants in the war for Texas independence. *Hail Hero* (1968) presents author John Weston's concern for the meaning of war as his student-soldier leaves an Arizona ranch for

Vietnam, blaming the older generation for the disillusionment of young men with the world as they find it.

Rudolph Mellard's *South by Southwest* (1960) has too little action for a historical romance and too little homelife for a domestic novel. However, it is descriptive of a historic period, and there is action of the historic outdoor type. The climax of the novel occurs in the Oklahoma land rush on April 22, 1889. The first half of the book is used to develop the character of "Pappy" Lee and to tell of his plans for staking a claim to a homestead at Willow Springs, which he had found when he was on the Chisholm Trail crossing Indian Territory. Now he knows that he can make a real home for his family. The race for the homestead is a vivid account of a desperate man striving to escape his competitors who learned his secret at a saloon on the previous night. Only brutal conflict resolves the race to Willow, in which Pappy is both victor and victim.

A race of a different kind is the climax for Conrad Richter's *The Lady* (1957). His heroine, Doña Ellen Sessions, is the daughter of a Mexican mother and an English father. When cattlemen invade the sheep ranch which has belonged to her family, she does not hesitate to live by the gun as her enemies have done. A fantastic race at the end of the story saves Doña Ellen from humiliation and underlines her English love for horses and her Spanish pride in the land of her forefathers. The artistry of Richter is displayed in this short novel as effectively as in any of his longer works.

Paul Wellman's *Iron Mistress* (1951) and his *Magnificent Destiny* (1962) draw upon biographical data in the lives of Jim Bowie and Sam Houston for plots in novels. *Iron Mistress* weaves both facts and folklore into Bowie's story. Research for either of these books could have established background for the other, for the two men were among the founders of the Texas Republic. Claud Garner's *Sam Houston, Texas Giant* (1969) is also a biographical novel dealing with General Houston and portraying him neither as an unblemished hero nor the anti-hero. Garner makes Houston a believable man, with large vices and larger virtues.

Historical romance can sometimes treat more seriously of personality flaws than concentrate on the broad sweep of events. *Divine Average* (1952) by Elithe Hamilton Kirkland deals with post-Texas Revolution times, a period less often dealt with than more dramatic eras. The plot is of cataclysmic evils of passion for land and of racial prejudice. These character flaws lead the anti-hero Range Templeton to alienate his son and daughter, Luke and Laska, and to destroy all happiness for himself and his gentle wife Luvisa. Mrs. Kirkland's *Love Is a Wild Assault* (1959) is a vivid re-creation of the tumultuous years on the Texas frontier in the life of the historic Harriet Page Potter. The lengthy novel is based on the autobiography of this brave woman and on court records of her attempt to establish the legality of her "bond marriage" to statesman-landowner Robert Potter.

Fire on the Mountain (1962) by Edward Abbey is a transition from a romantic Western to a domestic Western or story of family ties, those between John Vogelin and his grandson. Not only is their personal relationship involved, but the bond between both is found in the mountainous area where the family has lived for three generations. When Vogelin defies the efforts of the government to add his ranch to the White Sands Missile Range, the grandson joins him in resisting the sheriff's tear gas, even his gunfire. After the old rancher dies of a heart attack, his body is burned in the lookout cabin on top of the peak, and the fire becomes a symbol of the force that survived as long as it possessed the land. Abbey is also author of *The Brave Cowboy* (1956), which he calls "an old tale in a new time." By this he means that his narrative introduces a hero who is also a rebel against society. Jack Burns, the brave cowboy, is an anti-hero, because he is a criminal in the eyes of the law and a hero to his friends. Breaking out of jail, he escapes on horseback and is pursued up the side of a mountain. Both rider and horse escape their pursuers, but they are crushed by a tractor-trailer that bears down on them as they cross the highway on the other side of the mountain. *The Brave Cowboy* is an allegory of a society that destroys one set of incentives to encourage others.

The anti-hero is also celebrated in Larry McMurtry's *Horseman, Pass By* (1961). Although McMurtry grew up in a ranching family where cowboys were a reality, his experiences with ranch life destroyed more illusions than they created. His first novel begins with a sick animal instead of a healthy herd of Longhorns pushing through the mesquite. That single animal introduces the conflict on the ranch between Homer Bannon and his stepson, Hud. Others who breathe the air of this battlefield are Lonnie, Bannon's grandson; Jesse, a scarred ranchhand; and Halmea, the Negro cook. These make up the cast for a materialistic, somewhat sordid, chapter in Western storytelling. Hud is a cynical type untouched by the tradition of dignity and self-respect which characterize his stepfather. However, the brutality of Hud does not tarnish the power of Bannon, or the courage of the crippled ranchhand, or the wholesome nature of Lonnie and his love for his grandfather. McMurtry's story has a sinewy power which makes it a landmark in diversifying the cowboy myth rather than destroying it. His second work, *Leaving Cheyenne* (1963), is a novel combining three stories in one: the friendship of two cowboys; their love for the same girl; and the woman's own story involving her father, husband, lovers, and sons. As the summary suggests, the plot opens a wider horizon than *Horseman, Pass By,* and both novels stretch the definition of a standard Western. *The Last Picture Show* (1966) is a sordid tale of life in a West Texas town. The friendship of two high school boys and their compassion for the town half-wit relieves, to a degree, the distasteful plot. *Moving On* (1970), McMurtry's latest novel, is chiefly concerned with the sexual maladjustments of a dozen or more mating and non-mating couples who are constantly on the move, chiefly from rodeo to rodeo in Texas, Arizona, Idaho, Wyoming, and Nevada. However, detours are provided to academic circles and hippie colonies. The language used at all levels of society strains credibility with its coarseness.

"Standard" as a term to describe a Western indicates that hundreds of narratives have been written about the wide-open landscapes in the West and the people living there or moving around in them. At first, only ranchers, cowboys, and lawmen were described in these areas, plus rustlers and outlaws making trouble for the settlers. Gradually, sheepherders, miners, "nesters," health seekers, military men, "dudes," writers, clergymen, nuns, artists, movie stars, government officials, and educated Indians, not just the feather-and-tomahawk variety, appeared in both short story and novel-length Westerns.

The stories of Max Evans range from cowboy anecdotes to tales of sentiment, such as the "Musician of Marzal" in *Southwest Wind* (1958), a collection of short stories. The musician is a young violinist who earns fame as he plays the folk music of his native village. Later he is killed in an automobile accident while returning to that same village where he found his first inspiration. *The Rounders* (1960) and *Hi-Lo Country* (1961) are novels which deal with both humorous and grim events in line camps, rodeos, and on-trail drives. *The One-Eyed Sky,* a novelette completed in 1963, has a cow and a coyote as the central figures, along with a calf and four coyote pups which present a problem for a cowboy, who figures out a way to save them all. Two other novelettes, *The Great Wedding* and *My Pardner* appear in the same volume. *The Mountain of Gold* (1965) by Evans turns to one of the oldest Western themes, as Benito Anaya finds a lump of gold quartz on Black Mountain not far from the Anaya home. Seeking for the luxury of life in an adobe castle and the wealth to travel around the world, Benito returns time after time to search for the spot where the gold was found. The mountain becomes a great temptress, hunched over her vast treasure, which she protects with streams of water, rock slides, snow, and ice. Through youth into old age the struggle continues, while Benito labors until he loses an eye and a leg in the uneven contest. At last, the mountain claims her embittered lover without yielding the riches for which he sought.

Jack Schaefer is another writer whose artistry appears in a great variety of plots and characters. His best known book, *Shane* (1949), concerns life in a small Wyoming settlement where the transition from ranching to farming is just under way. His chief character is the gunman type who has reformed but has to return to his trade before the reformation is complete. When Schaefer's *Collected Stories* (1966) were published, he offered narratives about incidents in localities from Ft. McKay, Kansas, to Thermopolis, Wyoming. *Old Ramon* (1960), however, bears the stamp of the Southwest, for the Spanish sheepherder and his helper guide their flock in the shade of junipers and through arroyos characteristic of New Mexico and Arizona. The style of the book is as leisurely as the story, and both delight the reader who can share the drama of herders, young and old, as they train animals to win a battle against the elements, predatory beasts, and their own fears.

A Western close to the standard type is Will Henry's *Who Rides with Wyatt?* (1954). This volume reaches a kind of peak in the saga of Wyatt Earp as first told by Walter Noble Burns in *Tombstone* (1927). Somewhere between documentation and imagination, Henry describes Earp as "the last of the great lawmen" and "the greatest gunfighter of them all." His plot and his style lift the exploits of Earp to extravagant heights. Leslie Scott in *Tombstone Showdown* (1957) portrays Earp as a "loner," who nevertheless becomes the center of a gang of desperadoes and escapes from his past through drunkenness, gambling, and eventual suicide. In *The Hour of the Gun* (1967), Robert Kreps declares his story to be pure fiction, but he makes use of all the well-known figures and historical landmarks, permitting his publisher to announce that he has written a "story of the bloodiest feud in the West" which is now "told to its deadly end." Frank Waters identifies both the action and the participants with more fidelity in *The Earp Brothers of Tombstone* (1960).[2]

For the period from 1878 to 1881, the village of Lincoln, New Mexico, was as little to be envied from the standpoint of law and order as any place in the West. William Bonney, the Kid, has usually been the center of any treatment of gun play and violence in Lincoln, but Amelia Bean in *Time for Outrage* (1967) places him in perspective as she covers the entire warring period. Two factions, with cattle and supplies for a military outpost, and ranchers in the region provide the armies. The leaders are men with Scottish, English, and Irish names. The conflict is one which could have been fought in northern England or Ireland with as much reason as in New Mexico.

Novels dealing with the problems of Indians in contemporary non-Indian culture have never been considered as Westerns. They present the same questions calling for solution as does the domestic novel with a broader social background. Virginia Sorenson in 1951 wrote *The Proper Gods* about an Indian who moves from the Anglo-American way of life to an older social system in a Yaqui community of Mexico.

---

2. C. L. Sonnichsen, "Tombstone in Fiction," *The Journal of Arizona History* (1966), pp. 58-76.

When Adan Savala is living with Arizona relatives south of Tucson, he is called to service in the United States Army during World War II. After being wounded, he returns to an army hospital, then moves to the Mexican village from which Arizona Yaquis have migrated. There he encounters social patterns which represent enduring, if unprogressive, ways of life. Mrs. Sorenson's description of the ordered universe and colorful events among the Yaquis explains the choice made by Adan to become a leader of his people in their ancestral Mexican stronghold.

Edwin Corle's *In Winter Light* (1949) is a less serious study of Indians as they adjust to the white man's world. Two sets of characters develop the plot: the first, an Indian trader, Luke Stockwell, and his wife Ruby May; the second, a Navajo girl, Betty Squashblossom, and her sweetheart, Robert Two Crows. Linking the white couple and the red are Dr. Walterhouse, a dedicated Indian Service physician, and Miss Janice Talbot, a radio script writer, who is visiting the Arizona Reservation to find material for a new soap opera. Corle captures the Navajo attitude toward any culture other than their own, despite the effort of Dr. Walterhouse to find parallels between Christianity and the nature worship of the Navajos. Corle writes discerningly of the Indians as they seek security between two worlds.

In *A Woman of the People* (1966), Benjamin Capps presents the psychological dilemma of an Anglo-American girl who was kidnapped by Comanches and molded to their way of life. The realism with which the author writes of Helen Morrison, who was renamed Tehanita (Little Texan), creates the illusion that the book is a documentary about a real woman. When Tehanita has the chance to return to her relatives, she chooses to stay with her adopted people. She goes with her husband and their child to a reservation in southwestern Oklahoma. The reader feels that they will find the "good road" the Indian-Texan prays for. In *The White Man's Road* (1969), Capps deals with the problems of a young Comanche, Joe Cowbone, on the reservation near Fort Sill, Oklahoma. Now that hunting and fighting are denied him and his comrades, they wonder how they can win the favor of the girls. A horse-stealing raid, on which the plot hinges, is the attempt at an answer. The reader must understand the importance of horses to the Comanche to appreciate the tale. Capps, in *The Trail to Ogalalla* (1964) and *Sam Chance* (1965), uses his gift of storytelling to write of cowboys on the trail and the rise to fame of a cattle baron who has a community named in his honor. *The Trail to Ogalalla* may well be the best cattle-drive novel since Andy Adams wrote *Log of a Cowboy* (1903).

N. Scott Momaday, author of *House Made of Dawn* (1968), selected Jemez Pueblo as the location for the early and late scenes in his novel about Abel, an Indian youth who returns from World War II in the summer of 1945. On the feast day of Santiago, Abel is humiliated in one of the sports by a white man, and when they drink together a week later, he stabs the man to death. After a prison term, Abel is "relocated" in Los Angeles, where he meets a Navajo youth and other Indians at a Rescue Mission. The young Indians are aliens in a white society and they return to their reservations. Abel finds that his grandfather is dying. Alone in even his Indian world, he joins a group of men who are running a race toward the hills. He sings the song taught to him by his Navajo friend about a "house made of dawn" which is finished in beauty.

Oliver La Farge was an ethnologist who wrote fiction as well as scientific articles in his field. *Cochise of Arizona* (1953), a short narrative, does not rank with his earlier novels of Indian life, *Laughing Boy* and *The Enemy Gods*. But it does supply fact as well as imagination to the story of an Apache chieftain who held the United States Army at bay for ten years. Cochise was wounded after he was falsely accused of taking part in a raid on a white rancher. After this encounter, he carried on relentless warfare against the whites. Peace came only after a stagecoach operator named Jeffords arranged a conference with General O. O. Howard, the highest ranking officer ever to visit Arizona. La Farge presents Cochise in a sympathetic light, but omits the blood-brother compact reportedly made between Cochise and Jeffords by cutting veins and placing their arms together.

It is unusual to have an Indian background for a "novel of suspense" like Tony Hillerman's *The Blessing Way* (1970). Reports of a werewolf, a person capable of assuming a wolf's form, terrify the Indians on the Navajo Reservation. The accounts also interest Dr. Bergen McKee, a professor of anthropology. Called into the investigation is the chief of the Navajo Law and Order Division. Murder, the result of intrigue, mars the serenity of the cliffs and caves of the Anasazi or Ancient People before the mystery is solved, and a tinge of romance is added for the professor and a graduate student who finds herself involved in solving a crime instead of pursuing a research project.

In contrast to realistic writing about Indians is the fantasy of William Eastlake, who wrote three novels about the "Checkerboard" region of northwestern New Mexico. This area encompasses the western part of the Navajo Indian Reservation. Here Eastlake has created a special preserve for people and wildlife which owe their origin not only to nature, but to anthropology, philosophy, art, and literature as well. Only archaeology is untouched by the author's slant, as he employs the physical environment for his characters to enact their roles. The novels are *Go in Beauty* (1956), *The Bronc People* (1958), and *Portrait of an Artist with Twenty-six Horses* (1958), all of which stress the "pull" of Indian land to a better way of life. The first novel describes the conflict between two brothers, as it develops in a trading post near the reservation. The second treats of violence between two ranchers and the friendship that follows between their sons. The third is a potpourri of events centering chiefly about a trader's son who early in the narrative falls into quicksand while trying to pull his big, black horse across a stream. The horse is named Luto, the Spanish word for "grief." Both horse and man remain in the quicksand while the man's life passes in review. The Eastlake novels exist in the realm of fantasy, combining mysticism with romance. The setting of an Indian reservation with a trading post and a background of ranching is realistic, but Indians with names like My Prayer, Quicker-Than-You, President Taft, and Four Thumbs change the mood to caricature with a purpose, which is to introduce the reader to a state midway between the mechanized world of Big Reservation (the United States) and the actual stone age world of Indian faith and practice.

Richard Bradford's *Red Sky in the Morning* (1968) establishes a fictitious village of Sagrado, New Mexico, to provide amusing satire about both the artist colonies and the local populace in communities such as Santa Fe and Taos. The author went to junior high school in Santa Fe when his father, Roark Bradford, lived there in the 1930's. The story is told by Josh Arnold, who comes to Sagrado with his mother while his father serves as a naval commander in the South Pacific. Josh views the community chiefly through the eyes of his classmates: Marcia Davidson, daughter of an Episcopal minister; Steenie Stenopolous, an authority on human biology gleaned from his father's medical texts; Chango Lopez, who carries a switchblade; and Tarzan Velarde, a competitor in schoolroom terror. The plot is negligible, consisting of events such as a visit to a sculptor who has a nude model and a trip to the town dump to test the courage of anyone touching a dead horse, but the dialogue is inimitable. Wit and high comedy are sustained throughout the book.

Realistic fantasy of a tragic cast appears in *The Shallow Grass* (1968) by Tom Horn. The subject is the reinterment of the body of a serviceman who died in the Korean War. Through flashbacks that tell the story of Ronnie Parker, the reader follows a trail of sorrow beginning with Ronnie's fall from a giant windmill and ending with the opening of his casket in which only dirt is enclosed. A photographer from *Life* magazine has been sent to White Dove, Texas, to record the funeral in word and picture. He arrives in a winter storm, which establishes the mood of the story. In a lighter vein, Edwin Shrake releases his imagination to lift Peter Hermano McGill to the edge of sainthood by discovering his journal in a tin box buried in the fireplace of an adobe house in Taos. *Blessed McGill* (1968) is a grand spoof, mixing history, religion, and folklore to glorify not only McGill but also fabled Indian chieftains, buffalo hunters, treasure seekers, and missionary priests in a mock saga of the Southwest.

Robert Flynn's first novel, *North to Yesterday* (1967) puzzles the reader because it seems to be written partly as a satire and partly as romantic fiction about the old West. His hero is a storekeeper named Lampassas, who sells his store to a railroad agent in order to start a cattle drive in 1890, a decade after such overland treks were economically feasible.

The hazards of the trail, ludicrous at first, turn to mock heroic as the greenhorns become veterans. Even the typical touch of romance enters the story as one of the cowboys dreams of finding Diamond Anne, the beautiful blonde who lent him ten dollars in his youth. Amusing scenes concern the cowboys as they take turns playing nursemaid to the fatherless baby of a runaway girl who joins the outfit.

No such confusion of types mars Dillon Anderson's Claudie books: *I and Claudie* (1951) and *Claudie's Kinfolks* (1954). They are pure picaro. Clint Hightower, the "I" of the vagabond pair, and Claudie, who usually implements the shenanigans, wander over Texas living by their wits and staying just one step ahead of the law or irate citizens. Anderson's third novel, *The Billingsley Papers* (1961), spoofs the successful professional and businessman and his companions as they wheel and deal at work and work hard at play. University administrators and trustees come in, too, for subtle jibes about their generous conferring of honorary degrees upon wealthy alumni.

True Grit (1968) by Charles Portis contains all the elements of generous, good-humored laughter at the continuing popularity of the standard Western, whether in motion picture or in print. The heroine, Mattie Ross, a fourteen-year-old Arkansas girl, starts for Indian Territory to avenge the murder of her father. She persuades the marshal to let her join in pursuit of the murderers and rides to the capture and kill with sincerity and charm. *True Grit* is an amusing adventure story that becomes straight satire on books which portray law and order in the American West. The good and bad people who make up frontier society stand out in Victorian two-dimensional contrasts. The marshal swings a rifle not a revolver in the saddle, and he becomes a parody of the traditional law man. Mattie's earnest involvement in the maiming and bloodletting is treated with naive sincerity. The book will be read as a delightful hoax of a scene that has more often been poorly portrayed than well.

The hard-and-fast line between stories for juvenile readers and stories for older minds has never been clearly defined. Length of a book and the age of the principal characters have something to do with the distinction, but as young readers are interested in the actions of adults and adults maintain equal interest in young people, the books of Fred Gipson cross the age-interest line with effortless ease. *Hound-Dog Man* (1949) and *Old Yeller* (1956) are on reading lists for all ages. Whether the central figure is a vagabond like Blackie Scantling or a brother like Travis and Arlis Coates, the reader spreads his interest from the people to the animals they associate with, equally engrossed in the relations between them all. *Recollection Creek* (1959) concentrates on two youngsters who are released to run wild because the schoolhouse burns down. Their adventures and ingenious way of getting into trouble enliven country life in Texas in days before the automobile had made freeways and dragstrips more enticing than creeks and woods.

Novels of family or community life have usually dealt with the day-by-day efforts of people to enjoy security, love, and advancement. The efforts have often been fraught with danger and conflict. In *The Edge of Time* (1950) and *My Sky Is Blue* (1953), Loula Grace Erdman chooses West Texas and New Mexico for the scenes. However, the leading characters begin their lives in Missouri, and thus a background of contrasts is presented to the Southwestern area. Furthermore, as themes Miss Erdman selects those provided by regions everywhere: the loyalties of childhood, the promise of strange lands and the risks involved, the loss of old associations and the choice of new ones. The Camerons, Wade and Bethany, in *The Edge of Time*, fence their claim as a farm not as a cattle ranch and survive drought, a prairie fire, and sub-zero weather. Finally, they prosper and rear a family to enjoy the profits of their labor. By contrast, the Mungers in Al Dewlen's *The Bone Pickers* (1958) inherit wealth in a West Texas community, and manage to lose much of it through jealousy and decadence. The novel is massive and ends only when the Mungers are displaced by an outsider who marries into the family and shows more stability than any of its members. Dewlen's *Twilight of Honor* (1961) transforms a murder trial into a study of courtroom psychology that includes not only the criminal and the legal associates, but most of the community as well.

Madison Cooper's *Sironia, Texas* (1952) is one of the longest novels in the English language. Written in two volumes (which total 1,731 pages), the story centers on the interplay of privileged families living on the Hill and those less-favored residing on the flats. From the dozens of characters, Tammas Lipscomb and Launce Elliott (despite the defects in each) center the pride of their respective families, and Millicent Thaxton becomes the patriarch whose social invitations allot community prestige. No summary could cover the events which make up the plots and subplots in this novel, but no town was ever more thoroughly exposed to public view, including its sordid as well as its acceptable spheres of activity. The style of the narrative is evenly paced, as should be the pace of the reader who embarks on an experience in drama and melodrama, cruelty and kindness, jealousy and tolerance, with gossip as the medium of communicating it all.

Although the people in fictional Sironia (a thin disguise for Waco) clearly live in Central Texas, those who make up the population of the town in *The Wooden Horseshoe* (1964) by Leonard Sanders could have chosen almost any place in Texas or some other state to make their homes. The novelist's theme is a universal question: How honest are men in serving the public interest? The "horseshoe" is the table at which the City Council makes decisions. One of the members is buying land adjacent to a freeway exit on the outskirts of the town. Others have commercial projects to protect. How far will each go in permitting self-interest to outweigh justice? A decision is forced when the Chief of Police is threatened with dismissal for hearing evidence which is incriminating to members of the council.

In *So Long at the Fair* (1964), Bonner McMillion has written a novel of the domestic type which has as much action as any historical romance. The story is told by six-year-old Lanny Cargill, who lives on a farm near Waco, Texas, where his brother also resides. The older boy works for an aunt and uncle who are part of a large clan of relatives. Johnny Cargill is worshipped by his younger brother, and returns this fraternal devotion by taking Lanny with him wherever he goes, including a tryout in professional baseball, a career as a carnival barker at a fair, a trial with a troupe of actors, and a tour as a peddler which ends in success as an insurance salesman. The brothers survive a cyclone, an automobile wreck, even threats of a lynching when they protect a Negro friend. McMillion makes the unity of a family dominant to humor, pathos, and final happiness in the lives of his central characters.

In *Look to the River* (1963) by William A. Owens, a boy is also the storyteller. He is Jed, a backwoods, bottom land orphan who runs away from the overseer on a farm and is given a job by a kindly old couple who would like to keep him with them. The restlessness of youth leads the boy to join a Jewish-Dutch peddler, but before he completes this arrangement, he has experiences in a prison camp, and a chance encounter with a Negro boy leads both to strive to cross the Red River for a better life. In an earlier novel, *Walking on Borrowed Land* (1954), Owens has shown empathy for an educated Negro family in an Oklahoma town.

Two brothers are the center of interest in the Gordon family, as they appear in Tom Mayer's *Bubble Gum and Kipling* (1964). Johnny Gordon, the younger, is the hero in two of the nine stories. The first of these is "A Minute Forty-seven of the Second," referring to the round when a grade-school boxing match ends in Johnny's favor after Jerry, the older, trained him in the art of self-defense. Mayer has a gift of humor, illustrated by the way he has Jerry wisecrack his sessions in the school dispensary and the city hospital during an attack of appendicitis. The title story is a symbolic lead to an adolescent's introduction to sex.

Pathos is the dominant mood throughout *Summer on the Water* (1948) by David Westheimer. The water referred to is Pine Creek, emptying into a lake where families of wealthy Houston businessmen have their summer cottages. Uncle Talbot and Aunt M'Lou Carably are two of these vacationers, and with them lives a Negro maid and her illegitimate half-white child. The paternity of this child is the question which disturbs indulgent Aunt M'Lou. When it is solved, a drowning occurs as Pine Creek crawls "blindly and purposefully towards the sea." David Westheimer demonstrated his ability to write an action thriller in *Von Ryan's Express* (1964), which tells of the escape of American prisoners in Italy during World War II.

A novel similar in mood to *Summer on the Water,* though quite dissimilar in plot, is *The Dove Tree* (1961) by L. D. Clark. The morbid search for hidden gold on a cotton and corn growing farm results in the death of a young woman who accompanies her brothers in the search. She has been involved in sex with the farmer, who enters a stage of religious hysteria after her death. He is alienated from his son and the other members of his family. The dove nest is a symbol of the home which is destroyed by fire after death and discord have created a desolation of their own. Equally depressing is the story of Earl Kelly, as told in *A Shroud for a Journey* (1961) by Bill Casey. The central figure is no more admirable than his two brothers, Vernon and Corell, as all of them clash in violent quarrels and drunken brawls. A compulsion to discover whether their dead father was guilty of murder brings a certain amount of unity to Earl's search for the author of the crime, but death at the point of a pistol ends his search. References to a Bayou Club and the brown earth that produces bad cotton crops pinpoint the Texas Gulf Coast as the source of the folkways described.

Folkways are given a probing search in Benjamin Capps' *The Brothers of Uterica* (1967). Brotherhood is the universal dream of people everywhere, as experiments such as Brook Farm in New England and New Harmony, Indiana, exemplify. Similar colonies in Texas were the Icarian group in Denton County, 1849, and La Reunion in Dallas County six years later. Upon such backgrounds, novelist Capps constructs Uterica, or "Utopia in America." Brother Langley, an ex-Methodist minister (who had also learned the printer's trade), is the chief figure in the colony, as he mediates between the visionary founder, Brother Bossereau, and the practical farmer, Mr. Finch. Jealousy and selfishness contribute to internal conflict, and the antics of a feminist, Miss Harriet Edwards, are the chief relief to philosophical lectures and tragedy in the murder of Bossereau's daughter.

To describe Katherine Anne Porter's *Ship of Fools* (1962) as a domestic novel may seem a misnomer, but no reader can overlook the ship *Vera* as anything other than a house at sea, with its cabins as the scenes of private intimacies and its dining salon, lounges, and other gathering places as parts of a gigantic house, accommodating more than forty-two named characters and more than nine hundred other passengers, officers, and crew. There is no single thread of plot to this novel. Rather, there are a dozen plots, all dealing with personal conflicts, such as the aimless but impassioned love affair between two American artists; the anti-Semitism of a Nazi racist and his companion in the ladies garment business; the pathetic concern of the ship's doctor, a German, for an exiled Spanish countess; and the strange tension between a dying religious fanatic and his nephew. These and other absorbing problems reach a kind of resolution as the ship stops at ports in the Canary Islands, Spain, France, and Germany. Katherine Anne Porter was born in Brown County, Texas, and practiced journalism before she earned fame with her early stories, a number of which were written in Mexico. *The Collected Stories of Katherine Ann Porter* appeared in 1965.

The cast in Paul Horgan's *Whitewater* (1970) is limited in number and the action is localized in a Texas community named Belvedere, which is near a lake marked by seven islands. The lake was called Whitewater because the water from a dam covered a town by that name; the islands were formed by hills which had once surrounded the community. Since hunters and fishermen visit the lake and people find refreshment there, the standing pool separates the past from the present, this life from another, perhaps eternal life from the transitory. The plot centers about two boys, one active and athletic, the other sensitive and reflective. A wealthy widow guides the destinies of the reflective youth, who survives the tragic undertow that leads a man in physical illness and a girl in spiritual despair to seek escape by suicide in the lake. The incidents of family and community life in the book are very real, and although the stage is regional it can still be regarded as the earth anywhere. The people who move about in Belvedere are those who seek goals in this life and a life they believe lies beyond the present.

The Southwestern bookshelf is just beginning to have a number of books in the introspective or confessional category. Such works are devoted to personal and family revelations. In *The House of Breath* (1949) by William Goyen, Boy Ganchion discloses the inner secrets of a dozen people who live in a large old house at the place he calls Charity, East Texas. Once a prosperous farming village with a paper factory and a sawmill, the families wither as the town declines. Boy Ganchion, the storyteller, is a repressed adolescent who is withdrawn from others of his age and is absorbed with sex. The tortured nature of his efforts to find release is described with unusual frankness. Sensitive passages of beauty paint the wooded bottom land and the river near the town. Mack Thomas wrote *Gumbo* (1965) with less pessimism about the circumstances of a boy's life. Toby grew up in a Texas mill town where his world was a series of lively and amusing episodes inside a circle of parents, brother, sister, and grandparents. Then, too, life could always expand with flights of fantasy and the wonder of exploring the town and the countryside. A third book of adolescent experience is *Another Part of the House* (1970) by Winston M. Estes. In spite of economic hardships in the time of the Depression, nine-year-old Larry Morrison reacts to his surroundings with youthful optimism. He is secure in a close family relationship and idolizes his older brother, Ted. The conflict is produced by an uncle who lives with the family and steals from the boy's father. Larry's world is shattered when his brother dies tragically, but the wisdom of his parents helps him to regain his faith in what the future holds.

On a larger scale, *The Ordways* (1965) by William Humphrey is a family saga of four generations, their hardships and fun, feuds and foibles, and a kidnapping. It all began with a wounded Civil War veteran from Tennessee coming to Texas with his wife and children and the bones and headstones of his ancestors. Unity is preserved to a degree in the story by the search for little Ned Ordway, who was stolen by neighbors while his father and stepmother were on their once-a-month trip to Clarksville, their East Texas market town. Years later Ned is reunited with his family when sixty-five of his relatives travel in a caravan to visit him at his goat ranch on the Rio Grande. The novel is essentially the Ordways on the move, but wherever they live they belong to a plot of ground, and their sense of family ties leaves a mark in time and place. The book is rich in humor and, unlike much fiction of contemporary appeal, the story ends happily. *Home from the Hill* (1958), Humphrey's first novel, has an unnecessarily tragic ending. The novel is memorable for its handling of a strong father-son relationship.

Frank Waters touches on the world of mysticism in *The*

Woman at Otowi Crossing (1966), and mysticism is revelation, perhaps a form of confession. There really was a woman who lived near the bridge at Otowi, New Mexico, and that woman, Edith Warner, becomes the Helen Chalmers of the novel.[3] As Edith Warner did, she opens a tearoom where the scientists of Los Alamos Atomic Energy Research Center come for refreshment. As friend and counsellor of the Indians, she wins fame as a healer. She has a vision of a cataclysmic explosion that breaks the shell of the world asunder. Word of her vision is joined with the report of the atomic explosion at Trinity bombsite. She believes that the universe is a living thing, indivisible in its unity. When death comes to her by cancer, the Indians and the deer of the forest stand outside the house aware that her spirit had been one with theirs. Action in the novel moves from Otowi and Los Alamos to Washington, D. C., New York City, Las Vegas, the Grand Canyon, and the Marshall Islands in the Pacific, as the planning and testing occur for explosive atomic power. But the role of psychic power is also explored by the novelist, who expresses a clear conviction that man's greatest voyage of discovery lies in the final assertion of spirit over matter.

The troubled world of a minister of the Gospel, facing the problems of individual members of his congregation, is presented by Robert Flynn's novel, *In the House of the Lord* (1967). The Reverend Pat Shahan does not preach a single sermon in the book, but he tries to solve the frustrations of discordant families, the tragedy of unexpected death, bickerings about church funds, gossip about the morals of church members, and expressions of bigotry in interfaith councils. In a typical day of his ministry, his answers are courageous if sometimes skeptical, causing the reader to test his own faith and to seek answers for himself.

Examination of the world of the mind is related to confession inasmuch as it depends on personal analysis, and may be practiced by an individual upon others or upon himself. In C. F. Keppler's *The Other* (1964), the reader is gradually persuaded that analysis as prescribed by the central character, Dr. Gareth (Gary) Sheppard, a psychiatrist, is being practiced upon the doctor by one of his patients. Sheppard owns a pri-

3. For a factual narrative about this quiet woman, see Chapter II, pp. 197-98.

vate sanatorium in southern Arizona. Among his patients are a famous Long Island horsewoman, a writer of murder mysteries, an ex-gangster, a movie star, an industrial magnate, and a part-time chauffeur, typist, and filing clerk whose hallucination is the secret of a lost mine for which he holds maps and clues of history and location. The transformation of a scientist into a neurotic whose methods destroy almost as many as they cure makes an absorbing story.

Collections of short stories by Oliver La Farge and Katherine Anne Porter have previously been noted. William Peery's *21 Texas Short Stories* (1954) includes the work of writers dating back to O. Henry and proceeding to J. Frank Dobie, Dillon Anderson, Fred Gipson, and others. Walter Clemons' *The Poison Tree* (1959) consists of the sensitive sketches growing from a young boy's awareness of the adult world.

Old values have been reappraised and new ones established in the last two decades of Southwestern fiction. New themes have been added in these stories and novels. The plots make use of devices that increase interest, and style shapes language to heighten tension. The novelists enjoy a freedom that has lowered the moral tone of much of their writing. Perhaps writers in the past viewed the idealistic zone too narrowly, but if recent fiction has investigated subterranean depths in the exploration of character, the fullness of knowledge may disclose that light comes from above and is a necessary element for human survival.

IV

FOLK ART AND FOLKLORE

In the previous editions of *Southwest Heritage,* the materials of Indian and Spanish folklore were treated in a section apart from the Anglo-American ballads and frontier humor. This was justified both in terms of the chronology of each branch of popular literature and the separation of languages. Since 1948, these three areas of collecting have tended to coalesce somewhat, so that today collectors are likely to show an interest in more than one language, and anthologies of folklore are likely to publish non-English folklore with translations accompanying the original language. To represent adequately the activities of collectors and the literature of commentary as well, a digest of books and a survey of folklore societies are included in this chapter.

Folk art and folkcraft will be discussed here first, followed by commentary on books about folk medicine, folk song, tales of animals, and legends of lost mines and buried treasure. The mythology and folk tales about Indians will become a separate division as will the Spanish *cuentos* and other types of lore. Cowboy and non-cowboy English tales will be followed by Negro religious and workaday stories. A miscellaneous category containing books about place names and the publications of folklore committees or societies will conclude the chapter.

The oldest folkcraft in the Southwest may have been basketmaking, which Clara Lee Tanner in *Southwest Indian Crafts* (1968) states probably originated before 7,000 B.C. She discusses twined and coiled basketry, cordage, netting, and matting, not only in their prehistoric periods, but in the present day. She also discusses textiles, pottery, and silver work, and gives the final chapter to kachina dolls made by the Hopis of Arizona and Zuñis of New Mexico. Harold S. Colton's *Hopi Kachina Dolls* (1949) is entirely devoted to the carved religious dolls of these Pueblo kachina makers. Drawings and photographs for 125 figures are presented with a description of their significance. Kachinas are representations of super-

natural powers and sometimes of dead people. The dolls are
made by fathers to give to their daughters or nieces who hang
them on the wall as reminders of festivals held during the
year. Kachina dolls may be found in curio shops where they
vary in size from two to thirty inches. A reprint of Gene
Meany Hodge's *The Kachinas Are Coming* (1936, 1967) contains her beautiful drawings of these dolls as they represent
corn, snow, hummingbirds, eagles, and other natural objects
mentioned in the stories selected.

Eleven years before Mrs. Tanner wrote her book on the
Indian crafts, she prepared *Southwest Indian Painting* (1957),
a volume which begins with prehistoric decorations and covers
a period she calls transitional which pictures Spanish soldiers
as they pursue women and children in a battle dated for the
year 1805. Mrs. Tanner's book was followed by Dorothy
Dunn's monumental *American Indian Painting* (1968), which
has a subtitle, *Of the Southwest and Plains Area*. In her Foreword, Miss Dunn notes that paints, palettes, and engraving
tools have been found in American archaeological sites at the
lowest levels, corresponding to Mrs. Tanner's date for early
basketry. Both books mention Crescencio Martinez, who was
drawing eagle dancers on cardboard in 1910, perhaps the first
modern Indian artist. Miss Dunn also mentions the work of
Kiowa painters from Anadarko, Oklahoma, who sent paintings
to the International Congress of Folk Arts in Prague during
1928. Paintings from both Southwestern groups were included
in the Exposition of Indian Arts arranged for New York City
in 1931.

Masked Gods (1950) by Frank Waters gives an entire
section to Navajo and Pueblo dances, with the kachina dances
among them. This is folklore concerned with community religion which celebrates the changing of the seasons and the ro-
tation of life cycles from youth to old age. Waters compares
the Indian view of life with the Anglo-American and concludes
that the Indian view is closer to a universal concept. In his
Book of the Hopi (1963), Waters had a collaborator, Oswald
White Bear Fredericks, a well-informed Hopi. The two men
conferred with thirty elders of the Hopi tribe during three
years of tape recording and translation. As a result, the book

presents remarkably comprehensive data on mythology, legends, ceremony, and history about this tribe.

Spanish crafts in the Southwest are extensively defined by Roland Dickey and illustrated by Lloyd Lozes Goff in *New Mexico Village Arts* (1949, 1970). Small black-and-white designs appear on many of the pages with occasional full-page color drawings. Native houses, the tools and materials used, the furniture and religious paintings are shown to be expressions of the handcrafts and community thought in the Indian-Spanish period of Southwestern life. A book devoted to only one folk art is *Saints in the Valley* (1960), prepared by Jose E. Espinosa. This, too, is illustrated, showing photographs of the Christian sacred images which were produced by *santeros* or artisans in the period from about 1775 to 1875. An effort to revive the art of the *bulto* (carved in the round) and *retablo* (painted on board) has been made in recent years, but the products of ecclesiastical art studios have largely replaced those older products of folk art.

Carmen Espinosa's *Shawls, Crinolines, Filigree* (1970) describes the dress and adornment of the women of New Mexico in the period from 1739 to 1900. She relates the earliest fashions of the New World to those in the Spanish courts, where royal edicts governed the styles of bodice and neckpiece. Although few of the most elaborate of these garments appeared in the northernmost province of New Spain, the bustles, capes, mantillas, shawls, and ornate jewelry of gold and silver wire lent beauty to social occasions of every type. With the help of historical records, books, and family wills, Miss Espinosa documents her history, adding photographs in color and black and white to illustrate styles and designs. Much of the filigree work was locally produced in the nineteenth century. Craftsmen in Santa Fe, Taos, Las Vegas, and other communities cut and twisted materials for rings, pins, and necklaces, using scrolls and floral patterns originated as folk art in Egypt and India, then carried to Italy, Ireland, and Spain.

Healing herbs and plants have been associated with folklore from the beginning of time. In 1947, L. S. M. Curtin completed a study of medicinal plants which had been suggested by the folklorist and novelist Mary Austin. The book, *Healing Herbs of the Upper Rio Grande,* first published by the Laboratory of Anthropology in Santa Fe, was reprinted in 1965 by the Southwest Museum of Los Angeles. In the Preface, Maurice Ries wrote that plant medicine was legendary in the times of Aesculapius and Hippocrates, and that in the Southwest much of the folk information may have come from Spain after that country was occupied by the Moors who, in the late Middle Ages, were among the most advanced people in Europe in the sciences. Mrs. Curtin lists 225 plants that have been put to medicinal use in northern New Mexico. She refers to the Doctrine of Signatures, or the belief that plants may have some distinguishing mark that offers a clue to their quality as medicine. Her book is a valuable contribution to botanical science as well as to knowledge of the *médica* among the Spanish people. Isabel Kelly related the curing powers of Don Pedro Jaramillo in her *Folk Practices in North America, Birth Customs, Folk Medicine, and Spiritualism in the Laguna Zone* (1965). Don Pedro was called "the healer of Los Olmos," and his spiritualistic faith is also discussed by Ruth Dodson in the *Publications* of the Texas Folk-Lore Society, (Vol. XXIV, 1951). John Q. Anderson, while teaching folklore at Texas A. and M. University between 1961 and 1966, encouraged his students to collect information on herbs and preparations used in treating diseases. The results were organized and presented by Professor Anderson in *Texas Folk Medicine, 1,333 Cures, Remedies, Preventives, and Health Practices* (1970). The entire state with its different ethnic groups is represented.

With the deaths of two oustanding collectors, Jack Thorp in 1940 and John Lomax in 1948, the pioneer period of collecting cowboy songs may have ended. William A. Owens gave the Texas Folk-Lore Society its twenty-third volume, *Texas Folk Songs* (1950), and Harold W. Felton published *Cowboy Jamboree, Western Songs and Lore* (1951). Carl Carmer, in the Foreword to this volume, writes that the cowboy became "the leading character in a measureless tent-show, whose big top was the blue sky, and the villains to be overcome were the rattlesnake, cattle rustler, bad man, and the stampede." All the songs in Felton's book are well-known favorites, among them "The Chisholm Trail," "The Cowboy's Lament,"

"Home On the Range," and "Git Along Little Dogies." Each of these songs is introduced by an account of the circumstances under which it came to be written. However, Felton does not mention the authors of any of the songs, although Margaret A. Nelson in *Home on the Range* (1947) establishes that Dr. Brewster Higley and Dan Brewster were the writers of both lyric and music of the song for which her book is named; and Jack Thorp in *Songs of the Cowboys* (1921 edition) says that Troy Hale, of Battle Creek, Nebraska, was credited with writing "The Cowboy's Lament." Thorp gives other credits as he knew them. Felton was interested in descriptive background material, which his jamboree supplies, along with amusing drawings for each song.

Austin E. and Alta S. Fife reproduce a facsimile of Thorp's original volume in their *Songs of the Cowboys* (1966). When Thorp's small paperback pamphlet was published in 1908, it had a press run of only 2,000 copies. Very few of these booklets remain in either private or public libraries. The Fifes found variants for many of the songs, even those which Thorp himself wrote, the most famous of which was "Little Joe the Wrangler." In his Preface, Thorp had said, "I plead ignorant of the authorship of them" [the songs], but the facsimile shows that he penciled or inked the word "most" between "of" and "them" to correct his statement. In some ways, cowboy songs were the forerunners of country music, which has become a commercial bonanza in recent years.

John Donald Robb comments in his Foreword to *Hispanic Folk Songs of New Mexico* (1954) that many of the songs known in the villages of the Southwest are mutilated or incomplete and have to be given musical reconstruction. This is said despite his practice, as a folklorist, of authentic tape recordings for originals which he had collected during a quarter of a century of field work. In his volume, he discusses Hispanic *romances, corridos, canciones, inditas, relaciones,* and *letras* from the religious plays, adding the music and text to illustrate these types. Professor Robb plans an additional publication to include *cuandos, décimas, trovos,* and *alabados.* Juan B. Rael published *The New Mexican Alabado* (1951), with transcriptions of music as recorded by Eleanor Hague. In his Introduction, Professor Rael refers to Father Juan B. Ralliere's *Colección de Cánticos Espirituales* brought together in 1877 and often reprinted since that time. In addition to use in Spanish hymnals of the Roman Catholic Church, the *alabados* were part of the religious services held by the Penitentes in their chapter houses called *moradas*. A small collection of such *alabados* appears in Alice Corbin Henderson's study of the Penitentes called *Brothers of Light* (1937).

Animals, as subjects of folklore, are found in Aesop's *Fables* and *Sinbad the Sailor*. In Pueblo and Navajo story-telling, animals appear with people as conscious entities in nature with qualities of speech and feeling. Such is the world described by Helen Rushmore and Wolf Robe Hunt in *The Dancing Horses of Acoma* (1963). "Flint Bird," the first story, describes a contest between Long Hair, a mighty hunter, and a monstrous bird that has carried Long Hair's son to a house in the sky. In "The Battle at White Cliff House," the gods punish men for gambling and disrespect for each other and the gods. The neighborly communication between deities and men is not unlike the relationship between earthly and heavenly beings in the classic myths of Greece.

Miss Rushmore states in "A Note About the Acomas" that her story called "The Dancing Horses" shows non-Indian influence. La Verne Clark in *They Sang for Horses* (1966) explains the non-Indian background of horses. In what is now the territory of the United States, Indians first saw horses in 1540 when Coronado and his soldiers rode them into the Southwest. The Indians thought the animals were great dogs and capable of eating men. In time Indians captured horses and became horsemen themselves. However, Mrs. Clark does not believe that the Navajos acquired horses until late in the seventeenth century. Then the ownership of a horse became an item of prestige. She states that the Navajos decided that their gods always had horses but did not send them to the Navajos until the Indians needed them to fight the white man. In Navajo mythology, Johonai rides a turquoise horse across the sky when he brings the warm, white light to the people on earth. The horse became not only a gift of the gods, but in symbolic ways became significant in ceremonies, songs, and healing rites.

Snakes play important roles as messengers to the gods

among the Hopi Indians, neighbors to the Navajos. Contrary
to the attitudes of Europeans derived from the story in *Genesis,* the Southwestern Indians associate snakes with water and
other blessings of life. J. Frank Dobie's book *Rattlesnakes*
(1965) takes a neutral attitude; he states that "rattlesnakes,
though not harmless, are the most interesting of all snakes in
North America." Then he refuses to take sides in the argu-
ment: Do rattlesnakes swallow their young? However, he
must lean to the affirmative on this issue, because he reports
the statements of a dozen eyewitnesses corroborating the phenomenon. Other folk beliefs mentioned are that roadrunners
build a thorny fence around rattlesnakes and leave them to
starve or burn up in the heat of the sun; that rattlesnake fangs
kill after the snakes are dead; and that they have been known
to guard treasure in a cave or carry out a curse. Dobie's *The
Voice of the Coyote* (1949) is a more important book, but it
belongs to natural history more than to folklore. The coyote
or prairie wolf is known from Mexico to the Yukon and has
kept man company in the Indian world of myth and the white
man's world of homestead, cattle ranch, and hunting lodge.
Dobie's biography of the animal begins with an Aztec prince
whose name meant Hungry Coyote and then includes the enemies of the coyote known as the South Texas Wolf Hunters
Association. "Next to God the Coyote is the smartest person
on earth" say the country people of Mexico. Readers of Frank
Dobie's book will be likely to agree.

Folk narrative in the Southwest, both in English and Span-
ish, has emphasized treasure hunts, for concealed gold is a
source of wonder and mystery. Sims Ely develops this idea in
The Lost Dutchman Mine (1953), when he tells how he and a
partner tried for twenty-five years to find the mine visited by
Jacob Waltz and Jacob Weiser in 1870. A member of the
Peralta family first revealed the location of this mine in the
Superstition Mountains of Arizona, and after the death of
Jacob Waltz in 1891, the mine was widely sought. Weaver's
Needle, a high peak forty miles east of Phoenix, was a landmark always named by prospectors who claimed to have found
gold in or near the mine. Despite the deaths of twenty treasure hunters, some of them killed by Apaches, the search con-
tinues until the present day.

Apache gold is also one of the mysteries in *Tales of Old-Time Texas* (1955) by J. Frank Dobie. The location of his story is in the Guadalupe Mountains of New Mexico and Texas. A Mexican named Policarpio tells how he was captured by the Indians in the Big Bend of the Rio Grande and lived among them until he was eleven years old. He learned where they kept their gold and how they covered the entrance to the cave when the white men came. It is Policarpio's story and maps from Old Mexico that start the treasure hunting in the Guadalupes and other areas, one of which was on Shoal Creek where O. Henry dug in vain west of Austin, Texas. The stories in this book are among Dobie's best, varying from accounts that are historical to those that are "authentic" tall tales, meaning that they are tolerable because they bring out the characteristics of a situation and the persons placed there.

The Big Bend Country of Texas is the scene for *The Way I Heard It* (1959), by Walter Fulcher, whose parents bought a ranch at Terlingua, just west of what became the Big Bend National Park. Silver mines had once flourished at Terlingua and outlaws found hiding places in the caves of the Chisos Mountains or moved about openly on some of the big ranches where friends offered shelter. Fulcher's book not only has treasure tales, like the story of a mine protected by a wizard's curse, but it also has tales of traders from Old Mexico and bandits like Berry Ketchum (brother of Black Jack) and the ranchhands who robbed the mail coach on the Southern Pacific. Fulcher makes an interesting distinction between oral accounts without documentation and written records of such oral accounts. Verification of one is just as necessary as verification of the other, and folklore is valuable to confirm or interpret either. The book is ably edited by Elton Miles.

In the Preface to *Treasure of the Sangre de Cristos* (1963), the author, Arthur L. Campa, tells the stories he heard as a boy on his father's Texas ranch. One of these tales was about the Lost Padre Mine, discovered in New Mexico before Territorial days when a priest and his parishioners moved from Durango, Mexico. They found gold in Soledad Canyon, near St. Augustine's Pass. Attacked by soldiers, they covered the entrance to the mine. After the Treaty of Hidalgo, maps and memories sent treasure hunters to the site where even in modern times the search still goes on. The "Treasure of El Chato" is about a renegade who robbed a missionary caravan in the Mesilla Valley. Campa adds personality to some of his narratives by describing his own explorations, on one of which he became imprisoned in a cave and had to be rescued by the prospector who took him there. He concludes that there are fringe benefits to treasure hunts, such as artifacts or letters found in trunks and memories of abandoned houses which linger even when the mirage of wealth fades.

The folklore, as well as the history of Indians in Middle America, is preserved in Frances Gillmor's *Flute of the Smoking Mirror* (1949, 1968). She found the story of Nezahualcoyotl, co-ruler with Montezuma, in ancient Spanish chronicles and Aztec codices. The splendor of great temples, crowded market places, fine artists, musicians, and craftsmen shows in her pages as she describes the lifetime of this noted ruler, but conflict among his nobles, murder, human sacrifices, and social unrest contributed to the disunity which the Spaniards found when they arrived in Mexico some years after his death. Miss Gillmor is also the author of *The King Danced in the Market Place* (1964), another study making use of folklore and history to present Montezuma I to both English and Spanish readers.

Friends of Thunder (1964) is a collection of Cherokee folktales prepared by Jack F. and Anna G. Kilpatrick. Both the Kilpatricks are natives of Oklahoma, and she is a descendant of Sequoyah, who devised the written symbols used to transcribe Cherokee speech. The stories are divided into those about birds and animals; those about an early race of Little People who live in a world below this one and who can change into human beings at will; and those in which a trickster named Tseg'sgin' succeeds as much by stupidity as by cleverness. Some of the stories show intermingling of non-Indian materials with native Cherokee plots.

Alice Marriott also has a trickster as the central figure in *Saynday's People* (1963), which is a summary of her two previous books on Kiowa life and folk tales: *Winter-Telling Stories* (1947) and *Indians on Horseback* (1948). The first is devoted to the trickster tales and the second to the history and anthropology of the Kiowas, as they began their nomadic way of life on the steppes of Siberia and northern Asia. Sayn-day is a cousin of the Cherokee Tseg'sgin' and both are related to Ma'i, the coyote or roamer of the Navajos. Sayndy, like Ma'i, has a mythological role, since he contributes to bringing the sun to the Kiowa people and explains how the buffalo came to satisfy their need for food. Miss Marriott's *Greener Fields* (1953) offers her experiences among the American Indians in story form, and *American Indian Mythology* (1969), written in collaboration with Carol K. Rachlin, contains material from a good many Southwestern tribes: Tewa, Zuñi, Hopi, Navajo, Apache, and Kiowa.

N. Scott Momaday's *The Way to Rainy Mountain* (1969) is also a book about the Kiowa people, but it deals primarily with the cultural and psychological changes which occurred in their tribal migration three hundred years ago. During the long trek, these Indians found a stone image and named it the Tai-me, symbolic of the buffalo honored in the Sun Dance. Momaday retraced this pilgrimage, guided by the memories of his Kiowa grandmother. With the help of poetry and song, he conveys the aspirations of the tribe, as it became one of the foremost representatives of the hardihood of the Plains Indians.

Wilbur Sturtevant Nye's *Bad Medicine and Good* (1962) is a more literal picture of the Kiowa migrations than Scott Momaday's poetic transcription. The Kiowa informants of Colonel Nye also give his volume more realistic data than those Indians who were interviewed by Miss Marriott. Titles such as "Black Bear Becomes Chief," "White Horse Catches a Navaho," and "I Scalped a Man Once" go with accounts of a winter raid in eastern New Mexico where a wounded Kiowa nearly froze to death. The kidnapping of a Navajo boy and the scalping of a United States Army officer add oral history to folk-lore and give much to check with the previous volumes about the Kiowas. In *Bad Medicine and Good,* the pipe is smoked by Kiowas as a pledge to fight rather than to preserve the peace. In a great Sun Dance after a battle with Mexicans near El Paso, the Kiowas had three images of Tai-me, the sun doll, on their altar plus a wand or medicine stick with a carved head resembling the magic symbol. In the book, the word "medicine" is used to identify almost any type of policy or strategy adopted by an individual or a group. Planning any action which brought success became "good medicine" and that which failed became "bad."

Franc Johnson Newcomb, who lived among the Navajos as a teacher and as the wife of a merchant who owned a trading post, wrote some of the most informative books on Indian ceremonials: *Sandpaintings of the Navajo Shooting Chant,* in collaboration with Gladys Reichard (1937); *Navajo Omens and Taboos* (1940); *A Study of Navajo Symbolism* (1956), with Mary Wheelwright and Stanley Fishler; and *Navaho Folk Tales* (1967). The last named book recounts a version of the "coming up" myth when the Indian people were believed to have moved with the insects through four stages of life before reaching the final world stage where they found all that they needed for building their homes and establishing their families and clans. *Navaho Religion, A Study of Symbolism* (1950), by Gladys Reichard, is a detailed explanation of legends and rituals, emphasizing the exorcistic and sanctifying nature of their visual and auditory symbols.

Charles G. Newcomb, brother-in-law of Franc Johnson Newcomb, used the folklore he acquired on the Navajo Reservation to write a story called *The Smoke Hole* (1968). The central figure in the tale is an Indian trader who (like the author) had spent years among the Navajos. The "smoke hole" is the opening in the roof of an earth-covered hogan or house where the smoke escapes from an open fire. A young Navajo who has been brought up by the trader and his wife prompts the storytelling of his grandfather who remembers the lore of the *yei* or gods and wicked giants. Tales of the bear, the badger, the coyote and descriptions of clan ceremonies enter into the story line. *Thunderbird and Other Stories* (1964) by Henry Chafetz makes use of Navajo sand paintings to accompany three Indian legends. The first tells how the Great Spirit created the Thunderbird; the second explains why the bat flies at night; and the third describes the gift of the Peace Pipe to mankind as a way to end wars. Tribal origins of the tales are not given, but the spirit is Indian and the tone is authentic.

Literary Folklore of the Hispanic Southwest (1953) by Aurora Lucero White (Lea) is the only comprehensive survey of the Spanish folklore of New Mexico. Mrs. Lea entitles her book as "of the Hispanic Southwest," and the literary types which she traces in New Mexico are certainly represented wherever Spanish culture has survived in the region. In the first part of her book, she lists the religious dramas, such as the *Coloquios de los Pastores* (The Shepherds' Play), for which she edited a text in 1940. A more complete version of this text is to be found in *Music of the Spanish Folk Plays in New Mexico* (1969) by Richard B. Stark, assisted by T. M. Pearce and Ruben Cobos. Variants of this text of *Los Pastores* are to be found in *The Sources and Diffusion of the Mexican Shepherds' Plays* (1965), by Juan B. Rael. Seventy-seven manuscripts from northern Mexico, California, New Mexico, southern Colorado, and Texas are listed, many with casts of characters and excerpts from dialogue. Professor Rael also collected more than five hundred folktales and published them with English summaries in his *Cuentos Españoles de Colorado y de Nuevo Méjico* (1957).

The *corrido,* or Mexican ballad, which developed as a popular form of the Spanish *romance,* is well illustrated in Américo Paredes' volume *With His Pistol in His Hand* (1958). The title is a line in the poem written and sung in June of 1901 not long after the hero of the ballad Gregorio Cortez shot and killed the sheriff of Karnes County, Texas, as the official tried to arrest the man on the charge of stealing a mare. Paredes traces this story and presents the psychology of the *paisano* as he is confronted by mounted Rangers, defends himself, and escapes his pursuers by walking or riding more than five hundred miles before being betrayed by a countryman not far from the Mexican Border. In his final chapter, Professor Paredes discusses the social organization in which folklore flourished in frontier areas of New Spain, such as New Mexico and the communities of the lower Rio Grande.

La Conquistadora (1954) by Fray Angelico Chavez is an imaginary retelling of the facts confirmed in the author's historical novel *The Lady from Toledo* (1960). He dramatizes the journey of a statue of the Virgin Mary as it was brought to Santa Fe in 1625 by Fray Alonso de Benavidez, Father Custodian of the Franciscan Missions. The career of *La Conquistadora* included the retreat from the capital city with

Governor Otermin in 1680; the return with Governor-General De Vargas in 1692; and enthronement in six separate chapels before being placed in the present shrine at the Cathedral of St. Francis in Santa Fe. Changes in raiment, jewelry, and even in the wooden form itself are described with sustained interest for readers who are of *La Conquistadora's* faith as well as for those who are not. Alice Bullock's *Living Legends of the Santa Fe Country* (1970) also has stories about sacred images, one of which tells of a statue of San Jose which was first placed in a private chapel at a village fifteen miles south of New Mexico's capital. When the family tried to move the image to a chapel elsewhere, the figure became so heavy no one could carry it. Legends cannot be proved, observes Mrs. Bullock, but she presents twenty-three which became known about statues, bells, pictures, springs, houses, even a staircase, all of them associated with Indian or Spanish sources. They are recorded both for enjoyment and folk memory or belief.

More humor and realism appear in Sabine Ulibarri's *Tierra Amarilla, Stories of New Mexico* (1971), which was published in both Spanish and English. "My Wonder Horse" is a poetic treatment of a boy's fantasy associated with a wild stallion that is captured and lost again. "The Stuffing of the Lord" portrays a parish priest whose pronunciation of Spanish so astounds his congregation that he preaches constantly to churches packed with listeners. Mystery is not lacking, however, for the longest narrative, "Man Without a Name," concerns a youth who identifies with his dead father, and fights an imaginary battle to separate his own identity from the spirit of the man seen and heard as he speaks from their past associations. The psychological encounter is a revelation of the labyrinth of multiple aspects of reality and unreality recognizable in everyone.

The first edition of *Southwest Heritage* (1938) proclaimed Pecos Bill to be the "tallest folk hero" in the Southwest and the statement was repeated in the second edition ten years later. Harold W. Felton in *Pecos Bill, Texas Cowpuncher* (1949) supplies a complete bibliography of books and articles about Bill, who seems to have been invented by Tex O'Reilly in 1923. Cloyd Bowman's book in 1937 was a landmark in establishing a tradition, as were presentations by Mody Boatright, Irving Fiske, Carl Carmer, and others. Even poems, plays, and motion pictures are in the Pecos Bill repertoire. Felton remarks that his facts have been "truthened up" somewhat, but his account of the origins of Bill will satisfy every Southwesterner because Bill's parents first met in the Washita Valley of southern Oklahoma; Bill was born the day they crossed into Texas; and when Texas got crowded, the family built a corral in New Mexico and a calf ranch in Arizona. Felton ends his cycle with the news that after Pecos Bill invented chaps, the lasso, cowboy songs, and the Circle Mountain Ranch, he decided that he had done all he could for the West and retired to the Big Bend Country, which was wild and rough enough to suit him as long as he lived.

Although the parents of Pecos Bill met in Oklahoma, they probably came from Arkansas, the home of Vance Randolph, whose propensities for "truthening" the facts are illustrated in the following books: *We Always Lie to Strangers* (1951), *Who Blowed Up the Church House?* (1952), *The Devil's Pretty Daughter* (1955), *The Talking Turtle* (1957), and *Sticks in the Knapsack* (1958). In *We Always Lie to Strangers,* Randolph writes that the pioneer hated a liar, but he didn't see any harm in "stretchin' the blanket" or "spinnin' a windy" if it didn't injure anybody. Randolph's lies are authentic to the core and completely harmless, especially the one about the farm on an Arkansas hillside that was so steep the planting had to be done with a shotgun. Of course the rows were straight, being planted like that, and when harvest came, the farmer had the barn placed where the ears of corn could roll right in leaving the shucks on the hill. Razorback hogs that hunt wolves and root up oaks are normal in a land where twenty-foot lizards devour deer, sheep, and goats. *The Talking Turtle* and *Sticks in the Knapsack* contain a number of stories which are variants of tales found in Boccaccio and Chaucer, as the notes supplied by two well-known folklorists Herbert Halpert and E. W. Baughman convincingly demonstrate.

Joseph Leach in *The Typical Texan* (1952) analyzes the popular concept of a citizen of the Lone Star state as tall in the saddle, wearing a broad-brimmed hat that shades far-seeing eyes, whose gallantry to ladies contrasts with his scheming to outwit both cow and human critters. The myth, Leach points out, was born and bred on the frontier as far back as early days in Kentucky and has been kept alive by such prominent Texans as a recent Vice-President and even more recent President of the United States. Joe B. Frantz and Julian Ernest Choate, Jr., in *The American Cowboy, the Myth and the Reality* (1955) present comparison between the real cowhand and the glamorized cowboy of Western romances. In addition, and more importantly, scholars Frantz and Choate supply a fully annotated bibliography on the cowboy.

The vein of folklore staked out by Dorothy Pillsbury in *No High Adobe* (1950) and *Roots in Adobe* (1959) is the daily routine of people motivated by customs and guided by traditional attitudes and responses. When she went to live in Tenorio Flat in Santa Fe and participated in the *bailes* and festivals, she acquired a new code of neighborly behavior. Having heard the Spanish proverb *mi casa es suya* (my house is yours) she decided to share her orchard with the youngsters in the neighborhood before they raided it. Calling in the boy who delivered her newspaper, she made this known to him, and on the day the fruit was ready for harvesting, she invited the young marauders to divide it equally. To her surprise, they gave her a share for watering the trees. Then they gave her an additional basket which their relatives had brought from the country. In the two books, the reader meets the Spanish folk, young and old, city dwellers and country bred, adjusting old ways to new with native wit and good humor.

Herman Moncus in *Prairie Schooner Pirates* (1963) is one of the few folk historians and lorists to discuss the Comancheros, a group of Indian traders who started as peddlers but ended as bandits, preying on caravans and selling in any market where there was a demand. Moncus states that the Comancheros began in days of Spanish rule and lasted until after the Civil War. As a young druggist, Moncus collected and displayed guns, hunting knives, medicines, and other articles used in trade by the Comancheros. Later these articles became exhibits in the Tucumcari Historical Museum which he helped to establish.

Between the Neches and the Trinity rivers in Texas lies the Big Thicket, an area of cypress swamps, tievine and briar patches, canebrakes and prairies, where deer, bears, panthers, and a variety of snakes enjoy the same freedom as the hunter and the settler. Frances E. Abernathy in *Tales from the Big Thicket* (1966) records that people there once believed that a black panther would mount the gatepost of any house where there was the body of a deceased person awaiting burial. The piney woods rooter, a species of wild hog, was given credit for the discovery of oil in a county where a family saw the hogs come home covered with oil mud. When the muddy spot was found, an oil driller brought in a gusher. Old English ballads are still sung in the Big Thicket, such favorites as "Barbara Allen" and "The Hangman's Rope" enjoying special popularity.

Dorothy Jensen Neal has written two paperback books about the life and activities in the high, forested region of southern New Mexico. *Captive Mountain Waters* (1961) describes the building of pipelines from streams in the Sacramento Mountains to irrigate ranchland and to supply the railroad line leading to timber and recreation areas. *The Cloud-Climbing Railroad* (1966) is the story of engineering feats during which a roadbed was constructed on 28-degree curves and 200- to 300-foot-high trestles. "If the road has a wet spot, whittle a plug and stick it in the pipe" was a common saying of those who traveled the winding roads along the pipelines. "That snow was deeper than a tall man's thigh on an awful tall horse," reported a rancher in the days before the railroad went through the timber. Mrs. Neal relates that the switchback on the Alamogordo and Sacramento Railroad was suggested by the chief engineer's child who was playing with a set of toy blocks. He showed his father how to run an upper track parallel to a lower one and climb the steep grade. Another version has the demonstration by the lad at an older age and just returned from engineering college. Facts mingle with folklore of gunfights and suburban trains from El Paso in these two interesting booklets.

Folklore of the Oil Industry (1963) by Mody C. Boatright shows how some folklore is manufactured and some is truly created. The manufactured type is found in the Kemp Morgan stories modeled on the tall tales of Paul Bunyan. Kemp is a rotary well digger who once brought in a gusher in weather so cold that the oil froze as it came out of the well; so Morgan sawed it into sections and shipped the oil on flatcars. He even sawed up dry holes and sold them for postholes. The problem in rejecting Kemp Morgan as a parody of Paul Bunyan is that during the nineteenth century a well digger named Gib Morgan actually told such stories while he was operating in Pennsylvania. Boatright submits Gib Morgan stories that describe drilling an oil well on Pike's Peak and in the Fiji Islands. Oil folklore reported by Boatright as having authenticity concerns doodlebugs, dreams, and oil trompers, whose feet made tracks twice as deep when they walked over oil. The Doctrine of Signatures as applied to medicinal plants appears in oil well discovery, too, where some people thought that the shoestring cactus would reveal an oil field if its leaves pointed east. Others believed that evaporation over an oil field would give the topsoil more than normal content of hydrocarbon. Knowing plants with a hydrocarbon diet was all that was necessary to discover oil. As a matter of fact, some geochemists have had success with soil analysis as a clue to oil deposits. As with much folklore, the canny wit and the vein of humor in *Folklore of the Oil Industry* may touch pay dirt in more places than one.

Folklore by a Negro about Negroes is the exception rather than the rule. Joel Chandler Harris, Julia Peterkin, Charles C. Jones, and Samuel G. Stoney were well-known writers who have made the sagacity and humor of the black race known to white America in the South and throughout the nation. J. Mason Brewer is a Negro writer who grew up in the bottom lands of the Brazos, and the dialect in which he transcribes Negro storytelling is as Old South as that used by any of the Southern white transcribers. The phrases are of the pre- and post-Slavery periods. *The Word on the Brazos* (1953) consists of preacher tales filled with picturesque expressions, such as the "sinner man" who is going to hell "head fo'-most" on the "don'-care bandwagon." There are tales of religion, also, in *Dog Ghosts and Other Texas Negro Folk Tales* (1958), but the unusual stories are those about the "dog spirit," which is a benign ghost, a friend to man, helping people when they are in distress. All of Brewer's stories illustrate the personal, family-like nature of Negro relations with both the boss man and Higher Powers in workday, playday, and Sunday-go-to-meeting affairs.

Deep Like the River (1969) by Martha Emmons is also a memorial to a passing culture of the southern Negroes. Modernization and standardization have changed their way of life as refrigerators, sewing machines, and other motor-driven conveniences have taken the place of hand- and foot-powered tools. Ghosts that return to complete unfinished work or to protect someone from injury are confirmed as real in "Old Mean Tom" and "Miss Annie's Slap." Negro imagination can also be linguistic when parents describe children as "dis-loving them" and a woman as "slick-mouthed" when nobody can trust what she says. Stories of poltergeists and the sounds they make, revenants in animal forms and heavenly visitors with messages of hope or caution illumine the mores of a bygone day.

Mody C. Boatright in *Folk Laughter on the American Frontier* (1949, 1961) points out that exaggeration and incongruity were the staples for humor characteristic of backwoods America. The "half-horse and half-alligator" boaster, represented by types among the keelboat men and the fur-capped woodsmen, spawned tall tales which became entertainment at campfires, army posts, and trading places. Jim Bridger's glass mountain, a perfect telescope to see elk grazing twenty-five miles away, and Big-Foot Wallace's spider—"as big as a peck measure with a bite cured only by music"—stretch the imagination as well as tickle the risibles. Incongruities developed when refined travelers encountered the inconveniences of frontier accommodations and, in turn, the so-called yokels viewed gentility as ridiculous in rural surroundings. Boatright challenges a thesis presented by Albert Bigelow Paine, Lewis Mumford, and Van Wyck Brooks that frontier humor was born of despair. He sides with Bernard De Voto and Max Eastman who point to the exuberance and optimism behind the nonsense and absurdities in frontier tales. He also finds the mood rooted in basic democracy which survived the frontier, wars, and depressions that followed.

Publications on place names may be considered history rather than folklore, but the line between what can and what cannot be verified in place naming is frequently blurred. Virginia Madison and Hallie Stillwell discovered this when they wrote *How Come It's Called That?* (1958), a book dealing with place names in the Big Bend Country of Texas. Shot Tower, a peak resembling an instrument used in making lead shot, is said to have been named for this descriptive aspect, but a German geologist named Schott visited the region sometime before 1857 and, furthermore, a good many Big Bend people believed that a round hole at the top of the peak looked like the result of a cannon shot. The authors describe the Big Bend as "a chameleon region, a magnet to the adventuresome spirit." Some names are chameleon-like, adapting their meaning to any informant at his or her time and place.

Although comprehensive publications of place names for most of the Southwestern states are of recent date, earlier studies were prepared more than a quarter of a century ago. Charles N. Gould published a book of Oklahoma place names in 1933, and his work became the basis for *Oklahoma Place Names* (1965) prepared by George H. Shirk, president of the Oklahoma Historical Society. There are 3,500 names in this second publication, which gives locations in terms of county and a neighboring community, providing postal data and nomenclature as available. Collecting of material for *New Mexico Place Names* (1965), edited by T. M. Pearce, assisted by Ina Sizer Cassidy and Helen S. Pearce, began with the Writers' Program of the Work Projects Administration in 1936-40. Collecting was resumed by members of the New Mexico Folklore Society in 1948. Workers in a Spanish Place Name Project of the Modern Language Department, University of New Mexico, contributed material as did individuals who were reached through the News Bureau of that university. The volume is arranged alphabetically, giving locations by county, plus state or federal highways, and distance from outstanding landmarks. There are more than 5,000 entries with designation by language groups. An Introduction gives material on historic periods influencing names and the onomastic patterns followed as names were selected.

A year before the Writers' Program began to collect field and community names in New Mexico, Will C. Barnes published a collection of Arizona place names in the General

Bulletin Series of the University of Arizona. In his Foreword, Barnes states that he had spent more than thirty years gathering information, a remark supported by his bibliography and investigative details in the volume. In 1960, Byrd H. Granger revised and enlarged the work of Barnes for a new edition of *Arizona Place Names,* in which the names were grouped by counties, and elevations of towns and landmarks were added to the historical and statistical data previously supplied. Additional small-scale maps amplified the single map in the volume by Barnes. An Introduction was added to provide historical background for naming in the state.

The scope of place name studies in Texas surpasses the task of any other Southwestern state. Publication of Fred Tarpley's *Place Names of Northeast Texas* (1969) makes this clear. His volume contains 2,693 names collected in twenty-six counties. The total project for Texas will cover 254 counties and will extend to at least 24,000 names. Professor Tarpley made use of punch cards which were programmed for computer filing and summary. This made possible percentage data for derivations drawn from geographical features; names found in the Bible or other religious sources; those commemorating brand names as well as names for individuals; names from non-English sources; and names resulting from acronyms and misspellings. Numerous pictures distinctive of the Texas landscape, cities, academic institutions, and public monuments ornament the book, which was the result of eight years of labor by Professor Tarpley and his associates.

Folklore societies justify their existence by annual meetings and by encouraging the publication of research. *Publications* of the Texas Folk-Lore Society were edited from 1923 until 1943 by J. Frank Dobie, according to the Dedication to Dobie in Volume XXVI (1954). Volumes XXIV and XXV were edited by Wilson M. Hudson; then from 1953 until 1964, the editors were Mody C. Boatright, Wilson M. Hudson, and Allen Maxwell; Hudson and Maxwell served as editors for the volume in 1966; and Hudson became sole editor in 1968. These *Publications* treat such subjects as Kiowa-Apache, Mexican, and Negro folktales, Western ballads, cattle brands, remedies for arthritis, the gun-woman Belle Starr, tarantulas, cock fighting, horned toads, and cowboy comedians. It is not possible to do justice to this series, which is certainly the most distinguished collection of American folklore outside the volumes of the Bureau of American Ethnology and the issues of the *Journal of American Folklore*.

In 1947 the New Mexico Folklore Society began to publish the *New Mexico Folklore Record,* which appeared in ten volumes between 1947 and 1956 with the following editors: T. M. Pearce, 1947-52; E. W. Baughman, 1953-54; Julia M. Keleher, 1955-56. Additional volumes were published in 1964 and 1970, with T. M. Pearce again as editor. Articles deal with such topics as native tales from both Spanish and Indian languages; *corridos, chistes*, folk dramas, and *brujaría* or witchcraft from Spanish sources; ghost stories in English; the Lincoln County war and Billy the Kid; the cowboy boast; the border narcotic trade; the rainbow in Indian folklore; and the balladry of the sheep camp. The University of Arizona Folklore Committee, appointed in 1943 with Professor Frances Gillmor as chairman, has established an Arizona Folklore Archive to which manuscripts and tapes have been contributed by clubs, schools, and individual collectors. Folklore archives have also been established at the University of New Mexico and the University of Texas.

The efforts to uncover the riches of Southwestern folklore have been amply rewarded during the last two decades. The publications discussed in this chapter indicate this success and show where the treasure lies, sometimes concealed and at other times exposed. In libraries or in the field, the search can be as exciting in the future as in the past.

V

POETRY

Poetry has been classified as to verse form and subject matter. In the earliest periods, narrative poems were most popular in forms like the epic and metrical romance. Lyrics were represented by Hebrew psalms and Old English laments. Didactic poems in Old English were written as riddles and charms. Contemporary poetry has few narrative titles, but lyric poetry remains one of the largest groups of expression. In the pure sense, this is emotional exaltation in response to either an external or internal stimulus. With or without musical accompaniment, words in lyric form offer the same release to the newest generation of poets that they did to the oldest. Verse in drama has almost disappeared, but some forms of lyric describe people and places with dramatic imagination. They may be classified as a distinct poetic approach in the lyric form. Another type of modern verse may be found in the poetry of social protest. Usually somewhat formless and without rhyme, this group is justified as lyric in that it also offers release to an author through exuberant statement, not so much personal as social. The didactic and philosophic poem is still another type of poetry today, as are humorous or witty verses. Southwestern poets are active in four of these five areas of writing. The oldest and least active will be discussed first.

John Myers Myers in *Maverick Zone* (1961) has created a narrative account in verse about the Western Frontier. Gunfights in corrals take the place of medieval tournaments. Romantic antics in dance halls substitute for minstrel courtship within castle walls. "Red Conner's Night in Ellsworth" tells of the wooing of Prairie Rose by a lonesome cowboy and the robbery of Boston Joe's store by his niece and her accomplice, Happy Jack Morco. Surprise endings to both plots are told in verses that snap with vitality and rhyme in stanzas that carry the story forward with animation. S. Omar Barker has poems with storytelling in *Songs of the Saddlemen* (1954), such as "San Jacinto," where the reader sees the campfires of Santa

Anna's army gleaming in the distance while the Texans prepare to attack the next morning. Sam Houston withholds the order to attack, lulling the enemy into a siesta hour. When he gives the command, surprise is complete and the victory is won with the loss of only nine men. "Bruin Wooin' " and "Buckaroo's Squelch" have narrative interest, too, as one tells how a cowboy proved his bravery by riding a bear out of a cave, and the other points out how a cowboy rode the saddle instead of a horse. "Curly Wolf College" is in the true vein of cowboy humor, but "Old Time Cowboys" carries an undertone of melancholy for days that are gone. Vaida Montgomery's second volume of poetry, *Hail for Rain* (1948), contains a number of ballad-like poems, such as "The Two Bulls," in which a wild, unbranded bull named Samson encounters a pedigreed Hereford called Goliath. The battle which ensues holds the reader in suspense, as does the verse narrative "Cattle Brands," about a poker game won with a pair of sixes which thereafter became the winner's brand. "I Know Two Men" is a lyric with a quality of imagery and phrasing reminiscent of William Butler Yeats.

In *The Great Riding* (1966), Lily Peter pays tribute to Hernando de Soto, using a series of poems largely in flexible, long-lined free verse. She re-creates the story of his expedition from Florida to eastern Arkansas and into Texas, searching for the gold which had been reported earlier by Spanish chroniclers. "All their young, with the pith and plumage of youth," writes the poetess, "arrogant as young lions," they found frustration and buried their leader in an unmarked grave near the Mississippi River which they had been the first Europeans to explore. Although primarily narrative, *The Great Riding* is a meditation on time, history, and heroism as well. Lily Peter also has a collection of lyrics, *The Green Linen of Summer* (1964), which in the series "Considerations" shows further her interest in the past. Two long narratives by Roy Douglass Burrow question the universal stupidity of wars and human events. The first is *Trail of Tears* (1969) and the second, *The Battle of Pea Ridge* (1970). Both are written in long run-on lines governed by syntax rather than by rhythm or rhyme.

Chuck Haas, who was born in Topok, Arizona, in 1875, packs a cowpoke's experience into *Rhymes O' A Drifting Cow-*

boy (1969). He toured with Buffalo Bill and entertained the elite as well as the ordinary in Europe and America. His poems have the earthy rhythm of desert trails. Lyrical verse about winegrowers and winemakers have a narrative flow in Alvin Gordon's *Of Vines and Missions* (1971). The author tells of the vineyards when the early padres were building their missions along the Pacific Coast and in the Southwest. The Arizona artist Ted DiGrazia illustrates the text in watercolor sketches and paintings.

Poetic drama tells a story in verse, and Ramsey Yelvington in *A Cloud of Witnesses* (1959) retells the tragedy of the Alamo as he poses and resolves the question: Is Freedom worth dying for? The ghosts of the men, Anglo and Mexican, who gave their lives in defiance of Santa Anna, the dictator, answer, Yes. Only a deserter says, No. The play effectively combines elements of free verse in the dialogue with passages of poetic prose. The pitting of good against evil through characters that are both individuals and symbols suggests a medieval morality. *A Cloud of Witnesses* has been produced many times and published in a handsome permanent volume.

Everett A. Gillis presents a variety of themes and verse forms in *Sunrise in Texas* (1949) and *Angles of the Wind* (1954). Ballads are found in "Parson John," a rousing, shouting song-story of a parson who prayed while he fought and died in the Alamo; "Ballad of Big-Foot Wallace," "Sam Houston," "David Crockett," and "Bowie" are other heroes sung in ballad form. Some of the finest lyrics, such as "Light on the Tapestry," "Song for Caryl," and a group called "Heart Singly Vowed," are in the sonnet form. "The Water Finder" portrays a character from the poet's childhood in the Ozarks. "Estevanico The Black Sees Cibola" is a memorable portrait of the Spanish slave, puffed up by Indian adulation, whose search for treasure and freedom ended in tragedy. In each of these forms, Gillis is never at loss for poetic invention or skill.

One of the books published by Winfield Townley Scott after he moved to Santa Fe in 1954 is a long poem called *The Dark Sister* (1958). The narrative deals with Freydis, half-sister of Lief Ericson, and how she led a company of Icelanders and Norwegians to Vinland in North America in A.D. 1009. With long lines of rhythmic intervals, Scott brings his epic through battles with Skraelings and dissension between the ship folk, climaxed when Freydis slays her lover after he joins those who question her rule.

The second large class of poems in the Southwestern region presents lyrics of such variety that they could be divided into themes, such as nature, love, death, change, and other topics. Experiments in form and phrasing are most active here. Meter no longer conforms to recognizable measurement, and metaphors are more often paradoxical than not. Combining the images of one sense with those of another has become an artistic device. Fragmentary expression is meant to suggest more than is fully stated. The challenge of modern poetry resembles that of modern art and music, as all three media find room for mood or action in unrealistic as well as realistic forms.

Frances Alexander's *Time at the Window* (1948) is written in a variety of moods. There are lyrics of the seasons, trees, birds, the stars, portraits of people, and poems that have religious and philosophical themes. Among the portraits are those of a man named Willoughby, an antique dealer, and a high school girl. Occasionally the poet smiles at herself, as in "Numerator." All the poems are skillfully executed in a diversity of meters. Libby Stopple's *Singer in the Side* (1968) employs a lyric touch to explore man's presence in what seems to be a world of chaos where beauty is evanescent but restores faith for the moment. Frederic Will's poetic experience, as recorded in *A Wedge of Words* (1962), brings imagery from Sicily, Greece, Turkey, as well as from northern Europe. His idiom is modern, stressing the intensity of moments which recur in such poems as "Future" and "Answering." The insistent theme is that no certainty exists in love. Marvin Davis Winsett produces lyric autobiography in the poems of *Remembered Earth* (1962). Through loving and accurate detail, he re-creates the farm life he knew as a boy and young man. The sharply recalled images give conviction to his words. *April Always* (1956) and *Winding Stairway* (1953) are other books of poetry by Winsett. In them he introduces a stanza called the cyclus, which consists of twelve lines of graduating length rhyming in every third line.

Reflections on nature and the power of the earth dominate

Piecemeal and Gravel Green (1968), written by Eloise Johnston. Deceptively simple lyrics of her birthplace in Arkansas are found along with intricate French and Greek poetic forms. Tales of the pioneers are recalled by Bess Mae Sheets in "Heritage," one of her poems from *This Cry is Mine* (1970), but the pressure of present-day America is stressed in "Economitus," from an earlier volume called *Thread Your Thoughts* (1956). Very personal lyrics assume a social outlook in the work of Julius Lester Medlock. After careers in both teaching and farming, he found time for travel and writing two books of poetry: *Stray Hearts* (1956) and *Threads of Flame* (1960). His poems sing of discovering the artistry of the growing world and the countryside.

Lucille Adler, author of *The Travelling Out and Other Poems* (1967), makes use of synesthesia, combining sensations which produce unusual imagery. Metaphors like "knife-strong streams of snow" and "shards of wind" in her "Country School" and "Peace" challenge the reader's imagination. Jeanne DeLamarter Bonnette in *Oh, The Wide Sky* (1968) has a poem called "Vacant House," where tumbleweeds hide in corners of an abandoned yard, and rusty upside-down cars lie like "wingfolded shells of beetles on dry earth." "Vickers' Ranch" is a little drama in which a boy demonstrates his manhood in the branding pen. Mrs. Bonnette is the author of five other books of poetry, including *Chess Game and Other Poems* (1952) and *In This Place* (1971). Her work has appeared in a number of anthologies.

A volume called *The Poems of Alice Lavinia Long* (1967) was published eleven years after the author's death. In a Preface, her son Anton V. Long writes that his father, the poet Haniel Long, recognized his wife's gift and made a collection of her work, but the poems were never published during her lifetime. They are very personal lyrics which express her joy in both familiar and exotic experiences: the sound of a bell in Yokohama; the sight of a blue heron at the edge of a lake; awareness of a Pueblo Indian girl dipping water from a stream; and the view of sky and field in autumn. This type of lyric fullness is also found in *The Ultimate White Flower* (1958) by Eunice Carter Grabo, whose poem "Bird on the Night of Doom" shifts the mood from crescendos "articulate in mirth" to song that unlocks a dark door in the "jewelled wall of air." Sytha Motto's *Walk the High Places* (1968) crosses a horizon with haikus of spring and dawn to present "Santo Domingo Corn Dance" and "Battle Ground." In the second title she points to a rusted plow as a symbol of defeat by unyielding earth baked in the wind.

The early lyrics of Fray Angelico Chavez were more personal than those in *Eleven Lady-Lyrics* (1945) and *The Single Rose* (1948), and the reader is glad that a number of the poems found in his earliest volume, *Clothed with the Sun* (1939) are reprinted in *Selected Poems* (1970). In this later volume is also reproduced *The Virgin of Port Lligat* (1956), which was inspired by Salvador Dali's painting "The Madonna of Port Lligat." The poem interprets landscape, sea, and figures in the painting as symbols of mysteries in science and religion, fusing the Sphinx of Thebes, constellations within the atom, and themes from theology in lines of imaginative power and beauty. Both Dali and Chavez are of Hispanic origin, one in the old world, the other in the new.

The poems of Lautaro Vergara also bring the flow of Latin genius into Southwestern English. A native of Chile, Vergara has lived in the United States for more than forty years and in New Mexico since 1937. *Luz y Sombra* (1965) was first printed in Spanish; two years later it appeared in English translation. In the poem "Acoma," Vergara lauds the conquest of the rocky mesa by Spanish troops in January of 1599, but he also calls this pinnacle a symbol of harshness as well as of peace. Since the poet is a physician, "Microscope" is about the "skylight of the small world," where the blood cells devour each other and the bacteria of disease survive only at the expense of human life. Vergara is at once a humanist and a scientist. "The Old Physician" pays tribute to a country doctor who for fifty years dispensed wisdom with his medicine. The second volume by Dr. Vergara, *Ecos Serranos* or *Southwestern Poems* (1971), contains such titles as "Los Penitentes," "Bells of My Deserted Village," and Labyrinth Without Exit."

Poetry attempting to put chants or personal feelings of the American Indian into English words was given impetus in the 1920's when such poets as Alice Corbin Henderson, Mary Austin, and Witter Bynner made their collections of Indian material and wrote in the Indian manner themselves. In 1926, Eda Lou Walton published her *Dawn Boy, Blackfoot and Navajo Songs* which was followed by *Turquoise Boy and White Shell Girl* (1933). In between these books of regional poetry, Miss Walton published volumes of her personal lyrics. Her last book of poetry, *So Many Daughters* (1952), is a summary of her gifts, including the use of conceptual parallelism as illustrated by "Black Swan," in which a swan's movement is doubled by the changing image in water. "Twin Mirror" and "On the Lake" make use of this same duality when they offer an opportunity for psychological review of the objects examined. Although Eda Lou Walton lived most of her life in New York, her studies of Indian imagery and the desert landscape were always strong influences in her writing.

Witter Bynner also experimented early with native American rhythms, as his poems in *Indian Earth* (1929) signify, but his last two collections, *Book of Lyrics* (1955) and *New Poems* (1960), were experimental in quite different ways. Divided into groups entitled "Spring," "Summer," "Autumn," and "Winter," *Book of Lyrics* became a chronology of his periods of writing, thoughts, moods, and striving for perfection in poetic form. His themes are the delights in nature, the evanescence of beauty, and the mystery in human personality. Bynner's expression grew more subtle and quizzical as he grew older. Concealed in the cryptic and enigmatic phrasings of *New Poems* are meanings within meanings and statements that never completely come to a period—explaining why there is no punctuation anywhere. When the poet died on June 1, 1968, he had published fourteen volumes of poetry, nine of them after he came to Santa Fe in 1921. He also wrote plays, translations from the Chinese Jade Anthology, and two books of prose.

A type of lyric that is more dramatic than objective or introspective is found in a sonnet sequence called *The Ripened Fields*. It was written by Peggy Pond Church and appeared in a Quaker magazine, *Inward Light* (No. 46, Fall, 1954) and later issued in a privately printed booklet. These fifteen sonnets weave together the contests between two minds and hearts that hope to seal the contract of their marriage. The story begins in defiance, is maintained in strife, and is ended by the discovery that "love is two faces set toward one star . . . however far their separate paths may wander back and forth." *Ultimatum for Man* (1946, 1947) is Mrs. Church's statement that the frontiers for mankind have closed and men must learn to live within the boundaries of love or perish.

A number of Arizona writers with a surrealistic approach to poetry have published volumes in recent years. Peter Wild in *Mica Mountain Poems* (1968) and *Mad Night with Sunflowers* (1968) applies his image-creating mind to such phenomena as the moon over the desert, a deserted gas station, sand and cacti. His language draws upon both Spanish and English, and his feeling for Mexican village life is strong and explicit. Richard Shelton, too, is a regionalist who draws on the Sonoran desert near Tucson for themes. His first book *Journal of Return* (1969) contains a seventeen-poem series which incorporates Navajo symbology and myth. *The Tattooed Desert* (1970) has forty-eight poems using a wilderness tract to reflect a surrealistic quest for identity.

Lyrics of contrasting points of view are found in Neil Claremon's *East by Southwest* (1970) and Drummond Hadley's *The Webbing* (1967). Claremon brought his poetic gift from New York to Cortaro, Arizona. His poems have an Arizona setting, but his viewpoint is not that of a native in the region. Hadley is a longtime resident of Arizona, and his writing concerns the outdoor Southwest although he also writes short lyrics with personal themes. In style, Hadley's work shows the influence of the "projectionist" school of poets. *Alone I Wait* (1970) is a book of lyrical poems by Lynn Vanlandingham, a Phoenix architect, who finds in the Arizona landscape a mirror of man's moods and search for serenity. He illustrates his writing by pencil sketches and watercolors. The technical craftsman and the creative artist meet in words and drawings.

Jewels on a Willow Tree (1966), edited by Mabelle A. Lyon, is an anthology of poems in the haiku form. The subjects range from moments of meditation to moments of action, such as the haiku describing a little boy creating his own rainbow in a lawn sprinkler. C. Fayne Porter uses this poetic form to a purpose which is both lyric and narrative in his *Santa Fe in Haiku* (1970). The sections of the poem have a Prologue followed by five divisions, which are entitled "The Land," "The Indian," "The Spanish," "The Anglo," and "The Artist." The poem presents a panorama through imagery, memories, and lore found in the history of New Mexico's capital city. Alice Briley, editor of *Encore,* a poetry quarterly printed in Albuquerque, issued her own volume of poems in 1967 and named it *Program.* She added a subtitle with the words: "A Selection of Poems which I Frequently Choose for Reading Aloud," reminding readers that the first poetry was composed to be heard and was recited or read to listeners. Mrs. Briley's poems combine fantasy with amusing observation. "Need" is written about a town and a hill that seemed to belong together, and "Cherub" describes the transformation which occurs in a mischievous boy when he becomes an acolyte on Sunday.

John Gould Fletcher holds a secure place in the history of American poetry, both as an innovator in forms and as a traditionalist in cultural values. One of the leaders of the Imagist movement and the New Poetry in 1912 when *Poetry, A Magazine of Verse* appeared, Fletcher in his early years appeared to be more interested in aesthetics than in meaning as the purpose for writing poetry, and in his own words he states that his aim in writing was the "fusing of melody and vision," a definition of poetry beyond debate.[1] Born in Little Rock, student at Harvard, lecturer in many parts of the United States, and often a resident or visitor in Arkansas, Arizona, New Mexico, and Texas, his death on May 11, 1950, ended the enrichment he had brought to literature through his experimentation in free verse, lines of irregular length in rhyme artistically patterned, and in a type of elaborately rhythmed English called polyphonic prose.

In the year of Fletcher's death, Glenn Ward Dresbach, of Eureka Springs, Arkansas, published his *Collected Poems, 1914-1918,* the fruit of a long career. He had spent much of his life in the Southwestern states of New Mexico, Texas, and Arkansas, and the stamp of the environment is to be found in titles such as "A Desert Birdbath," "The Water-Finder," and "Valley of Gold." Lyrics descriptive of country life, along with

---

1. *Life Is My Song* (1937), p. 194.

portraits of individuals, often with observations which recall the method of Robert Frost, show the beauty and strength of his verse. The tradition of Ozark life was maintained by a younger poet, Edsel Ford, whose earlier volumes, *The Stallion's Nest* (1952), *The Manchild from Sunday Creek* (1956), *A Thicket of Sky* (1961), and *Love Is the House It Lives In* (1965), established him as one of the foremost interpreters of both past and present Arkansas. *Looking for Shiloh* (1968), a richer and more craftsmanlike volume, was published shortly before his death. Yet the message is the same: life is of one pattern; a boy's dreams are vibrant; and to one who returns, a native place may retain its charm.

Though some of her poems describe places and some constitute public statements, Sue Abbott Boyd is using her most typical expression when she conveys personal feelings through images sometimes from nature, sometimes from fantasy. She pictures people in "Abe" and "Three Hours Prior to a Poetry Day Banquet"; scenes in "Vacation" and "5 A.M."; and elusive moments in "A Knock at the Door" and "Many Fences to Mend." It is probable that in these mood pieces she finds her most individual voice. Such poems are to be found in *How It Is, Selected Poems, 1952-1968* (1968). Other books of poems by Mrs. Boyd are: *Of Sun and Stone* (1959), *Decanter* (1962), *The Sample Stage* (1964), and *Fort Smith and Other Poems* (1965).

Two young Arkansas poets with emotional and objective variety in poetic imagery are Eugenia Plunkett and John Wood. *If You Listen Quietly* (1969) by Miss Plunkett has sharp descriptions of scenes as the author employs apparently random but in fact carefully chosen details to portray humorous and wistful moments of human longing. Poems like "The Lesson Taken Out of Doors" and "The Moment Analyzed" display her gift for the unusual collocation of words and impressions of personalities. References to rich colors in *Orbs* (1968) allow Wood to provide a glittering surface for reactions to joy and love. Acrobatic wordplay and startling figures of imagination support Allen Ginsberg's reference, in his Introduction, to the "warm union phrases" found in Wood's poetry.

For over four decades, Rosa Zagnoni Marinoni wrote the

most popular poems in the Ozarks, publishing widely in periodicals and authoring several volumes of her sharp observations, sad and humorous, on emotions, on life, and especially on human types. A generous selection of her verse, *Timberline,* appeared in 1954, followed by *The Green Sea Horse* (1963) and *Lend Me Your Ears* (1965), a book of humorous poems published three years before her death. *Timberline* contains many of the comic epigrams and neatly stated familiar sentiments which appealed most to her reading public. *The Green Sea Horse* presents lyrics which in their complexity and imagery show an experimental departure from her earlier work: "A poet is a sea horse, never the perfect things; not mermaid with flowing hair, not Pegasus with wings." On March 3, 1969, the Arkansas legislature voted that October 15 be proclaimed Rosa Marinoni Day in the state.

Fantasy at the edge of reason characterizes the poetry of Clovita Rice, whose *Red Balloons for the Major* (1969) traces the patterns of thought and feeling from youth to maturity. Moreover, the balloons are symbolic of freedom, of the unclouded sky, the currents of air in which kites as well as balloons sail with controls of joy and pleasure. Yet poems entitled "Looking Back," "Aftermath," and "Portrait" tell a story of human relationships that make a family narrative interspersed with childhood games, trips to far places, and echoes of war.

Anna Nash Yarbrough is director of the Arkansas Writers Conference and a past president of the Poets' Roundtable. She is the author of *Flower of the Field* (1962) and of *Poetry Patterns* (1969), which contains both definitions of rhythms useful in writing English poetry and illustrations of stanza forms provided by the author. Variations of patterns in the sonnet, unusual rhyme schemes for lyrics, such as the villanelle, and exotic poetic measures like the haiku and senryu are discussed. Her poem "Wisdom of the Wood" has the lyric line: "This scarlet crimson, gold design is threaded through with gay bird song." Other members of the Poets' Roundtable and their publications are Lily Carmichael, *Across the Years* (1969); Etheree Armstrong, *The Willow Green of Spring* (1967); Marie Erwin Ward, *Swiftly the Years* (1968); Freda Hall, *The Spinner* (1967); May Gray, *The Voice of the Sea*

(1963); Laura Burnett Wessling, *Invisible Strings of Fate* (1970); Chester Bradley, *Nomad Fires* (1969); Addie Hedrick, *A Cup of Stars* (1969); and Etta Caldwell Harris, *Come Dreaming With Me* (1970). The work of these poets presents nature and mankind with faith and optimism, using traditional verse forms. Sybil Nash Abrams specializes in ballad measures for her contributions to *Laurel Branches* (1969), a book written with Lelus B. Nash and Anna Nash Yarbrough.

South and West is a literary association founded in 1962 with headquarters at Fort Smith, Arkansas. The association is devoted to the publication of books by poets and a poetry magazine named for the association. One of the founders of South and West is Betty Gosnell, who states in her booklet *The Poet Who Was a Painter of Souls* (1969) that poetry first sprang from village life where the boundaries of the world were those of the heart. She writes in free verse with occasional rhyme. Other members of South and West who have published books recently are Booker T. Jackson, *God Looks Down* (1968) and Marie Morris Rushing, *Five Golden Mice* (1969).

The poems in James Whitehead's *Domains* (1968) are almost equally divided between the lyric and the dramatic, often with social or philosophical overtones. Scenes of Mississippi as well as Arkansas appear in the unifying images, experiences, and characters of poems such as "One for the Road" and "The Opinions of an Interesting Old Man." "Tornadoes" is an example of the use of a brilliantly described event to reflect an attitude. Three books by Miller Williams present poetry ranging from themes about childhood to the violence of the contemporary scene. The titles are *A Circle of Stone* (1964), *So Long at the Fair* (1968), and *The Only World There Is* (1971). Many poems start with a lyric impulse that leads to a comment on a human situation, and some of the best, like "Notes on a Minister's Hymnbook" are pessimistic but sustained by hope. Williams' style, often difficult but never intentionally obscure, has the quality of both surprise and suspense. A careless reader may be impressed with Williams' cruelty and bitterness; a careful one will be left with a feeling of love and compassion.

People and places provoke a kaleidoscope of imagery by

the aspects of personality and the varieties of their back-grounds. Alice Gill Benton met Albert Schweitzer at a con-ference held in Aspen, Colorado, and she describes his "riot of unruly hair" and "brush of untamed eyebrows," calling the man "an honored fellow-pilgrim" who stood before his listen-ers as "a Titan, schooled in skill-carved hardihood." There are other memorable poems in her *Milestones* (1950). *See the Earth New* (1959) contains poems on the Penitentes of New Mexico, Malinche who served Cortez with courage, and the poet James Stephens. *Janus Had Two Faces* (1967) has word paintings in "Rio Grande" and "The Shalako Dance."

The poetry of Robert Lee Brothers is distinguished by pre-cision of phrase and by a keen, ironic insight into human charac-ter. Compression of utterance and an unexpected turn of language are qualities in which he excels. In *The Hidden Harp* (1952), this rancher poet has an eye for the strange and delicate in the outdoor scene, where he places such character studies as that of Deacon Dulby, who fatigues the saints with his long prayers, or of the family at Sunday dinner who gar-nish the servings with repressed resentments. Mr. Brothers has a quiet gift for irony in such poems as "Literary Tea" and "Possessed." The poems in this collection grow in significance with rereading, as do those in his *Democracy of Dust* (1947) and *Threescore and Ten* (1963).

Another poet who writes of ranch life, Walter E. Kidd (using the pen name "Conrad Pendleton"), employs no grandeur in *Slow Fire of Time* (1956) as he describes the harsh reality of cattle bawling against the first snow, or a cow calving in a snowstorm. *Time Turns West* (1961) continues themes from *Slow Fire of Time*: the hardships and courage of a dryland rancher, shown as a life of loneliness and frustration which sometimes erupts into violence. In this volume also appear a number of nature lyrics, of which perhaps the most moving describes a hanging mountain meadow. In *The Red Bull and Other Poems* (1963), Gene Shuford also writes of elemental things: the way a norther roars in on a wintry night, a flood beating down on the tent of an itinerant preacher, stallions thundering across the plains. He communicates the excitement of children discovering the joys of blackberrying, the desolateness of a sun sinking into a wintry landscape, and the anxiety of a world facing the threat of destruction. Shuford's images are bold, and he is equally the master of swinging rhythm, blank verse, and unfettered long lines. Faye Carr Adams, too, writes of scenes and characters in her native West Texas. The epic sweep of pioneer history is to be found in her volume of poems entitled *More Than a Loaf* (1968).

Rudolph Hill of Wewoka, Oklahoma, whose book *From Country Lanes to Space Age Dawn* (1968) contains ballads, narrative poems, and historical themes, finds imagery in dust storms becoming patterns for a square dance and war personified as an old man cutting a meadow with a scythe that separates no flower from grass or weeds. *Lariat Laughter and Other Poems* (1970) by Charles Price Green is also a volume of dynamic poems, a number of which picture life in the U.S. Navy. "Liberty Party" is one of these as its plot depends on vivid description of shore leave for twenty sailors with pay in their pockets and not a care in the world. Thomas Wellborn Hope's poetry reflects the freedom of America's way of life. In *The Great River and Other Poems* (1970) he lauds the early settlers and their efforts to forge a new state in Oklahoma. In "Times Square" he writes of cutting his ties with the West; yet he is still haunted by memories of "seas of grain and wild redbuds" when he buys a paper from home.

Winfield Townley Scott is another poet who associates people with places in many of his poems. Scott published eight books of poetry, but only two were written after he moved to Santa Fe in 1954. *The Dark Sister* (1958) has been discussed earlier in this chapter. *Scrimshaw* (1959) derives its title from a word naming the folk art of sailors who found time for bone carving with their jackknives on long ocean voyages. "Come Green Again," "Two Lives and Others," and "The Man at Mid-Century" are addressed to people the poet knew. Titles like "New Mexico" and "Frieda" (Lawrence) bear witness that Scott grew into the Southwestern environment. In *Exiles and Fabrications* (1961), a prose work, he has essays which deal with poets, some of whom lived for lengthy or short periods in New Mexico. He refers to poetry written in Taos by D. H. Lawrence as notable for "clusters of images"; to poems by Alice Corbin Henderson and Witter Bynner as distinctive for use of Indian culture; to lyrics by Haniel Long inspired by the countryside and narratives which interpret figures in the Spanish tradition. Scott concludes, however, that no single poet has possessed the land to the degree that Robinson Jeffers identified with the West Coast or Robert Frost with New England.

The titles of poems by Keith Wilson place him in the group who write of the conflicts people face and their struggles to find solutions. *Sketches for a New Mexico Hill Town* (1966) contains a gallery of portraits that become vivid for a reader: the grandmother whose stories keep her descendants mindful of warriors in the family and their women; the woodcarver who shapes cottonwood into images of the saints; the sheepherder standing in the rain; and black-shawled women who wait outside a church. *Homestead* (1969) has vivid episodes as Wilson re-creates scenes in the life he has lived in New Mexico, 1930-68: Indian ceremonials; a cowboy line camp; the branding fire; rustlers—one the victim of a rancher's bullet; boys no longer *compadres* but foes—Pachuco and Gringo; memories of Lincoln town—Billy the Kid; the scent of rain across the desert and in the hollow cones of lava beds. *The Old Car and Other Black Poems* (1967) and *Graves Registry* (1970) are two other books of Wilson's poetry.

William E. Bard writes of the Southwest landscape with firmly etched details and with bold, yet appropriate images. *This Land, This People* (1966) is written with a memory of the past, conscious of the history of the wilderness, recording events in depths of both space and time. Often Bard presents a broad canvas, and his best poems have a kind of epic sweep of detail and rhythm. Many of his poems deal with men and themes in Texas history; but he can write, too, delicately haunting lyrics, such as "This Is the Song."

Kneel from the Stone (1952) by William D. Barney shows striking originality in phrasing and liveliness of wit. In such precisely wrought lyrics as "Plainsman," "A State of Matter," "The Hill Hounds," and "Mosaic," the unexpected word and the fugitive image sharpen the impression. "The Gaffers" is a portrait poem which Barney develops with individual style. A second volume, *Permitted Proof* (1955), shows that he has mastered his spare, compressed line, and adapted it well to themes of the life that he knows. Many of the poems in this later volume appeal more to the intellect than to the senses.

Thomas Whitbread in *Four Infinitives* (1964) employs a variety of lyrical forms as he verbalizes his experiences and moods. The poems are grouped in a loose chronology as "To Observe," "To Remember," "To Enjoy," and "To Be." Whether about nature or people or people-made places and things, the poems are sensory and robust. There are also satirical poems, but without rancor or negativism. Many record the impressions of a mature man in the Southwest remembering his youth in the East. By contrast, most of the poems in Roger Shattuck's *Half Tame* (1964) are set in New England or in Europe, with only a few in the Southwest. He has a gift for capturing an unexpected experience, wherever the place: a French cafe with blind diners enjoying the orange marigolds; two boys playing ball, one standing in the sunshine, the other in the rain; his daughter, center of the world, at two, at nine, at nineteen.

Edgar Simmons in *Driving to Biloxi* (1968) writes also from a rich background of travel and study in America and Europe. A few poems in this volume are localized but most are of any time, any place. A number are addressed to or written about writers of the past and present: Chaucer, Whitman, Faulkner, John Crowe Ransom. All are original in concept and style. In R. G. Vliet's *Events and Celebrations* (1966) there are some thirty sense- and thought-appealing lyrics, plus a long character piece called "Clem Maverick" and two narrative prose poems, "The Journey" and "Ants." The poems are modern in structure and provocative in treatment. "Clem Maverick," about a country Western singer with his electric guitar and white Cadillacs, is a recital by his associates who, after his death at twenty-nine from an excess of adulation and liquor, recall experiences with their leader.

A group of poets consists of those who express protest and complaint, either by means of inner conflict or by carrying their discontent outside themselves against others. In these instances, literary objectives may be transferred to social objectives. In Robert Creeley's *For Love* (1962), the literary objective is certainly paramount, but internal protest with Creeley is expressed in the irony with which he views himself and others, as at once heroic and ridiculous, amusing and amused, exultant and suffering. In his Preface, he writes that his poems were "stumbled into" and recorded such experiences as warmth for a night or sudden instances of loving and being loved. In his second book, *Words* (1967), another introductory statement clearly indicates that, for Creeley, poetry is the feeling of a moment, a moment which he tries to capture in words. Yet such poems as "The Rhythm," "Variations," and "The Pattern" appear to be sustained reflection. *Pieces* (1969), a third book, is both cryptic and fragmentary. A number of the experimental, contemporary poets, Creeley among them, refer to their poems as "projections."[2] Protest is implicit in this concept of thrusting beyond an accepted line. Creeley's verse forms vary from traditional measures, and his poetic responses, in general, adhere to the doctrine of immediacy.

The themes in *Omphale's Wheel* (1966) by Archibald Henderson are disturbances in the psyche: the shock of encountering the facts of sex and tragedy at thirteen, the shame of disappointing a father by adolescent behavior, the conflict of moral restraint and desire in a sexual encounter. Dr. Henderson handles these situations with subtlety, and his effects are no less powerful for being indirect. His diction and images are arresting and appropriate to his bold probing of the subconscious. Another form of protest by irony is found in William Burford's *Man Now* (1954). The title poem, for example, shows in its spare, taut style awareness of the predicament of twentieth-century man and concern for the tremendous issues which confront him. Such selections as "The Sparrows" and "The Tomboy" achieve a powerful impact in a deceptively simple manner. Notable for economy of means are such poems as "The First Three Chapters," "Day of Sailing," and "The Solitary Man"; others, such as "At the Track" and "The Canebrake," are effective for their ironic twist. In this collection, as well as in two other books, *A World* (1962) and *A Beginning, Poems* (1966), Burford establishes himself as a strong poet with an individual style. *Messages from the Asylum* (1970) by Winston Weathers satirizes modern life in forty-eight sonnets that describe a world gone mad and the

---

2. *The New American Poetry* (1960), ed. Donald M. Allen, p. 409.

perverse definitions of what is beautiful, true, and good that hamper the development of his mind and spirit.

A didactic and philosophic point of view has dominated another group of Southwestern poets. "Didactic," as a term, may appear to be moralistic rather than imaginative, and "philosophic" will include the religious outlook. In both types of poetry, however, intellectual themes are sustained by imagination which explores imagery suggested by ideas. *This Way We Walk* (1964) by Robert Burlingame turns lyrics into sharply pointed meanings, as when a city park becomes the beginning of a good world for the poet strolling with his son, or when curbing nature with a sickle raises the ultimate problem of any restraint to natural growth, even by the dispatching of a weed. Burlingame's verses are turned out like sculptured strokes, smooth and unblemished. Goldie Capers Smith in *Deep in This Furrow* (1950) quotes Walt Whitman's line "In the faces of men and women I see God" before she outlines the grace of a performer in "Dancer." She describes the loneliness of Dorothy Wordsworth confiding in her *Journal.* Mrs. Smith's portraits of two presidents of the United States reveal the idealism deeply rooted in her thoughts and imagery. Jenny Lind Porter invokes the spirit of ancient philosophic quest in *The Lantern of Diogenes and Other Poems* (1954). In love with classic lore, she perfects her idiom in *Azle and the Attic Room* (1957) when she writes of the home place, the cedar trees fronting columns of the porch, and the place under the roof of the barn where books held more magic than at a desk in the house.

Edna Hull Miller, who was the wife of an Oklahoma Methodist minister, in her book, *Poems From a Parsonage* (1960), presents scenes that are serious with sorrow but also those that are joyous with the warmth and humor of living. Of the several hundred of poems in the book, all are reprinted from magazines to which she contributed for many years. In one of her poems, Mrs. Miller writes that she found subjects for poetry in "a trusting lover's heart, the sunset's wealth, the pocket of a bee, a songbird's lore, or a baby's first surmise." In "From a Hospital Window," she contrasts the "battle cry of birth" and surgery with the quiet comfort whispered by raindrops on the leaves.

Leslie A. McRill, patron and sponsor of poets in his home state, reflects the Oklahoma scene as well as a broader horizon in the nation. *Tales of the Night Wind* (1945) is a collection of poems on Indian lore. *Saga of Oklahoma* (1957) was written to celebrate the Semi-Centennial of the state. *Living Heritage* (1970) mirrors McRill's social concern as, in the poem "South Viet Nam," he questions whether "God's omniscient sight" wills that men wade in swamps and risk life for nameless and remote downtrodden men. Winston Weathers builds his *Indian and White, Sixteen Eclogues* (1970) on three themes: Indian history, the white man in Indian Territory, and the dissolution of the Old Southwest. Taken as a whole, these prose poems tell of a journey by a white narrator from the hills that embrace the Osage Nation to the country of other tribes in the state and then south into Texas. The narrator at lasts turns home having told the legends and characterized the peoples he has visited.

Thomas V. Calkins dedicates *Life in Many Facets* (1958) to "all folk who envisage—and strive together to create—a world life of peace and understanding for all people." Calkins was a strongly religious man, a counsellor to U.S. Army veterans, a man who felt concern over the pretence and error which could produce two World Wars. The "facets" in his book are labeled and they deal with human isolation, brotherliness, the compulsion of war, the ties between youth and age, the chain of existence. Calkins wrote poetry when he felt that he had something to say to his neighbors, family, and friends. What he said has affirmation and wisdom.

Into the view of human nature expressed by the poetry of Bryon Chew goes a mixture of faith and skepticism. His book *Strange Island* (1959) contains poems such as "Sea-Change" and "Storm" which stress loneliness, but "Leto" and "Voice in the Wind" share the joy of light and music. "To the Rebel Cain" expresses comradeship with the guilty one, not the innocent; yet "Duality" proclaims love for both. *Corrida and Other Poems* (1966) centers mainly on a colorful series of word pictures of the *plaza de toros* and the neighborhood where beggars, bars, and litter in the street accompany the fight inside the ring with its cheers, excitement and the death of the bull. Some of the other poems are "Mathematics Teacher,"

"The Evangelist," and "Antiphon for Tomorrow." Chew writes in stanzas that are rhymed and unrhymed, but with or without the echo of sound, his lines are always vivid.

Vassar Miller's poems are intensely spiritual. Her themes are the old ones of suffering, death, and love, but her language is always fresh and the imagery surprising. She makes use of traditional verse forms, giving them the force of controlled response and intensity of feeling. Four volumes represent her work in the last decade: *Adam's Footprint* (1956), *Wage War on Silence* (1960), *My Bones Being Wiser* (1963), and *Onions and Roses* (1968). There is constant development in technique, with an elaboration of some of her imagery that recalls the poetry of John Donne and the metaphysical poets of his time.

The poems in *Furrow with Blackbirds* (1951) by Arthur M. Sampley draw on the world of nature and events past and present in seeking answers to the riddles of life. One group of eight poems, called "Southwest by Sun," celebrates the infinite variety of the region from the Texas Big Bend to the Pacific. The title poem asserts the interdependence of all things: the earth, the plower, the horse, the blackbirds swooping down to peck the straw stubble and rising to "furrow the sky." Philosophic resolution to challenge the elements is the theme of two poems, "Desert Hunger" and "Night Flight," found in an earlier volume called *Of the Strong and the Fleet* (1947). Sampley's medium as a poet is both mature and eloquent.

Wit and humor have a never-ceasing appeal, encasing profundity as well as irony and always merriment. The penned gems of Mary M. Parrish in *How the World Wags* (1959) first appeared in periodicals as diverse as the *Saturday Review* and the *Wall Street Journal*. They are grouped under headings such as "The Fashion of These Times," "Frailty, Thy Name is Woman," and "Youth, I do Adore Thee," but whether observation covers the warm bath where the bather still wears her wrist watch or the birthdays she adores at fifteen, deplores at thirty, ignores as sixty, and restores at eighty, Mrs. Parrish is supremely in command of the elements of human comedy and the phrases to describe it.

A light-hearted series of poems called *Verse or Worse*

(1963) has all the solidity and wisdom nurtured by a human spirit that waited a lifetime for the courage to speak. The author, Cecil D. Basham of Phoenix, died in 1967, having lived to know that his poems were published and appreciated. The poem "Implications of Infinity" records speculation about what mortals would do if they were omnipotent. He concludes that they would be less responsive and effective than the God they have conceived and worship. History in the "present tense" and time as non-existent would leave only solitude without the "rules of finitude."

Editors of anthologies customarily make statements about their aims and procedures in planning a volume. In 1950 the editors of *Signature of the Sun, Southwest Verse, 1900-1950* stated that they were trying to discover the character of poetry in the region by beginning with what was created in the oldest settlements, Indian, and then proceeding to verses written in the Rio Grande country, the prairies, the woodlands, and the coastal plains. Following this statement in which nature seems to be conditioning certain poetic statements, the editors pointed to regional patterns that might be reflected in agriculture, ranching, oil fields, and even professional and educational fields. The book is divided into eight sections, each with a critical essay. Five of the sections are based on geographical regions, and the others have the sky and air flight, World War II, and subjective emotion to guide the selection of poems. One hundred and twenty-four poets contributed to *Signature of the Sun,* edited by Mabel Major and T. M. Pearce, and the Notes on Authors has been, perhaps, the best annotated bibliography available for books on poetry by writers living in the Southwest before 1950.

A more recent anthology, *Poems Southwest* (1968), edited by A. Wilber Stevens, includes poems from thirty contributors, ten of whom live in California, Nevada, Colorado, and Old Mexico—areas outside the five-state survey in *Southwest Heritage.* Eight of the twenty other writers have been considered separately in this chapter: Robert Burlingame, Witter Bynner, Arthur Sampley, Winfield Townley Scott, Edgar Simmons, Winston Weathers, Peter Wild, and Keith Wilson. Of the remaining twelve poets, four are from Texas: W. H. Acker, Haldeen Braddy, Judson Crews, and R. M. Russell;

five are from Arizona: Marilyn Francis, Paul Malanga, J. D.
McGeehee, Lester Ward Ruffner, and Harry Wood; and three
are from New Mexico: Joseph M. Fergusson, S. Stanley
Noyes, and Wendell Anderson. *Poems Southwest* represents
editorial preference for modes of statement and dimensions of
language in poetry defined by George Steiner in *Language and
Silence* (1967) as "light, music, and silence." The absence of
Indian and Spanish-American poets is admitted to be an omis-
sion to be repaired in a future volume.

The imagination of the poet feeds on what it finds, both
through the senses and through the mind. Every poet creates
an individual world, shaping it after his or her own fancy. He
expects the reader to enter this world and for this purpose he
gives his book a title which will arouse interest. Once the cover
of the book has been turned, the author hopes his guest will
find meaning and beauty in the world he has entered. This
chapter provides a guide to these varied worlds, each distinctive and each with its own type of poetic reality.

VI

LITERATURE FOR YOUNG READERS

In the second edition of *Southwest Heritage,* a new chapter was added which was called "Literature for Children." The editors of the third edition have chosen to call the chapter "Literature for Young Readers." Librarians no longer mark the catalogue cards according to the school grades for which the books may have been written, recognizing that neither authors nor librarians can determine what level of reading interest a child may have. Any young person should be free to choose any book on the shelf, selecting it by his own judgment and standards. We have, therefore, written this chapter to point out areas of subject matter and to direct young people to groups of books rather than to a level of vocabulary in them or their adaptability to elementary, junior, or senior high school libraries.

In 1948 we stated that literature for young readers in the Southwest was first written by folklorists who explored the Indian and Spanish backgrounds for stories about the customs, nature lore, folktales, work and play activities in rural communities and reservations where non-Anglos lived. There was also a section on pioneer Anglo-American explorers of forest and trail, and the early settlers who followed them into a country new to eastern travelers but old to people already living in the Southwest. Books of regional history and geography, stories of fantasy and imagination were available then, and additional titles in these areas of reading are recommended now.

What is new in this second survey of books for young people is the increased number of titles about the history of each individual state, their technical and cultural advances, with biographies of the individuals who have contributed to this progress. The division of Indian, Spanish, and Anglo traditions is still observed, but the intermingling is more noticeable today than it was twenty years ago. Organized sports have more space in the reading lists today than in the past. We repeat our comment that the cultures of many peoples in the

Southwest have provided writers with abundant materials, and we recommend their books to young people of all ages and tastes.

The earliest explorers of the Southwest were led to the region by rumors of treasure and great cities. In *Riding with Coronado* (1964), Robert Meredith and E. Brooks Smith quote Castañeda's eyewitness account in 1540: "We did not find the riches we had been told of, but time has given us a chance to understand where we were and what a good country we had in our hands." Camilla Campbell, in *Coronado and His Captains* (1958), after retelling the story of the explorer, states that he was "daring, competent, loyal, and humane." However, Coronado's men were not the first Europeans to explore the Southwest. Twelve years earlier, the Spanish governor of Cuba, Pamfilo de Narvaez, led a a company of six hundred men into Florida to explore the land. Disobeying orders, half of them returned in their ships to Cuba, and nearly all of the others were lost through sickness, battles with the Indians, or shipwreck in crude barges they had constructed without adequate tools or materials. Four men who were tossed up on the shore of Galveston Bay spent the next eight years among the Indians of West Texas and southern New Mexico, crossing through what is now Arizona before they arrived at the Gulf of California and returned to Mexico City.

An engrossing account of this journey is found in Betty Baker's *Walk the World's Rim* (1965), where Chakoh, an imagined Indian boy, is portrayed in the actual company of Cabeza de Vaca, Alonso Maldonado, Andres Dorantes, and his Negro slave Esteban. The slave becomes a hero to Chakoh as the Indian boy learns his desire for freedom. The slave leads two priests and a small company back to Cibola, which he had been told was a place of many storied houses and richer than the city of Mexico. When Esteban is killed by the Indians of Zuñi, who thought he was the forerunner of Spanish slave traders, his life ends a course which began in Spain, led to Cuba, to Florida, to Mexico, and at last to Cibola. He had walked the world's rim, "like a blind horse chained to a water wheel."

There are other fine histories for both elementary and high school readers. Walter Buehr's *The Spanish Conquistadores in North America* (1962) begins with the earliest European invaders who saw the glories of Montezuma's palace and the temples of Tenochtitlan; he tells how the missionaries in Mexico and the Southwest accomplished the religious conversion of the natives. Henry G. Castor in *The Spanish-American West* (1963) includes all the territory from the Red River to Cape Mendocino near San Francisco as the area traversed by the conquistadors. He points out how those who followed in their steps introduced sheepherding, cattle raising, advanced forms of agriculture, and other civilizing arts and crafts. Although they adopted much from the Indians, they contributed more to what they found in the native culture. Lynn I. Perrigo entitles his historical survey *Rio Grande Adventure* (1964) and defines the region in terms of the precipitation of moisture, the wildlife, and plant zones. This causes him to limit the study to New Mexico, Arizona, Texas, and the areas of California where similar environmental characteristics prevail.

A number of state histories give more detailed accounts of the streams of migration which filtered into the vastness of the Southwest. E. B. Mann and Fred E. Harvey in *New Mexico, Land of Enchantment* (1955) delve into the archaeological periods of human settlement 23,000 B.C. and then summarize written history during the sixteenth-century Spanish chronicles and the later Anglo-American accounts ending with statehood. *New Mexico* (1967) by Jack Schaefer is one of a series planned to show young readers the individuality of the various states in the Union. George and Mildred Fitzpatrick in *New Mexico for Young People* (1965) have chapters devoted to the mingling of Indian, Spanish, and Anglo-American cultures; and Ruth Armstrong's *New Mexico, From Arrowhead to Atom* (1969) begins with geologic time before summarizing the historic periods of conquest and colonization. For the youngest reader, *A Child's Story of New Mexico* (1960) by Ann Nolan Clark and Frances Carey awakens the imagination by describing the dinosaurs which left their tracks in fossil remains on the arid plains now being reclaimed by irrigation and explored for mineral wealth.

Siddie Joe Johnson in *Texas, the Land of the Tejas* first published in 1943 and republished in a revised edition in 1950, presents an overall view of the broad sweep of land between

the Rio Grande and the Red River. She remembers her childhood on the Gulf in *Feather in My Hand* (1967), a book of
thirty-nine graceful poems about seagulls, snails, kittens, kites,
ponies, boats, and all the other delights enjoyed by a child.
The poems are imaginatively illustrated by Barbara J. McGee.

J. Frank Dobie's *Up the Trail from Texas* (1955) shows
by its title how he means to define the individuality of his
native state. He notes that the cattle kingdoms of Europe were
transferred to Texas, but points out that there were no kings on
the unfenced lands where small frame houses were the center
of pioneer ways of living. William Weber Johnson begins *The
Birth of Texas* (1960) with the march of Santa Anna's army
toward San Antonio de Bejar in 1836. After the Mexican
general was defeated at San Jacinto on April 21, 1836, Texas
became a republic, one of two American states which ever
enjoyed this status. Vermont was the other, from 1777 to
1791. Texas entered the Union by decree of President Polk
on December 29, 1845. Robert Penn Warren in *Remember the
Alamo* (1958) tells the story of Texas beginning with the
situation which led to the revolt against Mexico. He stresses
the siege of the Alamo and concludes with the victory at San
Jacinto when the Texans were stirred by the battle cry which
is the title for his book.

Allan Carpenter is the author of a group of colorful,
outline-like histories in the Enchantment of America Series.
Each begins with "A True Story to Set the Scene," which is a
spectacular episode still remembered in that individual state.
Then, after this arresting flashback, sections of historic, economic, and sociological interest follow. Under the heading
"Human Treasures" are listed the best known people in each
state, such as those associated with politics, industry, and the
arts. Volumes for *Arizona* (1966), *Arkansas* (1967), *New
Mexico* (1967), *Oklahoma* (1965), and *Texas* (1965) have
appeared in the series.

Geography enriched with views of people and places is
found in Bernadine Bailey's series: *Picture Book of Texas*
(1950), *Picture Book of Arizona* (1960), and *Picture Book
of New Mexico* (1960). Virginia Moffitt introduces stories as
well as facts to inform young readers about Texas history in
Broad Skies of Freedom (1949). Stories also are the means

of conveying history in *True Tales of Texas* (1949) by Bertha May Cox. *Oklahoma, Footloose and Fancy Free* (1949) by Angie Debo is imaginative as well as factual. In the same year appeared Edward E. Dale's *Oklahoma, The Story of a State* (1949), a somewhat more classroom type of presentation. Both are excellent reference books.

Many books dealing with history in the Southwest describe events against the background of *llanos* or plains where water-holes are "far-between," where mountains fringe the sky, and where arroyos cut through wastelands. Few landscapes allure the eye as does the terrain of the Southwest. Writers find the scene absorbing and their books appear for readers of every age. *Elf Owl* (1958) by Mary and Conrad Buff looks at the desert and its inhabitants from the viewpoint of a giant saguaro cactus. Clear descriptions in words, supplemented by photographs of desert plants and animals, are presented by Harriet E. Huntington in *Let's Go to the Desert* (1949). Ann Nolan Clark takes the stranger with her in *Along Sandy Trails* (1969), where he will find the creatures living as described by Terry Shannon in *Desert Dwellers* (1958) and by Olive L. Earle in *Strange Lizards* (1964). George O. Whitaker confirms the existence of fantastic monsters by the information in *Dinosaur Hunt* (1965). All these stages of biology seem recent in the time cycle revealed by the Carlsbad Caverns described by Mabel Otis Robison in *The Hole in the Mountain* (1966). She tells how Jim White saw bats streaming from the entrance of the cave and pushed burning brands of dead cacti into the entrance to determine the depth. This was in 1901, long before he built cabins for travelers and served as a guide until the fame of the caverns grew to where the United States Government recognized them as a world marvel. In 1923 the site became a National Monument. These underground chambers and other national monuments are described by Frances Wood in *Rocky Mountain, Mesa Verde, Carlsbad Caverns* (1963).

Archaeology as history is written in people's handiwork, that is, how they designed and built their houses, furnished them, stored food and prepared it, defended their villages and attacked their foes, buried the dead and thought about life after death. The archaeologist uncovers these facts when he finds ruins in the earth, but he may also discover such artifacts above the earth and join the anthropologist in comparing pre-historic objects and beings with their historic and living coun-terparts. Gordon C. Baldwin traces the story of Southwestern archaeology in *The Ancient Ones* (1963). He dates the period of the earliest Basket Makers from A.D. 1-450 and begins the historic period of the Cliff Dwellers with the year 1600. He believes that the Navajos and the Utes may have been in the Southwest three hundred years earlier. The Pueblos began to build towers for defense as early as 1259 and abandoned their great villages at Chetro Ketl and Mesa Verde between 1276 and 1299. Oliver La Farge's *The American Indian* (1960), Special Edition for Young People, treats of the Pueblo Indians and the Plains Indians, discussing their pottery, weaving, jew-elry, and customs.

A closer look at the Pueblo builders is made by R. B. Marcus in *First Book of the Cliff Dwellers* (1968). He and Mary Elting, who wrote *The Secret Story of Pueblo Bonito* (1957), make the reader aware that these native peoples created their impressive architecture as part of their communal way of life. They had even created an elementary type of sky science to mark the seasons with ceremonies, altar drawings, and pictographs. However, they left no written language or books to commemorate their achievements. Today the great apartment houses stand free or under shelves of rock, silent and mysterious, but the onlookers can read in ruined kivas and towers stories perhaps as dramatic as those remaining from Asia Minor or the Orient.

L. Lee Floethe in *The Indian and His Pueblo* (1960) points out how the Southwestern climate has influenced the first Americans in their practices and beliefs. Sidney Fletcher makes use of brilliantly colored pictures in *Big Book of Indians* (1950) to illustrate the everyday life of various tribes. Harry James wrote *A Day in Oraibi, A Hopi Indian Village* (1959) to show how a white boy lives with Hopi children at the village; and Sonia Bleeker enables the reader to follow a Pueblo boy as he learns to work in the fields, hunt, and dance the cere-monies of his tribe as she reports them in *The Pueblo Indians, Farmers of the Rio Grande* (1965). Some other books on the Indians as craftsmen and artists are Sonia Bleeker, *The*

Navajo, Herders, Weavers, Silversmiths (1958); Ann Nolan Clark, *Little Indian Pottery Maker* (1955) and *Little Indian Basket Maker* (1957); Shirley Glubok, *Art of the North American Indian* (1964); and Robert Hofsinde, *Indian Music Makers* (1967).

Catherine Coblentz, writing about one of the best known Indian women of the Southwest in *Ah-yo-ka, Daughter of Sequoya* (1950), shows how the girl helps her father to spread knowledge of the Cherokee alphabet so that the Indians may learn of their origin and wanderings. A more general book on domestic arts and homelife of these Americans is *Indian Women* (1964) by Lela and Rufus Waltrip. A book which gives the background of Oklahoma Indians is Mary Elting's *First Book of Indians* (1950).

When a writer employs certain techniques of fiction in presenting history, the account gains a living quality, even though it may lose some factuality. People and events spring to life in Thelma C. Nason's *Under the Wide Sky* (1965). Historic personages such as the explorer Zebulon Pike, the commander Stephen Kearny, and the pioneering scientist Robert H. Goddard speak to their followers and friends, telling them of the hardships as well as the triumphs in the periods when these events occurred. Maude Davis Crosno and Charlie Scott Masters in *Discovering New Mexico* (1950) bring in facts, legends, and personal accounts with the thread of stories binding the whole together. If the young reader wants to learn about the earliest time of Anglo-American penetration into the Indian-Spanish Southwest, he should consult Don Berry's *Mountain Men* (1966), where he will meet the great trappers in the fur trade from 1822 to 1843, among them such famous men as Jim Bridger, Kit Carson, and Jedediah Smith. Marion T. Place animates the way of the traders, soldiers, and emigrants in *The Santa Fe Trail* (1966). The procession moves over a longer distance than the travelers on Chaucer's journey from London to Canterbury, but the events from Independence, Missouri, to Santa Fe, New Mexico, are more varied and the accommodations even less secure.

Samuel H. Adams in *The Pony Express* (1950) and Robert Pinkerton in *First Overland Mail* (1953) dramatize the hazardous route of the riders who carried messages through the Rocky Mountains to California from 1858 until 1861 when the Civil War sent soldiers on the same path as the couriers. The stations were called the Butterfield Line for the owner John Butterfield, an Albany, New York, expressman and organizer of the 2800-mile route from eastern points through El Paso and Tucson to Los Angeles. Horses and men fell victim both to the Confederates and to the Apaches, who were led by Cochise in Arizona and by Mangas Coloradas in New Mexico.

Overland Stage (1961) by Glen Dines has expert drawings of the Concord coaches and the loop harness used to draw the coaches in the 1860's. The carriages were colored vermilion, yellow, red, and black, with pictures of landscapes or famous people painted on the doors. Panels, wheels, and ironwork were marked with stripes, and even the undercarriage was painted and trimmed. Leather braces were used as "springs" on the coaches and gave a swinging motion, forward and back, over the roughest roads. All the passenger and freighting service ended when the continent was crossed by railroads. Wheels of hickory were succeeded by wheels of steel.

A broad stretch of the Southwest is covered in a tour by Anne Merriman Peck, as she reports in *Southwest Roundup* (1950). Her journal begins in San Antonio, a Texas shrine, and moves across the plains to El Paso, gateway to the North. Then the reader is carried up the Rio Grande Valley to Albuquerque and Santa Fe. The trip includes stops at Acoma and Zuñi; and passes into Arizona for stops at Bisbee, Phoenix, and Tucson. *Santa Fe* (1965) by Elizabeth L. Crandall is a book in the Cities of the World Series. Dallas is included among the choices made by Nina Brown Baker in *Ten American Cities* (1949). Perhaps no highway or guide is more universal than a river, and two books for young readers use the greatest stream in the Southwest for this purpose. Alexander L. Crosby in *The Rio Grande* (1966) and Armstrong Sperry in *Great River, Wide Land* (1967) trace the history of the Rio Grande in western America. The first book stresses pictorial and descriptive backgrounds; the second emphasizes cultural history in great detail.

More fiction about Indians appears in Arizona, Oklahoma, and New Mexico than in Arkansas or Texas. Few of the

Indians in Oklahoma, in contrast to those in Arizona and New Mexico, now live on reservations. Stories of Oklahoma Indians are likely to concern their advances toward integration into the whiteman's culture. The native Indians of Oklahoma, the Five Civilized Tribes (after they were transplanted to the Territory between 1817 and 1832), and tribes moved in after the Civil War experienced assimilation into Anglo-American civilization much earlier than did the Indians farther south and west. The Cherokees in Indian Territory began to print a newspaper in Cherokee and English as early as 1844. It was called the *Cherokee Advocate* and appeared a hundred years before any such publication was printed by other Southwestern Indians.

Lucille Mulcahy has written two novels which deal with families in the pre-European Southwest. The home of Flying Eagle, the central figure in *Dark Arrow* (1953), is in a cliff village at Posuge Canyon, which could be the site of present-day Bandelier National Monument north of Santa Fe. The scenes of Mrs. Mulcahy's *Natoto* (1960) may be Chetro Ketl or Pueblo Bonito, called the Great House in the novel, where a love affair occurs between Kimmu and the heroine for whom the novel is named. In both of Mrs. Mulcahy's stories the climax arrives when the Pueblans are invaded by people from the Plains who are called the Wanderers in one novel and the Long Heads in the other. The author makes this early civilization in America seem as real as life is today. Mary and Conrad Buff select the Four Corners area—where Utah, Colorado, New Mexico, and Arizona meet—as the home of a Ute boy who is deserted by his tribe and adopted by Pueblans in the canyons. The story, which is called *Hah-nee of the Cliff-Dwellers* (1965), takes place in the last half of the thirteenth century. A great drought occurs and the medicine men blame the adoption of an alien boy. With his foster parents, Hah-nee flees for refuge to people in a valley to the south, where a river flows which is later called the Rio Grande.

Some stories are written about a period that seems timeless, neither ancient nor modern. Terry Shannon's *Little Wolf, The Rain Dancer* (1954) presents a Zuñi boy who is chosen to dance as the Fire God in a ceremony to bring rain. Through his honesty and perseverance he is able to win this place and to help bring the much needed moisture. Shannon is also the

author of *Running Fox, The Eagle Hunter* (1957). Mary
Perrine's *Salt Boy* (1968) creates a boy who could exist at any
time in the Southwest. He wants to learn to handle a rope as
his father does; so he practices roping his sheep. When his
father watches Salt Boy use the rope to rescue a lamb from
drowning in an arroyo, he decides that the boy is ready to work
as a man with horses. Ann Nolan Clark has a Papago boy tell
about the old customs in *The Desert People* (1962). Betty
Baker recounts the transition time from independence to
reservation days for the Apache tribe in *Killer-of-Death*
(1963). Grace Moon reveals the emotions of any four-year-
old boy in *One Little Indian* (1950). When his mother offers
Ah-Di a surprise on his birthday, both of them are surprised by
what he finds outside the hogan. The story of an Indian boy
and his pony is told by Donald Worcester in *Lone Hunter's
First Buffalo Hunt* (1958). In the year when the scouts fail
to find a buffalo herd, Lone Hunter and his friend, Buffalo
Boy, succeed in locating not only buffalo but also enemy warriors waiting to attack. Using smoke signals they alert their
own warriors who drive off the enemy. Then the boys are
taken on their first hunt and are initiated as hunters and warriors as well.

During territorial days, the Oklahoma Indians were assigned tracts of land. Beginning in 1889 they saw Anglos
rush into all the unassigned parts of what had been called
Indian Territory. Historic scenes are detailed by Eugene
Campbell Barker and others in *Our New Nation* (1949).
Althea Bass, also an Oklahoma writer, portrays the present-
day Senecas in *The Thankful People* (1950), showing modern
Indians who hold to many of the former tribal ways. More
sympathy than conflict appears between old and young in her
book, and the "winter-telling" of legends lends constant interest. Conflict is revealed by Natachee Scott Momaday, whose
Owl in the Cedar Tree (1965) builds a plot around two an-
tagonisms, one of which is personal and another, cultural.
Haske, a Navajo boy, is led by his grandfather to believe that
the white man's school will mislead him, but Haske's parents
persuade the boy that he must learn the new customs. When
the schoolteacher urges the boy to draw with colored crayons,
he portrays a battle scene his grandfather once described. The

teacher sends the drawing to an exhibition where it wins a prize. With the money, the boy purchases a horse from the white trader, who gives the boy a saddle and a bridle in return for the next two pictures he paints.

Stories which show sympathy and helpfulness between the two races, Indians and white people, are more common today than they were twenty years ago. The title of Lois Duncan's book *Season of the Two-Heart* (1964) is symbolic as it shows how the best in two cultures can be combined. Ann Nolan Clark's story, *Medicine Man's Daughter* (1963), is also a novel that builds a bridge between the two worlds, Indian and non-Indian. *Magic Fingers* (1958) by Lucille Mulcahy discloses the secret of Indian pottery making, as well as provides a mystery story in which the theft of a silver-headed cane is solved. The cane had been given by President Lincoln as the staff of authority in Isleta Pueblo and the theft is tied to the jealous owner of a potter's wheel. *Fire on Big Lonesome* (1967), also by Miss Mulcahy, combines fiction with actual fire fighting in California by a Zuñi Indian company called the Red Hats. Photographs of parachuting behind the fire lines add realism to the story.

No reader, young or old, can understand the region in which he lives unless he knows about the animals that give that region identity and help to sustain human life there. Books dealing with animals vary from the purely biological to the fictional, and sometimes the line between the two can be close. George Franklin's informative books about the wild fauna in the Southwest are based on what he learned from the Indians when he lived in a cabin on Lake Fork River, a branch of the Gunnison in southern Colorado. His stories of the antelope, porcupine, coyote, bighorn sheep, and other beasts are reported in *Wild Animals of the Five Rivers Country* (1947). In *Wild Animals of the Southwest* (1950), he adds stories dealing with the black fox, buffalo, skunk, panther, lynx, grizzly, badger, and elk. All these animals are given names referring to their appearance or behavior, and the stories have plots appropriate to situations that are believable and exciting.

Loyd S. Tireman in 1943 began his Mesaland Series, stories chiefly about small animals with names like Jumping Jack Rabbit; Cocky, a roadrunner; Big Fat, a prairie dog;

and Quills, a porcupine. The final volume in the series is devoted to a larger creature, a coyote, whose adventures are
described in *3-Toes* (1950). William Morgan, also, has the
prairie wolf as the central character of his *Coyote Tales*
(1949), where legends are told of the prankster who, according to Navajo mythology, brought fire from the black gods
and scattered stars to make the Milky Way. It is difficult to
give a pleasant personality to a rattlesnake, but Robert Mc-
Clung comes as near as possible in *Buzztail* (1958). His
rattlesnake is the biggest on the mountainside and, as the story
develops, Buzztail defeats another rattler, mates and fathers
a brood of little rattlers, and survives a brush with a bobcat.
The fascination in the book depends on details about rattlesnakes, their swivel-jointed jaws and the venom channels in
their fangs. Rattlesnakes also appear in Betty B. Herndon's
Adventures in Cactus Land (1950) and in Allan R. Bosworth's *Rattlesnake Run* (1968). There are many more insects, birds, and mammals in Terry Shannon's *Desert Dwellers*
(1958), where the creatures that sleep during the hot days
come alive in the coolness of the nights.

Some animals just lend themselves to personification more
easily than do others. They are more like people, as was
Sancho, the central character in John H. Latham's *Lonesome
Longhorn* (1951). This spotted black-and-white steer became
a member of the Jess Cob family after they found him in a bog-
hole beside his dead mother. Not even a trail drive to Montana, with stampedes, flooded rivers, and wolves could separate
him from the people who were his friends. An old beaver fights
like a fierce grandfather to defend his colony from a lynx and
at the same time saves a boy's life in *Chip, the Dam Builder*
(1950) by James A. Kjelgard. The characters in Van Clark's
Peetie the Pack Rat (1950) have engaging personalities, as
Bennie the Burro finds his twenty-foot shadow the funniest
thing he has ever seen, and Sidney Centipede discovers his feet
can run faster without shoes.

To a degree, fiction about Spanish life in the Southwest has
a background similar to fiction about Indian life. The Pueblo
people resisted the Plains Indians, then traded with them and
shared a vast terrain, exchanging some ceremonies and customs,
some sports and pastimes, some techniques of hunting and fish-

ing. The Spanish, too, were invaders, and story plots grow from how they occupied the land, introduced livestock and agricultural plants, embraced what they could of the Indian civilization in America and later assimilated much that was useful in Anglo-American culture. Florence C. and Carl Means in *The Silver Fleece* (1950) place the Rivera children, Domingo and Lucia, as young settlers in colonial New Mexico. When they arrive with their uncle, Don José, and their mother, Doña Leonora, Santa Fe has just been reconquered by Don Diego de Vargas in 1692. Lucia's greatest possession is her pet lamb, *Tuson de Plata,* or "Silver Fleece." Events in the story tell how the new herd of sheep eventually is combined with the herd preserved during the decade of the family's exile. *Pancho, A Dog of the Plains* (1958) is the story of a sheep dog that guards the herd against the menace of Apaches. Bruce Grant, the author, tells how the Texas Rangers adopt both the dog and its young master before the Indian attacks come to an end.

Two delightful tales of sheepherding in the modern period are *And Now Miguel* (1953) by Joseph Krumgold and *Old Ramon* (1960) by Jack Schaefer. Miguel has the typical problems of any pre-teen boy. He is too big to play all the day and too young to go to the sheep camp with the herders. He does chores in the corral, but the mountains draw him as nothing else does. The climax comes when he carves his name on an old tree at the mountain crest, where the sheep men in his family have carved their names in the past. In the Schaefer book, the boy is about Miguel's age and his teacher at the sheep camp is an old herder who worked for the boy's grandfather. There is more of dogs and herding in Schaefer's book, and more of lambing and shearing in Krumgold's, but both are master works of the life which characterizes northern New Mexico in the way that cattle ranches dominate along the borders of the state to the east and west.

In the Spanish villages, there were contrasts to city ways as presented in *House Under the Hill* (1949), another Southwestern book by Florence Crannell Means. In this story, the young people want to exchange their old-fashioned homes for city apartments and when they do, the results are not entirely satisfactory. In *The Blue Marshmallow Mountains* (1959), Lucille Mulcahy combines mystery with problems of village communities, but in her book *Pita* (1954) all the problems are those of romance as her heroine overcomes family feuds and even troubles between the towns of Little Plaza and Three Coyotes over the ditch.

Uncomplicated, by contrast, is life in the Apodaca family, who in Margaret Embry's *Peg-Leg Willy* (1966) rescue one of their turkeys from the coyotes and become so devoted to him that they cannot sacrifice him on the *Día de Gracias* (Thanksgiving). *Amigo* (1968) by Byrd Baylor Schweitzer is another sympathetic story about children and pets, although only one boy is involved and the pet is a prairie dog, which he tames when his family cannot afford to let him have a real dog as a companion.

Stories of the Southwest where much of the population is Spanish illustrate the imagination and religious faith of young people. *Paco's Miracle* (1962) by Ann Nolan Clark centers about an orphan boy who is adopted by a French trapper living near Taos. Paco is friendly with the animals, and when a storm prevents delivery of packages for the festival on Christmas Eve, the animals show the boy where the piñon nuts are hidden and where to find cedar berries, wild honey, and mistletoe. The festival is merry and beautiful as a consequence. *Las Posadas* (1963) is the story of nine days before Christmas, as told by James Fraser, and *One Luminaria for Antonio* (1966) by Flora Hood concerns the one candle a boy lights for the Christ Child to bless. William Jones Wallrich tells stories of religious mysticism in *The Strange Little Man in the Chili-Red Pants* (1949).

Books in more than one language are rare, although such books should be in great demand in the Southwest. *Spanish Nuggets* (1968) by Rosemary Holman offers familiar quotations and proverbs with Spanish words on one page and English on the other. The half-tone drawings help the translations in both tongues. Two books written in Navajo as well as English encourage readers in each language. Hildegard Thompson's *Preprimer and Primer* (1953) in the Navajo Life Series is used by grade school children, and Jack L. Crowder's little story entitled *Stephanie and the Coyote* (1969) has beautiful pictures to lend graphic interest to his text.

If the average American—north, east, south, or west—

associates one word with the Southwest, it is likely to be the word "cowboy." That term includes all the other expressions that name what the cowboy wears, eats, and does day in and day out. He was called by various names: caballero, vaquero, buckaroo, cowpoke, cowhand, waddie, brush-popper, ranahan, and rannie. According to Mary Elting (whose pseudonym is Benjamin Brewster), a cowboy who lives all by himself is called a "sourdough." Michael Gorham in *The Real Book About Cowboys* (1952) lists the terms used in cowboy lingo as he informs the reader how rodeos began and the skills they call for. *Rodeo, Bulls, Broncos, and Buckaroos* (1949) by Glen Rounds is a practical manual of instruction, explaining the details of bareback and calf riding, wild cow milking, and a cutting horse contest. He states clearly that a rodeo is not a wild west show with hired hands in carnival costumes, but a genuine contest with authentic cowboys working with range stock not circus animals. Merritt Mauzey's *Texas Ranch Boy* (1955) describes a number of ranches in West Texas where the people he names actually live. Bruce Grant's *Cowboy Encyclopedia* (1951) begins with the word "aboard" for straddling a bucking horse and ends with "yucca," a plant with leaves that can be shredded to make rope. In between these two words are descriptions of dogies, cattle drives, remudas, and all the lingo and lore associated with the cowboy profession from Texas to California and from the Mexican border to the Canadian. Young people who like to sing about life on the range will find twenty songs in *Cowboy Jamboree* (1951) by Harold W. Felton. Such songs as "The Chisholm Trail," "The Cowboy's Lament," and "The Cowboy's Heaven" are among them.

Stories about rustlers and boys who help to capture them are popular in the library collections for young readers. *Ponca, Cowpony* (1952) by Helen Rushmore has a plot about both a young horse and a young rider. Chip Sanders is the rider and Ponca is the horse; Chip makes use of smoke signals and a giant firecracker to trap the cattle rustlers. Miss Rushmore is also the author of *The Shadow of Robbers' Roost* (1960), a tale based on the career of William Coe, who led a band of raiders in the Black Mesa country of western Oklahoma where cattlemen sent their herds to the markets in Kansas. Both

River Ranch (1949) by Doris Gates and *Secret of Lonesome Valley* (1949) by Elsie and Myriam Toles build stories about gangs of rustlers, with locations in Arizona.

Mystery books for young people need not be blood curdling with killing and other violence to create interest. A search for lost cattle and a turquoise mine keeps the reader turning the pages of *The Blue-Stone Mystery* (1963) by Eileen Thompson. Wanda J. Campbell sets two mystery novels in the Texas Panhandle. *The Museum Mystery* (1957) involves archaeological expeditions in Palo Duro Canyon, as well as the presence of a suspicious light in the museum. *The Mystery of Old Mobeetie* (1960) concerns a real town in the Panhandle that refuses to die when New Mobeetie is built nearer the railroad. The mystery involves vandalism, thefts, and fires in the old town. *Ten Cousins* (1963), another of Mrs. Campbell's stories, is a book rich in legends and farm customs. The setting is a rural community in East Texas during the early 1900's. Two girls, one a visitor in the home of her ten cousins, solve the mystery of stolen money, a horse, and a gamecock.

Ramona Maher's three mysteries will appeal to the slightly older boy and girl. The reader is introduced to material not usually employed in mystery tales. *The Abracadabra Mystery* (1961) makes use of a beautiful design for a typeface (used in printing) as a clue. In *Secret of the Sundial* (1966) the reader not only is involved in mystery, but he also learns the history of times and places where sundials were used. In *Mystery of the Stolen Fish Pond* (1969), history is a by-product of solving a strange theft. The all but forgotten art of the panorama contributes to the unusual nature of this tale.

Miss Maher's biographical novel, *Their Shining Hour* (1960), is based firmly on history. The story is told from the viewpoint of young Susanna Dickinson, who refused to leave the Alamo with the other wives when Santa Anna surrounded the fortress. She is taken prisoner and sent to General Sam Houston with the grim news that all the men within the fort are dead. The known facts of the heroic event needed no embellishment except the supplying of dialogue and sensory details to make this an engrossing novel.

Love, Bid Me Welcome (1964) by Janette Sebring Lowrey is for the young woman who still likes a good mystery, but likes a love story even better. She will find both in the momentous summer of Margaret McLeod's seventeenth year in a tradition-steeped Southern town.

Everyone thought the twins in Camilla Campbell's *Bartletts of Box B Ranch* (1949) were too young to take on any responsibility, but they find new motivation when Judy distinguishes herself as a rider and Glenn takes a hand in an old-fashioned cattle drive. Elizabeth Burleson tells the story of Speck—a skinny, five-foot, thirteen-year-old boy in *A Man of the Family* (1965). When drouth, flood, and accident beset his family, Speck wins the right to wear a Stetson and ride the fastest horse on the Texas ranch.

Thrills and dangers of the rodeo provide suspense in Leland Silliman's *Golden Cloud* (1950), the story of a Palomino horse. Ross Gordon, the central figure in *Fiddling Cowboy* (1949) by Adolph Regli is unusual in that the hero comes to Texas with a fiddle on his knee and wins his spurs as both cowboy and musician in a very fine Western. *The Top Hand of Lone Tree Ranch* (1960) by Anne Pence Davis is a realistic story set in West Texas when drouth creates problems for people and animals alike. Paddy Pence, a ten-year-old, is the chief character in the narrative, along with Tiny Miss, a Black Angus calf, and Moo-me, a Hereford. Paddy's finding of the new-born Angus calf, his hiding her, then losing and finding her again in an unexpected place make a plot constructed from human relationships and the relationships of people to animals in their charge during a time of hardship for both.

After the Mexican War in 1846-47, the U.S. Army guarded trails into the Southwest. Alice Mary Norton in *Stand to Horse* (1956) tells how the soldiers managed to cope with Apaches during a series of raids in New Mexico. Private Richie has to cope with his sergeant, too, but he negotiates successfully with both the military and the Indians. *Partners in the Saddle* (1950) describes skirmishes with Indians near Ft. Sill, Oklahoma. The author, Adolph Regli, knows the talk of soldiers as well as of horse wranglers. *Cyclone* (1959) by Bruce Grant is a humorous tale about an army mule. The author uses facts from Captain R. B. Marcy's expedition to establish the Comanche Reservation on the Brazos River.

Do Not Annoy the Indians (1968) is another type of

narrative in which Betty Baker uses an authentic situation for the fictitious family in charge of the Overland Mail station near Yuma, Arizona, in 1858. Experiences with the Indians who steal a stagecoach furnish high comedy. Miss Baker also wrote *The Treasure of the Padres* (1964), telling how the Bowdy family help restore a Spanish mission in Arizona while the children discover a cave, a mysterious bell, and an important archaeological site. *Ride the Pale Stallion* (1968) by Gus Tavo (a pseudonym for Gustave and Martha Ivan) is also a family story. The hero is Abraham Lincoln Jones, a boy of twelve, who comes with his father and mother to a ranch on Lobo Mountain, east of Taos. The boy's dog, Natty Bumpo, and his horse, Star, are companions in a world without playmates. When his father proposes to trade Star to Taos Indians in return for a bull, the boy is at first alienated but later understands the necessity for his sacrifice. The account of father-son interdependence and love is masterfully told, as is the adjustment of this family to the Taos Indians, their neighbors.

The families who pioneered in East Texas lived different lives than those who settled in the western part of the state, but they met adversities in much the same way. Carol Hoff, in three books with scenes in the neighborhood of Galveston, tells how some German families arrive there before Texas becomes a republic and build their cabins on homesteads with tools and equipment brought from the Old Country. *Johnny Texas* (1950) and *Johnny Texas on the San Antonio Road* (1953) are about the boy in the Friedcricks family who drove to Mexico to sell meal from the grist mill and returned with the money despite the dangers of Indians and robbers. In *Head to the West* (1957), Rosa and Franz von Dohn find old pirate gold.

Siddie Joe Johnson in two books writes of the present and the past of Fredericksburg, a German community where Old World traditions have survived, adding richness to modern America. *Rabbit Fires* (1951) describes the Easter bonfires commemorating the time when Indian campfires burned in the hills, and pioneer mothers quieted their frightened children by telling them that the rabbits were dyeing Easter eggs. *A Month of Christmases* (1952) takes two visiting children through the almost month-long festivities that begin on December 5, Saint Nicholas Day, and end with gala parties on the day after Christmas. Through the magic known only to children, the visitors, when they close their eyes, enter into the life of the town as it was a century ago.

Marian Cumming makes picnics and summer concerts in the park as momentous in *All About Marjory* (1950) as Fred Gipson makes the battles with coons and wild hogs exciting in his *Old Yeller* (1956). There is pathos in *Old Yeller* and the other Gipson books which concentrate upon the problems of people less exposed to the wide open spaces. Nature is equally hazardous, but people are more dependent on neighbors and closer to hunters like themselves. Gipson's *Hound-Dog Man* (1949) is an earlier tale which deals with a man, boys, and dogs in the woods. *The Trail Driving Rooster* (1955) establishes Fred Gipson not only as a master storyteller, but a yarn spinner with the touch of Mark Twain as well.

Loula Grace Erdman's stories treat the Southwest from the woman's point of view. In *The Wind Blows Free* (1952), although there are two boys and two girls in the Pierce family, the story is Melinda's as her feminine intuition guides her reactions to the schools, churches, animals, and ranch boys in her new West Texas home. Katie Pierce, the sister of Melinda, grows to teen age in *The Wide Horizon* (1956) to become as much a product of the Panhandle as her sister Melinda. *The Good Land* (1959) continues the saga of the Pierce family into a trilogy. *Room to Grow* (1962) likewise is a story of a pioneering West Texas family. The difference here is that the newcomers are from France with a brief stopover in New Orleans. Their learning to make a living in the treeless land and to be accepted as Texans makes a heartwarming tale. Again a girl is the leading character, with her slightly older brother at times stealing the star role. A woman schoolteacher solves the mysteries of land grabbing and community prejudice in *My Sky Is Blue* (1953).

Listen to the Mockingbird (1949) by Irmengarde Eberle is a charming book combining nature lore with the comings and goings of the Harper family through the seasons of the year. Three books stressing the joys and problems of caring for pets are *Choc, The Chachalaca* (1969) by Frances Alexander and *The Best of Friends* (1966) and *The Kittens and the Cardinals* (1969) by Charlotte Baker. The first book is about a rather rare South Texas and Mexican bird that is large and dusky green. He was hatched from one of two eggs bought from a Mexican boy by Clo and Leé Dickinson, a young ranch couple. As a pet, Choc becomes a personality to the reader through Clo's notes and the skill of the author in turning these notes into a book.

A dog is the central figure in one of Charlotte Baker's books. *The Best of Friends* centers about an abandoned animal whose puppies have been taken from her. Two little girls shelter and care for the dog, giving her the name "Rachel," after the Biblical mother who "wept for her children and would not be comforted." With this beginning, the dog becomes the center of a plot dealing with enlisting children in giving aid to lost, forsaken, and ill-treated animals. In *The Kittens and the Cardinals* groups of girls and boys are organized to promote activities for the Kindness Clubs.

Oil fields have had an impact in the Southwest within a relatively recent time, but no discovery of mineral wealth has brought more dramatic changes. Lois Lenski describes these changes in *Boom Town Boy* (1948), when she traces the life of the Robinson family from farming days to sudden riches. Their story illustrates how an industry can pollute the air and destroy the land while it is creating great wealth that can be applied to constructive ends. The Clays are another family altered by the search for "black gold" in Merritt Mauzey's *Oilfield Boy* (1957). A Cinderella story comes true for a Piney Woods girl through the wealth of oil in *Sylvan City* (1950) by Grace Trotter. *Spring in the Air* (1953) by the same author deals with the way Sadie Emerson becomes a landscape architect and transforms her Texas community into leafy vistas of flowering trees and shrubbery.

Sports, like scouting or boys' clubs, are universal and form common denominators for young people everywhere. Some books, however, show how young people adapt their sports to particular environments. The activities of the Boy Scout Troop in La Junta, Colorado, illustrate this point as Val Gendron in *Behind the Zuñi Masks* (1958) tells how the boys learn to perform Indian dances. Some problems arise when the Indians object that the dances are sacred, but a compromise is reached and non-Indian boys as well as the Indians are happy.

Wilfred McCormick's *Eagle Scout* (1952) has its setting at Philmont National Boy Scout Ranch, a 200-square-mile region in northeastern New Mexico, where camping, hiking, woodcraft, and Indian rituals are in the program. Mr. McCormick has written three series of boys' books, one dealing with baseball, a second with basketball, and a third with football. The stories not only relate to technique and performance, but they also refer to outstanding people and places in the development of the sports. Leland Silliman's *The Purple Tide* (1949) has a plot built around the rivalries of high school boys, as do most of Wilfred McCormick's books, but Silliman's *Bucky Forrester* (1951) treats of youths in a Boy's Club at Mills City, presumably in Oklahoma although it could be in any other state. The hero of this story wins the National Junior Citizenship Award, the highest honor of the Boys' Clubs of America, because of his contributions to leadership as well as to sports in the community.

Circus life can scarcely be considered a sport, but many of its activities have the nature of athletics, and Esse Forrester O'Brien's volume entitled *Circus, Cinders to Sawdust* (1959) will interest readers of all ages, even though it may have been aimed at the young generation. More than a hundred photographs document the text, which is historical as well as anecdotal. The book enables a reader to view a "world apart," the life of people and animals living in cages or coaches when they are not performing under the Big Top. Mrs. O'Brien's books for small children, *Animal Tots* (1956) and *Dolphins, Sea People* (1965) are engagingly illustrated with photographs.

Buford, The Little Bighorn (1967) qualifies as a book about sports because in it a scrawny little mountain sheep grows a pair of horns so big and round that they serve as skiis. They save Buford when the author, Bill Peet, shows how the bighorn escapes from hunters and lands on a ski run where he becomes a star and wins all the prizes. Dario, the chief character in Laura Atkinson's *The Horny-Toad Kite* (1957) gives a universal pastime a desert image. *Piñatas* (1966) by Virginia Brock includes both the history and "how to make" these marvellous candy jars which are broken in the piñata game. Southwestern festivals as well as sports are presented in *Big Meeting Day* (1950) by May Justus and other contributors.

Biography is a very special challenge to writers, since people worthy of having their histories told either live in a period calling for unusual action or become so active themselves that they stir up reaction in a period otherwise uneventful. Rosemary Buchanan's *Don Diego de Vargas* (1963) recounts the success of a distinguished military leader who reconquered the province of New Mexico in 1692 and then ruled as governor, but she failed to mention his heroic death in April of 1704 while campaigning against the Apaches in the valley below his capital city. *Sam Houston* (1953) by William Johnson is devoted to a man who, like De Vargas, combined military courage with talent for civilian leadership. Houston brought the Texas Republic to stability after the victory of his forces against the professionals of Santa Anna on April 21, 1836. Curtis Bishop in *Lone Star Leader* (1961) carries the man's biography forward from statehood to Houston's decision not to support the Southern cause in 1863. The largest city in Texas today honors the name of Sam Houston, who also represents the state in Statuary Hall in the National Capitol, Washington, D.C.

A book about a contemporary of Houston is *James Bowie* (1955) by Doris Shannon Garst, who dramatizes encounters with bears, pirates, and the invention of the famous dueling knife as her biography moves along to Bowie's death in the Alamo on March 6, 1836. The Texas Rangers, from their earliest days to the first decades of the twentieth century, are the subject of Lee McGiffin's *Ten Tall Texans* (1956). A man who might have been invited to join the Rangers if he had not lived in adjacent territory was Kit Carson, who is presented in three biographical accounts: Margaret E. Bell's *Kit Carson, Mountain Man* (1952), Ralph Moody's *Kit Carson and the Wild Frontier* (1955), and Donald Worcester's *Kit Carson, Mountain Scout* (1960). The first ends with Carson's fur-trapping trip to California from 1829 to 1831. The last treats Carson's early life in greater detail, and Moody's book carries the period in New Mexico to fuller development. Carson made Taos his home for nearly forty years. When he died in 1864, the mountains he had known as a trapper had been cut by the railroads, and the Old West was gone.

Two outstanding Indian leaders appeared on the Southwestern scene between 1860 and 1886. These were Cochise and Geronimo, both Apaches. Two books about Cochise came out in the same year: Oliver La Farge's *Cochise of Arizona* (1953), which is discussed in Chapter III, and Edgar Wyatt's *Cochise, Apache Warrior and Statesman* (1953). Both are suitable for juvenile as well as adult readers. They are, as La Farge states of his volume, "fiction based on fact." The imaginary conversations in each add drama to the outlines of real people in events that are historic. The books about the more famous of the two Apaches are Edgar Wyatt's *Geronimo, The Last Apache War Chief* (1952) and Ralph Moody's *Geronimo, Wolf of the Warpath* (1958). Geronimo's surrender brought to an end the Indian wars, a saga that reflects the courage of both Indians and whites but is also a melancholy commentary upon the relationships between them.

The Indians were a military problem when General Lew Wallace became governor of New Mexico in 1878. Lawless ranch gangs of Anglos and Spanish-Americans were also at war. Billy the Kid was the leader of one of the feuding bands. Disturbed though he was in facing such events, the governor, according to Martha E. Schaaf in *Lew Wallace, Boy Writer* (1961) found time to write the last pages of *Ben Hur* (1880) in the old adobe Palace. He also spoke at the opening of the Santa Fe Railroad before he left the Territory on June 4, 1881. William O'Neill was a lesser known literary figure at this time, but after practicing journalism in Phoenix and Tombstone, as told by Jeanette Eaton in *Bucky O'Neill of Arizona* (1949), he organized the Civil Patrol in Prescott and led them with others to join the Rough Riders in the Spanish-American War. He died a hero's death at San Juan Hill on July 1, 1898.

When Lew Wallace helped to celebrate the opening of the railroad, he knew that he was contributing to end the toll road built seventeen years earlier through the pass by Dick Wootton, an old-time mountain man. Wootton also operated a tavern for the comfort and security of coach travelers, as related by Doris Shannon Garst in her *Dick Wootton, Trail Blazer of Raton Pass* (1956). The family of Eugene Manlove Rhodes were among the passengers on the railroad in that first year. They rode south for 350 miles before they left the train to go to their homestead in the San Andres Mountains. Beth F. Day in *Gene Rhodes, Cowboy* (1954) tells how the young writer learned enough about the cowboy's occupation to write ten novels and more than a score of stories and articles after he left New Mexico and was living on his wife's farm in New York state. At the time he returned to New Mexico in 1929, another writer, Ernest Thompson Seton, was negotiating for the purchase of a large tract of piñon-forested land a few miles east of Santa Fe. He was the author of more than twenty books and famed as a lecturer and founder of the Boy Scouts of America. Doris Shannon and Warren Garst in *Ernest Thompson Seton, Naturalist* (1959) narrate the career of this remarkable man and how he founded Seton Village, now a National Historical Landmark bearing his name.

Perhaps no figure in modern times is more representative of the distinctive Southwestern qualities than William Penn Adair Rogers, whose given names as well as his surname completely disguise the fact that his father's grandmother was a Cherokee Indian and that Will was born in a place called Oologah twenty-nine years before Indian Territory became the state of Oklahoma in 1908. Doris Shannon Garst in *Will Rogers, Immortal Cowboy* (1950) stresses the energy and versatility of the man who found a pathway to greatness by capitalizing on his background of riding and roping, plus native wit and humor to win world fame. Donald and Beth Day in *Will Rogers, Boy Roper* (1950) develop his early life, when schoolmasters, parents, and acquaintances tried to shape an entirely different career than show business for young Will. Guernsey Van Riper's *Will Rogers, Young Cowboy* (1951) has chapter headings identifying the lad as part mule, part billy goat, and part rabbit, heading in directions away from the achievement as entertainer and commentator which made him great. More than a thousand people a day travel to Claremore, Oklahoma, to visit the Will Rogers Memorial, a tribute to the keen-sighted goodwill he brought to the spirit of America.

No clear line can be drawn between books written for readers who are young and those written for readers who are older. Idealism and romance are more characteristic of the early learning period in human life. Problems of a different sort develop with maturity and growing old. The books surveyed in this chapter are varied and vital. None of them reflect disillusion or pessimism about the goals young people may seek or the resources available to the seeker. There are more titles in the Bibliography, and young people are urged to make their own explorations in the nearest available library.

SELECTED SOUTHWESTERN BIBLIOGRAPHIES

1. TO FIRST AND SECOND EDITIONS

A. FOR GENERAL READERS

Acheson, Sam H., *et al.*, eds. *Texian Who's Who.* Dallas: Texian Co., 1937.
————. *30,000 Days in Texas.* N.Y.: Macmillan, 1938.
Adams, Andy. *A Texas Matchmaker,* N.Y.: Houghton, 1904.
————. *Cattle Brands.* Boston: Houghton, 1906.
————. *Log of a Cowboy.* Boston: Houghton, 1903, 1927.
————. *The Outlet.* Boston: Houghton, 1905.
————. *The Ranch on the Beaver.* Boston: Houghton, 1927.
————. *Reed Anthony, Cowman.* Boston: Houghton, 1907.
Adams, Ramon F. *Cowboy Lingo.* Boston: Houghton, 1936.
————. *Western Words.* Norman: University of Oklahoma Press, 1945.
Adams, Walter. *The Dead Lie Down.* Dallas: Kaleidograph Press, 1934.
Aikman, D., ed. *The Taming of the Frontier.* N.Y.: Minton, Balch & Co., 1925.
Aimard, Gustave. *The Bee Hunters.* London: Ward and Lock, n.d.
————. *Indian Scout.* London: Ward and Lock, 1861; N.Y.: Dutton, 1910; Everyman's Library, 1923.
————. *The Trappers of Arkansas.* London: G. Routledge, 1858; N.Y.: T. R. Dawley, 1858.
Alexander, Hartley Burr. *God's Drum and Other Cycles from Indian Lore.* N.Y.: Dutton, 1927.
Allan, Frances D., compiler. *Lone Star Ballads.* Galveston: J. D. Sawyer, 1874.
Allen, Hervey. *Anthony Adverse.* N.Y.: Farrar, 1933, 1934.
Allen, John Houghton. *Song to Randado.* Dallas: Kaleidograph Press, 1935.
Allen, Jules Verne. *Cowboy Lore.* San Antonio: Naylor, 1933.
Allsopp, Frederick William. *Albert Pike.* Little Rock: Parke-Harper Co., 1928. (Revised edition of author's *The Life Story of Albert Pike,* 1920.)
————. *Folklore of Romantic Arkansas.* N.Y.: Grolier Society, 1931.
————, ed. *The Poets and Poetry of Arkansas.* Little Rock: Central Printing Co., 1933.
Applegate, Frank G. *Indian Stories from the Pueblos.* Philadelphia: Lippincott, 1929.
————. *Native Tales of New Mexico.* Philadelphia: Lippincott, 1932.
Arkansas Traveller's Songster. N.Y.: Dick and Fitzgerald, 1864.
Armer, Laura. *Southwest.* N.Y.: Longmans, 1935.
————. *Waterless Mountain.* N.Y.: Longmans, 1931, 1933.
Arnold, Elliott. *Blood Brother.* N.Y.: Duell, 1947.
Arrington, Alfred W. ("Charles Summerfield"). *Poems.* Chicago: E. B. Myers Co., 1869.
————. *The Rangers and Regulators of the Tanaha, or Life among the Lawless.* N.Y.: Robert M. De Witt, 1856.
Astrov, Margot. *The Winged Serpent.* N.Y.: John Day, 1946.
Atkinson, Mary J. *Texas Indians.* San Antonio: Naylor, 1935.
Austin, Mary. *The American Rhythm.* N.Y.: Harcourt, 1923, 1930.
————. *The Children Sing in the Far West.* Boston: Houghton, 1928.
————. *Earth Horizon.* N.Y.: Houghton, 1932.

———. *Experiences Facing Death.* Indianapolis: Bobbs, 1931.
———. *The Flock.* Boston: Houghton, 1906.
———. *Land of Journeys' Ending.* N.Y.: Century, 1924.
———. *The Land of Little Rain.* Boston: Houghton, 1903.
———. *Lost Borders.* N.Y.: Harper, 1909.
———. *One-Smoke Stories.* Boston: Houghton, 1934.
———. *Starry Adventure.* Boston: Houghton, 1931.
Averitte, Ruth. *Salute to Dawn.* Dallas: Tardy, 1936.
———. *Cowboy Over Kiska.* Dallas: Avalon Press, 1945.
Aydelotte, Dora. *Trumpet's Calling.* N.Y.: Appleton, 1938.
Babb, Stanley E. *The Death of a Buccaneer.* Dallas: Southwest Press, 1927.
Baker, D. W. C. *A Texas Scrapbook.* N.Y. and Chicago: A. S. Barnes, 1875; reprint, Austin: Steck, 1935.
Baker, Karle Wilson. *The Birds of Tanglewood.* Dallas: Southwest Press, 1930.
———. *Blue Smoke.* New Haven: Yale University Press, 1919.
———. *Burning Bush.* New Haven: Yale University Press, 1922.
———. *Dreamers on Horseback.* Dallas: Southwest Press, 1931.
———. *Family Style.* N.Y.: Coward-McCann, 1937.
———. *Star of the Wilderness.* New York: Coward-McCann, 1942.
Bancroft, Herbert Howe. *Works.* San Francisco: History Co., 1882-90.
Bandelier, Adolph F. A. *The Delight Makers.* N.Y.: Dodd, 1890; reprint 1916.
———. *The Gilded Man.* N.Y.: Appleton, 1893.
———. *The Journey of Alvar Nuñez Cabeza de Vaca and His Companions from Florida to the Pacific, 1528-1536.* N.Y.: Allerton, 1905.
Bandelier, Adolph, and Edgar L. Hewett. *Indians of the Rio Grande Valley.* Albuquerque: University of New Mexico Press, 1937.
Bard, W. E. *A Little Flame Blown.* Dallas: Southwest Press, 1934.
Barker, E. C., ed. *The Austin Papers: October 1834—January 1837.* Washington: Government Printing Office, 1924-28; Austin: University of Texas, 1927.
———. *The Life of Stephen F. Austin, Founder of Texas, 1793-1836.* Nashville: Cokesbury Press, 1925.
Barker, Omar. *Buckaroo Ballads.* Santa Fe: New Mexican Pub. Co., 1928.
———. *Vientos de la Sierra.* Beulah, N.M.: 1924.
Barker, Ruth Laughlin. *Caballeros.* N.Y.: Appleton, 1931, 1937; Caldwell: Caxton Printers, 1945.
Barnard, E. G. *Rider of the Cherokee Strip.* Boston: Houghton, 1936.
Barnes, Nellie. *American Indian Love Lyrics.* N.Y.: Macmillan, 1925.
Barnes, William Croft. *Tales from the X-Bar Horse Camp; The Blue-roan Outlaw and Other Stories.* Chicago: Breeders Gazette, 1920.
Barr, Amelia E. *Remember the Alamo.* N.Y.: Dodd, 1888; reprint 1927.
Barrett, Monte. *The Tempered Blade.* N.Y.: Bobbs, 1946.
Barry, Ada Loomis. *Yunini's Story of the Trail of Tears.* London: Fudge and Co., 1932.
Bartlett, W. S. *My Foot's in the Stirrup.* Edited by Mabel Major and Rebecca W. Smith. Dallas: Dealey and Lowe, 1937.
Bass, Althea. *Cherokee Messenger.* Norman: University of Oklahoma Press, 1936.
Beach, Rex. *Flowing Gold.* N.Y.: Harper, 1922.
Bean, Ellis. *Memoirs.* 1856. New edition, Dallas: Book Club of Texas, 1930.
Beaty, John O., *et al.,* compilers. *Texas Poems.* Dallas: Dealey and Lowe, 1936.
Bechdoldt, Fred R. *Tales of the Old Timers.* N.Y.: Century, 1924.
———. *When the West Was Young.* N.Y.: Century, 1922.
Bedichek, Roy. *Adventures with a Texas Naturalist.* Garden City, N.Y.: Doubleday, 1947.

Benavides, Alonso de. *The Memorial of Fray Alonso de Benavides, 1630.* Chicago: Lakeside Press, 1916.
––––––. *Fray Alonso de Benavides' Revised Memorial of 1634.* Edited by F. W. Hodge, George P. Hammond, and Agapito Rey. Albuquerque: University of New Mexico Press, 1945.
Benedict, Ruth Fulton. *Patterns of Culture.* Boston: Houghton, 1934.
––––––. *Tales of the Côchiti Indians.* Washington: Government Printing Office, 1931.
Benefield, Barry. *Short Turns.* N.Y.: Century, 1926; reprint, London: George Allen & Unwin, 1932.
Benson, Elizabeth. *The Younger Generation.* N.Y.: Greenberg, 1927.
Bentley, Harold W., and H. J. Savage. *A Dictionary of Spanish Terms in English.* N.Y.: Columbia University Press, 1932.
Bishop, Morris. *Odyssey of Cabeza de Vaca.* N.Y.: Century, 1933.
Bizzell, William R. *Rural Texas.* N.Y.: Macmillan, 1924.
Blackmar, Frank W. *Spanish Institutions in the Southwest.* Baltimore: Johns Hopkins University Press, 1891.
Blake, Forrester. *Johnny Christmas.* N.Y.: Morrow, 1948.
Boatright, Mody C. *Gib Morgan, Minstrel of the Oil Fields.* El Paso: Texas Folklore Society, 1945.
––––––. *Tall Tales from Texas Cow Camps.* Dallas: Southwest Press, 1934.
Bolton, Herbert. *The Rim of Christendom.* N.Y.: Macmillan, 1936.
––––––. *The Spanish Borderlands.* New Haven: Yale University Press, 1921.
––––––. *Spanish Explorations in the Southwest, 1542-1706.* N.Y.: Scribner, 1916.
––––––. *Texas in the Middle Eighteenth Century.* Berkeley: University of California Press, 1915.
Botkin, Benjamin. *Play Party in Oklahoma.* Lincoln: University of Nebraska Press, 1937.
––––––, ed. *The Southwest Scene.* Oklahoma City: Economy Co., 1931.
Bowman, James C. *Pecos Bill.* Chicago: Whitman, 1937.
Bowyer, John W., and C. H. Thurman, eds. *The Annals of Elder Horn.* N.Y.: Richard R. Smith, 1930.
Boyer, Mary G., ed. *Arizona in Literature.* Glendale, Calif.: A. H. Clark, 1934.
Bracht, Viktor. *Texas in 1848. Texas im jahr 1848.* Elberfield U. Iserlohn, J. Bädeker, 1849. Translated by Chas. F. Schmidt. San Antonio: Naylor, 1931.
Bradford, Roark. *John Henry.* N.Y.: Harper, 1931.
Branch, Douglas. *The Cowboy and His Interpreters.* N.Y.: Appleton, 1926.
Breckenridge, W. M. *Helldorado.* Boston: Houghton, 1928.
Breithaupt, Thelma. *No Silence Heard.* Dallas: Tardy, 1937.
Brett, Dorothy. *Lawrence and Brett.* Philadelphia: Lippincott, 1933.
Brewer, J. Mason. *Negrito.* San Antonio: Naylor, 1933.
Bright, Robert. *The Life and Death of Little Joe.* Garden City, N.Y.: Doubleday, 1944.
Brinig, Myron. *All of Their Lives.* N.Y.: Farrar, 1941.
Brooks, Charles M., Jr. *Texas Missions.* Dallas: Dealey and Lowe, 1936.
Burlin, Natalie C. *The Indians' Book.* N.Y.: Harper, 1923.
Burnett, W. R. *Saint Johnson.* N.Y.: Dial Press, 1930.
Burns, Walter Noble. *The Saga of Billy the Kid.* Garden City, N.Y.: Garden City Pub. Co., 1926.
––––––. *Tombstone, An Iliad of the Southwest.* N.Y.: Doubleday, 1927; reprint, Garden City, N.Y.: Garden City Pub. Co., 1929.
Burr, Anna R. *The Golden Quicksand.* N.Y.: Appleton, 1936.
Bushby, D. Maitland, ed. *The Golden Stallion.* Dallas: Southwest Press, 1930.
––––––. *Mesquite Smoke, and other Poems.* Philadelphia: Dorrance, 1926.

Bynner, Witter. *Against the Cold*. N.Y.: Knopf, 1940.
———. *Indian Earth*. N.Y.: Knopf, 1929.
———. *Selected Poems*. N.Y.: Knopf, 1936.
———. *Take Away the Darkness*. N.Y.: Knopf, 1947.
Byrd, Sigman. *The Redlander*. N.Y.: Dutton, 1939.
———. *Tall Grew the Pines*. N.Y.: Appleton, 1936.
Callcott, Wilfrid Hardy. *Santa Anna*. Norman: Oklahoma University Press, 1936.
Calvin, Ross. *River of the Sun*. Albuquerque: University of New Mexico Press, 1946.
———. *Sky Determines*. N.Y.: Macmillan, 1934.
Campa, Arthur Leon. *Spanish Folk Poetry in New Mexico*. Albuquerque: University of New Mexico Press, 1946.
Campbell, Walter S. (pseud. Stanley Vestal). *Big-Foot Wallace*. Boston: Houghton, 1942.
———. *'Dobe Walls*. Boston: Houghton, 1929.
———. *Fandango. Ballads of the Old West*. Boston: Houghton, 1927.
———. *Kit Carson*. Boston: Houghton, 1928.
———. *Mountain Men*. Boston: Houghton, 1937.
———. *The Old Santa Fe Trail*. Boston: Houghton, 1939.
———. *Revolt on the Border*. Boston: Houghton, 1938.
———. *Short Grass Country*. American Folkways Series. Erskine Caldwell, ed. New York: Duell, 1941.
———. *Sitting Bull, Champion of the Sioux*. Boston: Houghton, 1932.
Cannon, Cornelia James. *The Fight for the Pueblo*. Boston: Houghton, 1934.
Canton, Frank M. *Frontier Trails*. Boston: Houghton, 1930.
Carb, David. *Sunrise in the West*. N.Y.: Brewer, 1931.
Carhart, Arthur. *Drum up the Dawn*. N.Y.: Dodd, 1937.
Carlisle, Irene. *Music by Lamplight*. La Porte, Ind.: Dierkes Press, 1945.
Carr, Lorraine. *Mother of the Smiths*. N.Y.: Macmillan, 1940.
Carr, Robert Van. *Cowboy Lyrics*. (Roundup edition) Boston: Small, 1912.
Carson, Christopher. *Kit Carson's Autobiography*. Edited by Milo M. Quaife. Chicago: Donnelley, 1935.
———. *Kit Carson's Own Story*. Edited by Blanche C. Grant. Taos, N.M.: Published by author, 1926.
Carter, Robert Goldthwaite. *On the Border with Mackenzie; or Winning West Texas from the Comanches*. Washington: Eynon Printing Co., 1935.
Castañeda, Carlos E. *The Mexican Side of the Texas Revolution*. Dallas: Turner, 1928.
Castañeda, Pedro de Nagera. *The Narrative of the Expedition of Coronado* in *Spanish Explorers in the Southern United States*. Edited by F. W. Hodge. N.Y.: Scribner, 1907.
———. *Narratives of The Coronado Expedition*. Edited by George P. Hammond and Agapito Rey. Albuquerque: University of New Mexico Press, 1940.
Cather, Willa. *Death Comes for the Archbishop*. N.Y.: Knopf, 1927.
Chabot, Frederick C. *The Alamo: Altar of Texas Liberty*. San Antonio: Published by author, 1931; The Leake Co., 1935.
Chamberlain, Mary Stuart. *We Inheritors*. N.Y.: Furman, 1937.
Chant, Elsie Ruth, and Julia Keleher. *The Padre of Isleta*. Santa Fe: Rydal Press, 1940.
Chapin, Katherine Garrison (Mrs. Francis Biddle). *Plain Chant for America*. N.Y.: Harper, 1942.
Chapman, Arthur. *The Pony Express*. N.Y.: Putnam, 1932.

Chapman, Kenneth M. *Pueblo Indian Pottery.* Nice: Szwedzicki, 1933; Santa
Fe: Clark's Studio, 1938.
Chavez, Fray Angelico. *Clothed with the Sun.* Santa Fe.: Writers' Editions, 1939.
———. *Eleven Lady Lyrics and other Poems.* Paterson, N.J.: St. Anthony Guild,
1945.
———. *New Mexico Triptych.* Paterson, N.J.: St. Anthony Guild, 1940.
Chittenden, Larry. *Ranch Verses.* N.Y.: Putnam, 1893, 1925.
Church, Peggy Pond. *Foretaste.* Santa Fe: Writers' Editions, 1933.
Clark, Badger. *Sun and Saddle Leather.* Boston: R. G. Badger, 1915; reprint,
Chapman & Grimes, 1936.
Clark, William Russell. *A Stained Glass Window and Other Poems.* Memphis:
Memphis Pub. Co., 1934.
Cleaveland, Agnes Morley. *No Life for a Lady.* Boston: Houghton, 1941.
Clum, Woodworth. *Apache Agent.* Boston: Houghton, 1936.
Coe, George W. *Frontier Fighter.* Boston: Houghton, 1934.
Cole, Maude E. *Wind Against Stone.* Los Angeles: Lyman House, 1941.
Collings, Ellsworth, and Alma Miller England. *The 101 Ranch.* Norman: Uni-
versity of Oklahoma Press, 1937.
Collins, Hubert E. *Warpath and Cattle Trail.* N.Y.: Morrow, 1928, 1933.
Comfort, Will Levington. *Apache.* N.Y.: Dutton, 1931.
———. *Mangas Coloradas.* London: Stein, 1931.
Cook, James Henry. *Fifty Years on the Old Frontier.* New Haven: Yale Uni-
versity Press, 1923.
Cook, Jim (Lane), and T. M. Pearce. *Lane of the Llano.* Boston: Little, 1936.
Coolidge, Dane. *Arizona Cowboys.* N.Y.: Dutton, 1938.
———. *The Navajo Indians.* Boston: Houghton, 1930.
———. *Texas Cowboys.* N.Y.: Dutton, 1937.
Coolidge, Mary Roberts. *The Rainmakers.* Boston: Houghton, 1929.
Cooper, Courtney Riley. *Oklahoma.* N.Y.: Little, 1926.
Copeland, Fayette. *Kendall of the Picayune.* Norman: University of Oklahoma
Press, 1943.
Corle, Edwin. *Desert Country.* American Folkways Series. Erskine Caldwell,
ed. N.Y.: Duell, 1941.
———. *Listen, Bright Angel.* N.Y.: Duell, 1946.
———. *People on the Earth,* N.Y.: Random House, 1937.
Crady, Kate McAlpin. *Free Steppin'.* Dallas: Mathis, Van Nort, 1938.
Crane, Leo. *Desert Drums.* Boston: Little, 1928.
———. *Indians of the Enchanted Desert.* Boston: Little, 1925.
Creel, George. *Sam Houston.* N.Y.: Cosmopolitan, 1928.
Crichton, Kyle S. *Law and Order Limited, The Life of Elfego Baca.* Santa Fe:
New Mexican Pub. Co., 1928.
———. *The Proud People.* N.Y.: Scribner, 1944.
Crockett, David. *Autobiography.* Philadelphia: T. K. and P. G. Collins, 1836;
reprint, N.Y.: Scribner, 1923.
Cronyn, George W., ed. *The Path of the Rainbow.* N.Y.: Liveright, 1918, 1934.
Cross, Ruth. *The Big Road.* N.Y.: Longmans, 1931.
———. *The Golden Cocoon.* N.Y.: Harper, 1924.
Crowell, Chester T. *Liquor, Loot and Ladies.* N.Y.: Knopf, 1930.
Crowell, Grace Noll. *Flame in the Wind.* Dallas: Southwest Press, 1930.
———. *Light of the Years.* N.Y.: Harper, 1936.
———. *Silver in the Sun.* Dallas: P. L. Turner, 1928.
———. *Some Brighter Dawn.* N.Y.: Harper, 1943.
———. *Songs of Courage.* Dallas: Southwest Press, 1930; reprint, N.Y.: Harper,
1938.

————. *Splendor Ahead.* N.Y.: Harper, 1940.

————. *Wind Swept Harp.* N.Y.: Harper, 1946.

Cunningham, Eugene. *Texas Sheriff.* Boston: Houghton, 1934; reprint, N.Y.: Triangle Books, 1944.

————. *Triggernometry.* N.Y.: Pioneer Press, 1934.

Cushing, Frank. *Zuñi Folk Tales.* N.Y.: Putnam, 1901; Knopf, 1931.

Custer, Elizabeth. *Tenting on the Plains: or General Custer in Kansas and Texas.* N.Y.: C. L. Webster and Co., 1887.

Dale, Edward Everett. *Prairie Schooner, and Other Poems.* Guthrie, Okla.: Cooperative Pub. Co., 1929.

————. *Range Cattle Industry.* Norman: University of Oklahoma Press, 1930.

———— and Morris L. Wardell. *History of Oklahoma.* N.Y.: Prentice-Hall, 1948.

Dasburgh, Marina Wister. *Fantasy and Fugue.* N.Y.: Macmillan, 1937.

Davis, Anne Pence. *The Customer Is Always Right.* N.Y.: Macmillan, 1940.

Davis, C. T. *Poems.* Little Rock: Arkansas Gazette, 1923.

Davis, Edward Everett. *The White Scourge.* San Antonio: Naylor, 1940.

Davis, J. Frank. *The Road to San Jacinto.* Indianapolis: Bobbs, 1936.

Davis, Mollie E. Moore. *Minding the Gap and Other Poems.* Houston: Cushing & Cane, 1867.

————. *Under the Man-Fig.* Boston: Houghton, 1895.

Davis, W. W. H. *El Gringo.* N.Y.: Harper, 1857; reprint, Santa Fe: Rydal Press, 1938.

————. *The Spanish Conquest of New Mexico.* Doylestown, Pa., 1869.

Dawson, Cleo. *She Came to the Valley.* N.Y.: Morrow, 1943.

Day, Donald. *Big Country Texas.* American Folkways Series. Erskine Caldwell, ed. N.Y.: Duell, 1947.

Debo, Angie. *And Still The Waters Run.* Princeton: Princeton University Press. 1940.

————. *Prairie City.* N.Y.: Knopf, 1944.

————. *Rise and Fall of the Choctaw Republic.* Norman: University of Oklahoma Press, 1934.

————. *Tulsa: From Creek Town to Oil Capital.* Norman: University of Oklahoma Press, 1943.

DeHuff, Elizabeth Willis. *Say The Bells of Old Missions.* St. Louis: Herder, 1943.

Dellenbaugh, Frederick S. *Breaking the Wilderness.* N.Y.: Putnam, 1905.

Densmore, Frances. *The American Indians and Their Music.* N.Y.: Woman's Press, 1926, 1936.

DeShields, James T. *Cynthia Ann Parker.* St. Louis, Mo.: published by author, 1886; reprint San Antonio: Naylor, 1934.

Dixon, Billy. *Life and Adventures of Billy Dixon.* Compiled by Frederick S. Barde. Guthrie, Okla.: Coöperative Pub. Co., 1914. Revised edition, Olive K. Dixon. Dallas: Turner, 1927.

Dixon, Sam H. *The Poets and Poetry of Texas.* Austin: Sam H. Dixon & Co., 1885.

Dobie, J. Frank. *Apache Gold and Yaqui Silver.* N.Y.: Little, 1939.

————. *Coronado's Children.* Dallas: Southwest Press, 1930. Garden City, N.Y.: Garden City Pub. Co., 1934.

————. *John C. Duval.* Dallas: Southwest Review, 1939.

————. *The Longhorns.* Boston: Little, 1941.

————. *Tales of the Mustang.* Dallas: Book Club of Texas, 1936.

————. *A Texan in England.* Boston: Little, 1945.

————. *Tongues of the Monte.* Garden City, N.Y.: Doubleday, 1935.

————. *Vaquero of the Brush Country.* Dallas: Southwest Press, 1929.

Doro, Edward. *The Boar and Shibboleth.* N.Y.: Knopf, 1933.

Dorsey, George. *Pawnee Mythology.* Washington: Carnegie Institute, 1906.

———. *Traditions of the Osage.* Washington: Carnegie Institute, 1904.

Douglas, C. L. *Gentlemen in the White Hats.* Dallas: Southwest Press, 1934.

Dresbach, Glenn Ward. *Cliff Dwellings and Other Poems.* Boston: Vinal, 1926.

———. *Star Dust and Stone.* Dallas: Turner, 1928.

Duffus, R. L. *Jornada.* N.Y.: Covici, 1935.

———. *The Santa Fé Trail,* N.Y.: Longmans, 1930.

Duval, John C. *The Adventures of Big-Foot Wallace.* Macon, Ga.: J. W. Burke, 1870. Edited by Mabel Major and Rebecca W. Smith. Dallas: Tardy, 1936; rev. ed. Lincoln: University of Nebraska Press, 1966.

———. *Early Times in Texas.* Austin: H. P. N. Gammel, 1892. Edited by Mabel Major and Rebecca W. Smith. Dallas: Tardy, 1936.

Eagleton, D. F. *Writers and Writings of Texas.* N.Y.: Broadway Pub. Co., 1913.

Ellis, Anne. *The Life of an Ordinary Woman.* Boston: Houghton, 1929.

———. *Sunshine Preferred.* Boston: Houghton, 1934.

Ellsworth Henry Leavitt. *Washington Irving on the Prairie.* Edited by Stanley T. Williams and Barbara D. Simison. N.Y.: American Book Co., 1937.

Elser, Frank B. *The Keen Desire.* N.Y.: Boni, Liveright, 1926.

Erdman, Loula Grace. *The Years of the Locust.* N.Y.: Dodd, 1947.

Espinosa, Aurelio. *Los Comanches.* Albuquerque: University of New Mexico, 1907.

———. *Cuentos, Romances y Cantares.* Boston: Allyn Bacon, 1925.

Espinosa, José M. *Spanish Folk Tales from New Mexico.* N.Y.: American Folklore Society, Steckert, 1937.

Evarts, Hal. *Tumbleweeds.* Boston: Little, 1923.

Falconer, Thomas. *Notes of a Journey Through Texas and New Mexico in the Years 1841 and 1842.* London: 1842(?) Reprinted as *Letters and Notes on the Texan Santa Fé Expedition, 1841-1842.* N.Y.: Dauber and Pine, 1930.

Farber, Lt. Colonel James. *Texas C. S. A.* New York and Texas: Jackson Co., 1947.

Faunce, Hilda. *Desert Wife.* Boston: Little, 1934.

Ferber, Edna. *Cimarron.* Garden City, N.Y.: Doubleday, 1930.

Ferguson, Mrs. Tom B. *They Carried the Torch.* Kansas City, Mo.: Burton Pub. Co., 1937.

Fergusson, Erna. *Albuquerque.* Albuquerque: Merle Armitage Editions, 1947.

———. *Dancing Gods.* N.Y.: Knopf, 1931.

———. *Our Southwest.* N.Y.: Knopf, 1940.

Fergusson, Harvey. *Followers of the Sun (Wolf Song, In Those Days, The Blood of the Conquerors).* N.Y.: Knopf, 1936.

———. *Footloose McGarnigal.* N.Y.: Knopf, 1930.

———. *Home in the West: An Inquiry into My Origins.* N.Y.: Duell, 1945.

———. *Rio Grande.* N.Y.: Knopf, 1933.

Ferril, Thomas Hornsby. *Westering.* New Haven: Yale University Press, 1934.

Ficke, Arthur Davison. *Mountain Against Mountain.* Garden City, N.Y.: Doubleday, 1929.

Finger, Charles J. *Adventure Under Sapphire Skies.* N.Y.: Morrow, 1931.

———. *Frontier Ballads.* Garden City, N.Y.: Doubleday, 1927.

———. *Ozark Fantasia.* Fayetteville, Ark.: Golden Horseman Press, 1927.

Fitzgerald, Mary S. *The Way of Beauty.* Dallas: Kaleidoscope Press, 1931.

Fletcher, Alice Cunningham. *Indian Story and Song from North America.* Boston: Small, 1900.

Fletcher, John Gould. *Arkansas*. Chapel Hill: University of North Carolina Press, 1947.
———. *Breakers and Granite*. N.Y.: Macmillan, 1921.
———. *Burning Mountain*. N.Y.: Dutton, 1946.
———. *Life Is My Song*. N.Y.: Farrar, 1937.
———. *Selected Poems*. N.Y.: Farrar, 1938.
———. *South Star*. N.Y.: Macmillan, 1941.
———. *XXIV Elegies*. Santa Fe: Writers' Editions, 1935.
Flint, Timothy. *Francis Berrien, or The Mexican Patriot*. 1826. (Second edition) Philadelphia: Key, Biddle, 1834.
Folk-Say: A Regional Miscellany. Edited by B. A. Botkin. *Publications* of Oklahoma Folk-lore Society. No. I, 1929; No. II, 1930; No. III, 1931; No. IV, 1932. Norman: University of Oklahoma Press.
Ford, Gus L. *Texas Cattle Brands*. Dallas: Cockrell, 1936.
Foreman, Grant. *The Five Civilized Tribes*. Norman: University of Oklahoma Press, 1934.
———. *A History of Oklahoma*. Norman: University of Oklahoma Press, 1942.
———. *Indian Removals*. Norman: University of Oklahoma Press, 1932.
———. *Indians and Pioneers*. New Haven: Yale University Press, 1930; rev. ed. Norman: University of Oklahoma Press, 1936.
Foster, O'Kane. *In the Night Did I Sing*. N.Y.: Scribner, 1942.
Fowler, Jacob. *Journal of Jacob Fowler*. N.Y.: Francis P. Harper, 1898.
Francis, May E., translator. *The Hermit of the Cavern*. San Antonio: Naylor, 1934.
Franciscan Fathers. *An Ethnologic Dictionary of the Navaho Language*. St. Michaels, Ariz.; printed in Germany, 1910, 1929.
French, Alice (pseud. Octave Thanet). *Knitters in the Sun*. Boston: Houghton, 1887.
Fulton, Maurice G., and Paul Horgan, eds. *New Mexico's Own Chronicle*. Dallas: Banks Upshaw, 1937.
Gallegly, Joseph. *The Adventures of Steve Waterhouse*. San Antonio: Naylor, 1947.
Gambrell, Herbert P. *Anson Jones, the Last President of Texas*. N.Y.: Doubleday, 1948.
———. *Mirabeau B. Lamar, Troubadour and Crusader*. Dallas: Southwest Press, 1934.
Gard, Wayne. *Sam Bass*. Boston: Houghton, 1936.
Garner, Claud. *Wetback*. N.Y.: Coward-McCann, 1947.
Garrard, Lewis H. *Wah-to-Yah and the Taos Trail*. Cincinnati: H. W. Derby; N.Y.: A. S. Barnes, 1850. Edited by Stanley Vestal, Oklahoma City: Harlow, 1927. Edited by Ralph P. Bieber, Glendale, Calif.: Arthur H. Clark, 1938.
Garrett, Julia Kathryn. *Green Flag Over Texas*. N.Y. and Dallas: Cordova Press, 1939.
Garrett, Pat F. *The Authentic Life of Billy the Kid*. Santa Fe: New Mexico Print. and Publ. Co., 1882. Edited by Maurice G. Fulton, N.Y.: Macmillan, 1927.
Geiser, Samuel W. *Naturalists of the Frontier*. Dallas: Southern Methodist University Press, 1937.
Gerstaecker, Frederick. *Wild Sports in the Far West*. London, N.Y.: G. Routledge, 1854. Philadelphia: Lippincott, 1876.
Gibson, Jewell. *Joshua Beene and God*. N.Y.: Random House, 1946.
Gillett, Jas. B. *Six Years With the Texas Rangers*. Austin: Von Boeckman-Jones, 1921. Edited by M. M. Quaife, New Haven: Yale University Press, 1925.

Gillis, Everett A. *Hello the House!* Dallas: Kaleidograph Press, 1944.

Gillmor, Frances. *Fruit Out of Rock.* N.Y.: Duell, 1940.

———. *Windsinger.* N.Y.: Minton, Balch & Co., 1930.

Gillmor, Frances, and Louisa Wade Wetherill. *Traders to the Navajos.* Boston: Houghton, 1934.

Gipson, Fred. *Fabulous Empire, 101 Ranch, Colonel Zack Miller's Story.* Boston: Houghton, 1946.

Glasscock, C. B. *Then Came Oil.* Indianapolis: Bobbs, 1938.

Goddard, P. E. *Indians of the Southwest.* N.Y.: American Museum of Natural History, 1913, 1927.

Goodwyn, Frank. *The Devil in Texas.* Dallas: Dealey and Lowe, 1936.

Graham, Philip. *Early Texas Verse.* Austin: Steck, 1936.

———. *Life and Poems of Miribeau B. Lamar.* Chapel Hill: University of North Carolina Press, 1938.

Grant, Blanche C. *Doña Lona.* N.Y.: Funk, 1941.

———. *When Old Trails Were New.* N.Y.: Press of the Pioneers, 1934.

Green, General Thomas Jefferson. *Journal of the Texian Expedition Against Mier.* N.Y.: Harper, 1845; facsimile reproduction, Austin: Steck, 1935.

Greer, Hilton Ross. *Ten and Twenty Aprils.* Dallas: Tardy, 1935.

———, ed. *Best Short-Stories From the Southwest.* First and Second Series. Dallas: Southwest Press, 1928, 1931.

———, ed. *Voices of the Southwest.* N.Y.: Macmillan, 1923.

Greer, Hilton Ross, and Florence E. Barns, eds. *New Voices of the Southwest.* Dallas: Tardy, 1934.

Greer, James K., ed. *Texas Ranger and Frontiersman, The Days of Buck Barry in Texas, 1845-1906.* Dallas: Southwest Press, 1932.

Gregg, Josiah. *Commerce of the Prairies.* N.Y.: H. G. Langley, 1844; reprint, edited by M. M. Quaife, Chicago: R. H. Donnelley, 1926; reprint, Dallas: Southwest Press, 1933.

———. *Diary and Letters of Josiah Gregg.* Edited by Maurice Garland Fulton. Norman: University of Oklahoma Press, 1941.

Gregory, Jackson. *Riders Across the Border.* N.Y.: Dodd, 1932.

Grey, Zane. *The Heritage of the Desert.* N.Y.: Harper, 1910; Grosset and Dunlap, 1920.

Grinnell, George Bird. *Indians of Today.* Chicago and N.Y.: H. S. Stone, 1900. Revised edition, N.Y.: Duffield, 1911.

———. *Pawnee Hero Stories and Folk Tales.* N.Y.: Forest and Stream, 1889; reprint, N.Y.: Scribner, 1916.

Hackett, Charles W. *Mexican Revolution and the United States, 1910-1926.* N.Y.: World Peace Foundation, 1926.

Haley, J. Evetts. *Charles Goodnight.* Boston: Houghton, 1936.

———. *George Littlefield, Texan.* Norman: University of Oklahoma Press, 1943.

———. *The XIT Ranch of Texas and the Early Days of the Llano Estacado.* Chicago: Lakeside Press, 1929.

Hall, D. J. *Enchanted Sand.* N.Y.: Morrow, 1933.

Hall, Sharlot. *Cactus and Pine.* Boston: Sherman, French, 1911. Revised edition, Phoenix: Republican Print Shop, 1924.

Hallenbeck, Cleve. *Spanish Missions of the Old Southwest.* N.Y.: Doubleday, 1926.

Hallenbeck, Cleve, and Juanita Williams. *Legends of the Spanish Southwest.* Glendale, Calif.: Clark, 1938.

Hammett, Samuel A. *In Piney Woods Tavern; or Sam Slick in Texas.* Philadelphia: T. B. Peterson, 1858.

Hammond, George P., ed. *Don Juan de Oñate and the Founding of New Mexico.* Santa Fe: El Palacio Press, 1927.

Hammond, G. P., and Agapito Rey. *Narratives of the Coronado Expedition, 1540-1542.* Albuquerque: University of New Mexico Press, 1940.

Hannun, Alberta. *Spin a Silver Dollar, The Story of a Desert Trading Post.* N.Y.: Viking, 1946.

Harrington, Isis. *Told in the Twilight.* N.Y.: Dutton, 1938.

Harris, Hazel Harper. *Wings of the Morning.* Dallas: Cockrell, 1930.

Harrison, Henry, ed. *Texas Poets.* N.Y.: Henry Harrison Co., 1936.

Henderson, Alice Corbin. *Brothers of Light.* N.Y.: Harcourt, 1937.

——. *Red Earth.* Chicago: Seymour, 1920.

——. *The Sun Turns West.* Santa Fe: Writers' Editions, 1933.

——. *The Turquoise Trail.* Boston: Houghton, 1928.

"Henry, O." *See* W. S. Porter.

Henry, Stuart. *Conquering Our Great American Plains.* N.Y.: Dutton, 1930.

L'Heroine du Texas in *The Story of Champ d'Asile.* Paris: 1819. Translated by Donald Joseph with Introduction by Fannie Ratchford. Dallas: Book Club of Texas, 1937.

Hewett, Edgar L. *Ancient Life in the American Southwest.* Indianapolis: Bobbs, 1930.

Hewett, Edgar L., and Adolph Bandelier. *Indians of the Rio Grande Valley.* Albuquerque: University of New Mexico Press, 1937.

Hewett, Edgar L., and Reginald G. Fisher. *Mission Monuments of New Mexico.* Albuquerque: University of New Mexico Press, 1943.

Hewett, Edgar L., and Wayne L. Mauzey. *Landmarks of New Mexico.* Albuquerque: University of New Mexico Press, 1940.

Hibben, Frank Cummings. *The Lost Americans.* N.Y.: Crowell, 1946.

Hill, Clyde Walton. *Shining Trails.* Dallas: Shining Trails Sales Co., 1926.

Hodge, Frederick W., ed. *Handbook of American Indians, North of Mexico.* Washington: Bulletin of Bureau of American Ethnology, 1907, 1912.

Hodge, Frederick W., and Theodore H. Lewis, eds. *Spanish Explorers in the Southwestern United States, 1528-1543.* N.Y.: Scribner, 1925.

Hoermann, P. Alto. *The Daughter of Tehuan.* Translated by Alois Braun. San Antonio: Standard Printing Co., 1935.

Hogan, Pendleton. *The Dark Comes Early.* N.Y.: Ives Washburn, 1934.

Hogan, William Ransom. *The Texas Republic, A Social and Economic History.* Norman: University of Oklahoma Press, 1946.

Hogner, Dorothy. *Navajo Winter Nights.* N.Y.: Nelson, 1935.

——. *South to Padre.* Boston: Lothrop, 1936.

Holden, William C. *Alkali Trails.* Dallas: Southwest Press, 1930.

Holley, Mary Austin. *Letters of an Early American Traveler.* Edited by Mattie Austin Hatcher. Dallas: Southwest Press, 1933.

——. *Texas.* Baltimore: Armstrong and Plaskitt, 1833; reprint, Lexington, Ky.: Clarke, 1836; reprint, Austin: Steck, 1935.

Horgan, Paul. *The Common Heart.* N.Y.: Harper, 1942.

——. *Far From Cibola.* N.Y.: Harper, 1938.

——. *Figures in a Landscape.* N.Y.: Harper, 1940.

——. *A Lamp on the Plains.* N.Y.: Harper, 1937.

——. *Main Line West.* N.Y.: Harper, 1936.

——. *No Quarter Given.* N.Y.: Harper, 1935.

——. *Return of the Weed.* N.Y.: Harper, 1936.

Hough, Emerson. *Heart's Desire.* N.Y.: Macmillan, 1905.

——. *North of '36.* N.Y.: Appleton, 1923, 1929.

House, Boyce. *Oil Boom; The Story of Spindletop, Burkburnett, Mexia, Smackover, Desdemona, and Ranger.* Caldwell, Idaho: Caxton Printers, 1941.
———. *Texas Rhythm.* Dallas: Regional Press, 1936.
———. *Were You In Ranger?* Dallas: Tardy, 1935.
Houston, Margaret Bell. *Lanterns in the Dusk.* N.Y.: Dodd, 1930.
———. *Magic Valley.* N.Y.: Appleton, 1934.
———. *The Singing Heart and Other Poems.* Nashville: Cokesbury Press, 1926.
Houston, Noll. *The Great Promise.* N.Y.: Reynal and Hichcock, 1946.
Hoyt, Henry F. *A Frontier Doctor.* Boston: Houghton, 1929.
Hughes, Dorothy Belle. *The Blackbirder.* N.Y.: Duell, 1943.
———. *Dark Certainty.* New Haven: Yale University Press, 1931.
———. *Ride the Pink Horse.* N.Y.: Duell, 1946.
Hunter, John Marvin, ed. *The Trail-Drivers of Texas.* San Antonio: Globe Printing Co., 1924; reprint, Nashville: Cokesbury Press, 1926.
Ickes, Anna Wilmarth. *Mesa Land.* Boston: Houghton, 1933.
Irving, Washington. *A Tour on the Prairies.* Philadelphia: Carey, Lea and Blanchard, 1835. Edited by George C. Wells. Oklahoma City: Harlow, 1926.
Jacobson, Oscar. *Kiowa Indian Art.* Nice: Szwedzicki, 1929.
James, Ahlee. *Tewa Firelight Tales.* N.Y.: Longmans, 1927.
James, George Wharton. *Arizona the Wonderland.* Boston: Page, 1917.
———. *New Mexico, The Land of the Delight Makers.* Boston: Page, 1920.
James, Marquis. *The Cherokee Strip, A Tale of an Oklahoma Boyhood.* N.Y.: Viking, 1946.
———. *The Raven.* Indianapolis: Bobbs, 1929; reprint, Texas Centennial Edition, N.Y.: Blue Ribbon Books, 1935.
James, Will. *Cowboys North and South.* N.Y.: Scribner, 1924.
———. *Lone Cowboy.* N.Y.: Scribner, 1930.
Jennings, Napoleon Augustus. *A Texas Ranger.* N.Y.: Scribner, 1899; reprint, Dallas: Southwest Press, 1930.
Johnson, Annie Fellows. *In the Desert of Waiting.* Boston: Page, 1905.
Johnson, Siddie Joe. *Agarita Berry.* Dallas: Southwest Press, 1933.
———. *Gallant the Hour.* Dallas: Kaleidograph Press, 1945.
Johnson, Spud. *Horizontal Yellow.* Santa Fe: Writers' Editions, 1935.
Johnson, Vance. *Heaven's Tableland.* N.Y.: Farrar, 1947.
Joseph, Donald. *Four Blind Mice.* N.Y.: Stokes, 1932.
———. *The Long Bondage.* N.Y.: Stokes, 1930.
———. *October's Child.* N.Y.: Stokes, 1929.
Kaufman, Kenneth C. *Level Land.* Dallas: Kaleidograph Press, 1935.
Keleher, W. A. *The Fabulous Frontier.* Santa Fe: Rydal Press, 1945.
———. *Maxwell Land Grant.* Santa Fe. Rydal Press, 1942.
Kendall, George Wilkins. *Narrative of the Texas-Santa Fe Expedition.* N.Y.: Harper, 1884; reprint, Austin: Steck, 1935.
Kennedy, William. *Texas.* London: R. Hastings, 1841; reprint, N.Y.: Benjamin and Young 1844; reprint, Fort Worth: Molyneau, 1925.
Kibbe, Pauline R. *Latin Americans in Texas.* Albuquerque: University of New Mexico Press, 1946.
Kidder, Alfred V. *Introduction to Southwest Archaeology.* New Haven: Yale University Press, 1924.
King, Charles. *Starlight Ranch and Other Stories of Army Life on the Frontier.* Philadelphia: Lippincott, 1890, 1905.
King, Mary. *Quincie Bolliver.* Boston: Houghton, 1941.
Kloss, Phillips. *Arid.* N.Y.: Macmillan, 1933.
———. *Realization.* Caldwell, Idaho: Caxton Printers, 1942.

Kluckhohn, Clyde. *Beyond the Rainbow*. Boston: Christopher, 1933.
———. *To the Foot of the Rainbow*. N.Y.: Century, 1927.
Kluckhohn, Clyde, and Dorothea Leighton. *The Navaho*. Cambridge: Harvard University Press, 1946.
Knibbs, Henry Herbert. *Songs of the Trail*. Boston: Houghton, 1920.
———. *Tonto Kid*. Boston: Houghton, 1936.
Krey, Laura. *And Tell of Time*. Boston. Houghton, 1938.
———. *On the Long Tide*. Boston: Houghton, 1940.
Kruger, Fania. *Cossack Laughter*. Dallas: Kaleidograph Press, 1937.
Kuipers, Cornelius. *Chant of the Night*. Grand Rapids: Zondervan, 1934.
Kupper, Winifred. *The Golden Hoof*. N.Y.: Knopf, 1945.
La Farge, Oliver. *All the Young Men*. Boston: Houghton, 1935.
———. *The Enemy Gods*. Boston: Houghton, 1937.
———. *Laughing Boy*. Boston: Houghton, 1929.
———. *Raw Material*. Boston: Houghton, 1945.
LaFlesche, Francis. *Osage Tribe—Songs of the Wa Xo'Be*. Washington: Government Printing Office, 1930.
Lake, Stuart N. *Wyatt Earp*. Boston: Houghton, 1931.
Lamar, Mirabeau B. *Verse Memorials*. N.Y.: Fetridge, 1857. Reprinted in *Life and Poems of Mirabeau B. Lamar* by Philip Graham, Chapel Hill: University of North Carolina Press, 1938.
Lanham, Edwin. *Banner at Daybreak*. N.Y.: Longmans, 1937.
———. *Thunder in the Earth*. N.Y.: Harcourt, 1941.
———. *The Wind Blew West*. N.Y.: Longmans, 1935.
Lanier, Sidney. *Retrospects and Prospects*. N.Y.: Scribner, 1899.
Larkin, Margaret. *El Cristo*, N.Y.: French, 1926.
———. *The Singing Cowboy*. N.Y.: Knopf, 1931.
Larned, W. T. *American Indian Fairy Tales*. Chicago: Volland, 1921.
Laut, Agnes. *Pilgrims of the Santa Fe*. N.Y.: Stokes, 1931.
———. *Through Our Unknown Southwest*. N.Y.: McBride, Nast, 1913.
Lawrence, D. H. *Mornings in Mexico*. N.Y.: Knopf, 1927.
———. *The Plumed Serpent*. N.Y.: Knopf, 1926.
Lawrence, Frieda. *"Not I, But the Wind . . ."* N.Y.: Viking, 1934.
Lehmann, Herman. *Nine Years with the Indians*. Edited by J. Marvin Hunter. Austin: Von Boeckmann-Jones, 1927.
Lewis, A. H. *Wolfville*. N.Y.: Stokes, 1897, 1923.
Lewis, Anna. *Along the Arkansas*. Dallas: Southwest Press, 1932.
Lewis, Judd Mortimer. *Sing the South*. Houston: Dealy, 1905.
Lindsey, Therese. *Blue Norther*. N.Y.: Vinal, 1925.
Lloyd, Everett. *Law West of the Pecos*. San Antonio: University Press, 1931; reprint, Naylor, 1936.
Lockwood, Frank C. *Arizona Characters*. Los Angeles: Times-Mirror Press, 1928.
———. *Pioneer Days in Arizona*. N.Y.: Macmillan, 1932.
———. *Tucson—The Old Pueblo*. Phoenix: Manufacturing Stationers, 1930; Tucson: Published by author, 1931
Loggins, Vernon. *Two Romantics and Their Ideal Life*. N.Y.: Odyssey, 1946.
Lomax, John A. *Adventures of a Ballad Hunter*. N.Y.: Macmillan, 1947.
Lomax, John Avery, ed. *Cowboy Songs and Other Frontier Ballads*. N.Y.: Macmillan, 1910; revised edition, with Alan Lomax, 1938.
———. *Songs of the Cattle Trail and Cow Camp*. N.Y.: Macmillan, 1919, 1927.
Lomax, John Avery, and Alan Lomax, eds. *American Ballads and Folk Songs*. N.Y.: Macmillan, 1935.
———. *Negro Folk Songs as Sung by Lead Belly*. N.Y.: Macmillan, 1936.

———. *Our Singing Country.* N.Y.: Macmillan, 1941.
Long, Haniel. *Atlantides.* Santa Fe: Writers' Editions, 1933.
———. *The Grist Mill.* Santa Fe: Rydal Press, 1945.
———. *Interlinear to Cabeza De Vaca.* Santa Fe: Writers' Editions, 1936.
———. *Malinche.* Santa Fe: Writers' Editions, 1939.
———. *Piñon Country.* American Folkways Series. Erskine Caldwell, ed. N.Y.: Duell, 1941.
Long Lance, Chief Buffalo Child. *Long Lance.* N.Y.: Cosmopolitan Book, 1928.
Luhan, Mabel Dodge. *Edge of Taos Desert.* N.Y.: Harcourt, 1937.
———. *Lorenzo in Taos.* N.Y.: Knopf, 1932.
———. *Taos and Its Artists.* N.Y.: Duell, 1947.
———. *Winter in Taos.* N.Y.: Harcourt, 1935.
Lummis, Charles Fletcher. *Flowers of Our Lost Romance.* Boston: Houghton, 1929.
———. *The Land of Poco Tiempo.* N.Y.: Scribner, 1893, 1925.
———. *Mesa, Cañon, and Pueblo.* N.Y.: Century, 1925.
———. *A New Mexico David.* N.Y.: Scribner, 1891, 1912.
———. *Pueblo Indian Folk Stories.* N.Y.: Century, 1910.
———. *Spanish Pioneers.* Chicago: McClurg, 1893, 1929.
Macleod, Norman. *Thanksgiving Before November.* N.Y.: Parnassus Press, 1936.
Magoffin, Susan Shelby. *Down the Santa Fe Trail and Into Mexico.* New Haven: Yale University Press, 1926.
Major, Mabel, and Rebecca W. Smith, eds. *The Southwest in Literature.* N.Y.: Macmillan, 1929.
Marcy, Col. Randolph B. *30 Years of Army Life on the Border.* N.Y.: Harper, 1866.
Marinoni, Rosa. *Behind the Mask.* N.Y.: Harrison, 1927.
Marriott, Alice. *The Potter of San Ildefonso.* Norman: University of Oklahoma Press, 1948.
———. *The Ten Grandmothers.* Norman: University of Oklahoma Press, 1945.
Marshall, James Leslie. *Santa Fe, The Railroad that Built an Empire.* N.Y.: Random House, 1945.
Mathews, John Joseph. *Sundown.* N.Y.: Longmans, 1934.
———. *Wah-kon-tah.* Norman: University of Oklahoma Press, 1932.
Matthews, Sallie Reynolds. *Interwoven.* Houston: Anson Jones, 1936.
Matthews, Washington. *The Mountain Chant.* Washington: Government Printing Office, 1887.
———. *Navajo Legends.* Boston: Houghton, 1897.
———. *Navajo Myths, Prayers, and Songs.* Berkeley: University of California Press, 1907.
Maverick, Mary Ann. *Memoirs.* San Antonio: Alamo Printing Co., 1921.
Maverick, Maury. *A Maverick American.* N.Y.: Covici, 1937.
McCampbell, Coleman. *Saga of a Frontier Seaport.* Dallas: Southwest Press, 1934.
McCarty, John Lawton. *Maverick Town, The Story of Old Tascosa.* Norman: University of Oklahoma Press, 1946.
McClure, John. *Airs and Ballads.* N.Y.: Knopf, 1918.
McConnell, H. H. *Five Years a Cavalryman.* Jacksboro, Texas: J. N. Rogers, 1889.
McCoy, Joseph G. *Historic Sketches of the Cattle Trails of the West and Southwest.* Kansas City: Ramsey, Millett, and Hudson, 1874. Edited by Ralph P. Bieber, Glendale, Calif.: A. H. Clark, 1940.
McDanield, H. F., and N. A. Taylor. *The Coming Empire or Two Thousand*

Miles in Texas on Horseback. N.Y., Chicago: A. S. Barnes, 1878; original edition, 1877; reprint, Dallas: Turner Co., 1936.

McDougal, Mary and Violet. *Wandering Fire.* Boston: Stratford, 1925.

McNeal, Tom H. *Motley's the Only Wear.* Dallas: Kaleidograph Press, 1942.

McNicol, Donald M. *The Amerindians.* N.Y.: Stokes, 1937.

Meine, Franklin, ed. *Tall Tales of the Southwest.* N.Y.: Knopf, 1930.

Melas, Roxylea. *Revival.* San Antonio: Naylor, 1934.

Milburn, George. *Catalogue.* N.Y.: Harcourt, 1938.

———. *Flannigan's Folly.* N.Y.: Whittlesey House, 1947.

———. *No More Trumpets and Other Stories.* N.Y.: Harcourt, 1933.

———. *Oklahoma Town.* N.Y.: Harcourt, 1931.

Miller, Helen Topping. *Never Another Moon.* N.Y.: Appleton, 1938.

Miller, Joaquin. *Collected Poems.* N.Y.: Putnam, 1923.

Montgomery, Vaida Stewart, ed. *A Century with Texas Poets and Poetry.* Dallas: Kaleidograph Press, 1934.

———. *Locoed and Other Poems.* Dallas: Kaleidograph Press. 1930.

Montgomery, Whitney. *Corn Silks and Cotton Blossoms.* Dallas: P. L. Turner, 1928.

———. *Hounds in the Hills.* Dallas: Kaleidograph Press, 1934.

———. *Joseph's Coat.* Dallas: Kaleidograph Press, 1946.

Moreland, Patrick. *Seven Song.* Garden City, N.Y.: Doubleday, 1936.

Morfi, Fray Juan Agustín. *History of Texas, 1673-1779.* Reprint, Albuquerque: Quivira Society, 1935.

Morris, Ann Axtell. *Digging in the Southwest.* Garden City, N.Y.: Doubleday, 1933.

Myers, John Myers. *The Alamo.* N.Y.: Dutton, 1948.

Nance, Berta Hart. *Cattle.* Dallas: Kaleidograph Press, 1932.

———. *Flute in the Distance.* Dallas: Kaleidograph Press, 1935.

Nelson, John Louw. *Rhythm for Rain.* Boston: Houghton, 1937.

Nuñez Cabeza de Vaca, Alvar. *The Narrative of Alvar Nuñez Cabeza de Vaca.* Edited by F. W. Hodge. N.Y.: Scribner, 1907.

Nuttall, Thomas. *A Journal of Travel into the Arkansas Territory During the Year 1819.* Philadelphia: T. H. Palmer, 1821; reprint, Glendale, Calif.: Clark, 1905.

O'Connor, Jack. *Boom Town.* N.Y.: Knopf, 1938.

———. *Conquest: A Novel of the Old Southwest.* N.Y.: Harper, 1930.

Oklahoma Folk-Lore Society, *Publications* of: *See Folk-Say.* . . .

Olmstead, Frederick. *A Journey Through Texas.* N.Y.: Dix, Edwards & Co., 1857.

Oskison, John M. *Brothers Three.* N.Y.: Macmillan, 1935.

Otero, Miguel Antonio. *My Life on the Frontier.* N.Y.: Press of the Pioneers, 1935.

———. *The Real Billy the Kid.* N.Y.: R. R. Wilson, 1936.

Otero, Nina. *Old Spain in Our Southwest.* N.Y.: Harcourt, 1936.

Otis, Raymond. *Fire in the Night.* N.Y.: Farrar, 1934.

———. *Miguel of the Bright Mountain.* London: Gollancz, 1936; Toronto: Ryerson Press, 1936.

Owens, W. A. *Swing and Turn.* Dallas: Tardy, 1936.

Paine, Albert Bigelow. *The Arkansas Bear.* Philadelphia: Altemus, 1902, 1929.

———. *Captain Bill McDonald, Texas Ranger.* Austin: Gammel, 1905; N.Y.: Little, Ives, 1909.

Parke, James H. *It Runs in the Family.* Philadelphia: Penn Pub. Co., 1928.

Parsons, Elsie, ed. *American Indian Life.* N.Y.: Viking, 1922.

Los Pastores. Translated with Introduction by M. R. Cole. Boston: Houghton, 1907.
Los Pastores. Edited by Mary R. Van Stone and Louise Morris. Cleveland: Gates Press, 1933.
Patterson, Norma. *Drums of the Night.* N.Y.: Farrar, 1935.
Pattullo, George. *The Untamed.* N.Y.: Desmond Fitzgerald, 1911.
Paul, Louis. *A Horse in Arizona.* Garden City, N.Y.: Doubleday, 1936.
Payne, Leonidas W. *A Survey of Texas Literature.* Chicago: Rand McNally, 1928.
Paytiamo, James. *Flaming Arrow's People.* N.Y.: Duffield, 1932.
Pearce, T. M. *The Beloved House.* Caldwell, Idaho: Caxton Printers, 1940.
———. *Cartoon Guide of New Mexico.* N.Y.: Augustin, 1939.
Pearce, T. M., with Jim (Lane) Cook. *Lane of the Llano.* Boston: Little, 1936.
Pearce, T. M., and Telfair Hendon, eds. *America in the Southwest.* Albuquerque: University of New Mexico Press, 1933.
Pearce, T. M., and A. P. Thomason, eds. *Southwesterners Write.* Albuquerque: University of New Mexico Press, 1947.
Peck, Leigh. *Pecos Bill and Lightning.* Boston: Houghton, 1940.
Perry, George Sessions. *Cities of America.* N.Y.: McGraw, 1947.
———. *Hackberry Cavalier.* N.Y.: Viking, 1944.
———. *Hold Autumn in Your Hand.* N.Y.: Viking, 1941.
———. *Texas, a World in Itself.* N.Y.: McGraw, 1942.
———, ed. *Roundup Time.* N.Y.: Whittlesey House, 1943.
Peyton, Green. *San Antonio, City in the Sun.* N.Y.: Whittlesey House, 1946.
Phillips, James (pseud. Philip Atlee). *The Inheritors.* N.Y.: Dial Press, 1940.
Phillips, Shine. *Big Spring, The Casual Biography of a Prairie Town.* N.Y.: Prentice-Hall, 1944.
Pierce, Evelyn Miller. *Hilltop.* N.Y.: King, 1931.
Pike, Albert. *Hymns to the Gods, and Other Poems.* Washington: Privately printed, 1873-82. Edited by Mrs. Lilian P. Roome. Little Rock: Allsopp, 1916.
———. *Lyrics and Love Songs.* Edited by Mrs. Lilian P. Roome. Little Rock. Allsopp, 1916.
———. *Prose Sketches and Poems Written in the Western Country.* Boston: Light & Horton, 1834.
Pike, Zebulon Montgomery. *Expedition of Zebulon Montgomery Pike.* Baltimore: John Binns, 1810. Edited by E. Coues. N.Y.: Francis P. Harper, 1895.
Poetry Society of Texas. *A Book of the Year.* Dallas, 1922-48.
Porter, Katherine Anne. *Flowering Judas and Other Stories.* N.Y.: Harcourt, 1935; Modern Library, 1940.
———. *The Leaning Tower.* N.Y.: Harcourt, 1944.
———. *Pale Horse, Pale Rider.* N.Y.: Harcourt, 1939.
Porter, William Sidney (pseud. O. Henry). *Heart of the West.* N.Y.: McClure, 1907; reprint, Garden City, N.Y.: Doubleday, 1918.
Porter, William Trotter, ed. *The Big Bear of Arkansas.* Philadelphia: Carey & Hart, 1845.
Posey, Alexander. *Poems.* Edited by Mrs. Minnie H. Posey. Topeka: Crane, 1910.
Postl, Karl (pseud. Charles Sealsfield). *Life in the New World.* N.Y.: New World Press, 1842.
Potter, Mrs. W. R. *Texas in History-Story-Legend.* Dallas: Southwest Press, 1933.
Priestley, J. B. *Midnight on the Desert.* N.Y.: Harper, 1937.

Prose and Poetry of the Live Stock Industry of the United States. Denver: National Live Stock Historical Association, 1904, 1905.

Pueblo Indian Painting. Introduction and notes by Dr. Hartley Burr Alexander. Nice: Szwedzicki, 1932.

Purchas, Samuel. *Purchas His Pilgrimage (1625).* Glasgow: Maclehose, 1906.

Quiett, Glenn Chesney. *They Built the West.* N.Y.: Appleton, 1934.

Quivira Society, *Publications* of. General editor, G. P. Hammond. Albuquerque: I. *The Espejo Expedition into New Mexico,* by Luxan, tr. and ed. by G. P. Hammond and Agapito Rey (1929); II. *Indian Uprising in Lower California, 1734-1737,* by Taraval, tr. and ed. by Marguerite Eyer Wilbur (1931, 1932); III. *The Mercurio Volante of Don Carlos Sigüenza y Gongora,* tr. with Introduction and Notes by Irving A. Leonard (1932); IV. *History of New Mexico, 1610, by Gaspar Perez de Villagrá,* tr. by Gilberto Espinosa, Introduction and Notes by F. W. Hodge (1933); V. *Diary of the Alarcón Expedition into Texas, 1718-1719,* by Fray Francisco Celiz, tr. and ed. by Fritz L. Hoffman (1935); VI. *History of Texas, 1673-1799,* by Fray Juan Augustín Morfi, tr. with Biographical Introduction and Annotations by Carlos E. Castañeda (1935); VII. *The Spanish Southwest, 1542-1794,* an annotated bibliography by Henry R. Wagner (1937); VIII. *New Mexico in 1602 or Juan de Montoya's Relation of the Discovery of New Mexico,* tr. and ed. by G. P. Hammond and Agapito Rey (1938); IX. *The Reconnaissance of Pensacola Bay, 1689-1693,* tr. and ed. by Irving A. Leonard (1938); XI. *Three New Mexico Chronicles,* tr. and ed. by H. Bailey Carroll and J. Villasana Haggard.

Radin, Paul. *Story of the American Indian.* N.Y.: Boni and Liveright, 1927; reprint, Garden City, N.Y.: Garden City Pub. Co., 1937.

Raine, William McLeod. *On the Dodge.* Boston: Houghton, 1938.

Raine, William McLeod, and Will C. Barnes. *Cattle.* Garden City, N.Y.: Doubleday, 1930.

Rainey, George. *The Cherokee Strip.* Enid, Okla., 1925; reprint, Guthrie, Okla.: Coöperative Pub. Co., 1933.

Rak, Mary Kidder. *A Cowman's Wife.* Boston: Houghton, 1934.

———. *Mountain Cattle.* Boston: Houghton, 1936.

Randolph, Vance. *Belle Star, The Bandit Queen.* N.Y.: Random House, 1941.

———. *From an Ozark Holler, Stories of Ozark Mountain Folk.* N.Y.: Vanguard, 1933.

———. *Ozark Mountain Folks.* N.Y.: Vanguard, 1932.

———. *Ozark Superstitions.* N.Y.: Columbia University Press, 1947.

Raymond, Dora Neill. *Captain Lee Hall of Texas.* Norman: University of Oklahoma Press, 1940.

Raynolds, Robert. *Brothers in the West.* N.Y.: Harper, 1931.

Read, Opie Percival. *An Arkansas Planter.* Chicago: Rand McNally, 1896, 1899.

———. *In the Alamo.* Chicago: Rand McNally, 1900.

Reichard, Gladys. *Prayer: The Compulsive Word.* N.Y.: Augustin, 1944. (American Ethnological Society, Monograph No. 7.)

———. *Spider Woman, A Story of Navajo Weavers and Chanters.* N.Y.: Macmillan, 1934.

Reid, Mayne. *The Lone Ranch.* N.Y.: Carleton, 1884; reprint, N.Y.: Dutton, 1908.

———. *The Scalp Hunters.* Philadelphia: Lippincott, Grimbo, 1851; reprint, N.Y.: Hurst, 1899.

Rhodes, Eugene Manlove. *Beyond the Desert.* Boston: Houghton, 1934.

———. *Good Men and True, and Hit the Line Hard.* N.Y.: Holt, 1910; Grosset and Dunlap, 1920.

——. *Once in the Saddle.* Boston: Houghton, 1927.

——. *Peñalosa.* N.Y.: H. K. Fly Co.; Grosset and Dunlap, 1917. Santa Fe: Writers' Editions, 1934.

——. *The Proud Sheriff.* Boston: Houghton, 1935.

——. *The Trusty Knaves.* Boston: Houghton, 1933.

——. *West is West.* N.Y.: H. K. Fly Co., 1917.

Rhodes, May D. *The Hired Man on Horseback: My Story of Eugene Manlove Rhodes.* Boston: Houghton, 1938.

Richardson, R. N. *Texas, the Lone Star State.* N.Y.: Prentice-Hall, 1943.

Richter, Conrad. *Early Americana and Other Stories.* N.Y.: Knopf, 1936.

——. *The Sea of Grass.* N.Y.: Knopf, 1937.

——. *Tacey Cromwell.* N.Y.: Knopf, 1942.

Rickman, Jesse C. *Racing Bits.* Boston: Badger, 1926.

Riggs, Lynn. *Green Grow the Lilacs.* N.Y.: French, 1931.

——. *The Iron Dish.* Garden City, N.Y.: Doubleday, 1930.

——. *A Lantern to See By and Sump'n Like Wings.* N.Y.: French, 1928.

——. *Russet Mantle* and *The Cherokee Night.* N.Y.: French, 1936.

Rister, Carl Coke. *Border Captives.* Norman: University of Oklahoma Press, 1940.

——. *Land Hunger.* Norman: University of Oklahoma Press, 1942.

——. *Robert E. Lee in Texas.* Norman: University of Oklahoma Press, 1946.

——. *Southern Plainsmen.* Norman: University of Oklahoma Press, 1938.

——. *Southwestern Frontier.* Cleveland: Clark, 1928.

Roark, Garland. *Wake of the Red Witch.* Boston: Little, 1946.

Robertson, Lexie Dean. *Acorn on the Roof.* Dallas: Kaleidograph Press, 1939.

——. *I Keep a Rainbow.* Dallas: Cockrell, 1932.

——. *Red Heels.* Dallas: P. L. Turner, 1928.

Robinson, Jacob S. *Journal of the Santa Fe Expedition under Colonel Doniphan* (1848). Portsmouth, N.H.: Portsmouth Journal Press, 1848; reprint, Princeton: Princeton University Press, 1932.

Robinson, William H. *Under Turquoise Skies.* N.Y.: Macmillan, 1928.

Roemer, Dr. Ferdinand. *Texas.* Translated by Oswald Mueller; reprint, San Antonio: Standard Printing Co., 1935.

Rogers, John William. *Judge Lynch.* N.Y.: French, 1924.

——. *Wedding Presents.* N.Y.: French, 1926.

——. *Women Folks.* N.Y.: French, 1927.

Rollins, Philip Ashton. *The Cowboy: His Equipment and His Part in the Development of the West.* N.Y.: Scribner, 1922; rev. ed., 1936.

——. *Jinglebob.* N.Y.: Scribner, 1927, 1930.

Roscoe, Burton. *Before I Forget.* Garden City, N.Y.: Doubleday, 1937.

——. *We Were Interrupted.* Garden City, N.Y.: Doubleday, 1947.

Rourke, Constance. *American Humor.* N.Y.: Harcourt, 1931.

——. *Davy Crockett.* N.Y.: Harcourt, 1934.

Russell, Charles M. *Trails Plowed Under.* Garden City, N.Y.: Doubleday, 1927.

Russell, David. *Sing With Me Now.* Dallas: Kaleidograph Press, 1946.

Ruxton, George Frederick. *Life in the Far West.* Edinburgh and London: Blackwood, 1849. Edited by Horace Kephart as *In the Old West.* N.Y.: Outing Pub. Co., 1915; *In the Old West,* reprint, N.Y.: Macmillan, 1920.

Ryan, Marah Ellis. *The Dancer of Tuluum.* Chicago: McClurg, 1924.

——. *The Flute of the Gods.* N.Y.: Stokes, 1909.

——. *For the Soul of Rafael.* Chicago: McClurg, 1906.

——. *The Treasure Trail.* N.Y.: Grosset, 1918.

Rye, Edgar. *Quirt and Spur.* Chicago: Conkey, 1909.

Rylee, Robert. *The Ring and the Cross.* N.Y.: Knopf, 1947.

Sabin, Edwin L. *Kit Carson Days, 1809-1868.* Chicago: McClurg, 1914; rev. ed., N.Y.: Press of the Pioneers, 1935.

Sampley, Arthur M. *Of the Strong and the Fleet.* Dallas: Kaleidograph Press, 1947.

———. *This Is Our Time.* Dallas: Kaleidograph Press, 1943.

Sandburg, Carl. *Good Morning, America.* N.Y.: Harcourt, 1928.

———. *Slabs of the Sunburnt West.* N.Y.: Harcourt, 1922.

Santee, Ross. *Apache Land.* N.Y.: Scribner, 1947.

———. *Cowboy.* N.Y.: Cosmopolitan Book, 1928.

Saxon, Lyle. *Lafitte the Pirate.* N.Y.: Century, 1930.

Scarborough, Dorothy. *Can't Get a Redbird.* N.Y.: Harper, 1929.

———. *Impatient Griselda.* N.Y.: Harper, 1927.

———. *In the Land of Cotton.* N.Y.: Macmillan, 1923.

———. *On the Trail of Negro Folk-Songs.* Cambridge: Harvard University Press, 1925.

———. *Stretchberry-Smile.* Indianapolis: Bobbs, 1932.

———. *The Wind.* N.Y.: Harper, 1925.

Schmitz, Joseph W. *Thus They Lived.* San Antonio: Naylor, 1935.

Scobee, Barry. *Old Fort Davis.* San Antonio: Naylor, 1947.

Sears, Paul B. *Deserts on the March.* Norman: University of Oklahoma Press, 1935.

Sedgwick, Mrs. William T. *Acoma, the Sky City.* Reprint, Cambridge: Harvard University Press, 1926.

Segale, Sister Blandina. *At the End of the Santa Fé Trail.* Columbus: Columbian Press, 1932; rev. ed. Milwaukee: Bruce Publishing Co., 1948.

Seton, Anya. *The Turquoise.* N.Y.: Houghton, 1946.

Seton, Ernest Thompson. *Lives of the Hunted.* N.Y.: Scribner, 1901.

Siemering, A. *The Hermit of the Cavern.* Translated by May Francis. San Antonio: Naylor, 1932.

Simpson, William Haskell. *Along Old Trails of New Mexico and Arizona.* Boston: Houghton, 1929.

Sinclair, John. *In Time of Harvest.* N.Y.: Macmillan, 1943.

Siringo, Charles A. *A Texas Cowboy; or Fifteen Years on the Hurricane Deck of a Spanish Cow Pony.* Chicago: Umbdenstock, 1885; Rand McNally, 1886; rev. ed. as *Riata and Spurs,* Boston: Houghton, 1912, 1927.

Sjolander, John P. *Salt of the Earth and Sea.* Dallas: P. L. Turner, 1928.

Smith, Dama Margaret. *Hopi Girl.* Palo Alto, Calif.: Stanford University Press, 1931.

———. *I Married a Ranger.* Palo Alto, Calif.: Stanford University Press, 1930.

Smith, Goldie Capers. *Sword of Laughter.* Dallas: Kaleidograph Press, 1932.

Smith, L. Walden. *Saddles Up.* San Antonio: Naylor, 1937.

Smith, Rebecca W. *See* Mabel Major and Rebecca W. Smith, eds.

Smithwick, Noah. *The Evolution of a State.* Austin: Gammel, 1900; reprint, Austin: Steck, 1935.

Sonnichsen, Charles Leland. *Billy King's Tombstone.* Caldwell, Idaho: Caxton Printers, 1942.

———. *Roy Bean, Law West of the Pecos.* N.Y.: Macmillan, 1943.

Sowell, A. J. *Life of Big-Foot Wallace.* 1899. Reprinted by *Frontier Times,* Bandera, Texas, 1934.

Spates, Virginia. *Enchanted Window.* Dallas: Kaleidograph Press, 1934.

Spinden, Herbert Joseph. *Songs of the Tewa.* N.Y.: Exposition of Indian Tribal Arts, 1933.

Stacey, May H. *Uncle Sam's Camels.* Edited by L. B. Lesley. Cambridge: Harvard University Press, 1929.
Standing Bear, Luther (Dakota Chief). *Stories of the Sioux.* Boston: Houghton, 1934.
St. Clair, George. *Young Heart.* N.Y.: Harrison, 1933.
Starkey, Marion L. *The Cherokee Nation.* N.Y.: Knopf, 1946.
Steinbeck, John. *Grapes of Wrath.* N.Y.: Viking, 1939.
Stilwell, Hart. *Border City.* N.Y.: Doubleday, 1945.
———. *The Uncovered Wagon.* Garden City, N.Y.: Doubleday, 1947.
Struther, Jan (Mrs. Joyce Maxtone Graham). *A Handful of Pebbles.* N.Y.: Harcourt, 1946.
Stuart, Ruth McEnery. *In Simpkinville.* N.Y.: Harper, 1897.
Summerhayes, Martha. *Vanished Arizona.* Philadelphia: Lippincott, 1908; reprint, Chicago: Lakeside Press, 1939.
Swan, Oliver G., ed. *Covered Wagon Days.* (Originally published as *Frontier Days.*) N.Y.: Grosset, 1928.
Sweet, Alexander E., and John Knox. *On a Mexican Mustang Through Texas.* Hartford: Scranton, 1883; reprint, N.Y.: Ogilvie, 1917.
Sylvester, Harry. *Dayspring.* N.Y.: Appleton, 1945.
Taylor, Ross M. *Brazos.* Indianapolis: Bobbs, 1938.
Taylor, T. U. *The Chisholm Trail and Other Stories.* Bandera, Texas: Frontier Times, 1936.
Tedlock, E. W., Jr. *The Frieda Lawrence Collection of D. H. Lawrence Manuscripts.* Albuquerque: University of New Mexico Press, 1948.
Texas Folk-Lore Society, *Publications* of. Edited by J. Frank Dobie, 1923-43; Mody Boatright, since 1943. Austin: I. (1916), ed. Stith Thompson; II. (1923); III. *Legends of Texas* (1924); IV. (1925); V. (1926); VI. *Texas and Southwest Lore* (1927); VII. *Follow de Drinkin' Gou'd* (1928); J. Frank Dobie's *Coronado's Children* (1929); VIII. *Man, Bird and Beast* (1930); IX. *Southwestern Lore* (1931); X. *Tone the Bell Easy* (1932); XI. *Spur of the Cock* (1933); Mody Boatright's *Tall Tales from Texas Cow Camps* (1934); XII. *Puro Mexicano* (1935); W. A. Owen's *Swing and Turn* (1936); XIII. *Straight Texas* (1937); XIV. *Coyote Wisdom* (1938); XV. *In the Shadow of History* (1939); XVI. *Mustangs and Cow Horses* (1940); XVII. *Texian Stomping Grounds* (1941); XVIII. *Backwoods to Border* (1943); XIX. *From Hell to Breakfast* (1944); XX. Mody Boatright's *Gib Morgan, Minstrel of the Oil Fields* (1945); XXI. *Mexican Border Ballads and Other Lore* (1946); Roy Bedicheck's *Adventures with a Texas Naturalist* (1947).
Thomas, Alfred B., ed. *Forgotten Frontiers.* Norman: University of Oklahoma Press, 1935.
Thomason, John W., Jr. *The Adventures of Davy Crockett.* Illustrated. N.Y.: Scribner, 1934.
———. *Fix Bayonets.* N.Y.: Scribner, 1926.
———. *Gone to Texas.* N.Y.: Scribner, 1937.
———. *Lone Star Preacher.* N.Y.: Scribner, 1941.
Thompson, Holland, ed. *The Book of Texas.* Dallas: Grolier Society, 1929.
Thorp, N. Howard (Jack), ed. *Songs of the Cowboy.* Estancia, N.M.: Published by author, 1908; rev ed., Boston: Houghton, 1921.
———. *Tales of the Chuck Wagon.* Santa Fe: New Mexican Pub. Co., 1926.
Thorp, N. Howard, and Neil McCullough Clark. *Pardner of the Wind.* Caldwell, Idaho: Caxton Printers, 1945
Thorpe, T. B. *The Hive of the Bee-Hunter.* N.Y.: Appleton, 1854.

Thrall, H. S. *A History of Texas.* N.Y.: University Pub. Co., 1876.

Three Southwest Plays: "We Are Besieged," by Sam Acheson; "Where the Dear Antelope Play," by John William Rogers; "Jute," by Katherine Witherspoon. With an Introduction by John Rosenfield. Dallas: Southwest Press, 1942.

Thwaites, Reuben Gold, ed. *Early Western Travels, 1748-1846.* Cleveland: Clark, 1904-07.

Tilghman, Zoe A. *Dugout.* Oklahoma City: Harlow, 1925.

———. *Prairie Winds.* Oklahoma City: Harlow, 1930.

Twitchell, Ralph E. *Leading Facts of New Mexican History.* Cedar Rapids: Torch Press, 1911-17.

Underhill, Ruth M. *First Penthouse Dwellers of America.* N.Y.: Augustin, 1938. Second edition, revised and redesigned, Santa Fe: Laboratory of Anthropology, 1946.

———. *Singing for Power.* Berkeley: University of California Press, 1938.

Underwood, John Curtis. *Trail's End, Poems of New Mexico.* Santa Fe: Santa Fe Pub. Co., 1921.

Van Dyke, John C. *Grand Canyon of the Colorado.* N.Y.: Scribner, 1920.

Van Stone, Mary R. *Spanish Folk Songs of New Mexico.* Chicago: Seymour, 1926.

Van Stone, Mary R., and Louise Morris. *Los Pastores.* Cleveland: Gates Press, 1933.

Vestal, Stanley. *See* Walter S. Campbell.

Villagrá, Gaspar Perez de. *History of New Mexico, 1610.* Translated by G. Espinosa. Los Angeles: Quivira Society, 1933.

Wade, Mary Donaldson. *The Alabama Indians of East Texas.* Livingston, Texas: Enterprise Press, 1931, 1936.

Wallace, Lew. *The Fair God; or The Last of the 'Tzins.* Boston: Osgood, 1873; reprint, Boston: Houghton, 1927.

Wallace, Susan E. *The Land of the Pueblos.* N.Y.: John B. Alden, 1888.

Walter, Paul A. F. *Old Santa Fe and Vicinity.* Albuquerque: University of New Mexico Press, 1936.

Walton, Eda Lou. *Dawn Boy. Black Foot and Navajo Songs.* N.Y.: Dutton, 1926.

Warner, Louis H. *Archbishop Lamy.* Santa Fe: New Mexican Pub. Co., 1936.

Waters, Frank. *The Man Who Killed the Deer.* N.Y.: Farrar, 1942.

———. *People of the Valley.* N.Y.: Farrar, 1941.

Weaver, Augusta. *Oklahoma Wildcat.* N.Y.: Macaulay, 1938.

Webb, J. J. *Adventures in the Santa Fé Trade.* Cleveland: Clark, 1931.

Webb, Walter Prescott. *Divided We Stand.* Boston: Houghton, 1937.

———. *The Great Plains.* Boston: Ginn, 1931.

———. *The Texas Rangers.* Boston: Houghton, 1935; second ed. with Foreword by Lyndon B. Johnson, Austin: University of Texas Press, 1965.

———, ed. *The Handbook of Texas.* Austin: Texas State Historical Association, 1952.

Wellman, Paul. *Death in the Desert.* N.Y.: Macmillan, 1935.

———. *Death on the Prairie.* N.Y.: Macmillan, 1934.

Wharton, Clarence. *Santana, the Great Chief of the Kiowas.* Dallas: Banks Upshaw, 1935.

Wheeler, Homer W. *Buffalo Days.* Indianapolis: Bobbs, 1925.

White, Owen P. *My Texas 'Tis of Thee.* N.Y.: Putnam, 1936.

———. *Trigger Fingers.* N.Y.: Putnam, 1926.

White, Stewart Edward. *Arizona Nights.* N.Y.: McClure, Grosset, 1907; Garden City, N.Y.: Sun Dial Press, 1937.
———. *The Long Rifle.* Garden City, N.Y.: Doubleday, 1932.
Whitman, William. *Navaho Tales.* Boston: Houghton, 1925.
Wilbarger, J. W. *Indian Depredations in Texas.* Austin: Hutchings Printers, 1889; reprint, Austin: Steck, 1935.
Williamson, Thames. *The Woods Colt.* N.Y.: Harcourt, 1933.
Wilson, Augusta Evans. *Inez, a Tale of the Alamo.* N.Y.: Harper, 1855; N.Y.: G. W. Carleton, 1882.
Winship, George Parker, ed. *The Journey of Coronado, 1540-42.* N.Y.: A. S. Barnes, 1904; reprint, N.Y.: Allerton, 1922.
Winslow, Thyra Samter. *My Own, My Native Land.* Garden City, N.Y.: Doubleday, 1935.
Wissler, Clark. *The American Indian.* N.Y.: D. C. McMurtree, 1917; reprint, N.Y.: Oxford Press, 1932.
Wooten, Dudley. *A Comprehensive History of Texas.* Dallas: Scarff, 1898.
Wright, Harold Bell. *Long Ago Told, Legends of the Papago Indians.* N.Y.: Appleton, 1929.
Yauger, Fay. *Planters' Charm.* Dallas: Kaleidograph Press, 1935.
Yoakum, Henderson. *History of Texas From Its First Settlement.* N.Y.: Redfield Co., 1855; reprint, Austin: Steck, 1935.
Young, Stark. *Street of the Islands.* N.Y.: Scribner, 1930.
Zavala, Adina de. *History and Legends of the Alamo and Other Missions.* San Antonio: Published by author, 1917.
Ziegler, Jesse A. *Wave of the Gulf.* San Antonio: Naylor, 1938.

B. BIBLIOGRAPHIC GUIDES

Agatha, Sister Mary. *Texas Prose Writings.* Dallas: Banks Upshaw, 1936.
Barns, Florence E. *Texas Writers of Today.* Dallas: Tardy, 1935.
Dobie, J. Frank. *Guide to Life and Literature of the Southwest.* Dallas: Southern Methodist University Press, 1943.
Dobie, J. Frank, and John William Rogers. *Finding Literature on the Texas Plains.* Dallas: Southwest Press, 1930.
Marable, Mary Hays, and Elaine Boylan. *A Handbook of Oklahoma Writers.* Norman: University of Oklahoma Press, 1939.
Matthews, Jim P., and V. L. Jones. *Arkansas Books.* Fayetteville: University of Arkansas Bulletin, 1927.
Munk, Joseph A. *Bibliography of Arizona.* Los Angeles: Southwest Museum, 1900, 1914.
Parsons, Mabel. *A Courier in New Mexico.* Tesuque, N.M.: Tesuque Printers, 1936.
Raines, C. W. *A Bibliography of Texas.* Austin: Gammel, 1896, 1934.
Raines, Lester. *Writers and Writings of New Mexico.* Las Vegas, N.M.: Mimeograph, 1934.
Saunders, Lyle. *A Guide to Materials Bearing on Cultural Relations in New Mexico.* Albuquerque: University of New Mexico Press, 1944.
Smith, Goldie Capers. *The Creative Arts in Texas. A Handbook of Biography.* Nashville: Cokesbury Press, 1926.
Tucker, Mary. *Books of the Southwest. A General Bibliography.* N.Y.: Augustin, 1937.

C. FOR CHILDREN

Abeita, Louise. *I Am a Pueblo Indian Girl.* N.Y.: Morrow, 1939.
Adams, Andy. *Ranch on the Beaver.* Boston: Houghton, 1927.
————. *Wells Brothers, the Young Cattle Kings.* Boston: Houghton, 1911.
Alexander, Frances. *Mother Goose on the Rio Grande.* Dallas: Banks Upshaw, 1944.
Altsheler, Joseph A. *Apache Gold.* N.Y.: Appleton, 1913.
————. *Texan Scout.* N.Y.: Appleton, 1913.
————. *Texan Star.* N.Y.: Appleton, 1912.
————. *Texan Triumph.* N.Y.: Appleton, 1913.
Armer, Laura Adams. *Dark Circle of Branches.* N.Y.: Longmans, 1933.
————. *Traders' Children.* N.Y.: Longmans, 1937.
————. *Waterless Mountain.* N.Y.: Longmans, 1931.
Austin, Mary Hunter. *Basket Woman.* Boston: Houghton, 1904.
————. *Children Sing in the Far West.* Boston: Houghton, 1928.
————. *Trailbook.* Boston: Houghton, 1918.
Baker, Elizabeth W. *Stocky, A Boy of West Texas.* Philadelphia: Winston, 1945.
Baker, Karle Wilson. *Texas Flag Primer.* Yonkers-on-Hudson, N.Y.: World Book Co., 1925.
————. *Two Little Texans.* Yonkers-on-Hudson, N.Y.: World Book Co., 1932.
Bosworth, Allan. *Sancho of the Long, Long Horns.* Garden City, N.Y.: Doubleday, 1947.
Bowman, James C. *Pecos Bill.* Chicago: Whitman, 1937.
Brock, Emma L. *One Little Indian Boy.* N.Y.: Knopf, 1932.
Buff, Mary. *Dancing Cloud.* (Lithographs by Conrad Buff.) N.Y.: Viking, 1937.
Campbell, Camilla. *Galleons Sail Westward.* Dallas: Mathis Van Nort, 1939.
————. *Star Mountain and Other Legends of Mexico.* (Illustrations by Ena McKinney.) N.Y.: Whittlesey House, 1946.
Cannon, Cornelia. *Fight for the Pueblo.* Boston: Houghton, 1934.
————. *Lazaro in the Pueblo.* Boston: Houghton, 1931.
————. *Pueblo Boy.* Boston: Houghton, 1926.
————. *Pueblo Girl.* Boston: Houghton, 1929.
Charnley, Mitchell V. *Jean Lafitte, Gentleman Smuggler.* N.Y.: Viking, 1934.
Clark, Ann Nolan. *In My Mother's House.* N.Y.: Viking, 1941.
————. *Little Navajo Bluebird.* N.Y.: Viking, 1943.
Coblentz, Catherine Cate. *Blue and Silver Necklace.* Boston: Little, 1937.
Crowell, Grace Noll. *Miss Humpety Comes to Tea and Other Poems.* N.Y.: Harper, 1938.
Crownfield, Gertrude. *Lone Star Rising.* N.Y.: Crowell, 1940.
De Huff, Elizabeth. *Five Little Katchinas.* Boston: Houghton, 1930.
————. *Hoppity Bunny's Hop.* Caldwell, Idaho: Caxton Printers, 1939.
————. *Little Boy Dance.* Chicago: Wilcox and Follette, 1946.
————. *Taytay's Memories.* N.Y.: Harcourt, 1924.
————. *Taytay's Tales.* N.Y.: Harcourt, 1922.
Dobie, J. Frank. *On the Open Range.* Dallas: Southwest Press, 1931.
Duplaix, Lily. *Pedro, Niña and Perrito.* (Illustrations by Barbara Latham.) N.Y.: Harper, 1939.
Eberle, Irmengarde. *The Very Good Neighbors.* Philadelphia: Lippincott, 1945.
Erdman, Loula Grace. *Separate Star.* N.Y.: Longmans, 1944.
Fellows, Muriel H. *Land of Little Rain.* Philadelphia: Winston, 1936.
Finger, Charles. *Tales from Silver Lands.* Garden City, N.Y.: Doubleday, 1924.
Harrington, Isis L. *Komoki of the Cliffs.* N.Y.: Scribner, 1934.
————. *Nah-le Kah-de.* N.Y.: Dutton, 1937.

Hayes, Florence S. *Hosh-Ki, the Navajo.* N.Y.: Random House, 1943
Hogner, Dorothy Childs. *Navajo Winter Nights.* N.Y.: Nelson, 1935.
Hooker, Forrestine. *Cricket, A Little Girl of the Old West.* N.Y.: Doubleday, 1925.
Hubbard, Margaret Ann. *Seraphina Todd.* N.Y.: Macmillan, 1941.
Jacobs, Caroline E. *Texas Bluebonnet.* Boston: Page, 1910.
James, A. *Tewa Firelight Tales.* N.Y.: Longmans, 1927.
James, Bessie R. *Six-Feet-Six.* Indianapolis: Bobbs, 1931.
Johansen, Margaret A. *Hawk of Hawk Clan.* N.Y.: Longmans, 1941.
Johnson, Siddie Joe. *Cathy.* N.Y.: Longmans, 1945.
——. *Debby.* N.Y.: Longmans, 1940.
——. *New Town in Texas.* N.Y.: Longmans, 1942.
——. *Texas, the Land of the Tejas.* (Illustrations by Fanita Lanier.) N.Y.: Random House, 1943.
Johnston, Annie Fellows. *Little Colonel in Arizona.* Boston: Page, 1919.
——. *Mary Ware in Texas.* Boston: Page, 1910.
Kaler, James Otis. *Phillips of Texas.* N.Y.: American Book Co., 1913.
Kelly, Eric P. *On the Staked Plain.* N.Y.: Macmillan, 1940.
——. *Treasure Mountain.* N.Y.: Macmillan, 1937.
Ladd, Ileta Kerr. *Seeing Texas.* Dallas: Mathis Van Nort, 1943.
Lockwood, Myna. *Beckoning Star,* N.Y.: Dutton, 1943.
——. *Up With Your Banner.* N.Y.: Dutton, 1945.
Lowrey, Janette Sebring. *Annunciata and the Shepherds.* N.Y.: Harper, 1938.
——. *Lavender Cat.* N.Y.: Harper, 1944.
——. *Rings on Her Fingers.* N.Y.: Harper, 1941.
——. *Silver Dollar.* N.Y.: Harper, 1940.
——. *Tap-A-Tan.* N.Y.: Harper, 1942.
Lummis, Charles F. *Pueblo Indian Folk-Stories.* N.Y.: Appleton, 1910.
Malkus, Alida. *Dragon Fly of Zuñi.* N.Y.: Harcourt, 1933.
——. *Stone Knife Boy.* N.Y.: Harcourt, 1928.
Marriott, Alice. *Winter-Telling Stories.* N.Y.: William Sloane Associates, 1947.
Marshall, Helen L. *New Mexican Boy.* N.Y.: Holiday House, 1940.
Means, Florence C. *Adella Mary in Old New Mexico.* Boston: Houghton, 1930.
——. *Shadow Over Wide Ruin.* Boston: Houghton, 1942.
——. *Tangled Waters.* Boston: Houghton, 1936.
——. *Whispering Girl.* Boston: Houghton, 1941.
Moon, Grace. *Book of Nah-Wee.* N.Y.: Doubleday, 1932.
——. *Chi-Wee.* N.Y.: Doubleday, 1925.
——. *Chi-Wee and Loki of the Desert.* N.Y.: Doubleday, 1926.
——. *Lost Indian Magic.* N.Y.: Stokes, 1918.
——. *Magic Trail.* N.Y.: Doubleday, 1929.
——. *Missing Katchina.* N.Y.: Doubleday, 1930.
——. *Nadita.* N.Y.: Doubleday, 1927.
——. *Runaway Papoose.* N.Y.: Doubleday, 1928.
Moran, George. *Kwahu, the Hopi Indian Boy.* N.Y.: American Book Co., 1913.
Morris, Ann A. *Digging in the Southwest.* N.Y.: Doubleday, 1933.
Nusbaum, Aileen. *Zuni Indian Tales.* N.Y.: Putnam, 1926.
Nusbaum, Deric. *Deric in Mesa Verde.* N.Y.: Putnam, 1926.
——. *Deric with the Indians.* N.Y.: Putnam, 1927.
Paschal, Nancy. *Magnolia Heights.* N.Y.: Thomas Nelson, 1947.
Peck, Leigh. *Don Coyote.* Boston: Houghton, 1942.
——. *Pecos Bill and Lightning.* Boston: Houghton, 1940.
Pilgrim, Thomas. *Live Boys or Charley and Nasho in Texas.* Boston: Lee and Shepard, 1878.

————. *Live Boys in the Black Hills or Young Texas Gold Hunters.* Boston: Lee and Shepard, 1880.

Porter, Wm. Sydney. *Ransom of Red Chief and Other O. Henry Stories for Boys.* N.Y.: Doubleday, 1918.

Ranson, Nancy R. *Texas Wildflower Legends.* Dallas: Kaleidograph Press, 1933.

Sayers, Frances Clarke. *Bluebonnets for Lucinda.* N.Y.: Viking, 1934.

————. *Tag-A-Long Tooloo.* N.Y.: Viking, 1941.

Scacheri, Mario and Mabel. *Indians Today.* N.Y.: Harcourt, 1936.

Scott, Lena B. *Dawn Boy of the Pueblos.* Philadelphia: Winston, 1935.

Shapiro, Irwin. *John Henry and the Double Jointed Steam Drill.* N.Y.: Messner, 1945.

Sheahan, Henry Beston. *Sons of Kai.* N.Y.: Macmillan, 1926.

Simon, Charlie May. *Bright Morning.* N.Y.: Dutton, 1939.

————. *Faraway Trail.* N.Y.: Dutton, 1940.

————. *Lost Corner.* N.Y.: Dutton, 1935.

————. *Robin on the Mountain.* N.Y.: Dutton, 1934.

————. *Teeny Gay.* N.Y.: Dutton, 1936.

Smith, Nora A. *Bee of the Cactus Country.* Boston: Houghton, 1932.

Sperry, Armstrong. *Little Eagle.* Philadelphia: Winston, 1938.

Stratemeyer, Edward. *For the Liberty of Texas.* Boston: Estes, 1900; Boston: Lothrop, 1909.

————. *Under Scott in Mexico.* Boston: Estes, 1902; Boston: Lothrop, 1909.

————. *With Taylor on the Rio Grande.* Boston: Estes, 1901; Boston: Lothrop, 1909.

Strong, Phil. *Cowhand Goes to Town.* N.Y.: Dodd, 1939.

Tireman, Loyd. *Baby Jack and Jumping Jack Rabbit.* Mesaland Series. Albuquerque: University of New Mexico Press, 1943.

————. *Big Fat.* Albuquerque: University of New Mexico Press, 1947.

————. *Cocky.* Albuquerque: University of New Mexico Press, 1946.

————. *Dumbee.* Albuquerque: University of New Mexico Press, 1945.

————. *Hop-A-Long.* Albuquerque: University of New Mexico Press, 1944.

Toepperwein, Emilie and Fritz A. *I Want to Be a Cowboy.* Boerne, Texas: Highland Press, 1947.

————. *The Little Valley Quail.* Boerne, Texas: Highland Press, 1945.

Tousey, Sanford. *Cowboy Tommy.* N.Y.: Doubleday, 1932.

Whitman, Wm. *Navajo Tales.* Boston: Houghton, 1925.

Wilder, Laura Ingalls. *Little House on the Prairie.* N.Y.: Harper, 1935.

Youmans, Eleanor. *The Forest Road.* Indianapolis: Bobbs, 1939.

2. TO THIRD EDITION

A. FOR GENERAL READERS

Abbey, Edward. *The Brave Cowboy.* N.Y.: Dodd, 1956.

————. *Fire on the Mountain.* N.Y.: Dial Press, 1962.

Abernathy, Frances E. *Tales from the Big Thicket.* Austin: University of Texas Press, 1966.

Abrams, Sybil Nash. *We Are What We Think All the Day.* Dallas: Triangle Pub. Co., 1970.

Adams, Faye Carr. *More Than a Loaf.* San Antonio: Naylor, 1968.

Adams, Ramon F. *Burs Under the Saddle. A Second Look at Books and Histories of the West.* Norman: University of Oklahoma Press, 1964.

————. *The Cowboy and His Humor.* Austin: University of Texas Press, 1968.
————. *A Fitting Death for Billy the Kid.* Norman: University of Oklahoma Press, 1960.
————. *Old Time Cowhand.* N.Y.: Macmillan, 1961.
Adler, Lucille. *The Travelling Out and Other Poems.* N.Y.: Macmillan, 1967.
Aldington, Richard. *D. H. Lawrence, Portrait of Genius, But . . . .* London: Heinemann, 1950; N.Y.: Duell, 1950.
Alexander, Frances. *Time at the Window.* Dallas: Kaleidograph Press, 1948.
Allen, John Houghton. *Southwest.* Philadelphia: Lippincott, 1952.
Anderson, Clinton P., with Milton Viorst. *Outsider in the Senate.* N.Y.: Houghton, 1970.
Anderson, Dillon. *Claudie's Kinfolks.* Boston: Little, 1954.
————. *The Billingsley Papers.* N.Y.: Simon and Schuster, 1961.
————. *I and Claudie.* Boston: Little, 1951.
Anderson, John Q. *Texas Folk Medicine.* Austin: Encino Press, 1970.
Angelou, Maya (pen and stage name of Marguerite Johnson). *I Know Why the Caged Bird Sings.* N.Y.: Random House, 1970.
Armstrong, Etheree. *The Willow Green of Spring.* Long Island, N.Y.: J. R. Dicks, 1967.
Arnold, Elliot. *The Time of the Gringo.* N.Y.: Knopf, 1953.
Arnold, Oren. *The Golden Chair.* Houston: Elsevier Press, 1954.
————. *Savage Son.* Albuquerque: University of New Mexico Press, 1951.
Atkinson, Mary Jourdan. *Indians of the Southwest.* San Antonio: Naylor, 1963.
Ball, Eve. *In the Days of Victorio.* Tucson: University of Arizona Press, 1970.
————. *Ma'am Jones of the Pecos.* Tucson: University of Arizona Press, 1969.
————. *Ruidoso: The Last Frontier.* San Antonio: Naylor, 1963.
Bard, William E. *Feather in the Sun.* Dallas: Kaleidograph Press, 1949.
————. *This Land, This People.* San Antonio: Naylor, 1966.
Barker, S. Omar. *Rawhide Rhymes.* Garden City, N.Y.: Doubleday, 1968.
————. *Songs of the Saddlemen.* Denver: Sage Books, 1954.
Barnes, Will. C. *Arizona Place Names.* 1935; revised and enlarged by Byrd C. Granger. Tucson: University of Arizona Press, 1960.
Barney, William D. *Kneel from the Stone.* Dallas: Kaleidograph Press, 1952.
————. *Permitted Proof.* Dallas: Kaleidograph Press, 1955.
Barrett, Velma, and Hazel Oliver. *Odessa, City of Dreams.* San Antonio: Naylor, 1952.
Basham, Cecil D. *Verse or Worse.* Flagstaff, Ariz.: Northland Press, 1963.
Bean, Amelia. *Time for Outrage.* Garden City, N.Y.: Doubleday, 1967.
Bedichek, Roy. *Karankaway Country.* Garden City, N.Y.: Doubleday, 1950.
————. *The Sense of Smell.* Garden City, N.Y.: Doubleday, 1960.
Bell, Thomas W. *A Narrative of the Capture and Subsequent Sufferings of the Mier Expedition in Mexico.* Printed for the author at the Press of R. Morris and Co., De Soto County, Miss., 1845. Reproduced with Introduction and Notes by James M. Day, Waco: Texian Press, 1964.
Benton, Alice Gill. *Janus Had Two Faces.* Albuquerque: Privately printed, 1967.
————. *Milestones.* Eureka Springs, Ark.: New Dimension Press, 1950.
————. *See the Earth New.* Alpine, Texas: Round Table Press, 1959.
Blacker, Irwin R. *Taos.* Cleveland: World, 1959.
Boatright, Mody C. *Folk Laughter on the American Frontier.* N.Y.: Macmillan, 1949; Collier Books, 1961.
————. *Folklore of the Oil Industry.* Dallas: Southern Methodist University Press, 1963.
Boatright, Mody C., and W. A. Owens. *Tales from the Derrick Floor.* Garden City, N.Y.: Doubleday, 1970.

Bode, Winston. *A Portrait of Pancho, The Life of a Great Texan: J. Frank Dobie.* Austin: Pemberton Press, 1965.

Bolton, Herbert E. *Coronado, Knight of Pueblos and Plains.* Albuquerque: University of New Mexico Press, 1949, 1964.

Bonnette, Jeanne DeLamarter. *Chess Game and Other Poems.* Chicago: Seymour, 1952.

——. *In This Place.* Fort Smith, Ark.: South and West, 1971.

——. *Oh, The Wide Sky.* Albuquerque: Roy E. Thompson Graphic Arts, 1968.

Bosworth, Allan R. *Ozona Country.* N.Y.: Harper, 1964.

Boyd, Sue Abbott. *Decanter.* Fort Smith, Ark.: South and West, 1962.

——. *Fort Smith and Other Poems.* Fort Smith, Ark.: Border Press, 1965.

——. *How It Is, Selected Poems, 1952-1968.* Homestead, Fla.: Olivant Press, 1968.

——. *Of Sun and Stone.* Crescent City, Fla.: Epos Press, 1959.

——. *The Sample Stage.* Fort Smith, Ark.: South and West, 1964.

Bradford, Richard. *Red Sky at Morning.* Philadelphia: Lippincott, 1968.

Bradley, Chester. *Nomad Fires.* Little Rock: Probeck Printing Co., 1969.

Brewer, J. Mason. *Dog Ghosts and Other Texas Negro Folk Tales.* Austin: University of Texas Press, 1958.

——. *The Word on the Brazos.* Austin: University of Texas Press, 1953.

Briley, Alice. *Program.* Albuquerque: Privately printed, 1967.

Brothers, Robert Lee. *Democracy of Dust.* Dallas: Kaleidograph Press, 1947.

——. *The Hidden Harp.* Dallas: Kaleidograph Press, 1952.

——. *Threescore and Ten.* San Antonio: Naylor, 1963.

Broussard, Ray F. *San Antonio During the Texas Republic.* El Paso: Texas Western Press, 1967.

Browne, Lina Fergusson, ed. *J. Ross Browne, Letters, Journals, Writings.* Albuquerque: University of New Mexico Press, 1969.

Bryan, Jack Y. *Come to the Bower.* N.Y.: Viking, 1963.

Bullock, Alice. *Living Legends of the Santa Fe Country.* Denver: Green Mountain Press, 1970.

Burford, William. *A Beginning, Poems.* N.Y.: Norton, 1966.

——. *Man Now.* Dallas: Southern Methodist University Press, 1954.

——. *A World.* Austin: University of Texas Press, 1962.

Burlingame, Robert. *This Way We Walk.* Parker, Colo.: Thelma and John R. Evans, 1964.

Burrow, Roy Douglass. *The Battle of Pea Ridge.* Charleston, Ill.: Prairie Press Books, 1970.

——. *Trail of Tears.* Fayetteville, Ark.: Burro Books, 1969.

Bynner, Witter. *Book of Lyrics.* N.Y.: Knopf, 1955.

——. *Journey with Genius, Recollections and Reflections Concerning the D. H. Lawrences.* N.Y.: Day, 1951.

——. *New Poems.* N.Y.: Knopf, 1960.

Byrd, Sigman. *Sig Byrd's Houston.* N.Y.: Viking, 1955.

Cabeza de Baca, Fabiola (Mrs. Carlos Gilbert). *We Fed Them Cactus.* Albuquerque: University of New Mexico Press, 1954.

Cahill, Mary. *The Desert Speaks.* Dallas: Naylor, 1968.

Calkins, Thomas V. *Life in Many Facets.* N.Y.: Exposition Press, 1958.

Campa, Arthur L. *Treasure of the Sangre de Cristos.* Norman: University of Oklahoma Press, 1963.

Campbell, Walter S. (pseud. Stanley Vestal). *Dodge City, Queen of Cowtowns.* N.Y.: Harper, 1952.

——. *Warpath and Council Fire, The Plains Indians' Struggle for Survival in War and in Diplomacy, 1851-1891.* N.Y.: Random House, 1948.

Capps, Benjamin. *The Brothers of Uterica.* N.Y.: Meredith, 1967.
————. *Sam Chance.* N.Y.: Duell, 1965.
————. *The Trail to Ogallala.* N.Y.: Duell, 1964.
————. *The White Man's Road.* N.Y.: Harper, 1969.
————. *A Woman of the People.* N.Y.: Duell, 1966.
Carmichael, Lily. *Across the Years.* Little Rock: Balfour Pub. Co., 1969.
Carpenter, Liz. *Ruffles and Flourishes.* Garden City, N.Y.: Doubleday, 1970.
Carpenter, Will Tom. *Lucky 7, A Cowman's Autobiography.* Edited by Elton
    Miles. Austin: University of Texas Press, 1957.
Carter, Harvey Lewis. *"Dear Old Kit," The Historical Christopher Carson.
    With a New Edition of the Carson Memoirs.* Norman: University of Okla-
    homa Press, 1968.
Carver, Charles. *Brann and the Iconoclasts.* Austin: University of Texas
    Press, 1957.
Casey, Bill. *A Shroud for a Journey.* Boston: Houghton, 1961.
Cavitch, David. *D. H. Lawrence and the New World.* N.Y.: Oxford Press,
    1969.
Chafetz, Henry. *Thunderbird and Other Stories.* Norman: University of Okla-
    homa Press, 1964.
Chavez, Fray Angelico. *La Conquistadora, The Autobiography of an Ancient
    Statue.* Paterson, N.J.: St. Anthony Guild Press, 1954.
————. *The Lady from Toledo.* Fresno: Academy Library Guild, 1960.
————. *Selected Poems.* Santa Fe: Press of the Territorian, 1970.
————. *The Single Rose.* Santa Fe: Santa Fe Press, 1948.
————. *The Virgin of Port Lligat.* Fresno: Academy Library Guild, 1956.
Chew, Byron. *Corrida and Other Poems.* Tyler, Texas: Merchants Press, 1966.
————. *Strange Island.* San Antonio: Naylor, 1959.
Church, Peggy Pond. *The House at Otowi Bridge: The story of Edith Warner
    and Los Alamos.* Albuquerque: University of New Mexico Press, 1959.
————. *The Ripened Fields.* Philadelphia: Inward Light, 1954.
————. *Ultimatum for Man.* Stanford University, Calif.: James Ladd Delkin,
    1946, 1947.
Claremon, Neil. *East by Southwest.* N.Y.: Simon and Schuster, 1970.
Clark, Ann Nolan. *These Were the Valiant, A Collection of New Mexico Pro-
    files.* Albuquerque: Calvin Horn, 1969.
Clark, James Anthony, and Michael T. Halbouty. *Spindletop.* N.Y.: Random
    House, 1952.
Clark, L. D. *The Dove Tree.* Garden City, N.Y.: Doubleday, 1961.
Clark, La Verne. *They Sang for Horses.* Tucson: University of Arizona Press,
    1966.
Clarke, Mary Whatley. *David G. Burnet, First President of Texas.* Austin:
    Pemberton Press, 1969.
Clemons, Walter. *The Poison Tree.* Boston: Houghton, 1959.
Coe, Wilbur. *Ranch on the Ruidoso.* N.Y.: Knopf, 1968.
Collinson, Frank. *Life in the Saddle.* Edited by Mary Whatley Clarke. Nor-
    man: University of Oklahoma Press, 1963.
Colquitt, Betsy Feagan, ed. *A Part of Space, Ten Texas Writers.* Fort Worth:
    Texas Christian University Press, 1969.
Colton, Harold S. *Hopi Kachina Dolls.* Albuquerque: University of New
    Mexico Press, 1949.
Connor, Seymour V., ed., The Saga of Texas Series: I. *A Successful Failure,
    1519-1810* by Odie B. Faulk; II. *The Revolutionary Decade, 1810-1836* by
    David M. Vigness; III. *Adventure in Glory, 1836-1849* by Seymour V.
    Connor; IV. *Texas in Turmoil, 1849-1875* by Ernest Wallace; V. *The*

Search for Maturity, 1875-1900 by Billy M. Jones; VI. *Texas after Spindle-top, 1901-1965* by Seth S. McKay and Odie B. Faulk. Austin: Steck-Vaughn, 1965.

Cooper, Madison, Jr. *Sironia, Texas.* N.Y.: Houghton, 1952.

Corle, Edwin. *In Winter Light.* N.Y.: Duell, 1949.

Cosulich, Bernice. *Tucson.* Tucson: Arizona Silhouettes, 1953.

Cowan, James C. *D. H. Lawrence's American Journey, A Study in Literature and Myth.* Cleveland: Case Western Reserve Press, 1970.

Creeley, Robert. *For Love.* N.Y.: Scribner, 1962.

————. *Pieces.* N.Y.: Scribner, 1969.

————. *Words.* N.Y.: Scribner, 1967.

Crosby, Thelma, and Eve Ball. *Bob Crosby, World Champion Cowboy.* Clarendon, Texas: Clarendon Press, 1966.

Current-Garcia, Eugene. *O. Henry* (William Sydney Porter). N.Y.: Twayne, 1965.

Curry, George. *An Autobiography.* Edited by H. B. Hening. Albuquerque: University of New Mexico Press, 1958.

Curtin, L. S. M. *Healing Herbs of the Upper Rio Grande.* Los Angeles: Southwest Museum, 1965; published originally by Laboratory of Anthropology, Santa Fe, 1947.

Dale, E. E. *Ranching on the Great Plains, 1865-1925.* Norman: University of Oklahoma Press, 1960.

Dawson, Joseph Martin. *Jose Antonio Navarro, Co-Creator of Texas.* Waco: Baylor University Press, 1970.

————. *A Thousand Months to Remember.* Waco: Baylor University Press, 1964.

Day, James M. *Black Beans and Goose Quills, Literature of the Texas Mier Expedition.* Waco: Texian Press, 1970.

Dearing, Frank V., ed. *The Best Short Stories of Eugene Manlove Rhodes.* Boston: Houghton, 1949.

Dewlen, Al. *The Bone Pickers,* N.Y.: McGraw, 1958.

————. *Night of the Tiger.* N.Y.: McGraw, 1956.

————. *Twilight of Honor.* N.Y.: McGraw, 1961.

Dickey, Roland. *New Mexico Village Arts.* Albuquerque: University of New Mexico Press, 1949.

Dobie, J. Frank. *Cow People.* Boston: Little, 1964.

————. *The Mustangs.* Boston: Little, 1952.

————. *Rattlesnakes.* Boston: Little, 1965.

————. *Some Part of Myself.* Boston: Little, 1967.

————. *Tales of Old-Time Texas.* Boston: Little, 1955.

————. *The Voice of the Coyote.* Boston: Little, 1949.

Dresbach, Glenn Ward. *Collected Poems, 1914-1948.* Caldwell, Idaho: Caxton Printers, 1950.

Dugger, Ronnie, ed. *Three Men in Texas: Bedichek, Webb, Dobie.* Austin: University of Texas Press, 1967.

Dunn, Dorothy. *American Indian Painting of the Southwest and Plains Area.* Albuquerque: University of New Mexico Press, 1968.

Durham, Philip, and Everett L. Jones. *The Negro Cowboys.* N.Y.: Dodd, 1965.

Duval, John C. *The Adventures of Big-Foot Wallace.* Edited by Mabel Major and Rebecca W. Smith. Dallas: Tardy, 1936; Lincoln: University of Nebraska Press, 1966.

Eastlake, William. *The Bronc People.* N.Y.: Harcourt, 1958.

————. *Go in Beauty.* N.Y.: Harper, 1956.

————. *Portrait of an Artist with Twenty-Six Horses.* N.Y.: Simon and Schuster, 1958.

Eaves, Charles Dudley, and C. A. Hutchinson. *Post City, Texas; C. W. Post's Colonizing Activities in West Texas.* Austin: Texas State Historical Association, 1952.

Ely, Sims. *The Lost Dutchman Mine.* N.Y.: Morrow, 1953.

Emery, Emma Wilson. *Aunt Puss and Others, Old Days in the Piney Woods.* Austin: Encino Press, 1969.

Emmett, Chris. *Shanghai Pierce, A Fair Likeness.* Norman: University of Oklahoma Press, 1953.

Emmons, Martha. *Deep Like the River, Stories of My Negro Friends.* Austin: Encino Press, 1969.

Erdman, Loula Grace. *Another Spring.* N.Y.: Dodd, 1966.

————. *The Edge of Time.* N.Y.: Dodd, 1950.

————. *The Good Land.* N.Y.: Dodd, 1959.

————. *Life Was Simpler Then.* N.Y.: Dodd, 1963.

————. *Many a Voyage,* N.Y.: Dodd, 1960.

————. *My Sky Is Blue.* N.Y.: Longmans, 1953.

————. *The Short Summer.* N.Y.: Dodd, 1955.

————. *A Time to Write.* N.Y.: Dodd, 1969.

Espinosa, Carmen. *Shawls, Crinolines, and Filigree.* El Paso: Texas Western Press, 1970.

Espinosa, Gilberto, and Tibo J. Chavez. *El Rio Abajo.* Pampa, Texas: Pampa Print Shop, 1966.

Espinosa, Jose E. *Saints in the Valley.* Albuquerque: University of New Mexico Press, 1960.

Estergreen, M. Morgan. *Kit Carson: A Portrait in Courage.* Norman: University of Oklahoma Press, 1962.

Estes, Winston. *Another Part of the House.* Philadelphia: Lippincott, 1970.

Evans, Max. *Hi-Lo Country.* N.Y.: Macmillan, 1961.

————. *The Mountain of Gold.* Dunwoody, Ga.: N. S. Burg, 1965.

————. *The One-Eyed Sky.* Boston: Houghton, 1963.

————. *The Rounders.* N.Y.: Macmillan, 1960.

————. *Shadow of Thunder.* Chicago: Swallow, 1969.

————. *Southwest Wind.* San Antonio: Naylor, 1958.

Faulk, Odie B. *Arizona: A Short History.* Norman: University of Oklahoma Press, 1970.

————. *Land of Many Frontiers, History of the American Southwest.* N.Y.: Oxford Press, 1968.

Fehrenbach, T. R. *Lone Star: A History of Texas and the Texans.* N.Y.: Macmillan, 1968.

Felton, Harold W. *Cowboy Jamboree, Western Songs and Lore.* N.Y.: Knopf, 1951.

————. *Pecos Bill, Texas Cowpuncher.* N.Y.: Knopf, 1949.

Ferber, Edna. *Giant.* Garden City, N.Y.: Doubleday, 1952.

Fergusson, Erna. *Murder and Mystery in New Mexico.* Albuquerque: Merle Armitage, 1948.

————. *New Mexico, A Pageant of Three Peoples.* N.Y.: Knopf, 1951.

Fergusson, Harvey. *The Conquest of Don Pedro.* N.Y.: Morrow, 1954.

————. *Grant of Kingdom.* N.Y.: Morrow, 1950.

Fife, Austin E. and Alta S. *See* Howard N. (Jack) Thorp.

Flanagan, Sue. *Sam Houston's Texas.* Austin: University of Texas Press, 1964.

Flynn, Robert. *In the House of the Lord.* N.Y.: Knopf, 1967.

———. *North To Yesterday.* N.Y.: Knopf, 1967.

Foote, Horton. *The Chase.* N.Y.: Rinehart, 1956.

Ford, Edsel. *Looking for Shiloh.* Columbia: University of Missouri Press, 1968.

———. *Love Is the House It Lives In.* Fort Smith, Ark.: Homestead House, 1965.

———. *The Manchild from Sunday Creek.* Dallas: Kaleidograph Press, 1956.

———. *The Stallion's Nest.* Fayetteville, Ark.: Privately printed, 1952.

———. *A Thicket of Sky.* Fort Smith, Ark.: Homestead House, 1961.

———. *This Was My War.* Privately printed, 1955.

Fornell, Earl W. *The Galveston Era, The Texas Crescent on the Eve of Secession.* Austin: University of Texas Press, 1961.

Francis, Marilyn. *Mirror Without Glass.* Flagstaff, Ariz.: Northland Press, 1964.

———. *Space for Sound.* San Antonio: Naylor, 1962.

———. *Symbols for Instants.* San Antonio: Naylor, 1965.

———. *Tangents at Noon.* San Antonio: Naylor, 1961.

Frantz, Joe B. *Gail Borden, Dairyman to a Nation.* Norman: University of Oklahoma Press, 1951.

Frantz, Joe B., and J. E. Choate, Jr. *The American Cowboy, the Myth and the Reality.* Norman: University of Oklahoma Press, 1955.

Friend, Llerena. *Sam Houston, The Great Designer.* Austin: University of Texas Press, 1954.

Frontier Forts of Texas. Introduction by Rupert N. Richardson. Historical coordinator, Colonel Harold B. Simpson. Chapters by Kenneth F. Neighbors, *et al.* Waco: Texian Press, 1966.

Fuermann, George. *The Face of Houston.* Houston: Press of Premier, 1963.

———. *Houston, The Feast Years.* Houston: Premier Printing Co., 1962.

———. *Houston, Land of the Big Rich.* Garden City, N.Y.: Doubleday, 1952.

———. *Reluctant Empire, The Mind of Texas.* Garden City, N.Y.: Doubleday, 1957.

Fulcher, Walter. *The Way I Heard It.* Edited by Elton Miles. Austin: University of Texas Press, 1959.

Fulton, Maurice G. *History of the Lincoln County War.* Edited by Robert N. Mullin. Tucson: University of Arizona Press, 1968.

Gambrell, Herbert, ed. *Texas Today and Tomorrow.* Essays by W. St. John Garwood, *et al.* Dallas: Southern Methodist University Press, 1962.

Gambrell, Herbert and Virginia. *A Pictorial History of Texas.* N.Y.: Dutton, 1960.

Gard, Wayne. *The Chisholm Trail.* Norman: University of Oklahoma Press, 1954.

———. *Fabulous Quarter Horse, Steel Dust.* N.Y.: Duell, 1958.

———. *Frontier Justice.* Norman: University of Oklahoma Press, 1949.

———. *The Great Buffalo Hunt.* N.Y.: Knopf, 1959.

———. *Rawhide Texas.* Norman: University of Oklahoma Press, 1965.

Garner, Claud. *Sam Houston, Texas Giant.* San Antonio: Naylor, 1969.

Gaston, Edwin W., Jr. *Conrad Richter.* N.Y.: Twayne, 1965.

———. *The Early Novel of the Southwest.* Albuquerque: University of New Mexico Press, 1961.

Geue, Chester William and Ethel Hander. *A New Land Beckoned, German Immigration to Texas, 1844-1847.* Waco: Texian Press, 1967.

Gillis, Everett A. *Angles of the Wind.* Dallas: Kaleidograph Press, 1954.

———. *Sunrise in Texas.* San Antonio: Fotolith Corporation, 1949.

Gillmor, Frances. *Flute of the Smoking Mirror.* Albuquerque: University of

New Mexico Press, 1949; Tucson: University of Arizona Press, 1968.
——. *The King Danced in the Market Place.* Tucson: University of Arizona Press, 1964.
Gilpin, Laura. *The Rio Grande, River of Destiny.* N.Y.: Duell, 1949.
Gipson, Fred. *Recollection Creek.* N.Y.: Harper, 1959.
Goodwyn, Frank. *Life on the King Ranch.* N.Y.: Crowell, 1951.
——. *Lone Star Land.* N.Y.: Knopf, 1955.
Gordon, Alvin. *Of Vines and Missions.* Flagstaff, Ariz.: Northland Press, 1971.
Gosnell, Betty. *The Poet Who Was a Painter of Souls.* Fort Smith, Ark.: South and West, 1969.
Goyen, William. *The House of Breath.* N.Y.: Random House, 1949.
Grabo (Calkins), Eunice Carter. *The Ultimate White Flower.* Highgate, Jamaica, W.I.: Walker's Printing, 1958.
Granger, Byrd H. *See* Will C. Barnes.
Graves, John. *Goodbye to a River.* N.Y.: Knopf, 1960.
Gray, May. *The Voice of the Sea.* Fort Smith, Ark.: South and West, 1963.
Green, Ben K. *Horse Trading.* N.Y.: Knopf, 1967.
——. *Wild Cow Tales.* N.Y.: Knopf, 1969.
Green, Charles Price. *Lariat Laughter and Other Poems.* London: Mitre Press, 1970.
Greene, A. C. *A Personal Country.* N.Y.: Knopf, 1969.
Gregory, Jack, and Rennard Strickland. *Sam Houston with the Cherokees, 1829-1833.* Austin and London: University of Texas Press, 1967.
Griffin, John Howard. *Black Like Me.* Boston: Houghton, 1961.
——. *Land of the High Sky.* Midland, Texas: First National Bank of Midland, 1959.
Haas, Chuck. *Rhymes O' A Drifting Cowboy.* Flagstaff, Ariz.: Northland Press, 1969.
Hackleman, Wauneta. *Soliloquies in Verse.* N.Y.: Vantage Press, 1966.
Hadley, Drummond. *The Webbing.* San Francisco: Four Seasons Foundation, 1967.
Haley, J. Evetts. *XIT Ranch of Texas.* Chicago: Lakeside Press, 1929; new edition, Norman: University of Oklahoma Press, 1953.
Hall, Colby D. *The Gay Nineties.* San Antonio: Naylor, 1961.
Hall, Freda. *The Spinner.* Fayetteville, Ark.: Ozark Sunlight Series, 1967.
Hallenbeck, Cleve. *Land of the Conquistadores.* Caldwell, Idaho: Caxton Printers, 1950.
Halsell, Grace. *Soul Sister.* Cleveland: World, 1969.
Hanke, Lewis U. *Aristotle and the American Indian, A Study in Race Prejudice in the Modern World.* London: Hollis and Carter, 1959.
Hannett, Arthur Thomas. *Sagebrush Lawyer.* N.Y.: Pageant Press, 1964.
Hano, Arnold. *Western Roundup.* N.Y.: Bantam Books, 1948.
Hardwicke, Robert. *The Oilman's Barrel.* Norman: University of Oklahoma Press, 1958.
Harris, Etta Caldwell. *Come Dreaming With Me.* Dallas: Triangle Pub. Co., 1970.
——. *Lest The Harvest Be Not Grapes.* Little Rock: Allard House, 1960.
——. *Let This Be Home.* Dallas: Triangle Pub. Co., 1963.
——. *The Marked Path.* Dallas: Triangle Pub. Co., 1958.
Harris, William Foster. *The Look of the Old West.* N.Y.: Viking, 1955.
Hayes, Jess G. *Apache Vengeance.* Albuquerque: University of New Mexico Press, 1954.

Hedrick, Addie. *A Cup of Stars*. Francestown, N.H.: Golden Quill Press, 1969.

Henderson, Archibald. *Omphale's Wheel*. Francestown, N.H.: Golden Quill Press, 1966.

Henderson, Richard B. *Maury Maverick, A Political Biography*. Austin: University of Texas Press, 1970.

Hendrick, George. *Katherine Anne Porter*. N.Y.: Twayne, 1965.

Hendricks, George D. *Mirrors, Mice, and Mustaches, A Sampling of Superstitions and Popular Beliefs in Texas*. Austin: Encino Press, 1966.

Henry, Will. *Who Rides with Wyatt?* N.Y.: Random House, 1954.

Hill, Rudolph N. *From Country Lanes to Space Age Dawn*. San Antonio: Naylor, 1968.

Hillerman, Tony. *The Blessing Way*. N.Y.: Harper, 1970.

Hodge, Gene Meany. *The Kachinas Are Coming*. Flagstaff, Ariz.: Northland Press, 1967; reprint of original by Bruce McAllister, Los Angeles, 1936.

Hogan, Ray. *Jackman's Wolf*. Garden City, N.Y.: Doubleday, 1970.

Holland, Ellen Bowie. *Gay as a Grig, Memories of a North Texas Girlhood*. Austin: University of Texas Press, 1963.

——. *Quiet Please!* Fort Worth: Branch-Smith, 1968.

Hollon, W. Eugene. *The Great American Desert, Then and Now*. N.Y.: Oxford Press, 1966.

——. *The Southwest, Old and New*. N.Y.: Knopf, 1961; Lincoln: University of Nebraska Press, 1968.

Hope, Thomas Wellborn. *The Great River and Other Poems*. Norman: University of Oklahoma Press, 1970.

Horgan, Paul. *The Centuries of Santa Fe*. N.Y.: Dutton, 1956.

——. *Conquistadors*. N.Y.: Farrar, 1963; Fawcett World Library, 1965.

——. *A Distant Trumpet*. N.Y.: Farrar, 1960.

——. *Great River, The Rio Grande in North American History*, 2 vols. N.Y.: Rinehart, 1954.

——. *The Heroic Triad, Background of Our Three Southwestern Cultures*. N.Y.: Holt, 1970.

——. *Humble Powers*. Garden City, N.Y.: Doubleday, 1954.

——. *Memories of the Future*. N.Y.: Farrar, 1966.

——. *Peter Hurd, A Portrait Sketch from Life*. Amon Carter Museum of Western Art, Fort Worth. Austin: University of Texas Press, 1965.

——. *Whitewater*. N.Y.: Farrar, 1970.

Horn, Calvin. *New Mexico's Troubled Years*. Albuquerque: Horn and Wallace, 1963.

Horn, Tom. *The Shallow Grass*. N.Y.: Macmillan, 1968.

House, Boyce. *City of Flaming Adventure, the Chronicle of San Antonio*. San Antonio: Naylor, 1949.

——. *Roaring Ranger*. San Antonio: Naylor, 1951.

Hubbard, Louis H. *Recollections of a Texas Educator*. Salado, Texas: Anson Jones Press, 1965.

Hudson, Wilson. *Andy Adams, His Life and Writings*. Dallas: Southern Methodist University Press, 1964.

Humphrey, William. *Home from the Hill*. N.Y.: Knopf, 1958.

——. *The Ordways*. N.Y.: Knopf, 1965.

Hunt, Wolf Robe. *The Dancing Horses of Acoma*, as told to Helen Rushmore. Cleveland: World, 1963.

Hurd, Peter. *Portfolio of Landscapes and Portraits*. Albuquerque: University of New Mexico Press, 1950.

Hutchinson, W. H. *A Bar Cross Man, The Life and Personal Writings of Eugene Manlove Rhodes*. Norman: University of Oklahoma Press, 1956.

Jackson, Booker T. *God Looks Down*. Fort Smith, Ark.: South and West, 1968.
Jenkinson, Michael. *Ghost Towns of New Mexico*. Albuquerque: University of New Mexico Press, 1967.
Johnson, Lady Bird. *A White House Diary*. N.Y.: Holt, 1970.
Johnston, Eloise. *Piecemeal and Gravel Green*. Oklahoma City: Times-Journal, 1968.
Jones, Douglas C. *The Treaty of Medicine Lodge*. Norman: University of Oklahoma Press, 1966.
Jones, Oakah L. *Pueblo Warrior and Spanish Conquest*. Norman: University of Oklahoma Press, 1966.
Keith, Noel L. *The Brites of Capote*. Fort Worth: Texas Christian University Press, 1950.
Keleher, William A. *Turmoil in New Mexico*. Santa Fe: Rydal Press, 1952.
————. *Memoirs, 1892-1969, A New Mexico Item*. Santa Fe: Rydal Press, 1969.
————. *Violence in Lincoln County, 1869-1881*. Albuquerque: University of New Mexico Press, 1957.
Kelly, Isabel. *Folk Practices in North America, Birth Customs, Folk Medicine, and Spiritualism in the Laguna Zone*. Austin: University of Texas Press, 1965.
Kennon, Bob. *From the Pecos to the Powder,* as told to Ramon F. Adams. Norman: University of Oklahoma Press, 1965.
Kent, Ruth, ed. *Oklahoma, A Guide to the Sooner State*. Norman: University of Oklahoma Press, 1957.
Keppler, C. F. *The Other*. N.Y.: Houghton, 1964.
Kidd, Walter E. (pseud. Conrad Pendleton). *Slow Fire of Time*. Denver: Allan Swallow, 1956.
————. *Time Turns West*. Cleveland: American Weave Press, 1961.
Kilpatrick, Jack F. and Anna G. *Friends of Thunder, Folktales of the Oklahoma Cherokees*. Dallas: Southern Methodist University Press, 1964.
Kirkland, Elithe Hamilton. *Divine Average*. Boston: Little, 1952.
————. *Love Is a Wild Assault*. Garden City, N.Y.: Doubleday, 1959.
Knight, Oliver. *Fort Worth, Outpost on the Trinity*. Norman: University of Oklahoma Press, 1953.
Kreps, Robert. *The Hour of the Gun*. N.Y.: Fawcett, 1967.
Krutch, Joseph Wood. *The Best of Two Worlds*. N.Y.: Sloane, 1953.
————. *The Desert Year*. N.Y.: Sloane, 1952.
————. *Grand Canyon: Today and All Its Yesterdays*. N.Y.: Sloane, 1958.
————. *The Voice of the Desert: A Naturalist Interpretation*. N.Y.: Sloane, 1955.
La Farge, Oliver. *Cochise of Arizona*. N.Y.: Dutton, 1953.
————. *The Door in the Wall*. Boston: Houghton, 1965.
————. *A Pause in the Desert*. N.Y.: Houghton, 1957.
————. *Santa Fe: The Autobiography of a Southwestern Town*. Norman: University of Oklahoma Press, 1959.
Lange, Charles H. *Cochiti: A New Mexico Pueblo, Past and Present*. Austin: University of Texas Press, 1959; Carbondale and Edwardsville: Southern Illinois University Press, 1969.
Langford, Gerald. *Alias O. Henry, A Biography of William Sidney Porter*. N.Y.: Macmillan, 1957.
Langford, J. Oscar. *Big Bend*. Austin: University of Texas Press, 1953.
Larson, Robert W. *New Mexico's Quest for Statehood, 1846-1912*. Albuquerque: University of New Mexico Press, 1968.
Lasswell, Mary, in collaboration with Bob Pool. *I'll Take Texas*. Boston: Houghton, 1958.

Laughlin, Ruth. *The Wind Leaves No Shadow*. N.Y.: Whittlesey House, 1948.

Lea, Aurora Lucero White. *Literary Folklore of the Hispanic Southwest*. San Antonio: Naylor, 1953.

Lea, Tom. *The Brave Bulls*. Boston: Little, 1949.

——. *The Hands of Cantu*. Boston: Little, 1964.

——. *The King Ranch*. Boston: Little, 1957.

——. *A Picture Gallery*. Boston: Little, 1968.

——. *Tom Lea, A Portfolio of Six Paintings*. Austin: University of Texas Press, 1953.

——. *The Wonderful Country*. Boston: Little, 1952.

Leach, Joseph. *The Typical Texan*. Dallas: Southern Methodist University Press, 1952.

Leath, Marcelle Chancellor. *Awake in the Night*. San Antonio: Naylor, 1948.

Lee, Rebecca Smith. *Mary Austin Holley, A Biography*. Austin: University of Texas Press, 1962.

Leslie, Warren. *Dallas, Public and Private, Aspects of an American City*. N.Y.: Grossman, 1964.

Long, Alice Lavinia. *The Poems of Alice Lavinia Long*. Naples, N.Y.: Haniel Long Fund, 1967.

Long, E. Hudson. *O. Henry, The Man and His Work*. Philadelphia: University of Pennsylvania Press, 1949.

Long, Haniel. *If He Can Make Her So*. Anthology of works of Long, edited by Ron Caplan. Pittsburgh: Frontier Press, 1968; N.Y.: Small Publishers, 1968.

——. *Interlinear to Cabeza de Vaca*. Reprint. Pittsburgh: Frontier Press, 1969.

Loomis, Noel M., and Abraham P. Nasatir. *Pedro Vial and the Roads to Santa Fe*. Norman: University of Oklahoma Press, 1967.

Looney, Ralph. *Haunted Highways, The Ghost Towns of New Mexico*. N.Y.: Hastings House, 1968.

Lyon, Mabelle A., ed. *Jewels on a Willow Tree*. Charleston, Ill.: Prairie Press, 1966.

——. *Melodies from a Jade Harp*. Charleston, Ill.: Prairie Press, 1968.

Madison, Virginia. *The Big Bend Country of Texas*. Albuquerque: University of New Mexico Press, 1955.

Madison, Virginia, and Hallie Stillwell. *How Come It's Called That?* Albuquerque: University of New Mexico Press, 1958.

Major, Mabel, and T. M. Pearce, eds. *Signature of the Sun, Southwest Verse, 1900-1950*. Albuquerque: University of New Mexico Press, 1950.

Marinoni, Rosa Zagnoni. *The Green Sea Horse*. Francestown, N.H.: Golden Quill Press, 1963.

——. *Lend Me Your Ears*. Fayetteville, Ark.: Ozark Sunlight Series, 1965.

——. *Timberline*. Cedar Rapids, Iowa: Torch Press, 1954.

Marriott, Alice. *Greener Fields, Experiences Among the American Indians*. N.Y.: Crowell, 1953.

——. *Hell on Horses and Women*. Norman: University of Oklahoma Press, 1953; Garden City, N.Y.: Dolphin Books, 1962.

——. *Indian Annie, Kiowa Captive*. N.Y.: McKay, 1965.

——. *Indians of the Four Corners*. N.Y.: Crowell, 1952.

——. *Maria, The Potter of San Ildefonso*. Norman: University of Oklahoma Press, 1948.

——. *Saynday's People*. 1963 reprint of *Winter-Telling Stories*, 1947, and *Indians on Horseback*, 1948. Lincoln: University of Nebraska Press, 1963.

Marriott, Alice, and Carol K. Rachlin. *American Epic, The Story of the American Indian*. N.Y.: Putnam, 1969.

———. *American Indian Mythology.* N.Y.: Crowell, 1968.
Martin, Robert L. *The City Moves West, Economic and Industrial Growth in Central West Texas.* Austin: University of Texas Press, 1969.
Mason, Herbert Molloy, Jr. *The Great Pursuit.* N.Y.: Random House, 1970.
Mathews, John Joseph. *Life and Death of an Oilman, The Career of E. W. Marland.* Norman: University of Oklahoma Press, 1951.
———. *The Osages, Children of the Middle Waters.* Norman: University of Oklahoma Press, 1961.
———. *Wah'Kon-Tah, The Osage and the White Man's Road.* Reissue of 1932 edition. Norman: University of Oklahoma Press, 1968.
Maudslay, Robert. *Texas Sheep Man.* Edited by Winifred Kupper. Austin: University of Texas Press, 1951.
Mayer, Tom. *Bubble Gum and Kipling.* N.Y.: Viking, 1964.
Mayhall, Mildred P. *Indian Wars of Texas.* Waco: Texian Press, 1965.
———. *The Kiowas.* Norman: University of Oklahoma Press, 1962.
McCallum, Henry D. and Frances T. *The Wire That Fenced the West.* Norman: University of Oklahoma Press, 1965.
McCarty, John L. *Maverick Town, The Story of Old Tascosa.* New and enlarged edition. Norman: University of Oklahoma Press, 1968.
McComb, David G. *Houston, the Bayou City.* Austin: University of Texas Press, 1969.
McLean, Malcolm D. *Fine Texas Horses, Their Pedigrees and Performance, 1830-1845.* Fort Worth: Texas Christian University Press, 1966.
McMillion, Bonner. *So Long at the Fair.* Garden City, N.Y.: Doubleday, 1964.
McMurtry, Larry. *Horseman, Pass By.* N.Y.: Harper, 1961.
———. *In a Narrow Grave, Essays on Texas.* Austin: Encino Press, 1968.
———. *The Last Picture Show.* N.Y.: Dial Press, 1966.
———. *Leaving Cheyenne.* N.Y.: Harper, 1963.
———. *Moving On.* N.Y.: Simon and Schuster, 1970.
McReynolds, Edwin C. *The Seminoles.* Norman: University of Oklahoma Press, 1957.
McRill, Albert. *And Satan Came Also.* Oklahoma City: Burron Pub. Co., 1955.
McRill, Leslie A. *Living Heritage.* Oklahoma City: Dunn Pub. Co., 1970.
———. *Okalona, Valley of Peace.* Oklahoma City: Dunn Pub. Co., 1967.
———. *Saga of Oklahoma.* Oklahoma City: Privately printed, 1957.
———. *Tales of the Night Wind.* Oklahoma City: Dunn Pub. Co., 1945.
Medlock, Julius L. *Stray Hearts.* Oklahoma City: Harlow Pub. Co., 1956.
———. *Threads of Flame.* Oklahoma City: Northwest Pub. Co., 1960.
Mellard, Rudolph. *South by Southwest.* Denver: Sage, 1960.
Meriwether, David. *My Life in the Mountains and on the Plains.* Edited by Robert A. Griffen. Norman: University of Oklahoma Press, 1965.
Mertins, Louis. *The Blue God.* Los Angeles: Ward Ritchie Press, 1968.
Miller, Edna Hull. *Poems From a Parsonage.* Oklahoma City: Northwest Pub. Co., 1960.
Miller, Vassar. *Adam's Footprint.* New Orleans: New Orleans Poetry Journal, 1956.
———. *My Bones Being Wiser.* Middletown, Conn.: Wesleyan University Press, 1963.
———. *Onions and Roses.* Middletown, Conn.: Wesleyan University Press, 1968.
———. *Wage War on Silence.* Middletown, Conn.: Wesleyan University Press, 1960.
Momaday, N. Scott. *House Made of Dawn.* Evanston and N.Y.: Harper, 1968.
———. *The Way to Rainy Mountain.* Albuquerque: University of New Mexico Press, 1969.

Moncus, Herman. *Prairie Schooner Pirates.* N.Y.: Carlton Press, 1963.

Montgomery, Vaida. *Hail for Rain.* Dallas: Kaleidograph Press, 1948.

Mooney, Harry John, Jr. *The Fiction and Criticism of Katherine Anne Porter.* Pittsburgh: University of Pittsburgh Press, 1957.

Moore, Harry T., ed. *The Collected Letters of D. H. Lawrence,* 2 vols. N.Y.: Viking Press, 1962.

————. *D. H. Lawrence: His Life and Works.* N.Y.: Twayne, 1951; rev. ed., 1964.

————. *The Intelligent Heart, The Story of D. H. Lawrence.* London: Heinemann, 1955; N.Y.: Farrar, 1955.

Moorhead, Max. *The Apache Frontier.* Norman: University of Oklahoma Press, 1968.

Morang, Alfred. *Santa Fe.* Denver: Sage Books, 1955.

Morris, Willie. *North Toward Home.* Boston: Houghton, 1967.

Motto, Sytha. *No Banners Waving.* N.Y.: Vantage Press, 1966.

————. *Walk the High Places.* Appalachia, Va.: Young Publications, 1968.

Myers, John Myers. *Doc Holliday.* Boston: Little, 1955.

————. *Maverick Zone.* N.Y.: Hastings House, 1961.

Nance, William L. *Katherine Anne Porter and the Art of Rejection.* Chapel Hill: University of North Carolina Press, 1963.

Neal, Dorothy Jensen. *Captive Mountain Waters.* El Paso: Texas Western Press, 1961.

————. *The Cloud-Climbing Railroad.* Alamogordo, N.M.: Alamogordo Printing Co., 1966.

Nehls, Edward, ed. *D. H. Lawrence, A Composite Biography,* 3 vols. Madison: University of Wisconsin Press, 1957, 1958, 1959.

Newcomb, Charles G. *The Smoke Hole.* San Antonio: Naylor, 1968.

Newcomb, Franc Johnson. *Hosteen Klah, Navajo Medicine Man and Sandpainter.* Norman: University of Oklahoma Press, 1964.

————. *Navajo Bird Tales. As Told by Hosteen Clah Chee.* Wheaton, Ill.: Theosophical Publishing House, 1970.

————. *Navaho Folk Tales.* Santa Fe: Museum of Navaho Ceremonial Art, 1967.

————. *Navaho Neighbors.* Norman: University of Oklahoma Press, 1966.

Newcomb, Franc Johnson, with Stanley Fishler and Mary C. Wheelwright. *A Study of Navajo Symbolism.* Cambridge: The Museum, 1956.

Newcomb, W. W., Jr. *The Indians of Texas.* Austin: University of Texas Press, 1961.

New Mexico Folklore Record. T. M. Pearce, ed. I-VI, 1947-52; E. W. Baughman, ed. VII-VIII, 1953-54; Julia M. Keleher, ed. IX-X, 1955-56; T. M. Pearce, ed. XI, 1964, and XII, 1970. Albuquerque: University of New Mexico.

Newton, Violette. *Moses in Texas.* Fort Smith, Ark.: South and West, 1967.

Nolan, Frederick W. *John Henry Tunstall.* Albuquerque: University of New Mexico Press, 1965.

Nordyke, Lewis. *Cattle Empire.* N.Y.: Morrow, 1949.

————. *Great Roundup.* N.Y.: Morrow, 1955.

————. *The Truth about Texas.* N.Y.: Crowell, 1957.

Nunn, W. C. *Escape from Reconstruction.* Fort Worth, Ark.: Leo Potishman Foundation, 1956.

Nye, Wilbur Sturtevant. *Bad Medicine and Good.* Norman: University of Oklahoma Press, 1962.

————. *Plains Indian Raiders.* Norman: University of Oklahoma Press, 1968.
O' Brien, Esse Forrester. *Circus: Cinders to Sawdust.* San Antonio: Naylor, 1959.
————. *The First Bulldogger.* San Antonio: Naylor, 1961.
————. *Reindeer Roundup.* Austin: Steck, 1959.
O'Connor, Jack. *A Boyhood on the Last Frontier.* N.Y.: Knopf, 1969.
O'Connor, Richard. *O. Henry, The Legendary Life of William S. Porter.* Garden City, N.Y.: Doubleday, 1970.
Oliva, Leo E. *Soldiers on the Santa Fe Trail.* Norman: University of Oklahoma Press, 1967.
O'Meara, Walter. *The Spanish Bride.* N.Y.: Putnam, 1954.
Owens, William A. *Fever in the Earth.* N.Y.: Putnam, 1958.
————. *Look to the River.* N.Y.: Athenaeum, 1963.
————. *Texas Folk Songs.* Austin: Texas Folk-Lore Society, 1950.
————. *This Stubborn Soil.* N.Y.: Scribner, 1966.
————. *Three Friends: Bedichek, Dobie, Webb.* Garden City, N.Y.: Doubleday, 1969.
————. *Walking on Borrowed Land.* N.Y.: Bobbs, 1954.
Pare, Madeline Ferren. *Arizona Pageant, A Short History of the 48th State.* Phoenix: Historical Foundation, 1965.
Paredes, Americo. *With His Pistol in His Hand, A Border Ballad and Its Hero.* Austin: University of Texas Press, 1958.
Parrish, Mary M. *How the World Wags.* Philadelphia: Dorrance, 1959.
Patterson, Paul. *Pecos Tales.* Austin: Encino Press, 1967.
Pearce, T. M. *Mary Hunter Austin.* N.Y.: Twayne, 1965.
————. *Oliver La Farge.* N.Y.: Twayne, 1971.
Pearce, T. M., assisted by Ina Sizer Cassidy and Helen S. Pearce. *New Mexico Place Names, A Geographical Dictionary.* Albuquerque: University of New Mexico Press, 1965.
Peery, William, ed. *21 Texas Short Stories.* Austin: University of Texas Press, 1954.
Pendleton, Conrad. *See* Walter E. Kidd.
Pendleton, Tom (pseud.). *Husak.* N.Y.: McGraw, 1969.
————. *The Iron Orchard.* N.Y.: McGraw, 1966.
————. *The Seventh Girl.* N.Y.: McGraw, 1970.
Perry, George Sessions. *My Granny Van.* N.Y.: McGraw, 1949.
————. *Tale of a Foolish Farmer.* N.Y.: McGraw, 1951.
Peter, Lily. *The Great Riding.* Nashville: R. M. Allen, 1966.
————. *The Green Linen of Summer and Other Poems.* Nashville: R. M. Allen, 1964.
Pillsbury, Dorothy. *No High Adobe.* Albuquerque: University of New Mexico Press, 1950.
————. *Roots in Adobe.* Albuquerque: University of New Mexico Press, 1959.
Plunkett, Eugenia. *If You Listen Quietly.* Fort Smith, Ark.: South and West, 1969.
Poetry Society of Texas. *A Book of the Year.* Dallas, 1949-71.
Porter, C. Fayne. *Santa Fe in Haiku.* Santa Fe: Ortiz Printing Shop, 1970.
Porter, Jenny Lind. *Azle and the Attic Room.* Los Angeles: Ward Ritchie Press, 1957.
————. *The Lantern of Diogenes and Other Poems.* San Antonio: Naylor, 1954.
Porter, Katherine Anne. *The Collected Stories of Katherine Anne Porter.* N.Y.: Harcourt, 1965.
————. *Ship of Fools.* Boston: Little, 1962.

Portis, Charles. *True Grit.* N.Y.: Simon and Schuster, 1968.

Powell, Lawrence Clark. *Books in My Baggage, Adventures in Reading and Collecting.* Cleveland: World, 1960.

——. *West Southwest, Essays on Writers, Their Books and Their Lands.* Los Angeles: Ward Ritchie Press, 1957.

Procter, Ben H. *Not Without Honor, The Life of John Reagan.* Austin: University of Texas Press, 1962.

Rael, Juan B. *Cuentos Españoles de Colorado y de Nuevo Méjico.* Spanish Originals with English Summaries, 2 vols. Stanford: Stanford University Press, 1957.

——. *The New Mexico Alabado,* with transcriptions of music by Eleanor Hague. Stanford: Stanford University Press, 1951.

——. *The Sources and Diffusion of the Mexican Shepherds' Plays.* Guadalajara, Mexico: Librería La Joyita, 1965.

Ramsdell, Charles. *San Antonio: A Historical and Pictorial Guide.* Austin: University of Texas Press, 1960.

Randolph, Vance. *The Devil's Pretty Daughter.* Oxford: Oxford Press, 1955.

——. *Sticks in the Knapsack.* N.Y.: Columbia University Press, 1958.

——. *The Talking Turtle, And Other Ozark Folk Tales.* N.Y.: Columbia University Press, 1957.

——. *We Always Lie to Strangers.* N.Y.: Columbia University Press, 1951.

——. *Who Blowed Up the Church House?* N.Y.: Columbia University Press, 1952.

Reeve, Frank D., and Alice Ann Cleveland. *New Mexico, Land of Many Cultures.* Boulder, Colo.: Pruett, 1969.

Reichard, Gladys A. *Navajo Religion, A Study of Symbolism.* N.Y.: Pantheon Books, 1950.

Rice, Clovita. *Red Balloons for the Major.* Fort Smith, Ark.: South and West, 1969.

Richardson, Rupert N., Ernest Wallace, and Adrian N. Anderson. *Texas, the Lone Star State.* Third edition. Englewood Cliffs, N.J.: Prentice-Hall, 1970.

Richter, Conrad. *The Lady.* N.Y.: Knopf, 1957.

Rister, Carl Coke. *Oil, Titan of the Southwest.* Norman: University of Oklahoma Press, 1949.

Robb, John Donald. *Hispanic Folk Songs of New Mexico.* Albuquerque: University of New Mexico Press, 1954.

Roberts, Warren. *A Bibliography of D. H. Lawrence.* London: Rupert Hart-Davis, 1963.

Robertson, Lexie Dean. *Answer in the Night.* Dallas: Kaleidograph Press, 1948.

Robinson, Cecil. *With the Ears of Strangers, The Mexican in American Literature.* Tucson: University of Arizona Press, 1963.

Rogers, John William. *The Lusty Texans of Dallas.* N.Y.: Dutton, 1951.

Rothe, Aline. *Kalita's People, A History of the Alabama-Coushatta Indians of Texas.* Waco: Texian Press, 1963.

Rushing, Marie Morris. *Five Golden Mice.* Salem, N.H.: Allard House, 1969.

Russell, David. *The Incredible Flower.* Dallas: Kaleidograph Press, 1953.

Ryden, Hope. *America's Last Wild Horses,* N.Y.: Dutton, 1970.

Sagar, Keith. *The Art of D. H. Lawrence.* Cambridge: Cambridge University Press, 1966.

Sampley, Arthur M. *Furrow with Blackbirds.* Dallas: Kaleidograph Press, 1951.

——. *Of the Strong and the Fleet.* Dallas: Kaleidograph Press, 1947.

Sanders, Leonard. *The Wooden Horseshoe.* Garden City, N.Y.: Doubleday, 1964.

Schaefer, Jack. *Collected Stories of Jack Schaefer*. Boston: Houghton, 1966.
Schockley, Martin, ed. *Southwest Writers Anthology*. A collection of folk songs, folktales, stories, poems, and essays by Southwest writers. Austin: Steck-Vaughn, 1967.
——. *Old Ramon*. Boston: Houghton, 1960.
Scott, Leslie. *Tombstone Showdown*. N.Y.: Arcadia House, 1957.
Scott, Winfield Townley. *The Dark Sister*. N.Y.: New York University Press, 1958.
——. *Exiles and Fabrications*. Garden City, N.Y.: Doubleday, 1961.
——. *Scrimshaw*. N.Y.: Macmillan, 1959.
Scully, Francis J. *Hot Springs, Arkansas, and Hot Springs National Park*. Little Rock: Hansen Co., 1966.
Seiffert, Shirley. *The Turquoise Trail*. Philadelphia: Lippincott, 1950.
Sekaquaptewa, Helen. *Me and Mine*, as told to Louise Udall. Tucson: University of Arizona Press, 1969.
Shattuck, Roger. *Half Tame*. Austin: University of Texas Press, 1964.
Sheets, Bess Mae. *This Cry is Mine*. Oklahoma City: Privately printed, 1970.
——. *Thread Your Thoughts*. Oklahoma City: Harlow Pub. Co., 1956.
Shelton, Richard. *Journal of Return*. San Francisco: Kayak Press, 1969.
——. *The Tattooed Desert*. Pittsburgh: University of Pittsburgh Press, 1970.
Sherman, James E. and Barbara H. *Ghost Towns of Arizona*. Norman: University of Oklahoma Press, 1969.
Shirk, George H. *Oklahoma Place Names*. Norman: University of Oklahoma Press, 1965.
Shirk, Lucyl. *Oklahoma City, Capital of Soonerland*. Oklahoma City: City Board of Education, 1957.
Shrake, Edwin. *Blessed McGill*. Garden City, N.Y.: Doubleday, 1968.
Shuford, Gene. *The Red Bull and Other Poems*. Fort Smith, Ark.: South and West, 1964.
Simmons, Edgar. *Driving to Biloxi*. Baton Rouge: Louisiana State University Press, 1968.
Simon, Charlie May (Mrs. John Gould Fletcher). *Johnswood*. N.Y.: Dutton, 1953.
Slayden, Ellen Maury. *Washington Wife, Journal from 1897-1919*. N.Y.: Harper, 1963.
Small, Joe Anstell, ed. *The Best of True West*. N.Y.: Simon and Schuster, 1964.
Smith, Goldie Capers. *Deep in This Furrow*. Dallas: Kaleidograph Press, 1950.
Smith, Henry Nash. *Virgin Land, The American West as Symbol and Myth*. Cambridge: Harvard University Press, 1950; N.Y.: Vintage Books, 1957, 1959, 1961.
Sonnichsen, C. L. *Cowboys and Cattle Kings*. Norman: University of Oklahoma Press, 1950.
——. *The El Paso Salt War, 1877*. El Paso: Carl Herzog, 1961.
——. *I'll Die Before I'll Run, The Story of the Great Feuds of Texas*. N.Y.: Harper, 1951.
——. *The Mescalero Apaches*. Norman: University of Oklahoma Press, 1958.
——. *Outlaw*. Denver: Sage Books, 1965.
——. *Pass of the North*. El Paso: Texas Western Press, 1968.
——. *Ten Texas Feuds*. Albuquerque: University of New Mexico Press, 1957.
——. *Tularosa: Last of the Frontier West*. N.Y.: Devin, 1960.
——. ed., *The Southwest in Life and Literature*. N.Y.: Devin, 1962.
Sorenson, Virginia. *The Proper Gods*. N.Y.: Harcourt, 1951.
Southwest Writers Series. James W. Lee, ed. Authors and the commentators: *Andy Adams,* Wilson M. Hudson; *Mary Austin,* Jo W. Lyday; *Roy Bedi-*

chek, Eleanor James; *Mody Boatright,* Ernest B. Speck; *J. Mason Brewer,* James W. Byrd; *J. Frank Dobie,* Frances E. Abernathy; *John C. Duval,* John Q. Anderson; *William Eastlake,* Gerald Haslam; *Loula Grace Erdman,* Ernestine P. Sewell; *Erna Fergusson,* David A. Remley; *Harvey Fergusson,* James K. Folsom; *Wayne Gard,* Ramon F. Adams; *Reminiscences of Range Life,* Wayne Gard; *Fred Gipson,* Sam H. Henderson; *John Howard Griffin,* Jeff H. Campbell; *A. B. Guthrie, Jr.,* Thomas W. Ford; *Alice Corbin Henderson,* T. M. Pearce; *Paul Horgan,* James M. Day; *Emerson Hough,* Delbert E. Wylder; *William Humphrey,* James W. Lee; *Oliver La Farge,* Everett A. Gillis; *Tom Lea,* John O. West; *John and Alan Lomax,* Roger Abrahams; *Alice Marriott,* Turner S. Kobler; *Larry McMurtry,* Thomas Landess; *George Milburn,* Steve Turner; *William A. Owens,* William T. Pilkington; *George Sessions Perry,* Stanley G. Alexander; *Katherine Anne Porter,* Winfred S. Emmons; *Eugene Manlove Rhodes,* Edwin W. Gaston, Jr.; *Conrad Richter,* Robert G. Barnes; *Lynn Riggs, Southwest Playwright,* Thomas A. Erhard; *Ross Santee,* Neal B. Huston; *Charles A. Siringo,* Charles D. Peavy; *Southwest Humorists,* Elton Miles; *John W. Thomason, Jr.,* William D. Norwood, Jr.; *Frank Waters,* Martin Bucco; *Walter Prescott Webb,* Walter Rundell, Jr. Austin: Steck-Vaughn, 1967-71.

Spencer, Bessie Saunders. *Out of This Dust.* Iowa City: Prairie Press, 1967.

Spratt, John S. *The Road to Spindletop.* Dallas: Southern Methodist University Press, 1955.

Stanton, Robert Brewster. *Down the Colorado.* Edited by Dwight L. Smith. Norman: University of Oklahoma Press, 1965.

Stark, Richard B., assisted by T. M. Pearce and Ruben Cobos. *Music of the Spanish Folk Plays in New Mexico.* Santa Fe: Museum of New Mexico Press, 1969.

Stephens, Edna B. *John Gould Fletcher.* N.Y.: Twayne, 1967.

Stevens, A. Wilber, ed. *Poems Southwest.* Prescott, Ariz.: Prescott College Press, 1968.

Stopple, Libby. *Singer in the Side.* Chicago: Windfall Press, 1968.

Strong, Julia Hurd. *Postlude to Mendelssohn.* Philadelphia: Dorrance, 1964.

Tanner, Clara Lee. *Southwest Indian Crafts.* Tucson: University of Arizona Press, 1968.

———. *Southwest Indian Painting.* Tucson: University of Arizona Press, 1957.

Tarpley, Fred. *Place Names of Northeast Texas.* Commerce: East Texas State University, 1969.

Tedlock, E. W., Jr. *D. H. Lawrence, Artist and Rebel.* Albuquerque: University of New Mexico Press, 1963.

———. ed., *Frieda Lawrence, The Memoirs and Correspondence.* N.Y.: Knopf, 1964.

Texas Folk-Lore Society, *Publications* of. Editors: Mody C. Boatright, 1949; William A. Owens, 1950; Wilson M. Hudson, 1951; Boatright, Hudson, and Allen Maxwell, 1953-64; Hudson and Maxwell, 1966; Hudson, 1968. XXII. *The Sky is My Tipi* (1949); XXIII. *Texas Folk Songs* (1950); XXIV. *The Healer of Los Olmos and Other Mexican Lore* (1951); XXV. *Folk Travelers: Ballads, Tales, and Talks* (1953); XXVI. *Texas Folk and Folklore* (1954); XXVII. *Mesquite and Willow* (1957); XXVIII. *Madstones and Twisters* (1958); XXIX. *And Horns on the Toads* (1959); XXX. *Singers and Storytellers* (1961); XXXI. *The Golden Log* (1962); XXXII. *A Good Tale and a Bonnie Tune* (1964); XXXIII. *The Sunny Slopes of Long Ago* (1966); XXXIV. *Tire Shrinker to Dragster* (1968). XXXV. *Hunters and Healers* (1971). Austin: Texas Folk-Lore Society.

Thomas, Mack. *Gumbo.* N.Y.: Grove, 1965.

Thomason, John William. *A Thomason Sketchbook.* Edited by Arnold Rosenfeld. Austin: University of Texas Press, 1969.

Thorp, Howard N. (Jack). *Songs of the Cowboys.* Facsimile reprint of 1921 edition with variants and commentary by Austin E. and Alta S. Fife. N.Y.: Clarkson N. Potter, 1966.

Tinkle, Lon. *Mr. De., A Biography of Everette Lee DeGolyer.* Boston: Little, 1970.

————. *13 Days to Glory, Siege of the Alamo.* N.Y.: McGraw, 1958; reprint titled *The Alamo,* N.Y.: New American Library, 1960.

Tolbert, Frank X. *The Day of San Jacinto.* N.Y.: McGraw, 1959.

————. *An Informal History of Texas.* N.Y.: Harper, 1961.

————. *The Staked Plains.* N.Y.: Harper, 1958.

Turner, Martha Anne. *The Life and Times of Jane Long.* Waco: Texian Press, 1969.

————. *Sam Houston and His Twelve Women.* Austin: Pemberton Press, 1966.

Ulibarrí, Sabine. *Tierra Amarilla, Stories of New Mexico.* In Spanish and English. Translated by Thelma Campbell Nason. Albuquerque: University of New Mexico Press, 1971.

Underhill, Ruth M. *The Navajos.* Norman: University of Oklahoma Press, 1956.

Vanlandingham, Lynn. *Alone I Wait.* Flagstaff, Ariz.: Northland Press, 1970.

Van Zandt, K. M. *Force Without Fanfare.* Edited by Sandra L. Myres. Fort Worth: Texas Christian University Press, 1968.

Vasquez, Richard. *Chicano.* Garden City, N.Y.: Doubleday, 1970.

Vergara, Lautaro. *Luz y Sombra.* Thirteen English Translations, 1965. Placitas, N.M.: Tumbleweed Press, 1967.

————. *Ecos Serranos or Southwestern Poems.* Placitas, N.M.: Tumbleweed Press, 1971.

Vestal, Stanley. *See* Walter S. Campbell.

Vliet, R. G. *Events and Celebrations.* N.Y.: Viking, 1966.

Walker, Stanley. *The Dallas Story.* N.Y.: Harper, 1956.

————. *Home to Texas.* N.Y.: Harper, 1956.

————. *Texas.* N.Y.: Viking, 1962.

Walton, Eda Lou. *So Many Daughters.* N.Y.: Bookman Associates, 1952.

Ward, Elizabeth. *No Dudes, Few Women.* Albuquerque: University of New Mexico Press, 1951.

Ward, Marie Erwin. *Swiftly the Years.* Dallas: Triangle Pub. Co., 1968.

Waters, Frank. *Book of the Hopi.* N.Y.: Viking, 1963.

————. *The Earp Brothers of Tombstone.* N.Y.: Clarkson N. Potter, 1960.

————. *Masked Gods, Navaho and Pueblo Ceremonialism.* Albuquerque: University of New Mexico Press, 1950; Denver: Sage Books, 1962.

————. *The Woman at Otowi Crossing.* Denver: Alan Swallow, 1966.

Waugh, Julia Nott. *The Silver Cradle.* Austin: University of Texas Press, 1955.

Weathers, Winston. *Indian and White, Sixteen Ecologues.* Lincoln: University of Nebraska Press, 1970.

————. *The Lonesome Game.* N.Y.: David Lewis, 1970.

————. *Messages from the Asylum.* Tulsa: Joseph Nichols, 1970.

Webb, Walter Prescott. *The Great Frontier.* Boston: Houghton, 1952; Austin: University of Texas Press, 1964.

————. *The Texas Rangers, A Century of Frontier Defense.* Boston: Houghton, 1935; Austin: University of Texas Press, 1965.

Weddle, Robert S. *San Juan Bautista, Gateway to Spanish Texas.* Austin: University of Texas Press, 1968.

Weems, John Edward. *Men Without Countries.* Boston: Houghton, 1969.

———. *Weekend in September.* N.Y.: Holt, 1957.

Wellman, Paul I. *Glory, God, and Gold.* Garden City, N.Y.: Doubleday, 1954.

———. *Iron Mistress.* Garden City, N.Y.: Doubleday, 1951.

———. *Magnificent Destiny.* Garden City, N.Y.: Doubleday, 1962.

Wessling, Laura Burnett. *Invisible Strings of Fate.* Fayetteville, Ark.: Burro Books, 1970.

West, Ray B. *Katherine Anne Porter.* Minneapolis: University of Minnesota Press, 1963.

Westheimer, David. *Summer on the Water.* N.Y.: Macmillan, 1948.

Weston, John. *Hail Hero.* N.Y.: McKay, 1968.

Wheeler, Kenneth. *To Wear a City's Crown, The Beginnings of Urban Growth in Texas.* Cambridge: Harvard University Press, 1968.

Wheeler, Thomas C., ed. *A Vanishing America, The Life and Times of the Small Town.* N.Y.: Holt, 1964.

Whitbread, Thomas. *Four Infinitives.* N.Y.: Harper, 1964.

White, C. C., and Ada Morehead Holland. *No Quittin' Sense.* Austin: University of Texas Press, 1969.

Whitehead, James. *Domains.* Baton Rouge: Louisiana State University Press, 1968.

Wild, Peter. *The Good Fox.* Chicago: Adams Press, 1967.

———. *Mad Night with Sunflowers.* Sacramento: The Runcible Spoon, 1968.

———. *Mica Mountain Poems.* Chapel Hill, N.C.: Lillabulero Press, 1968.

———. *Sonnets.* San Francisco: Cranium Press, 1967.

Will, Frederic. *Planets.* Francestown, N.H.: Golden Quill Press, 1967.

———. *A Wedge of Words.* Austin: University of Texas Press, 1962.

Williams, George Guion. *The Blind Bull.* N.Y.: Abelard, 1952.

Williams, Miller. *A Circle of Stone.* Baton Rouge: Louisiana State University Press, 1964.

———. *The Only World There Is.* N.Y.: Dutton, 1971.

———. *So Long at the Fair.* N.Y.: Dutton, 1968.

Wilson, Keith. *Graves Registry.* N.Y.: Grove Press, 1970.

———. *Homestead.* San Francisco: Kayak Press, 1969.

———. *The Old Car and Other Black Poems.* Sacramento: Grande Ronde Press, 1967.

———. *Sketches for a New Mexico Hill Town.* Portland, Ore.: Portland State University, 1966.

Winsett, Marvin Davis. *April Always.* Dallas: Wilkinson Pub. Co., 1956.

———. *Remembered Earth.* San Antonio: Naylor, 1962.

———. *Winding Stairway.* Dallas: Wilkinson Pub. Co., 1953.

Wise, Dan, and Marietta Maxfield. *The Day Kennedy Died.* San Antonio: Naylor, 1964.

Wolfenstine, Manfred R. *The Manual of Brands and Marks.* Edited by Ramon F. Adams. Norman: University of Oklahoma Press, 1970.

Wood, John. *Orbs.* Jonesboro, Ark.: Apollyon Press, 1968.

Woodward, Grace Steele. *The Cherokees.* Norman: University of Oklahoma Press, 1963.

———. *Pocahontas.* Norman: University of Oklahoma Press, 1969.

Wright, Muriel H. *Guide to the Indian Tribes of Oklahoma.* Norman: University of Oklahoma Press, 1951.

Yarbrough, Anna Nash. *Flower of the Field.* Dallas: Triangle Pub. Co., 1962.

———. *Poetry Patterns.* Dallas: Triangle Pub. Co., 1969.

Yarbrough, Anna Nash, co-author with Sybil Nash Abrams and Lelus B. Nash. *Laurel Branches.* Dallas: Triangle Pub. Co., 1969.

Yelvington, Ramsey. *A Cloud of Witnesses, The Drama of the Alamo.* Austin: University of Texas Press, 1959.

B. BIBLIOGRAPHIC GUIDES AND DICTIONARIES

Adams, Ramon F. *The Rampaging Herd, A Bibliography of Books and Pamphlets on Men and Events in the Cattle Industry.* Norman: University of Oklahoma Press, 1959.
————. *Six-Guns and Saddle Leather, A Bibliography of Books and Pamphlets on Western Outlaws and Gunmen.* Norman: University of Oklahoma Press, 1954.
————. *Western Words, A Dictionary of the American West.* New edition, revised and enlarged. Norman: University of Oklahoma Press, 1968.
Campbell, Walter S. *A Book Lover's Southwest, A Guide to Good Reading.* Norman: University of Oklahoma Press, 1955.
Dobie, J. Frank. *Guide to Life and Literature of the Southwest.* Revised edition. Dallas: Southern Methodist University Press, 1952.
Dykes, J. C. *Billy the Kid, The Bibliography of a Legend.* Albuquerque: University of New Mexico Press, 1952.
Jenkins, John Holmes. *Cracker Barrel Chronicles, A Bibliography of Texas Town and County Histories.* Austin: Pemberton Press, 1965.
Powell, Lawrence Clark. *Heart of the Southwest, A Selective Bibliography of Novels, Stories, and Tales Laid in Arizona and New Mexico.* Los Angeles: Plantin Press, 1955.
————. *Southwestern Book Trails, A Reader's Guide to the Heartland of New Mexico and Arizona.* Albuquerque: Horn and Wallace, 1963.
Saunders, Lyle. *Guide to the Literature of the Southwest.* Albuquerque: University of New Mexico Press, 1952.
Streeter, Thomas Winthrop. *Bibliography of Texas, 1795-1845.* Cambridge: Harvard University Press, 1955-60.
Tarpley, Fred. *From Blinky to Blue-John, A Word Atlas of Northeast Texas.* Wolfe City, Texas: University Press, 1970.
Taylor, J. Golden. *The Literature of the American West.* N.Y.: Houghton, 1971.
Winkler, Ernest William. *Check List of Texas Imprints,* vol. I, 1846-60. Austin: Texas State Historical Association, 1964.

C. FOR YOUNG READERS

Adams, Samuel H. *The Pony Express.* N.Y.: Random House, 1950.
————. *Santa Fe Trail.* N.Y.: Random House, 1951.
Alexander, Frances. *Choc, The Chachalaca.* Austin: Von Boeckmann-Jones, 1969.
Allen, Allyn. *Lone Star Tomboy.* N.Y.: Watts, 1951.
Armstrong, Ruth. *New Mexico, From Arrowhead to Atom.* N.Y.: Barnes, 1969.
Arnold, Oren. *Young People's Arizona.* San Antonio: Naylor, 1968.
Atkinson, Laura. *The Horny-Toad Kite.* Austin: Steck, 1957.
Bailey, Bernadine. *Picture Book of Arizona.* Chicago: Whitman, 1960.
————. *Picture Book of New Mexico.* Chicago: Whitman, 1960.
————. *Picture Book of Texas.* Chicago: Whitman, 1950.
Bailey, Flora. *Between the Four Mountains.* N.Y.: Macmillan, 1949.
Baker, Betty. *Do Not Annoy the Indians.* N.Y.: Macmillan, 1968.
————. *Killer-of-Death.* N.Y.: Harper, 1963.

————. *Shaman's Last Raid.* N.Y.: Harper, 1963.
————. *The Treasure of the Padres.* N.Y.: Harper, 1964.
————. *Walk the World's Rim.* N.Y.: Harper, 1965.
————, ed. *Great Ghost Stories of the Old West.* N.Y.: Four Winds Press, 1948.
Baker, Charlotte. *The Best of Friends.* N.Y.: McKay, 1966.
————. *The Kittens and the Cardinals.* N.Y.: McKay, 1969.
Baker, Nina Brown. *Ten American Cities.* N.Y.: Harcourt, 1949.
Baldwin, Gordon C. *The Ancient Ones.* N.Y.: Norton, 1963.
Bannon, Laura. *Hop-High, the Goat.* Indianapolis: Bobbs, 1960.
Barker, Eugene Campbell, et al. *Our New Nation.* Evanston, Ill.: Row, 1949.
Bass, Althea. *The Thankful People.* Caldwell, Idaho: Caxton Printers, 1950.
Beebe, Burdette Faye. *Coyote, Come Home.* N.Y.: McKay, 1963.
————. *Little Red.* Chicago: Follett, 1966.
————. *Run, Light Buck, Run!* N.Y.: McKay, 1962.
Behn, Harry. *Painted Cave.* Eau Claire, Wis.: Hale, 1957.
Bell, Margaret E. *Kit Carson, Mountain Man.* N.Y.: Morrow, 1952.
Benton, Patricia. *Arizona, The Turquoise Land.* N.Y.: Fell, 1958.
Berry, Don. *Mountain Men.* N.Y.: Macmillan, 1966.
Bialk, Elisa. *Tizz in Cactus Country.* Chicago: Children's Press, 1964.
Bishop, Curtis. *Lone Star Leader, Sam Houston.* N.Y.: Messner, 1961.
Bleeker, Sonia. *The Apache Indians.* N.Y.: Morrow, 1952.
————. *The Navajo, Herders, Weavers, Silversmiths.* N.Y.: Morrow, 1958.
————. *The Pueblo Indians, Farmers of the Rio Grande.* N.Y.: Morrow, 1965.
Bosworth, Allan R. *Rattlesnake Run.* Chicago: Follett, 1968.
Bracken, Dorothy K. *Doak Walker, Three Time All-American.* Austin: Steck, 1950.
Brock, Virginia. *Piñatas.* Nashville: Abingdon, 1966.
Buchanan, Rosemary. *Don Diego de Vargas.* N.Y.: Kenedy, 1963.
Buehr, Walter. *The Spanish Conquistadores in North America.* N.Y.: Putnam, 1962.
Buff, Mary. *Dancing Cloud.* N.Y.: Viking, 1958.
Buff, Mary and Conrad. *Elf Owl.* N.Y.: Viking, 1958.
————. *Hah-nee of the Cliff-Dwellers.* N.Y.: Houghton, 1965.
Buffler, Esther. *Rodrigo and Rosalita.* Austin: Steck, 1949.
Bulla, Clyde. *Indian Hill.* N.Y.: Crowell, 1963.
Burleson, Adele Steiner. *Toughey.* Austin: Steck, 1950.
Burleson, Elizabeth. *A Man of the Family.* Chicago: Follett, 1965.
Burroughs, Jean M. *The Punkin That Didn't Turn Yellow.* Portales, N.M.: Plexico Press, 1970.
Burt, Olive. *Camel Express.* Philadelphia: Winston, 1954.
Campbell, Camilla. *Barletts of Box B Ranch.* N.Y.: Whittlesey House, 1949.
————. *Coronado and His Captains.* Chicago: Follett, 1958.
Campbell, Wanda J. *The Museum Mystery.* N.Y.: Dutton, 1957.
————. *The Mystery of Old Mobeetie.* N.Y.: Dutton, 1960.
————. *Ten Cousins.* N.Y.: Dutton, 1963.
Carpenter, Allan. Enchantment of America Series. *Arizona* (1966), *Arkansas* (1967), *New Mexico* (1967), *Oklahoma* (1965), *Texas* (1965). Chicago: Children's Press.
Castor, Henry G. *The Spanish-American West.* N.Y.: Watts, 1963.
Chastain, Madye Lee. *Loblolly Farm.* N.Y.: Harcourt, 1950.
Clark, Ann Nolan. *Blue Canyon Horse.* N.Y.: Viking, 1954.
————. *Along Sandy Trails.* N.Y.: Viking, 1969.
————. *The Desert People.* N.Y.: Viking, 1962.
————. *Little Indian Basket Maker.* Chicago: Melmont, 1957.

————. *Little Indian Pottery Maker.* Chicago: Melmont, 1955.

————. *Medicine Man's Daughter.* N.Y.: Farrar, 1963.

————. *Paco's Miracle.* N.Y.: Farrar, 1962.

————. *Summer Is for Growing.* N.Y.: Farrar, 1968.

————. *This for That.* San Carlos, Calif.: Golden Gate Junior Books, 1965.

————. *Tia Maria's Garden.* N.Y.: Viking, 1963.

Clark, Ann Nolan, and Frances Carey. *A Child's Story of New Mexico.* Lincoln, Nebr.: University Publishing Co., 1960.

Clark, Van. *Peetie the Pack Rat and Other Desert Stories.* Caldwell, Idaho: Caxton Printers, 1960.

Coblentz, Catherine. *Ah-yo-ka, Daughter of Sequoya.* Evanston, Ill.: Row, 1950.

Cox, Bertha May. *True Tales of Texas.* Dallas: Turner, 1949.

Crandall, Elizabeth L. *Santa Fe.* Chicago: Rand McNally, 1965.

Crosby, Alexander L. *The Rio Grande.* Champaign, Ill.: Garrard, 1966.

Crosno, Maude D., and Charlie Scott Masters. *Discovering New Mexico.* Austin: Steck, 1950.

Cross, Jack Lee. *Arizona, Its People and Resources.* Tucson: University of Arizona Press, 1960.

Crowder, Jack L. *Stephanie and the Coyote.* In Navajo and English. Bernalillo, N.M.: Published by author, 1969.

Crowell, Ann. *A Hogan for the Bluebird.* N.Y.: Scribner, 1969.

Cumming, Marian. *All about Marjory.* N.Y.: Harcourt, 1950.

Dale, Edward E. *Oklahoma, The Story of a State.* Evanston, Ill.: Row, 1949.

Davis, Anne Pence. *The Top Hand of Lone Tree Ranch.* N.Y.: Crowell, 1960.

Day, Beth F. *Gene Rhodes, Cowboy.* N.Y.: Messner, 1954.

Day, Donald and Beth. *Will Rogers, Boy Roper.* N.Y.: Houghton, 1950.

Debo, Angie. *Oklahoma, Footloose and Fancy Free.* Norman: University of Oklahoma Press, 1949.

Dewey, Anne Perkins. *Robert Goddard, Space Pioneer.* Boston: Little, 1962.

Dines, Glen. *Overland Stage.* N.Y.: Macmillan, 1961.

Disney, Walt. *Living Desert.* N.Y.: Simon and Schuster, 1954.

Dobie, J. Frank. *Up the Trail from Texas.* N.Y.: Random House, 1955.

Duncan, Lois. *Season of the Two-Heart.* N.Y.: Dodd, 1964.

Earle, Olive L. *State Birds and Flowers.* N.Y.: Morrow, 1951.

————. *Strange Lizards.* N.Y.: Morrow, 1964.

Eaton, Jeanette. *Bucky O'Neill of Arizona.* N.Y.: Morrow, 1949.

Eberle, Irmengarde. *Listen to the Mockingbird.* N.Y.: Whittlesey House, 1949.

Elting, Mary (pseud. Benjamin Brewster). *First Book of Cowboys.* N.Y.: Watts, 1950.

————. *First Book of Indians.* N.Y.: Watts, 1950.

————. *The Secret Story of Pueblo Bonito.* Irvington-on-Hudson, N.Y.: Harvey House, 1957.

Embry, Margaret. *Peg-Leg Willy.* N.Y.: Holiday House, 1966.

Erdman, Loula Grace. *The Good Land.* N.Y.: Dodd, 1959.

————. *My Sky Is Blue.* N.Y.: Longmans, 1953.

————. *Room to Grow.* N.Y.: Dodd, 1962.

————. *The Wide Horizon.* N.Y.: Dodd, 1956.

————. *The Wind Blows Free.* N.Y.: Dodd, 1952.

Evans, Edna. *Written with Fire.* N.Y.: Holt, 1962.

Felton, Harold W. *Bowleg Bill, Seagoing Cowpuncher.* N.Y.: Prentice-Hall, 1957.

Fenner, Phyllis R., compiler. *Cowboys, Cowboys, Cowboys.* N.Y.: Watts, 1950.

Fenton, Carroll Lane. *Cliff Dwellers of Walnut Canyon.* N.Y.: Day, 1960.

Fitzpatrick, George and Mildred. *New Mexico for Young People.* Lincoln, Nebr.: University Pub. Co., 1965.

Fletcher, Sidney E. *Big Book of Cowboys.* N.Y.: Grosset, 1950.

————. *Big Book of Indians.* N.Y.: Grosset, 1950.

Floethe, L. Lee. *The Indian and His Pueblo.* N.Y.: Scribner, 1960.

Franklin, George Cory. *Pancho.* Boston: Houghton, 1953.

————. *Pedro, the Roadrunner.* N.Y.: Hastings House, 1957.

————. *Pioneer Horse.* Boston: Houghton, 1960.

————. *Son of Monte.* Boston: Houghton, 1956.

————. *Trails West.* Boston: Houghton, 1960.

————. *Tuffy.* Boston: Houghton, 1954.

————. *Wild Animals of the Five Rivers Country.* Boston: Houghton, 1947.

————. *Wild Animals of the Southwest.* Boston: Houghton, 1950.

————. *Wild Horses of the Rio Grande.* Boston: Houghton, 1951.

————. *Zorra.* Boston: Houghton, 1957.

Fraser, James. *Las Posadas.* Flagstaff, Ariz.: Northland Press, 1963.

Frazer, Steve. *First Through the Grand Canyon.* N.Y.: Holt, 1961.

Garst, Doris Shannon. *Dick Wootton, Trail Blazer of Raton Pass.* N.Y.: Messner, 1956.

————. *James Bowie.* N.Y.: Messner, 1955.

————. *Will Rogers, Immortal Cowboy.* N.Y.: Messner, 1950.

Garst, Doris Shannon and Warren. *Ernest Thompson Seton, Naturalist.* N.Y.: Messner, 1959.

Gates, Doris. *River Ranch.* N.Y.: Viking, 1949.

Gendron, Val. *Behind the Zuñi Masks.* N.Y.: Longmans, 1958.

George, Jean Craighead. *The Moon of the Wild Pigs.* N.Y.: Crowell, 1968.

Gessner, Lynne. *Lightning Slinger.* N.Y.: Funk, 1958.

————. *Trading Post Girl.* N.Y.: Fell, 1968.

Gipson, Fred. *Cowhand.* N.Y.: Harper, 1953.

————. *The Cow Killers.* Austin: University of Texas Press, 1956.

————. *Hound-Dog Man.* N.Y.: Harper, 1949.

————. *Old Yeller.* Evanston, Ill.: Harper, 1956.

————. *The Trail Driving Rooster.* N.Y.: Harper, 1955.

Glubok, Shirley. *Art of the North American Indian.* N.Y.: Harper, 1964.

Gorham, Michael (pseud. for Mary Elting). *The Real Book About Cowboys.* Garden City, N.Y.: Garden City Books, 1952.

Grant, Bruce. *Cowboy Encyclopedia.* Chicago: Rand McNally, 1951.

————. *Cyclone.* Cleveland: World, 1959.

————. *Pancho, A Dog of the Plains.* Cleveland: World, 1958.

Grote, William. *J. P. and the Apaches.* N.Y.: Meredith, 1967.

Halsey, D. S. *Sky on Fire!* N.Y.: Macmillan, 1965.

Harris, Harry. *Billy Joe and the Rangers.* N.Y.: Hastings, 1965.

Harter, Helen. *Carmelo.* Chicago: Follett, 1962.

Harvey, James O. *Beyond the Gorge of Shadows.* N.Y.: Lothrop, 1965.

Hayes, Florence S. *Chee and His Pony.* N.Y.: Houghton, 1950.

Henry, Marguerite. *Brighty of the Grand Canyon.* N.Y.: Rand McNally, 1953.

Herndon, Betty B. *Adventures in Cactus Land.* Caldwell, Idaho: Caxton Printers, 1950.

Hoff, Carol. *Head to the West.* Chicago: Follett, 1957.

————. *Johnny Texas.* Chicago: Follett, 1950.

————. *Johnny Texas on the San Antonio Road.* Chicago: Follett, 1953.

————. *Wilderness Pioneer, Stephen F. Austin of Texas.* Chicago: Follett, 1955.

Hofsinde, Robert. *Indian Fishing and Camping.* N.Y.: Morrow, 1963.

————. *Indian Music Makers.* N.Y.: Morrow, 1967.

Holbrook, Stewart H. *Davy Crockett*. N.Y.: Random House, 1955.
Holland, Ellen B. *Gay as a Grig*. Austin: University of Texas Press, 1963.
Holman, Rosemary. *Spanish Nuggets*. In Spanish and English. San Antonio: Naylor, 1968.
Hood, Flora. *One Luminaria for Antonio*. N.Y.: Putnam, 1966.
Huntington, Harriet E. *Let's Go to the Desert*. N.Y.: Doubleday, 1949.
Hyde, Wayne. *What Does a Cowboy Do?* N.Y.: Dodd, 1963.
Ivan, Martha and Gustave (pseud. Gus Tavo). *Ride the Pale Stallion*. N.Y.: Knopf, 1968.
James, Harry. *A Day in Oraibi, A Hopi Indian Village*. Chicago: Melmont, 1959.
———. *A Day with Poli, A Hopi Indian Girl*. Chicago: Melmont, 1957.
———. *Ovada, An Indian Boy of the Grand Canyon*. Los Angeles: Ward Ritchie Press, 1969.
Jensen, Ann. *The Time of Rosie*. Austin: Steck, 1967.
Johnson, James Ralph. *Camels West*. N.Y.: McKay, 1964.
Johnson, Siddie Joe. *Feather in My Hand*. N.Y.: Athenaeum, 1967.
———. *A Month of Christmases*. N.Y.: Longmans, 1952.
———. *Rabbit Fires*. Boerne, Texas: Highland Press, 1951.
———. *Texas, the Land of the Tejas*. N.Y.: Random House, 1943; Dallas: Cokesbury Book Store, 1950.
Johnson, William Weber. *Sam Houston, The Tallest Texan*. N.Y.: Random House, 1953.
———. *The Birth of Texas*. Boston: Houghton, 1960.
Justus, May, *et al. Big Meeting Day and Other Festival Tales*. N.Y.: Aladdin, 1950.
Kjelgard, James A. *Chip, the Dam Builder*. Eau Claire, Wis.: Hale, 1950.
———. *Coyote Song*. N.Y.: Dodd, 1969.
———. *Hi Jolly*. N.Y.: Dodd, 1969.
Krumgold, Joseph. *And Now Miguel*. N.Y.: Crowell, 1953.
La Farge, Oliver. *The American Indian*. Special Edition for Young People. N.Y.: Golden Press, 1960.
Lampman, Evelyn. *Navajo Sister*. Garden City, N.Y.: Doubleday, 1958.
Latham, Jean Lee. *Sam Houston, Hero of Texas*. Champaign, Ill.: Garrard, 1965.
Latham, John H. *Lonesome Longhorn*. Philadelphia: Westminster, 1951.
Lazarus, Keo Felker. *Rattlesnake Run*. Chicago: Follett, 1968.
Lenski, Lois. *Boom Town Boy*. Philadelphia: Lippincott, 1948.
———. *Cowboy Small*. N.Y.: Oxford, 1949.
———. *Texas Tomboy*. Philadelphia: Lippincott, 1950.
———. *We Live in the Southwest*. Philadelphia: Lippincott, 1962.
Livingston, Myra Cohn. *I'm Not Me*. N.Y.: Harcourt, 1963.
Lowrey, Janette Sebring. *Love, Bid Me Welcome*. N.Y.: Harper, 1964.
———. *Margaret Hopper*. N.Y.: Harper, 1950.
———. *Mr. Heff and Mr. Ho*. Eau Claire, Wis.: Hale, 1952.
Maher, Ramona (Mrs. Tim Weeks). *Mystery of the Stolen Fish Pond*. N.Y.: Dodd, 1969.
———. *Secret of the Sundial*. N.Y.: Dodd, 1966.
———. *Their Shining Hour*. N.Y.: Day, 1960.
———. *The Abracadabra Mystery*. N.Y.: Dodd, 1961.
Mann, E. B., and Fred E. Harvey. *New Mexico, Land of Enchantment*. East Lansing: Michigan State University Press, 1955.
Marcus, R. B. *First Book of the Cliff Dwellers*. N.Y.: Watts, 1968.
Marriott, Alice. *Sequoyah, Leader of the Cherokees*. N.Y.: Random House, 1956.

Mauzey, Merritt. *Oilfield Boy.* N.Y.: Abelard-Schuman, 1957.
——. *Texas Ranch Boy.* N.Y.: Abelard-Schuman, 1955.
McClung, Robert. *Buzztail, The Story of a Rattlesnake.* N.Y.: Morrow, 1958.
McCormick, Wilfred. (Fifty books appear in the Bronc Burnett and Rocky McCune Scouting, Baseball, Basketball, and Football Series, of which the following are selected titles:)
——. *Bases Loaded.* Bronc Burnett Baseball. N.Y.: Putnam, 1950.
——. *The Bigger Game.* Rocky McCune Football. N.Y.: McKay, 1958.
——. *The Captive Coach.* Rocky McCune Football. N.Y.: McKay, 1956.
——. *Eagle Scout.* Bronc Burnett Scouting. N.Y.: Putnam, 1952.
——. *Fielder's Choice.* Bronc Burnett Baseball. N.Y.: Putnam, 1949.
——. *Five Yards to Glory.* Rocky McCune Football. N.Y.: McKay, 1959.
——. *Man in Motion.* Bronc Burnett Football. N.Y.: McKay, 1961.
——. *One Bounce Too Many.* Bronc Burnett Baseball. Indianapolis: Bobbs, 1967.
——. *The Play for One.* Rocky McCune Basketball. N.Y.: McKay, 1961.
McGriffin, Lee. *Ten Tall Texans.* N.Y.: Lothrop, 1956.
McNeer, May. *The Story of the Southwest.* N.Y.: Harper, 1948.
——. *War Chief of the Seminoles.* N.Y.: Random House, 1954.
Meadaris, Mary. *Big Doc's Daughter.* Philadelphia: Lippincott, 1950.
Meadowcraft, Enid La Monte. *Texas Star.* N.Y.: Crowell, 1950.
Means, Florence C. *House Under the Hill.* N.Y.: Houghton, 1949.
Means, Florence C. and Carl. *The Silver Fleece.* Philadelphia: Winston, 1950.
Meredith, Robert, and E. Brooks Smith, eds. *Riding with Coronado.* Boston: Little, 1964.
Moffitt, Virginia May. *Broad Skies of Freedom.* Dallas: Banks, 1949.
——. *The Jayhawker.* Boston: Page, 1949.
Momaday, Natachee Scott. *Owl in the Cedar Tree.* N.Y.: Ginn, 1965.
Moody, Ralph. *Geronimo, Wolf of the Warpath.* N.Y.: Random House, 1958.
——. *Kit Carson and the Wild Frontier.* N.Y.: Random House, 1955.
Moon, Grace P. *One Little Indian.* Chicago: Whitman, 1950.
Moore, Dwight M. *Trees of Arkansas.* Fayetteville: University of Arkansas, 1950; rev. ed., Little Rock: Arkansas Forestry Commission, 1960.
Morgan, William. *Coyote Tales.* Lawrence, Kan.: Haskell Institute, 1949.
Mulcahy, Lucille. *The Blue Marshmallow Mountains.* N.Y.: Nelson, 1959.
——. *Dark Arrow.* N.Y.: Coward-McCann, 1953.
——. *Fire on Big Lonesome.* Los Angeles: Elk Grove Press, 1967.
——. *Magic Fingers.* N.Y.: Nelson, 1958.
——. *Natoto.* N.Y.: Nelson, 1960.
——. *Pita.* N.Y.: Coward-McCann, 1954.
Munch, Theodore. *Road Runner.* Austin: Steck, 1958.
Nason, Thelma C. *Under the Wide Sky.* Chicago: Follett, 1965.
Norton, Alice Mary. *Stand to Horse.* N.Y.: Harcourt, 1956.
O'Brien, Esse Forrester. *Animal Tots.* Austin: Steck, 1956.
——. *Circus: Cinders to Sawdust.* San Antonio: Naylor, 1959.
——. *Dolphins, Sea People.* San Antonio: Naylor, 1965.
Olguin, Joseph. *Sam Houston and His Indian Friends.* N.Y.: Houghton, 1958.
Parish, Peggy. *Let's Be Indians.* N.Y.: Harper, 1962.
Paschal, Nancy. *See* Grace Trotter.
Peck, Anne Merriman. *Jo Ann of the Border Country.* N.Y.: Dodd, 1952.
——. *Southwest Roundup.* N.Y.: Dodd, 1950.
Peet, Bill (pseud. William Bartlett). *Buford, The Little Bighorn.* Boston: Houghton, 1967.
Perrigo, Lynn I. *Rio Grande Adventure.* Chicago: Lyons and Carnahan, 1964.

Perrine, Mary. *Salt Boy*. N.Y.: Houghton, 1968.
Perry, George Sessions. *The Story of Texas*. Garden City, N.Y.: Garden City Books, 1956.
Phelps, Margaret. *Jaro and the Golden Colt*. Philadelphia: Smith, 1954.
———. *Territory Boy*. Philadelphia: Smith, 1953.
Pinkerton, Robert. *First Overland Mail*. N.Y.: Random House, 1953.
Place, Marion T. *The Santa Fe Trail*. N.Y.: Watts, 1966.
Price, Joan. *A Very Special Burro*. San Antonio: Naylor, 1966.
Regli, Adolph. *Fiddling Cowboy*. N.Y.: McKay, 1949.
———. *Partners in the Saddle*. N.Y.: Watts, 1950.
Rice, Elizabeth. *Rodeo*. Austin: Steck, 1949.
Robinson, Dorothy F. *Arizona for Boys and Girls*. Tempe, Ariz.: Connolly, 1959.
———. *Navajo Indians Today*. San Antonio: Naylor, 1966.
Robison, Mabel O. *The Hole in the Mountain*. N.Y.: Dodd, 1966.
Rosvear, Marjorie. *The Secret Cowboy*. N.Y.: Messner, 1955.
Rounds, Glen. *Rodeo; Bulls, Broncos, and Buckaroos*. N.Y.: Holiday House, 1949.
Rushmore, Helen. *Cowboy Joe of the Circle S*. N.Y.: Harcourt, 1950.
———. *Ponca, Cowpony*. N.Y.: Harcourt, 1952.
———. *The Shadow of Robbers' Roost*. Cleveland: World Pub. Co., 1960.
Russell, Solveig Paulson. *Navajo Land, Yesterday and Today*. Chicago: Melmont, 1961.
Sasek, M. *This is Texas*. N.Y.: Macmillan, 1967.
Schaaf, Martha E. *Lew Wallace, Boy Writer*. Indianapolis: Bobbs, 1961.
Schaefer, Jack. *New Mexico*. State of the Nation Books. N.Y.: Coward-McCann, 1967.
———. *Old Ramon*. N.Y.: Houghton, 1960.
Schweitzer, Byrd Baylor. *Amigo*. N.Y.: Houghton, 1968.
———. *One Small Bead*. N.Y.: Macmillan, 1965.
Shannon, Terry. *Desert Dwellers*. Chicago: Whitman, 1958.
———. *Little Wolf, The Rain Dancer*. Chicago: Whitman, 1954.
———. *Running Fox, The Eagle Hunter*. Chicago: Whitman, 1957.
Shireffe, Gordon. *Rebel Trumpet*. Philadelphia: Westminster, 1960.
Silliman, Leland. *Bucky Forrester*. Philadelphia: Winston, 1951.
———. *Golden Cloud, Palomino of Sunset Hill*. Philadelphia: Winston, 1950.
———. *The Purple Tide*. Philadelphia: Winston, 1949.
Soule, Gardner. *Gemini and Apollo*. N.Y.: Duell, 1964.
Sperry, Armstrong. *Great River, Wide Land, The Rio Grande Through History*. N.Y.: Macmillan, 1967.
Spies, Victor C. *Sun Dance and the Great Spirit*. Chicago: Follett, 1954.
Sutton, Ann and Myron. *Life of the Desert*. N.Y.: McGraw, 1966.
Tavo, Gus. *See* Martha and Gustave Ivan.
Thompson, Eileen. *The Apache Gold Mystery*. N.Y.: Abelard, 1965.
———. *The Blue-Stone Mystery*. N.Y.: Abelard, 1963.
Thompson, Hildegard. *Preprimer and Primer* (1953). Navajo Life Series. Window Rock, Ariz.: Navajo Service, 1949-53.
Tireman, Lloyd S. *3-Toes*. Mesaland Series. Albuquerque: University of New Mexico Press, 1950.
Toepperwein, Fritz and Emilie. *Little Deputy*. Boerne, Texas: Highland Press, 1949.
Toles, Elsie and Myriam. *Secret of Lonesome Valley*. San Francisco: Wagner, 1949.
Trotter, Grace (pseud. Nancy Paschal). *Spring in the Air*. N.Y.: Viking, 1953.
———. *Sylvan City*. N.Y.: Viking, 1950.

Ullman, James R. *Down the Colorado with Major Powell.* Boston: Houghton, 1960.

Van Riper, Guernsey. *Will Rogers, Young Cowboy.* Indianapolis: Bobbs, 1951.

Wallrich, William J. *The Strange Little Man in the Chili-Red Pants.* Fort Garland, Colo.: Cottonwood Press, 1949.

Waltrip, Lela. *Purple Hills.* N.Y.: Longmans, 1961.

——. *Quiet Boy.* N.Y.: Longmans, 1961.

Waltrip, Lela and Rufus. *Indian Women.* N.Y.: McKay, 1964.

Ward, Don. *Cowboys and Cattle Country.* N.Y.: American Heritage, 1961.

Warren, Betsy. *Indians Who Lived in Texas.* Austin: Steck-Vaughn, 1970.

Warren, Robert Penn. *Remember the Alamo.* N.Y.: Random House, 1958.

Webb, George. *A Pima Remembers.* Tucson: University of Arizona Press, 1959.

Webb, Walter Prescott. *The Texas Rangers.* N.Y.: Grosset, 1957.

Whitaker, George O. *Dinosaur Hunt.* N.Y.: Harcourt, 1965.

Wier, Estes. *The Wind Chasers.* N.Y.: McKay, 1967.

Wilson, Ellen. *Ernie Pyle, Boy from Back Home.* Indianapolis: Bobbs, 1955.

Wood, Frances. *Rocky Mountain, Mesa Verde, Carlsbad Caverns.* Chicago: Follett, 1963.

Woodward, Mary Tyson. *A Day with Becky.* Dallas: Kaleidograph Press, 1950.

——. *Birthday Kittens.* Dallas: Kaleidograph Press, 1949.

Worcester, Donald E. *Kit Carson, Mountain Scout.* N.Y.: Houghton, 1960.

——. *Lone Hunter's First Buffalo Hunt.* N.Y.: H. Z. Walck, 1958.

——. *War Pony.* N.Y.: H. Z. Walck, 1961.

Wormser, Richard. *The Kidnapped Circus.* N.Y.: Morrow, 1968.

Wright, Frances F. *Sam Houston, Fighter and Leader.* Dallas: Cokesbury Book Store, 1953.

Wyatt, Edgar. *Geronimo, The Last Apache War Chief.* N.Y.: McGraw, 1952.

Wyatt, Geraldine. *Wronghand.* N.Y.: Longmans, 1949.

INDEX